The Atonal Music of Arnold Schoenberg

Eugène Delacroix, *Jacob Wrestling with the Angel* (1856–61), Church of St. Sulpice, Paris. Courtesy of Art Resource.

The
Atonal Music of
ARNOLD SCHOENBERG
1908–1923

BRYAN R. SIMMS

OXFORD
UNIVERSITY PRESS

2000

OXFORD
UNIVERSITY PRESS

Oxford   New York
Athens   Auckland   Bangkok   Bogotá   Buenos Aires   Calcutta
Cape Town   Chennai   Dar es Salaam   Delhi   Florence   Hong Kong   Istanbul
Karachi   Kuala Lumpur   Madrid   Melbourne   Mexico City   Mumbai
Nairobi   Paris   São Paulo   Shanghai   Singapore   Taipei   Tokyo   Toronto   Warsaw

and associated companies in
Berlin   Ibadan

Copyright © 2000 by Oxford University Press

Published by Oxford University Press, Inc.
198 Madison Avenue, New York, New York 10016

Oxford is a registered trademark of Oxford University Press.

Library of Congress Cataloging-in-Publication Data
Simms, Bryan R.
The atonal music of Arnold Schoenberg, 1908–1923
/ Bryan R. Simms.
p.   cm.
Includes bibliographical references and index.
ISBN 0-19-512826-5
1. Schoenberg, Arnold, 1974–1951—Criticism
and interpretation.   2. Atonality.   I. Title.
ML410.S283S45   2000
780'.92—dc21   99-35938

For permission to reprint copyrighted material,
acknowledgment is gratefully made to the following:

Artists Rights Society, New York, and VBK, Vienna,
for Arnold Schoenberg's paintings "The Burial of Gustav Mahler"
and untitled scene drawing for *Erwartung*.

Belmont Music Publishers, for excerpts from Schoenberg,
String Quartet No. 2, Op. 10; Three Piano Pieces, Op. 11;
Two Songs, Op. 14; Fifteen Poems from *Das Buch der hängenden Gärten*
by Stefan George, Op. 15; *Erwartung*, Op. 17; *Die glücklicke Hand*,
Op. 18; *Die Jakobsleiter; Pierrot lunaire*, Op. 21.

C. F. Peters Corporation, for excerpts from
Schoenberg, Five Orchestral Pieces, Op. 16.

Edition Wilhelm Hansen AS, Copenhagen, for excerpts
from Schoenberg, Five Piano Pieces, Op. 23; and Serenade, Op. 24.

Lawrence Schoenberg, for manuscripts, letter excerpts,
and paintings by Arnold Schoenberg.

Museum of Fine Arts, Boston, for a photograph
of Kokoschka, "Self-Portrait as a Warrior."

1 3 5 7 9 8 6 4 2
Printed in the United States of America
on acid-free paper

Preface

This book contains a historical and analytic portrait of Arnold Schoenberg's atonal music, a body of some fifteen major compositions and numerous fragments created between 1908 and 1923. These include such masterpieces as *Pierrot lunaire*, the opera *Erwartung*, Five Orchestra Pieces, Op. 16, and songs from Stefan George's *Book of the Hanging Gardens*. The atonal works are distinguished from the composer's earlier compositions by their lack of traditional key, among many other innovative features, and stand apart in style and compositional technique from his later works composed according to his twelve-tone method.

My presentation of this complex musical oeuvre rests both on a close analytic study of the works themselves and a review of the historical circumstances through which they came into being, by which I hope to show how the musical language of this period in Schoenberg's creative life continually evolved to reflect his personal circumstances and changing artistic outlook. The music is also a product of its time, coming on the heels of the collapsing romantic style, persisting through the angst-ridden period before and after World War I, and reaching its own end in the materialistic and cynical atmosphere of the 1920s. This book is shaped also by an assessment of the many writings that already exist on the subject. In attempting to cope with the remarkably large literature on each of Schoenberg's atonal compositions (see the Bibliography for examples), I have attached the greatest importance to Schoenberg's own writings, in which the composer provocatively addresses the constructive and expressive content of his music, including its atonal phase. To the extent possible I also comment upon and synthesize other important critical and analytic points of view, despite the great diversity of method and objective that characterizes this literature.

Schoenberg was himself well aware of the ambiguities and limitations inherent in any analysis of a musical work, especially an atonal composition. In a lecture of 1932 on the Four Orchestral Songs, he cautioned his listeners in a way that the author of this book can only echo: "I would not have you believe, ladies and gentlemen, that with this analysis all aspects of this section have been elucidated. . . . I state what I see, as far as I am able to express it. Yet in the end, this is still a path on which one must feel one's way, step by step, with the tip of one's toes."[1]

I am indebted in the writing of this book to the staff of the Arnold Schoenberg Institute at the University of Southern California, especially to Leonard Stein, director of the institute, and to its archivists Clara Steuermann (1922–82), Jerry McBride, and R. Wayne Shoaf. Their work since 1976 with the composer's literary and musical legacy has been indispensable to every major study of Schoenberg undertaken after that time. I am also grateful for the assistance of my wife, Charlotte E. Erwin, who read the entire manuscript and had many recommendations for its improvement, and for the help of Eika Vorndran, who checked the accuracy of the German texts.

Los Angeles   B.R.S.
August 1998

Contents

Abbreviations

AGS   Theodor W. Adorno. *Gesammelte Schriften*. Edited by Rolf Tiedemann, et al. Frankfurt: Suhrkamp, 1970– .

ASL   *Arnold Schoenberg Letters*. Edited by Erwin Stein. Translated by Eithne Wilkins and Ernst Kaiser. New York: St. Martin's Press, 1965.

AZB   Alexander Zemlinsky. *Briefwechsel mit Arnold Schönberg, Anton Webern, Alban Berg und Franz Schreker*. Edited by Horst Weber. Briefwechsel der Wiener Schule, vol. 1. Darmstadt: Wissenschaftliche Buchgesellschaft, 1995.

BSC   *The Berg-Schoenberg Correspondence: Selected Letters*. Edited and translated by Juliane Brand, Christopher Hailey, and Donald Harris. New York and London: Norton, 1987.

BSL   Ferruccio Busoni. *Selected Letters*. Translated and edited by Antony Beaumont. New York: Columbia University Press, 1987.

FMC   Arnold Schoenberg. *Fundamentals of Musical Composition*. Edited by Gerald Strang and Leonard Stein. New York: St. Martin's Press, 1967.

HL   Arnold Schoenberg. *Theory of Harmony*. Translated by Roy E. Carter. Berkeley and Los Angeles: University of California Press, 1978.

JASI   *Journal of the Arnold Schoenberg Institute*, 1976–96.

JMS   Jan Maegaard. *Studien zur Entwicklung des dodekaphonen Satzes bei Arnold Schönberg*. 3 vol. Copenhagen: Wilhelm Hansen Musikforlag, 1972.

SFH   Arnold Schoenberg, *Structural Functions of Harmony* Revised edition with corrections. Edited by Leonard Stein, New York: Norton, 1969.

SI   Arnold Schoenberg. *Style and Idea*. Edited by Leonard Stein. Translated by Leo Black. Berkeley and Los Angeles: University of California Press, 1984.

SSW   *Arnold Schönberg Sämtliche Werke*. Rudolf Stephan, general editor. Mainz: Schott; Vienna: Universal Edition, 1966– .

The Atonal Music of Arnold Schoenberg

1

Atonality and the Critical Imagination

In a letter addressed in 1909 to Ferruccio Busoni, Schoenberg described his recent compositions as works that demand "belief and conviction."[1] They were products of pure imagination, he said, not objects to be judged by outward appearance, and they were intended only for those who take "the side of all who seek."[2] With these generalizations he described a new style of music with which he had been experimenting for about a year. It was an outgrowth of the post-Brahmsian and post-Wagnerian musical languages that Schoenberg had cultivated earlier, although its differences from these idioms were so pronounced that they would soon isolate him from the leading German modernist composers—from Richard Strauss, Gustav Mahler, Max Reger, and even his teacher, Alexander Zemlinsky.

Schoenberg never settled on a name for the style of music about which he spoke to Busoni, although others called it atonal. But this term scarcely did justice to the far-reaching diversity and multifaceted originality of the works that Schoenberg began to compose in 1908. The word points to the absence of key, certainly a striking characteristic of the new approach, but even in 1908 traditional tonality was hardly perceptible in new music from many contemporaries— Debussy, Reger, and Strauss among others. The newness was more pervasive: "New sounds were produced, a new kind of melody appeared, a new approach to expression of moods and characters was discovered," Schoenberg wrote.[3] "From the very beginning," he concluded, "such compositions differed from all preceding music, not only harmonically but also melodically, thematically, and motivally."[4]

Throughout a period of fourteen years after he wrote to Busoni, Schoenberg constantly rethought and reworked the new idiom. By 1923 it had little in common with what it had been in 1909; in the interim it had grown and matured, and it was then ripe to be superseded by the twelve-tone method of composition, which initiated yet another major period in Schoenberg's restless musical development. At first Schoenberg's atonal music was touched by angst and spurred on by a need for liberation from the past; it erupted from the same energetic creativity that was evident in literature and painting in the years before World War I. But gradually it lost its spontaneous and emotional character, and it came to rely on methodic controls in the fashioning of its materials. After about 1912 its explosive subjectivity dissipated in a more objective atmosphere; its expressive content had cooled by then to a level that could admit even parody and humor.

A musical style of such diversity and originality could only provoke diverging critical interpretations. During Schoenberg's lifetime the historian-writers who analyzed it usually found it to be a necessary expression of its time—the evolutionary outgrowth of a crisis in music at the turn of the century or the product of a vigorous revolution that swept aside the remnants of an exhausted romanticism. Kurt Westphal, writing in 1928, interpreted Schoenberg's atonality as a consequence of Debussy's nonfunctional harmony, which was itself a response to the "stressful crisis in which music was found at the turn of the century."[5] Hans Mersmann found in Schoenbergian atonality not so much an isolated or individual development as the symptom of a broad revolution felt throughout the world of art in the first decade of the century: "It was the problem of an entire generation that he was grappling with. Everywhere, throughout all of Europe, the battle was taken up by the young, the advance guard, the bold ones. Parties were formed, slogans coined, denunciations hurled, manifestos issued. Music entered a stage of revolution whose spiritual leader was Schoenberg."[6]

Some critics of this time saw in atonal music an outpouring of anxiety, a manifestation of trauma within the composer himself, or a resounding echo of the social antinomies of the pre– and post–World War I periods. Theodor W. Adorno, for example, emphasized the connection of atonality to a historical process that had produced a degraded capitalistic society. Schoenberg's music, according to Adorno's view, grew from a senseless world. Its effect upon the listener would always be to shock and to unsettle, to awaken him to the brutality of the society in which he lived. It was the first genuinely "new music," Adorno wrote, and it had little to do with musical evolution or with the innovations of predecessors such as Debussy. Instead, it "breaks from the continuity of musical development. It is shockingly alienated from [normal] musical speech, and it declares war upon the dispassionate, hedonistic popular taste."[7]

Ernst Krenek recast Adorno's argument by underscoring the individuality that lay behind Schoenberg's atonal music. It was a unique expression of the composer's thought, Krenek asserted, so intensely and directly personalized that it left the listener with a sense that all mankind lived in similar isolation:

> Atonality has always aimed straight at the substance, the gist, of musical expression, eliminating all intervening associations, all nonessential elements, and all the ornaments of handicraft. . . . Atonality has given speech to the individual, liberating him from delusive chains and seductive illusions. By intensifying the expression of personal emotion to the utmost, it has demonstrated the loneliness and alienation of humanity as clearly as possible.[8]

Among the early critical writings on Schoenberg's atonal oeuvre, the most authoritative and enlightening of all are the composer's own. These are plainly indispensable for an understanding of his music, although they are themselves often in need of interpretation, since they stem from a restless imagination that produced a constantly changing and sometimes conflicting body of insights. Very often with Schoenberg, an important technical essay was written at about the same time that its ideas were applied in a musical composition, but these ideas may be irrelevant or misleading if they are used to interpret his music outside the same chronological context. Many examples of the limited sphere of reference of a given essay are found in Schoenberg's *Harmonielehre,* written in 1910 and 1911. The book ostensibly deals with tonal composition, although the relevance of this idiom to the early atonal style is a subtext that runs throughout the treatise. A simple example arises in the final chapter, where the composer writes: "The artist's creative activity is instinctive. Consciousness has little influence on it."[9] This statement aptly characterizes Schoenberg's music written at about the same time as the *Harmonielehre,* when he experimented with composition in a stream of consciousness and relied almost entirely on artistic instinct. But it has little relevance to the late tonal style and no pertinence at all to his atonal music composed after about 1914, when his works were methodically constructed and reveal the highest degree of "consciousness."

A more complex example is found in the essay "Das Verhältnis zum Text," which was published in *Der blaue Reiter* in 1912.[10] Here the composer theorizes that a musical setting of a poetic text could bypass the expressive relations between words and tones that normally exist in vocal music, provided that a deeper congruence is established between the sound or tone of the music and the comparable quality in the poem. Schoenberg experiments with just this type of vocal music in works such as the Four Orchestral Songs, Op. 22, which were composed in 1913 and 1914. The doctrine is highly misleading if applied to his works composed prior to 1912, such as the George songs, Op. 15, which are expressive to the fullest measure.

Closer to the present day, the critical interpretation of Schoenberg's atonal music has flowed into two separate streams, one of which extends the thinking of Adorno and Krenek and seeks in the music a statement about the world and man's fate within it, while the other ignores the music's ideational content altogether, in an attempt to elucidate the music as an abstract formal structure. Writers who occupy the first category have tended to revive Adorno's ontological reading by an assessment of atonality as a historical record, an artifact of a turbulent century nearing its end. For Alexander L. Ringer, Schoenberg the atonalist was a prophet of the future, whose music foretold the dismal outlook for European Jews. The mission of the prophet, Ringer asserts, "is precisely to confront us with the human condition in all its terrifying ramifications as well as in its ubiquitous hopes."[11]

> Schoenberg assaults the listener with often devastating dramatic force engendered by all manner of extreme contrasts—rhythmic, melodic, textural, and harmonic. From a psycho-historical perspective, therefore, stylistic inroads like the much-misunderstood "emancipation of dissonance" represent but very specific aspects of a comprehensive effort to extricate music from the realm of beauty, in nineteenth-century eyes the eternal preserve of all art, for the sake of naked truth, where compromise is no longer tolerated.[12]

The formalist position on Schoenberg's atonal oeuvre, advanced by both American and German writers since the 1960s, has portrayed the music primarily as an expression of highly unified and integrated structures created by tones and other basic musical elements. An example is "set theory," advanced by Allen Forte and refined by several other writers. For Forte, atonality itself can be defined by a body of common structural principles that are manifest in twentieth-century works by many composers. It is not a style, nor does it partake of any particular expressive content. In his book *The Structure of Atonal Music* (1973), Forte writes: "Any composition that exhibits the structural characteristics that are discussed, and that exhibits them throughout, may be regarded as atonal."[13] Forte's outlook is quite the opposite of an analytic viewpoint held by George Perle, Robert Morgan, and Ethan Haimo, for whom Schoenberg's atonal works are all essentially "free" or "contextual" in their structure and meaning. According to this interpretation, as George Perle writes in his *Serial Composition and Atonality*, "the 'free' atonality that preceded dodecaphony precludes by definition the possibility of a statement of self-consistent, generally applicable compositional procedures."[14] Each composition, that is, creates its own unique assumptions, relationships, and meaning.

Now at the end of the twentieth century, Schoenberg's atonal music remains as elusive as it has ever been, still among the most complex phenomena in the entire world of art. Its popular acceptance is small, and this has not increased appreciably in the years since 1908. But the music endures. Although written for a small audience and making no concession to the popular taste, Schoenberg's atonal works continue to grasp and hold the musical imagination, speaking plainly to a state of human consciousness that is not addressed by other forms of artistic utterance. Pieces such as *Pierrot lunaire*, the opera *Erwartung*, and the Five Orchestra Pieces, Op. 16, remain today as masterpieces of the modern repertory, as unsettlingly relevant to artistic thought at the end of the twentieth century as when they were composed near its beginning. Without them, most of the works of Anton Webern and Alban Berg could not have been written; the return to modernism in music by Pierre Boulez, Milton Babbitt, and Olivier Messiaen that followed World War II would be unthinkable; and the persistence of modernism in contemporary works by Elliott Carter and Wolfgang Rihm would scarcely be possible. Given this vitality, it seems certain that the prophetic voice in Schoenberg's atonal music will continue to speak as urgently to the twentieth-first century as it did to the twentieth.

2

Schoenberg's Evolution toward Atonality

Schoenberg's reasons for adopting the atonal style have never been fully explained. They are wound together in a tangle of historical, technical, and personal factors so tightly intertwined that they were probably not fully known even to the composer himself. Schoenberg often said that his transition to atonal composition was unwilled, even unplanned, the result of an unconscious or instinctive process. Other explanations that he put forward contain more than a few contradictions. Near the time of his move to atonality, he cited Dionysian factors—the "ecstatic" inspiration found in poetry, the wish for a new intensity of expression, a powerful urge to be released from all formal restrictions in music. "I am obeying an inner compulsion, which is stronger than any upbringing; I am obeying the formative process which, being the one natural to me, is stronger than my artistic education," he wrote in 1910.[1] Later he described the evolution to atonality in a more Apollonian voice: "I was driven onward by the need for *brevity, precision, definition and clarity.* I had the sense that I was now saying it *better,* more *clearly,* more *unambiguously,* more *personally.*"[2]

Schoenberg's adoption of the atonal style of composition in 1908 was also a symptom of a larger historical evolution that engaged progressive composers throughout the world. Béla Bartók's Fourteen Bagatelles, Aleksandr Scriabin's *Prometheus,* and Charles Ives's Set No. 1 for Small Orchestra—all composed, at least partly, in 1908—share the same free treatment of dissonance, attenuation or removal of key, and outré expressivity that also characterize Schoenbergian atonality. This remarkable coordination of such widespread but interrelated experiments suggests, as Schoenberg often contended, that the birth of atonality resulted from a deeply rooted evolution in musical structure and means of expression.

The Term and Concept of Atonality

If Schoenberg was uncertain about how he came to atonality, he was quite sure that the word itself was inappropriate. The term *atonal* began to appear sporadically in German technical writing on music in various contexts early in the twentieth century. It was probably first used to describe Schoenberg's new style by his student Egon Wellesz.[3] In an article published in September 1911, Wellesz divided Schoenberg's music to that time into three style periods, of which the Three Piano Pieces, Op. 11, initiated the last. "These are atonal [pieces] and do away with the concept of dissonance," Wellesz wrote.[4] An expanded version of the same paper was published in 1916 in *The Musical Quarterly*, in which the translator, Otto Kinkeldey, rendered the term *atonal* as "atonic." Perhaps because the essay was to be published in a foreign country, Wellesz was emboldened to aim a fair measure of criticism at recent works both by Schoenberg and by Wellesz's own fellow students. Schoenberg's Six Little Piano Pieces, Wellesz wrote, were hardly comprehensible, "apparently amorphous products of very few measures." Aphoristic orchestral works by other students—Wellesz was no doubt thinking about Berg's Op. 6 and Webern's Op. 6—were "without aesthetic justification." He concluded that Schoenberg's "musical language has become so complicated that he himself can offer no theoretical explanation of his latest works and must rely entirely upon his intuitive musical feeling."[5]

Martin Thrun has shown that the term *atonal* was soon widely and approvingly used by many in Schoenberg's circle.[6] But Schoenberg himself apparently took little note of it until 1921, when he discovered that the word had been co-opted by Josef Matthias Hauer to describe his own highly eccentric music. In his treatise *Vom Wesen des Musikalischen* (1920), Hauer defined "atonal music" as a style in which

> there is no longer tonic, dominant, subdominant degrees, resolutions, consonances, dissonances, instead, only the twelve intervals of equal temperament. Its "scale" consists of the twelve tempered half steps. In atonal melody the purely physical, sensual, also the trivial and sentimental are, so far as possible, ruled out. Its "law," its "nomos" is that within a specified succession of tones, no note is repeated and none is omitted.[7]

If we judge from the dates attached to Schoenberg's marginal notes in his copy of Hauer's book, he encountered this description of atonality during the summer of 1921, just at the time that he was at work revising his own *Harmonielehre*. Not wanting his brand of atonality to be confused with Hauer's, Schoenberg then completely rejected the term.[8] In the margins of Hauer's book he wrote:

> The expression "atonal music" is nonsense. Tonal is that which *pertains* to tone; tonality is used in the sense of a special application of this concept; since it must mean that in a musical piece everything is referable back to one tone (the tonic), there is a significant verbal imprecision here. Such a piece [as Hauer describes] would have to be called *monotonal*. "Atonal" cannot be something in which tones occur, [instead] something that does not pertain to tone, having no connection to it. Even in the sense in which tonality is [commonly] used, atonal cannot be applied since a succession of tones that in no way relate to one another is not a succession. One could perhaps say *polytonal*. In any event: the expression atonal would have been applied before my music to Reger, Mahler and

Strauss, since the relation to a single tonic is not evident. Just as wrongly! I have always rejected the term.[9]

In a footnote that he added at about this time to the new edition of the *Harmonielehre*, Schoenberg paraphrased these remarks, again putting forward "polytonal," also "pantonal," as better alternatives for what others called atonal.[10] These two words suggest that the new idiom made free and equal use of the entire chromatic scale of tones, not just the seven notes of a major or minor scale. In the first edition of the *Harmonielehre* Schoenberg had already alluded to the twelve-tone chromatic scale as the basic "conceptual unit" of ultramodern harmony, and by the early 1920s he was all the more inclined to suggest a connection between this twelve-tone element in his atonal works and twelve-tone composition per se.

This important association is evident in the contents of a fragmentary and anonymous typescript titled "Komposition mit zwölf Tönen," found in the Berg Collection in the Austrian National Library, which almost certainly consists of notes made from a lecture given by Schoenberg in 1922 or 1923 concerning twelve-tone composition in its early stage of development.[11] Here the author describes the beginnings of atonality as an imperfect and primarily intuitive forerunner of twelve-tone composition, the two types of music even sharing the same name:

> With the onset of twelve-tone composition [i.e., atonality], one was suddenly confronted by the void. The old way was rejected, but a new form had still not been found. At first one had to compose by instinct. But the search for a conscious profile for this formal intuition could not be given up, instead, it became a necessity. These first essays resulted in something that was similarly necessary—brevity. When motivic repetition and motivic development were abandoned, it became impossible to write longer compositions.[12]

Atonality in Schoenberg's Writings

Although Schoenberg wrote no theory of atonal music, his literary oeuvre still offers an invaluable entrée into this repertory, one that is especially rich in information about the separation of atonal from tonal music. In such essays as the *Harmonielehre* (1911), *Structural Functions of Harmony* (published in 1954), and the lecture "Problems of Harmony" (1927, revised 1934), the composer addressed in detail the subject of tonality as a compositional tool, and he also traced the historical process by which it was expanded, weakened, and ultimately abandoned.

He distinguished, to begin with, between tonality (*Tonalität*) and key (*Tonart*). Tonality was the broader concept of which key was a specific example. "Everything implied by a series of tones constitutes tonality, whether it be brought together by means of direct reference to a single fundamental or by more complicated connections," he wrote.[13] "Tonality is a formal possibility that emerges from the nature of the tonal material, a possibility of attaining a certain completeness or closure by means of a certain uniformity."[14] Since all tones have some degree of interrelationship, he wrote, all music must have a tonality, including the ostensibly "atonal."

Key, however, was a specific system of scalar and chordal allegiances to a tonic note. As a practical application of tonality, it endured from the time of Bach to the early twentieth century. Its main characteristic was the persistence of a "tonal center" or "common fundamental tone," to which the chords and lines throughout a work referred by well-defined hierarchical and functional relationships. Key provided the composer with two properties that allowed music to be better understood: a unity of structure that flowed from the pervasive allegiances of lines and chords to the tonal center and a means to readily achieve differentiation, contrast, and articulation. Key also produced an integration of the horizontal and vertical dimensions of a work, as Schoenberg explained:

> Whenever all chords of a complete piece of music appear in progressions that can be related to a common fundamental tone, one can then say that the idea of the musical chord (which is conceived as vertical) is extended to the horizontal plane. Everything following it [the chord] springs from this fundamental postulate, refers back to it, even when antithetical to it, elaborates and complements it, and finally leads back to it, so that this fundamental is treated in every respect as central, as embryonic.[15]

The composer was quick to observe that the system of relationships that defined a key was not a product of natural law or eternally valid; it was subject to the same evolution that changing ideas in music enacted upon all forms of expression. The unity, contrast, and multidimensional integration that key could produce, for example, could also be achieved by motivic or thematic practices.[16] Although he allowed that his own music after 1908 probably possessed some still-unformulated principle of tonality, he repeatedly emphasized that it had no key.

The historical movement in which traditional tonality was set aside, Schoenberg said, reached back at least to the time of Bach; it gained strength in the romantic period and came to a climax at the turn of the twentieth century. The process was not one of rebellion or rejection but instead the result of a continuing enrichment of harmony that was driven, especially in its later stages, by the ever more vivid expression of extramusical ideas. This relentless change in harmonic language led to a style, prefigured even in the early history of tonal harmony, that the composer called "extended tonality." It was produced by two distinct but related phenomena. First was an ever greater variety in the makeup of chords themselves, as triads and simple seventh chords gradually gave up their exclusive status as basic harmonies. Second was the progressive freeing of these chords from their functions within a key, a weakening and finally an abandonment of their relationship to a tonic note or chord.

A style that was especially characteristic of nineteenth-century music that suggested a weakening of functional harmony was what Schoenberg called *Stufenreichtum* (richness of degrees). It was evident in a multiplicity of roots ("degrees") in a harmonic progression in a prevailing key. In *Structural Functions of*

Example 2.1. Bruckner, Symphony No. 7, Adagio, measures 1–9, with Schoenberg's analysis

Harmony Schoenberg admiringly cited the opening of the main theme of Bruckner's Symphony No. 7, second movement, as an example of tonality extended by *Stufenreichtum.* According to his analysis (Example 2.1), every degree in the key of C♯ minor is represented by one or more chords.[17] He also noted the presence of passing tones, marked with a cross, as elements that further enriched the harmony and extended the key.

Another and even greater means by which composers weakened functional harmonic progressions, Schoenberg said, was the accumulation in a work of "vagrant" chords. These were nondiatonic harmonies that were capable of suggesting a relationship to two or more tonal centers. If used in large numbers they could weaken or even remove the perceptible existence of a tonic. Schoenberg wrote about them often, and he was plainly fascinated by their capacity to extend normative tonal structures:

> The pupil will best take all these vagrant chords for what they are, without tracing them back to a key or a degree: homeless phenomena, unbelievably adaptable and unbelievably lacking in independence; spies, who ferret out weaknesses and use them to cause confusion; turncoats, to whom abandonment of their individuality is an end in itself; agitators in every respect, but above all: most amusing fellows.[18]

The primary vagrant chords that Schoenberg discussed in his pedagogical writings were the diminished seventh, half-diminished seventh (to which he gave no name), augmented triad and larger whole-tone chords (including the French sixth), fourth chords, Neapolitan sixth, German sixth (which he called the "aug-

Example 2.2. Beethoven, String Quartet in E minor, Op. 59, No. 2, Allegro, measures 1–10, with Schoenberg's analysis

mented 4/3"), and two of its inversions, which he referred to as the "augmented 6/5" and "augmented 2."[19] Other chords could also be vagrant; in fact, Schoenberg held that any chord could be such depending on its use. In *Structural Functions of Harmony* he analyzed numerous works of the eighteenth and nineteenth centuries in order to illustrate the ways that vagrant chords extended tonality. The occurrence of these harmonies in the standard literature suggested to him that traditional tonality was always in flux, always contending with the seeds of its own destruction. He wrote: "The question of endangering tonality becomes acute at that stage where, in addition to the diatonic, key-determining chords, an excessive number of chords occur within a composition, whose use the key at best permits but which no longer definitely refer to it. This danger manifested itself rather early in musical history."[20]

He found this endangerment of tonality even in passages where a key was usually strictly presented, as in the exposition of a classical main theme. One such was in the opening of Beethoven's String Quartet in E minor, Op. 59, No. 2, first movement.[21] The first ten measures of the theme are supported, according to Schoenberg's analysis (Example 2.2), by a succession of tonic and dominant chords, with the exception of measures 6–7, where the "Neapolitan" tonal region of F major is evident. Since the F-major triad functions simultaneously as a representative of the supertonic in E minor and the tonic of the Neapolitan region itself, it is a vagrant chord that, Schoenberg concludes, weakens the key of E minor.

Schoenberg's analysis of the Beethoven quartet shows that his theory of tonal harmony was not always adequate to explain expanded tonal structures; in fact, what he interpreted as a weakening of tonality in nineteenth-century music was often the product of a defective theory faced with an enriched harmonic language. Schoenberg based his concept of harmony on a pedagogical tradition that rigidly isolated harmony per se from counterpoint and voice leading, and in doing so it made relatively few concessions to how the music actually sounds. In Schoenberg's view, any simultaneity of tones creates a harmony, whose function in a key is determined solely by a root tone. His analytic observations were also almost entirely directed at small, even minute, time spans within a work, ignoring larger units of musical thought.[22] There was no possibility in his system, for example, of relating the bass note F in measures 6 and 7 to the bass of the preceding tonic triad, E, and to the F♯ on the downbeat of measure 9, although these notes have a plainly audible connection that is linear rather than harmonic in origin. The localized I–V–I progression in measures 6–7 prolongs the triadic harmonization of the passing tone F, and although the tonality of E minor in the theme is enlarged and enriched by this nondiatonic passage, it is not at all weakened by the passage or by the introduction of chromatic tones. In fact, the tonal coherence is reinforced by an interweaving of contrapuntal and harmonic motions, from which neither one can be meaningfully isolated.

Schoenberg was on firmer ground when he pointed to three phenomena in late-nineteenth-century music that represented the final stages in the weakening of functional harmonic progressions. Two of these—tonality that he called *aufgehoben* (suspended) and *schwebend* (wavering)—have special relevance to his own music, and they will be discussed later in this chapter. The third concerns the "impressionistic" or "coloristic" use of chords, which he found in music by Claude Debussy and in certain passages by Richard Strauss, especially from *Salome.* In order to communicate extramusical content, Debussy wrote harmonies that essentially eliminated root progressions:

> His harmonies, without constructive meaning, often served the coloristic purpose of expressing moods and pictures. Moods and pictures, though extra-musical, thus became constructive elements, incorporated in the musical functions; they produced a sort of emotional comprehensibility. In this way, tonality was already dethroned in practice, if not in theory.[23]

Schoenberg rarely analyzed specific works by Debussy, although what he refers to as Debussy's "harmonies, without constructive meaning," can be readily observed in Debussy's music from the 1890s and later. The opening of the Sarabande from *Pour le piano* will provide an example.[24] The piece is ostensibly in the key of C♯ minor (it ends on a C♯-minor triad). In the opening passages (Example 2.3), the beginnings and ends of phrases refer to primary functional harmonies in that key—the minor dominant chord, for example, is placed at the end of measures 2 and 4, the dominant of the relative major at measure 8, and the bass of the first measure arpeggiates a II chord in C♯ minor. Furthermore, the outer sections of the piece rest almost entirely on triads and various seventh chords drawn from the key of C♯. The form and texture of the Sarabande are also highly regular, reminiscent of earlier tonal music, in their simple phrasing, melodiousness, and persistent, unvaried repetitions of small phrases. But despite these conventional elements of style, the chords of the piece are not essentially or-

Example 2.3. Debussy, Sarabande from *Pour le piano*, measures 1–8

ganized by tonal syntax. Most of them are laid out in parallel streams, and cadencelike pauses occur on degrees that do not consistently suggest the functions of tonic, dominant, or dominant preparation. Schoenberg went directly to this issue when he declared that tonality in Debussy's music had already been eliminated, well in advance, that is, of his own quite different tonal experiments of the first decade of the century.

Schoenberg emphasized that his own evolution toward atonality had more to do with the makeup of the chords in his harmonic vocabulary than with Debussy's impressionistic removal of harmonic function. Schoenberg's chords, like those of other German modernists of his day, were more varied in sound and structure than Debussy's largely tertian harmonies, a distinction that Schoenberg attributed to the dissonance and chromatic content that had long increased in the harmonic dimension of German music. One explanation that the composer gave for these differences was the prevalence in German music of "transformed" (i.e., altered) chords, which are diatonic harmonies in which one or more tones are displaced by a note a step away.[25] Unlike vagrant chords, altered chords retain a single diatonic function, although both types of harmonies introduce a richness of dissonance and an increase in chromatic pitch content.

The chromaticism that stemmed from the accumulation of vagrant and transformed chords tended, in Schoenberg's view, to equalize all twelve chromatic tones, removing the priority naturally accorded to the seven diatonic notes of a prevailing scale and dissipating the hierarchical distinctions among scale degrees. "It is evident that chords remote from the key, appearing in large numbers, will favor the establishment of a new *conceptual unit:* the chromatic scale," Schoenberg wrote. "It is not to be ignored that through accumulation of such phenomena the solid structure of tonality could be demolished."[26] Schoenberg's generalization rang true to Béla Bartók, who later echoed Schoenberg's conclusion in his own analysis of the onset of atonality. In 1920 Bartók wrote:

> The complete adoption of atonality began only . . . when the necessity was first felt for an equalization of the twelve different tones of our twelve-tone system, that is, when composers first attempted to use the twelve tones both vertically and horizontally in any configuration whatever, not deployed according to an established scale system in which some tones are always accorded greater or lesser weight.[27]

Schoenberg held that modern harmony was also brought to the frontier of atonality by the higher profile of dissonance. He found in dissonance—far more than in Debussy's removal of harmonic function—a portentous indication of the future. Debussy's nonfunctional harmonies, on the contrary, "would perhaps not have caused a radical change in compositional technique. Such a change became necessary when there occurred simultaneously a development which ended in what I call the *emancipation of dissonance*."[28] This term, whose origins Robert Falck credits to the theorist Rudolf Louis in his *Die deutsche Musik der Gegenwart* (1909),[29] was used by Schoenberg to describe a progressive loss of the power of dissonant chords to disrupt the listener. In his view, they gradually became equivalent to consonant chords in their structural role and comprehensibility, no longer in need of special treatment such as preparation or resolution, and inherently neither harsh nor beautiful. Schoenberg had broached the concept of the emancipation of dissonance in 1911 in his *Harmonielehre* in the context of seventh and ninth chords that were equivalent in use to consonant harmonies.[30] In his own music composed after 1908 he declared a full liberation of dissonance, which finalized the elimination of a tonal center: "The term *emancipation of dissonance* refers to its comprehensibility, which is considered equivalent to the consonance's comprehensibility. A style based on this premise treats dissonances like consonances and renounces a tonal centre."[31]

But for Schoenberg the emancipation of dissonance that accompanied the early atonal style did not immediately mean the creation of a completely new harmonic vocabulary. Instead, the composer brought forward the same enriched chords that already existed in his late tonal style. These included—in addition to a few triads and seventh chords—altered chords and some of the vagrant harmonies that had characterized the style of extended tonality. Other atonal chords found in passing in the late tonal repertory are described in the final chapters of the *Harmonielehre*, specifically, in passages that deal with nonharmonic tones, whole-tone chords, and fourth chords.[32] Although these categories of chords were evident in the style of extended tonality, they have much more relevance to the atonal style, in which they are fully "emancipated" rather than merely unstable and passing phenomena. Schoenberg apparently wished to underscore that such chords coexisted in both types of music so that early atonality would be seen as cut from the same cloth as the more familiar and widely accepted post-Wagnerian idiom. "I believe that in the harmony of us ultramodernists will ultimately be found the same laws that obtained in the older harmony, only correspondingly broader, more generally conceived," Schoenberg concluded. "Therefore, it seems to me of great importance that we conserve the knowledge and experience of the past. Precisely this former knowledge and experience will show, I hope, how correct is the path along which we are searching."[33]

The greater relevance of the concluding chapters of the *Harmonielehre* for atonal rather than tonal harmony is seen nowhere more plainly than in Schoenberg's discussion of nonharmonic tones.[34] In this chapter the composer denies even the possibility that melodic motion or rhythmic dislocation can produce tones that are foreign or unessential to a chord: "Non-harmonic tones do form chords, hence are not non-harmonic; the musical phenomena they help to create are harmonies, as is everything that sounds simultaneously."[35] This interpretation, which subsequently brought on him a fair measure of ridicule,[36] can only be understood in the context of posttonal music. As it concerns the structure of tonal music, Schoenberg's denial of the existence of nonharmonic tones is plainly untenable. But as a projection into the future—a statement about atonal harmony—it is an important assessment that touches on the origin of the chords that he was using in that style even as the *Harmonielehre* was being written.

A virtual catalog of the most prominent harmonies in Schoenberg's early atonal music is given out in his discussion of nonharmonic tones. In the *Harmonielehre* these are shown as chords formed primarily by melodic motions supported by triads; in the atonal style the resolutions and preparations are usually absent and the underlying triad no longer has structural priority, but the dissonant chordal structures themselves remain and characterize the sound of the new idiom. The chords that Schoenberg illustrates in this chapter are mainly four-note figures, only occasionally enlarged to five or six tones, and three of the tones almost always form a major or minor triad. Since they are interelated by the presence of the triad, they will henceforth be called *triadic tetrachords*. The family is basic to Schoenberg's early atonal harmonic practices.

If transpositions and the ordering of notes are discounted, there are only nine possible tetrachords that contain a major triad. These are illustrated in Example 2.4A, using a C-major triad (shown with open note heads in the example) as a basis. Some of these have a familiar sound in tonal harmony—no. 8 is equivalent to a dominant seventh chord, no. 7 to a minor seventh—while the others arise there less frequently, usually as linear chords that contain passing, auxiliary, or suspended tones. In his chapter on nonharmonic tones in the *Harmonielehre*, Schoenberg used virtually every one of them in his examples, there as harmonies that arise through melodic embellishment. With the exception of the dominant seventh, he used them all copiously in his early atonal music.

There are also nine possible tetrachords that contain a minor triad, as shown in Example 2.4B. A measure of redundancy exists between the two subgroups. Nos. 3, 7, and 9 from Example 2.4A contain both a major and a minor chord—they are the same as nos. 3, 8, and 6 from Example 2.4B, only reordered and transposed. The remaining six tetrachords from each group can, at least in theory, also be linked into pairs that share a common intervallic profile. For example, the notes of no. 1A are separated by a semitone, minor third, and minor

Example 2.4. Triadic tetrachords

third—the same as no. 5B, although in reverse order that suggests an intervallic inversion. The sound of the two elements of these pairs, however, may not be especially similar; still, Schoenberg sometimes alternated the two elements of a pair as a means of variation.

One of them, no. 9B, seemed especially to capture his attention.[37] It is discussed in several different contexts within the *Harmonielehre*[38] and reappears as one of the most prominent of chords in Schoenberg's early atonal music. He found it in the form G B G$\sharp$ E$\flat$, in the first movement of Mozart's G-Minor Symphony, K. 550 (measures 150–52), where it arises as a prefix to a dominant seventh in the home key, to which it is connected by stepwise motion in all voices.[39] "But the theorists told Mozart during his lifetime what a dissonance chaser he was, and how all too often he gave in to the passion to write something ugly," he added wryly.[40] Later in the *Harmonielehre*, Schoenberg returned to this chord in the context of enriched diatonic harmony, and he gave no fewer than seven sample harmonic progressions in which it occurs, each time as an altered chord that represented a functional degree. These illustrations underscore a property of the chord that clearly fascinated the composer—it contains both a minor and an augmented triad. As can be seen from Example 2.4B, it is the only one of the nine tetrachordal types having this property. Except for his discussion of the chord in the context of nonharmonic tones, as in Mozart, Schoenberg was not especially successful at finding a normative use for the chord in tonal harmony. It can, he says, have a diatonic function as a seventh chord on the first degree in minor (for example, A C E G$\sharp$ in A minor).[41]

One of the many prominent occurrences of the chord in Schoenberg's early atonal music—in the company of other triadic tetrachords and vagrant harmonies—is in the first section of the song "Hain in diesen Paradiesen," Op. 15, No. 2 (Example 2.5). This opening passage, like several in the George cycle, has

Example 2.5. Schoenberg, "Hain in diesen Paradiesen," Op. 15, No. 2, measures 1–5

a distinctly tonal flavor, here alluding to the key of D minor by vestigial functional progressions. In fact, the style and tonal structure of these five measures alone are very similar to Schoenberg's songs from as early as 1903. References to tonal harmonic progressions are much reduced later in this song, as though Schoenberg wanted to ease his listener into the atonal environment. The first chord in the piano is a form of triadic tetrachord 9B, the "seventh chord on the first degree of [D] minor," as Schoenberg was later to describe it. Its triadic component is reinforced by the nearly diatonic motion in D minor in the voice in measures 1–2; the augmented triad that it contains is then dwelled upon in measure 3, where all of the notes are whole-tone related. A dominant-seventh chord in the key of D minor is heard briefly over the bass tone E at the beginning of measure 4, but the harmonic motion quickly turns away and reaches a cadence on a B-major triad, at which point the section ends.

   After the early phase of his atonal experiment in the George songs and the first two Piano Pieces, Op. 11, Schoenberg moved away from the repertory of atonal chords that he had borrowed from late tonal music. He then almost completely ruled out even the passing use of triads and familiar seventh chords and adopted larger basic harmonies that have more than four tones, which had little, if any, resonance in the tonal literature. He alluded briefly to these resources in the final chapter of the *Harmonielehre*, subtitled "Aesthetic Evaluation of Chords with Six or More Tones," a passage written in 1911 at about the time that he was himself experimenting with larger harmonies in *Die glückliche Hand.* But he had relatively little to say about them. In fact, Schoenberg's writings— so illuminating about late romantic harmony and the transition to atonality— include remarkably little technical information about atonal music after its earliest stages.[42] He seemed reluctant to theorize about a movement that arose so much from instinctive impulse. Concerning a harmony in Berg's Four Songs, Op. 2, for example, Schoenberg remarked: "Why is it that way and why is it correct, I cannot yet explain in any detail."[43] "Laws apparently prevail here," he continued. "What they are, I do not know. Perhaps I shall know in a few years. Perhaps someone after me will find them. For the present the most we can do is describe."[44]

Approaches to Atonality in Schoenberg's Early Songs

Just as Schoenberg's theoretical writings provide important information on the weakening and downfall of tonality, his music before 1908 contains a virtual encyclopedia of harmonic and tonal practices that prefigure the outright adoption of atonality. But this preliminary development followed no straight or coherent path. Especially during the years from 1903 until 1905, works that are filled with innovations, such as the song "Verlassen," Op. 6, No. 4, often stand chronologically beside others—the Wolfian "Traumleben," Op. 6, No. 1, is an example—that are relatively conventional in their tonal structure. Schoenberg's almost constantly shifting orientation toward tonality is especially observable in the songs from his late tonal period, as the expression of a text apparently drove the composer in the most divergent of directions. The genre of song was an especially useful laboratory in which to try out new ideas. Its inherent expressivity provided an environment in which harmonic and tonal experiments needed no further justification than their alliance with heightened emotions and new poetic ideas. The presence of a text was an especially powerful stimulus for Schoenberg's imagination—"extramusical influences produced the concept of extended tonality," he later asserted.[45] It was perhaps inevitable that Schoenberg's earliest atonal compositions would be vocal works.

During the early tonal period that followed his apprenticeship under Alexander Zemlinsky, Schoenberg wrote songs mainly in three chronological phases. The first took place from 1898 until 1900, during which time he worked within inherited styles, using expressive principles shared with his late romantic contemporaries. He later chose songs from these years to be published as his Opp. 1 and 2. He returned to the genre of song in 1903, when most of his Six Songs, Op. 3, were composed, and again in 1905 in the songs of Opp. 6 and 8, these two collections composed just after he completed the First String Quartet. His songs from these years show an important degree of independence from any existing models within their genre.

Although Schoenberg did not create a distinct or consistent musical language in each of these periods, a study of selected songs from 1899 to 1905 will show characteristic aspects of his thinking about key and form. These brought him to the very limits of tonality and led him by 1908 almost effortlessly to the atonal style of the George songs, Op. 15. A few generalizations about Schoenberg's early songs are first in order. Their expressive principles are shared with the late romantic German lied, in which models by Brahms and Wolf are especially evident. Schoenberg seemed comfortable with almost any style of poetry—the high language of Goethe, Dehmel, or Nietzsche coexisted on his workbench with folklike verse and with sentimental doggerel. The topics addressed in the poetry that he chose for musical treatment often have a resonance with events in his personal life—including his courtship of Mathilde Zemlinsky and the strain that later entered his marriage. Schoenberg said that he chose a poem for a song because it produced "inspiration, a state of feverish excitement; preceding the real conception of ideas."[46]

Virtually every early song uses a traditional large-scale architecture, most often a varied ternary design that was frequently enlarged by a piano postlude. A highly varied strophic form is another recurring formal archetype. Even the earliest songs show careful attention to organic unity achieved by pervasive variations upon motives and phrases, whose subtle recurrences link otherwise contrasting sections. The piano is usually an equal partner of the voice in carrying the burden of expression. It is often entrusted with the exposition and development of the main melodic materials, and, as in "Dank" and "Abschied" from Op. 1, it sometimes takes the character of a bombastic orchestral reduction. The voice line is principally concerned with declaiming the poem, underscoring its emotions, and, for certain texts, creating a lyrical melody. The music of both the voice and piano is typically filled with many word paintings.

The song "Erwartung," Op. 2, No. 1 (1899), is rightly celebrated among Schoenberg's earliest important compositions for its originality and provocatively expressive language.[47] It is one of eight completed songs, all composed between 1897 and 1905, that adopt poetry by Richard Dehmel, Schoenberg's first great poetic muse. In addition to its inspired level of expressivity, the song illustrates the capacity of tonality to organize Schoenberg's early music and to further the coherent presentation of ideas, although it also shows a great flexibility that could accommodate an enriched mode of expression.

The five strophes of the text and a piano postlude are symmetrically distributed to create a large ternary form (the three sections begin at measures 1, 11, and 26), and each section has two subdivisions (the junctures are at measures 6, 18, and 31). The middle section of the ternary form stands apart from the outer ones by conventional means of contrast—a distinct tempo, new surface design, and thematic materials that are only distantly related to those of the opening passage. Schoenberg also applied distinctive harmonic techniques to give the middle part an even clearer contrasting status. Both tonality and motivic development act as formative principles in the music, binding the whole song together into an organic unit. Unlike most of Schoenberg's songs, however, "Erwartung" contains a number of immediate and unvaried recurrences

Example 2.6. Schoenberg, "Erwartung," Op. 2, No. 1, measures 2–3

of small phrases, which give the music a resemblance to contemporary works by Debussy, a kinship that may have been suggested to Schoenberg by Dehmel's decidedly impressionistic text.

Schoenberg's chordal vocabulary in the song conforms in general to the expanded harmonic language of modern German and French composers of 1899, which Schoenberg was to describe later in his *Harmonielehre*. In addition to triads and seventh chords from prevailing keys, it also includes the enriched dissonances of vagrant and transformed chords. Freely used ninth chords, 6/4 chords, whole-tone formations, and diminished and minor sevenths are all present, and the song is also characterized by a colorful five-note chord ($E^\flat$ A D $G^\flat$ $C^\flat$), heard on the downbeat of the first measure (see Example 2.6). This harmony is an embellishment of the tonic $E^\flat$ triads that surround it, although—characteristic of Schoenberg's boldness in using dissonant harmony—its repeated appearance, elongation, and metric stress call more attention to it than to the structural triad from which it takes its origin. But the derivation of this chord—explicitly as an embellishment of a triad—suggests that dissonance in the song is not yet "emancipated," not structurally equivalent to consonant harmony. The structural framework of the whole song is provided by triads, mainly those with primary functions in the key of $E^\flat$ major. Dissonant chords, despite their great variety and quantity, are unstable entities that take their meaning and origin from consonances.

Tonal harmonic progressions that stretch over different spans of the song control and integrate its harmonic and melodic motion in a way that is similar to music by other modern German composers at the turn of the century. On a large scale the song is organized by a single circular harmonic progression that departs from the initial tonic $E^\flat$, passes through the submediant region that begins in measure 6, arrives at a dominant harmony in measure 21, and finally returns to the tonic from measure 26. These harmonic pillars coincide with major structural junctures in the ternary form and with the principal divisions of the text. Between these structural points, however, the control exerted by key is looser, generally remote from functional triads within the prevailing keys. The

Example 2.7. Schoenberg, "Erwartung," Op. 2, No. 1: (a) measures 30–31; (b) measures 7–10; (c) measures 11–17

(a)

(b)

intervening passages suggest a technique of expansion and embellishment of simple harmonic or cadential progressions, but one that was still familiar to many of the modern composers of 1900.

Specifically, diatonic chords are embellished or connected by three primary means of enlargement. In the first and simplest of these, seen in measures 30–31 (Example 2.7a), a single chord (here a dominant seventh) is sustained and ornamented by simultaneous movements in the upper voices. The harmony does

Example 2.7. Continued

not change in these two measures, remaining instead continually on the domi-nant. The second and highly characteristic connective device is encountered in measures 7–10 (Example 2.7b) in a region of the song in which C is the local tonic. Here the music moves from a statement of a C triad in measure 7 to the dominant ninth chord on G at the end of measure 10. The connection between these framing structural points is guided not by harmonic processes per se, but by a stepwise descending bass line that moves from C down to G while the upper voices create altered or vagrant chords by stepwise movement or common tones, incorporating motivic recurrences as always.

   The third technique used by Schoenberg to expand conventional harmonic progressions—the harmonic sequence—was a tool that had been used with great expressivity by Wagner. An example in "Erwartung" is found in the first half of the song's middle section (measures 11–17), whose harmony is entirely created by sequence (Example 2.7c). The sequential model is the succession of ninth chords on G and D, first heard in measure 12, which moves upward to A and E (measures 14–15), then to B, where the pattern is broken. Here the har-monic motion is left in medias res, the outcome of harmonic movement that serves primarily to underscore the text, which at this point speaks of sinking colors that radiate from jewels in the man's ring. This passage is probably an ex-ample of what Schoenberg in the *Harmonielehre* described as tonality that was *aufgehoben*, meaning suspended or set aside, a phenomenon that he found espe-

cially characteristic of music by Bruckner and Wolf.[48] Key is briefly annulled
here in the sense that the ascending pattern itself governs the passage, not harmonic processes inherent in any particular key. The suspension of key is only
local and temporary. When the seventh chord on B is reached in measure 17,
the harmony is redirected toward the key of E♭, in which this chord functions as
an enharmonically spelled German sixth chord on the lowered sixth scale degree (C♭). The listener's attention is thus directed toward the dominant harmony
in E♭, which is finally regained in measure 21.

"Erwartung" also shows the great expressive power that Schoenberg derived
from elliptical and incomplete harmonic progressions. Frequently in cadential
formations in his early songs, Schoenberg suppressed the dominant chord, moving directly from a dominant preparation or from some other harmony directly
to the tonic. He alluded to this and other forms of ellipsis in the *Harmonielehre:* "We
can now even omit the middle parts of the [cadential harmonic] formula, set beginning and end right together, 'abbreviate,' so to speak, the whole pattern, set
it down merely as premise and conclusion."[49] This elliptical treatment is highly
characteristic of "Erwartung," as Walter Frisch has pointed out.[50] The phenomenon is seen most clearly in the approach to the tonic E♭ triad at the reprise
in measure 26, which is prefixed by a cadential 6/4 chord on the bass tone B♭
and by the exotic pentad of the opening, but not by an authentic dominant. The
incomplete harmonic progression is also a pronounced feature of Schoenberg's
early songs, as in the nontonic openings of both songs of his Op. 1. In "Erwartung" the phenomenon occurs most plainly at the end of the first section in
measure 10 (shown in Example 2.7b), where a progression in the main secondary key of C major is left incomplete, resting on its dominant.

The four years that separated "Erwartung" from the song "Die Aufgeregten,"
Op. 3, No. 2, witnessed a great evolution in Schoenberg's harmonic thinking, so
much so that this and many other works of 1903 have relatively little resemblance to Schoenberg's earlier models from the late romantic period and move
instead in a decidedly experimental direction. "Die Aufgeregten" is a setting of
a poem by Gottfried Keller, the nineteenth-century Swiss writer whose works
Schoenberg was much involved with in his music of 1903 and 1904. The tone
of the poem is partly ironic. The smallest creatures of nature, Keller writes,
seem to enact in their lives a passion that mankind can only witness with indifference. The reader is left to think that the great passions of men are equally insignificant when viewed from a still higher level.

Schoenberg's setting ignores Keller's ironic twist and dwells upon the *Leiden-
schaft* and *Schmerz* mentioned at the outset. The song embodies a more complex
architecture than "Erwartung," as it combines elements of both ternary and
strophic form. Keller brings back the first two lines of the first stanza at the end
of the concluding third stanza, and Schoenberg simply repeats the music of this
refrain to create the outer sections of an *ABA* plan. The middle part is freely
strophic, with divisions at measures 7, 10, and 17.

The ambiguities that characterize the tonal plan of the song are evident from
the very outset (Example 2.8). This example contains the refrain, which is made
from a chain of primarily vagrant chords whose progression is guided solely by

Example 2.8. Schoenberg, "Die Aufgeregten," Op. 3, No. 2, measures 1–6

a descending stepwise bass line. The listener has no way of relating the passage definitely to any key. Toward the end it alludes to G major, the supertonic of the principal tonality of F minor, to whose tonic it abruptly moves in measure 7. The passage is thus similar to measures 11–17 of "Erwartung," in which tonality was suspended by a linear pattern that temporarily superseded the control of a key. But in "Die Aufgeregten" the suspension of key is placed front and center, at the very beginning of the work, so that the listener has no tonal context in which to interpret it. The opening is a clear signal that the organizing power of tonality will be greatly transformed in what is to come.

"Die Aufgeregten," like most of Schoenberg's songs from 1903 to 1907, also exhibits an experimental and nontraditional use of key that the composer described as *schwebend,* the term implying that the definition of key was wavering or undecided.[51] Its use in his songs from 1903 to 1907 marks off a major transitional stage in his evolution toward atonality, although its full implications are nowhere explained in his writings. His account of it was brief:

> The sense of form of the present does not demand this exaggerated intelligibility produced by working out the tonality. A piece can also be intelligible to us when the relationship to the fundamental is not treated as basic; it can be intelligible even when the tonality is kept, so to speak, flexible, fluctuating [*schwebend*]. Many examples give evidence that nothing is lost from the impression of completeness if the tonality is merely hinted at.[52]

In the *Harmonielehre* and *Structural Functions of Harmony*, Schoenberg analyzes the phenomenon in three songs from Opp. 6 and 8,[53] and these musical examples suggest that tonality became *schwebend* in short phrases where the root progressions suggested two or more keys simultaneously. In these passages vagrant chords are prominent and other harmonies are so obscured by alterations and so weakened by elliptical and incomplete progressions that no single key is firmly established.

Although Schoenberg's analyses focused on small spans within a composition, the use of wavering tonality produced its most fundamental disruption in the macrostructure of a work, weakening the unifying capacity of a key throughout the entirety of a composition. The change can be observed by comparing "Die Aufgeregten" to "Erwartung." Despite its moments of suspended tonality, "Erwartung" rests on a single normative harmonic progression, circulating through regions that correspond to I–VI–V–I in the key of E♭. There is no such large, tonally unified plan at work in "Die Aufgeregten." The opening passage alludes to a harmonic environment of G major; the middle of the song, F minor; the passage from measures 17 to 19, G♭ minor; G is again suggested at the reprise (measures 20–26); and the song concludes on an F-major triad. The order in which these tonal areas occur and the presence of elliptical and incomplete progressions prevent the listener from deducing any one key that controls the totality of the piece. Certainly Schoenberg conceived of the work as moving within the key of F minor. After all, he chose a key signature of four flats for the whole song, which progresses ultimately to a conclusion on the major tonic in that key. But even the most astute listener cannot trace the persistence of the key from beginning to end, as he can the E♭ tonality of "Erwartung." Here traditional tonality wavers to the point of fragmentation and is relegated to dim and localized references to the distant regions of F, G♭, and G. No longer does Schoenberg use key to produce a unified and integrated structure.

An especially advanced and complex application of wavering and suspended tonality is also apparent in "Der Wanderer," Op. 6, No. 8, composed in April 1905. This song brings Schoenberg's harmonic language to the very limit of conventional tonality; indeed, it extends that language partially into atonal practices. The work contains a setting of Nietzsche's poem as it appeared in his collection of *Gedichte und Sprüche*. A nightingale, singing for its mate, pities the lonely wanderer, whose fate is to journey through the world alone. The song again rests on a ternary plan in which the contrasting middle section (measures 17–70) has two parts, divided at the change of tempo at measure 40. As in "Erwartung," the reprise is prefigured by a short transition (beginning in measure 67) in which the initial motives gradually return.

Certain isolated features of the early atonal style of 1908 and 1909 present themselves immediately in this remarkable song. An ostinato figure in the pianist's right hand runs relentlessly through its outer sections, prefiguring the great importance that Schoenberg would later attach to ostinato. The passage from measures 17 to 39 makes no consistent reference to any key, although it contains the same repertory of altered and vagrant chords from the earlier songs, establishing a mixed style that was the hallmark of Schoenberg's early atonal-

Example 2.9. Schoenberg, "Der Wanderer," Op. 6, No. 8, measures 43–53, with Schoenberg's analysis

ity—a mixture interpreted by Edward T. Cone as an inconsistency among chordal sonority, succession, and harmonic syntax.[54]

The tonal macrostructure of "Der Wanderer" is more conventional than that of "Die Aufgeregten," as the music moves from the tonic G minor at the beginning to the dominant region by measure 40 and back to the tonic from measure 82 to the end. But coherence provided by these closely related regions is clouded by long passages, spanning almost the entire middle of the song, in which the key is *schwebend*. The composer's own analysis of measures 43–53 (Example 2.9) emphasizes the simultaneous presence of D major (abbreviated "T," the local tonic) and B♭ major (abbreviated "♭SM," its flatted submediant region), which are represented by small-scale motions among tonics, dominant preparations, and dominants, all highly embellished by a complex voice leading that produces many enriched and altered chords.[55] At most of the primary structural junctures in the song—measures 16–17, 39, and 70, for example— the listener hears only vagrant chords that can point to several keys but definitively to no one. The return to G minor at the very end of the song has a certain arbitrariness, although it is a moving symbol of the aimless and perpetual wandering of Nietzsche's journeyer.

Wavering and suspended tonality represent Schoenberg's final stages in the evolution of tonal harmony prior to its abandomment in 1908. They relegate functional harmonic progressions to a decidedly small, localized, and relatively arbitrary status, and make the return to a triad at the conclusion of a work almost a symbolic choice. With the removal of large-scale diatonic progressions, the structural distinction between triadic and dissonant chords evaporates; the dissonant harmonies themselves increase in number, and they are no longer the mere instrument by which triads are prolonged or connected. This emancipation of dissonance allows the motions of lines to become ever more chromatic. The seven tones of a diatonic scale no longer maintain a hierarchy of meaning within the entire chromatic gamut, whose twelve notes become equal in their structural standing, rendering the use of key signature superfluous and even misleading.

After 1905 Schoenberg's production of new songs waned. But his search for new expressive resources that could restimulate his musical imagination intensified, leading him almost inevitably to realize more fully the implications of his highly extended tonal language—to remove the arbitrary triad at the end of a piece, to eliminate the redundant key signature, to further suppress the now localized and almost insignificant references to tonics and dominants. The stage was finally set for the emergence of the early atonal style.

3

Settings of the Poetry of Stefan George
Opp. 10, 14, and 15

Schoenberg began to write atonal music in a series of songs and songlike works composed from 1907 to 1909 to the poetry of Stefan George (1868–1933). Just as the lyric verse of Richard Dehmel a decade earlier had beckoned to the composer from the frontiers of modernism, George's words now provoked Schoenberg to cross over into unexplored territory in his search for new expressive resources. He often described this change of style as uncalculated, a musical response to the "state of feverish excitement" that certain poetry could awaken within him. The transition to atonality, he wrote, "happened gradually, in accordance not with any wish or will, but with a *vision,* an *inspiration;* it happened perhaps instinctively."[1] In another essay he connected this change of musical idiom explicitly to one poet:

> I was inspired by poems of Stefan George, the German poet, to compose music to some of his poems and, surprisingly, without any expectation on my part, these songs showed a style quite different from everything I had written before. . . . New sounds were produced, a new kind of melody appeared, a new approach to expression of moods and characters was discovered.[2]

Schoenberg and the Poetry of Stefan George

George's career as a lyric poet was launched after a sojourn in Paris in 1889, during which he came into contact with the circle of Stéphane Mallarmé. The experience rendered George a devoted adherent of French symbolist attitudes and a trenchant opponent of the utopian naturalism that was prevalent then in German literature. He first attracted attention with three poetic collections—*Hymnen, Pilgerfahrten,* and *Algabal*—which appeared in rapid succession between 1890 and 1892 and were later published as a single cycle. Other cycles soon followed, including *Das Buch der hängenden Gärten* (1895), *Das Jahr der Seele* (1897), *Der Teppich des Lebens* (1899), and *Der siebente Ring* (1907). In these works George created a mythic world of the imagination in which the poet often assumed the persona of a solitary pilgrim estranged from his true homeland of the spirit.

A handsome example of George's formal precision and richness of tone is provided by the poem "Sprich nicht immer" from *Das Buch der hängenden Gärten,* which Schoenberg set to music in 1908 or 1909:

Sprich nicht immer	Hush your tale
Von dem laub,	Of the leaves
Windes raub;	Wind unweaves,
Vom zerschellen	Quince that lies
Reifer quitten,	Ripe and bled,
Von den tritten	And the tread
Der vernichter	Of the vandals,
Spät im jahr,	Fall of year,
Von dem zitttern	Of the brightning
Der libellen	Dragonflies
In gewittern	In the lightning,
Und der lichter	Of the candles
Deren flimmer	That in frail
Wandelbar.	Glimmers veer.[3]

The rigid curtailment of line length and cryptic syntax in this poem—which leave little more than a succession of disjunct and alien images in an atmosphere of foreboding—underscore its differences from the poetic language of Dehmel. Certainly Dehmel's verse is more deeply rooted in the real world than is George's. Virtually all of Dehmel's poems that Schoenberg selected as song text concern women, who are presented in a mundane and sometimes cynical guise as sensual creatures alternately desired and hated by men. Dehmel's women run the gamut of familiar types—saints ("Jesus bettelt"), sensualists ("Mädchenfrühling"), sinners ("Mannesbangen," "Im Reich der Liebe"), muses ("Erhebung"), and coy mistresses ("Nicht doch!"). His poetic language was direct and realistic, although sometimes self-consciously flamboyant (as in the poem "Erwartung"). George is quite the opposite. In his verse every word hints at a transcendental state. The language is maximally compressed and devoid of either the mundane or the purely embellishing.

The rich sonority and elegant language of George's poetry left a decidedly musical impression on those who heard the author speak it aloud. Oddly, though, it had little impact on German composers of the first rank outside Schoenberg's school. A George cycle by Conrad Ansorge, *Waller im Schnee,* had been performed in Vienna in 1904 and was probably known to Schoenberg,[4] but not a single leading German musician had set George's writings to music prior to Schoenberg's song "Ich darf nicht dankend" of 1907. One reason for the distance between George and the musician was the poet's well-known opposition to having his verse used as musical text; another was his arcane and highly compressed language, which left little room for music to expand and to enhance.

For Schoenberg, however, these were minor hindrances in comparison to the inspiring music that he heard in George's verse. For Schoenberg the sound of a poem was the initial stimulus that led to a musical treatment. In a letter to Dehmel of 16 November 1913, the composer praised this quality in poetry above all others. "We were instructed by the sound of your verse, which we fully assimilated," he wrote. "I always approached your verse by understanding through sound, and I was thus successful in penetrating it mentally."[5]

Schoenberg's discovery in 1907 of the musical stimulation inherent in George quickly brought an end to a period of silence in terms of songwriting. Since 1905, when most of the songs of Opp. 6 and 8 were written, his inspiration for composing songs had flagged. Many attempts at new songs had ended unsuccessfully in fragments, and only in the hope of winning a competition for new musical ballads could he manage to complete the two songs of Op. 12 (1907). He turned from one poet to the next—Goethe, Heinrich Ammann, Victor Klemperer, Hermann Löns, Gottfried Keller, Theodore von Rommel, Conrad Ferdinand Meyer—plainly unable to find a writer who could invigorate him in the way that Dehmel had earlier.

Schoenberg's search for a new poetic muse became all the more urgent in the waning months of 1907, when he was faced with an emotional crisis provoked by a series of personal and professional setbacks. His financial situation was dire, and his marriage was apparently under strain. His music had been performed in several major concerts in Vienna earlier in that year, and the response to it, outside his circle of friends and students, had been crushingly negative. Stating an attitude shared by many Viennese musicians, Heinrich Schenker wrote in his diary after hearing Schoenberg's D-minor String Quartet in February: "If there are criminals in the world of art, this composer, whether by birth or his own making, would have to be counted among them."[6]

Schoenberg's waning prospects for acceptance as a composer suffered another blow later in 1907 when Gustav Mahler left Vienna for New York. Schoenberg had come to revere Mahler not only as a "saint" and one of his few influential supporters but also as central to his hopes for future success in the practical world of music. Shortly after Mahler departed Vienna on December 9, Schoenberg turned to *Das Jahr der Seele*—one of many George volumes in his library—and discovered a poem, "Ich darf nicht dankend," that must have seemed almost fatefully perfect as an expression of his feelings following Mahler's abandonment, perfect in its sound, imbued with just the "supremely imaginative music" that Mallarmé had found in George's collection as a whole. The poem, inspiring music that flowed quickly from his pen, in all likelihood turned Schoenberg's attention decisively to George as a proven source of inspiration that could simultaneously give voice to his innermost emotions—at this time highly tumultuous—and inspire him musically to create works with an expressivity greater than ever before.

But Schoenberg's enthusiasm for George was as brief as it was intense, spanning little more than one year. After "Ich darf nicht dankend" he returned to George's writings in March 1908, when he began to compose songs on verse from *Das Buch der hängenden Gärten*. In July of 1908, after composing at least five songs in the George cycle and at the height of a marital crisis, he returned to his Second String Quartet, on which he had been working sporadically for more than a year. He then reconceived the work to include voice in its last two movements, using texts from George's newly published anthology, *Der siebente Ring*, that spoke directly to his emotional dilemmas. The quartet was quickly completed, probably by late July or August 1908, whereupon Schoenberg returned to the song cycle, which he finished, in the estimation of Christian Martin Schmidt, during March 1909.[7]

Except for a translation of Ernest Dowson's "Seraphita" used in a song from 1913, Schoenberg never returned to George's poetry. "After a certain point I didn't like it anymore," he wrote in 1932 (a time when the writer was unfairly implicated as a supporter of National Socialism).[8] One reason for his sudden abandonment of George in 1909 may have been the persistent rivalry that Schoenberg felt with his students, especially with Anton Webern. George's poetry had been enthusiastically taken up by Webern in 1908, shortly after Schoenberg had done so, and used in no fewer than fourteen songs and the chorus "Entflieht auf leichten Kähnen," all composed before the end of 1909. Alban Berg was more circumspect. Although an avid reader of literature in the symbolist vein, Berg only later used George texts in his compositions and then only George's translations of poems by Charles Baudelaire. Schoenberg later complained about his students' trying "to outdo what I offer, which puts me in danger of becoming their imitator,"[9] so instead of competing with Webern after the George cycle, Schoenberg redirected his attention to instrumental composition, although he retained the new atonal style that George's verse had inspired.

Two Songs, Op. 14, and "Am Strande"

George's *Das Jahr der Seele* is a large collection of verse marked by an intensely personal tone of loneliness and melancholy. Many of its poems—"Ich darf nicht dankend" is an example—were addressed in the form of confessions to Ida Coblenz, George's muse of the time. The poem echoes Schoenberg's feelings of gratitude to Mahler, and, at the same time, it addresses the theme of reaching out for love and suffering rejection, an idea repeatedly encountered in the verse that the composer set to music in all of his earlier song collections.

Ich darf nicht dankend an dir niedersinken.	I must not kneel in thanks before you.
Du bist vom geist der flur, aus der wir stiegen:	You came from the spirit of the fields, from which we rose:
Will sich mein trost an deine wehmut schmiegen,	If I try to ease your melancholy,
So wird sie zucken, um ihm abzuwinken.	You turn away in rejection.
Verharrst du bei dem quälenden beschlusse,	Must you remain with your agonizing decision,
Nie deines leides nähe zugestehen,	Never to acknowledge the nearness of your sorrow,
Und nur mit ihm und mir dich zu ergehen	And only to walk with it and me
Am eisigklaren tiefentschlafnen flusse?[10]	Along the river trapped in icy sleep?

There is much about Schoenberg's music for this poem, completed on 17 December 1907, that points to it as his earliest atonal composition. The composer said as much in his article "My Evolution" (1949), since the song is the earliest from the three works—Opp. 11, 14, and 15—that he cited there as his "first step" in atonality.[11] Still, the evolutionary character of Schoenberg's approach to the early atonal style prevents the fixing of any single or definitive point for the onset of atonality. The early atonal style was, first and foremost, a mixed idiom, bringing together elements from the composer's existing tonal language but also continuing the process—which he had begun as early as 1903 in the songs of Op. 3—of eliminating crucial elements of that very style. The song plainly retains characteristics of the late phase of tonality. It has a key signature of two sharps, a final cadence on a B-minor triad, and references to the major and minor chord on F$^\sharp$, the dominant harmony in B minor, at the structural junctures at measures 8, 16, and 20. Otherwise the harmonies—mainly vagrant chords, fourth chords, and triadic tetrachords—are similar to those that he had used in his songs from 1903 to 1907 and that he would soon discuss in a tonal context in his *Harmonielehre.* An important traditionalism also resides in the overall form of the work, which adheres to the varied strophic model. The second stanza of the poem (beginning in measure 16) returns to a recognizable variant of the melody and harmonic material of the first stanza, although a far-reaching process of variation quickly disguises the resemblance between the two passages.

Also familiar from the composer's earlier music is a subtle reference at the beginning of the song to a triad on D, which is still perceptible, though hidden beneath chromatic part writing, alterations, and appoggiaturas. Such references to the D triad are exceedingly common in Schoenberg's early atonal music from 1907 and 1908, continuing to appear even until *Die glückliche Hand* in 1913. They are apparently related to Schoenberg's earlier preference for the key of D major or minor in his tonal compositions, which is so prominent in his early music as to suggest a personal motto.[12] Beginning with "Ich darf nicht dankend," allusions to the triad on D placed at the beginning of an atonal work continue to suggest a personal signature. In the atonal style, Schoenberg—like his student Alban Berg—also reinforced his personal identity and voice within his music by the special use of musical letters contained in his own name, especially in works or passages that had a closely personal meaning.

But the reminiscences of tonality that are so evident in "Ich darf nicht dankend" retain only a symbolic status in the song, as key is not its central structural or syntactic principle. The dissonant chords do not arise as prolongations or connectives between consonant triads but intermingle with them as equals. The seven tones of the B-minor scale have no special priority in the work, in which all twelve tones circulate freely and equally, and it is virtually impossible for the listener to trace functional harmonic progressions except in a few isolated instances. The musical coherence of the song relies instead primarily on the variation of motives, phrases, and harmonies that are freed from tonal functions.

The variational method in this song is especially far-reaching, disposed in ways that seem geared to compensate for the absence of functional chords and modulations. The song is filled with motivic recurrences—some simple repetitions, others highly varied—as the composer apparently looked to motivic practices to find an alternative to the formative power of tonality. Schoenberg normally defined a motive as a small but distinctive rhythmic-intervallic figure that was repeated or varied. "The features of a motive are intervals and rhythms," he wrote in *Fundamentals of Musical Composition*, "combined to produce a memorable shape or contour which usually implies an inherent harmony."[13] The basic motives of "Ich darf nicht dankend" are expanded by a process that Schoenberg later called *developing variations,* by which he meant that their formative power was exerted throughout large spans of a composition. He first defined the phenomenon in 1917:

> One can distinguish *two methods of varying* a motive. With the first, usually the changes virtually seem to have nothing more than an *ornamental* purpose; they appear in order to create variety and often disappear without a trace. . . . The second can be termed *developing variation.* The changes proceed more or less directly toward the goal of allowing new ideas to arise.[14]

The process of developing variation in Schoenberg's music has two objectives: it can help to create a sophisticated and artful melody by the rapid growth of initial motivic elements, and it can link together seemingly different melodies on the basis of continually evolving motive forms. In a note to Ferruccio Busoni in 1910, Schoenberg compared the expansive development of motives in a musical composition both to an embryonic process and to the unfolding of a dramatic action: "A hero who is to be shot in the third act [of a play] should be depicted in the first so that the astute observer can foresee his fate. But he doesn't have to be brought onstage in the first act already shot—I mean first the egg, then the chicken."[15]

The opening of the song (Example 3.1) illustrates a developing variation of the motive G♯–G, which first appears in the right hand in measure 1. Characteristic of Schoenberg's melodic structures, the motive immediately reappears in a series of sophisticated transformations. It is transposed, inverted, and given a new rhythmic context in the left hand also in measure 1; that rhythm is then varied by augmentation in the right hand in measure 2, whereupon the intervallic profile is expanded into the shape E♯–F♯–D♯; and this new configuration is further varied as the figure A♯–B–F♯ in the right hand in measure 4. The process of variation also "allows new ideas to arise" in that the basic motive continues to unfold within the apparently new vocal melody in measures 6–8. This passage begins with the eighth-note rhythm of the left hand of measure 1, and the descending semitone then reemerges within ever more remote motive forms.

In this song Schoenberg finds numerous ways of marking the ends of units of thought despite the absence of tonal cadences. In his works that stand at the frontier of atonality, such as "Ich darf nicht dankend" or the latter movements of his Second String Quartet, Op. 10, structural junctures are usually marked by the placement of triads, and these often have a distantly functional relation to the tonality suggested by the final chord. In the song, for example, an F♯-minor triad occurs on the downbeat of measure 8 and a D-minor triad arises in

Example 3.1. Schoenberg, "Ich darf nicht dankend," Op. 14, No. 1, measures 1–8

measure 11—the two familiar sounds placed at the end of the second and third poetic lines of the first stanza, respectively. These help to clarify the structure of the piece as well as to create a dimly or vestigial functional relationship with the "tonic" B-minor triad at the end.

The recurrence of nontriadic, nonfunctional chords also contributes to a clarity of form, and here Schoenberg initiates ways of varying or interrelating such chords that will be highly significant for his atonal harmonic practices. An example occurs in the framing of the very first structural unit of the song in measures 1–5, which contain a brief piano introduction followed by a setting of the first line of the text (see Example 3.1). Schoenberg apparently wished to relate the cadential figure in measure 5 closely to the opening gesture in measure 1, just as the composer of tonal music would typically begin and end the first structural unit of a piece with a statement of the tonic chord. Similarly, the two chords from the right hand in measure 1 return in the left hand in measure 5, at which point they are transposed down a fifth and slightly changed in their motivic setting.

But the simplicity of this recurrence is also carried to a more complex level by the way that the chords meet the quicker-moving melodic lines in the two passages to create a symmetrical parallelism, or an "inversional balance," to use the

term coined by David Lewin.[16] This mirrrorlike relationship between the two
passages can be readily seen in their motivic similarities, as the two hands exchange their materials. It also exists on a more abstract level solely in the pitch
content of the two figures. This more conceptual relationship can be assessed by
extracting the tones of the two passages from their musical context and comparing their intervallic profiles. One way of doing so is to place the notes of each
passage in a compact scalewise order, whereupon the relationship of their con-
stituent intervals becomes apparent. For example, the fourth chord that ends
the phrase in measure 5 (D G C) meets the final two tones from the line in the
right hand line (E–D♯) to form the five-note collection C D D♯ E G. Compare it to
the collection A G F♯ E♯ D, which underlies the parallel figure in measure 1,
where the fourth chord, A D G, accompanies the melodic tones E♯–F♯ in the left
hand. The succession of intervals in both scales is equivalent to a major second,
minor second, minor second, and minor third, descending in the former instance and ascending in the latter. The two passages are thus related not only
motivically and transpositionally but also by the symmetrical or "intervallic"
inversion of their pitch content. Throughout his atonal period, this type of inversion of notes within lines and chords remained an important variational tool
on Schoenberg's workbench.

   At about the time that he composed "Ich darf nicht dankend," Schoenberg
began another George song, "Der Jünger," whose text reveals a similar theme of
gratitude and discipleship. Schoenberg may again have had Mahler in mind
when he chose this poem from George's *Der Teppich des Lebens* (1899); it speaks
in a religious tone of a disciple willingly following his lord, despite many dan-
gers. The music was left as an undated fragment of six measures, and, like "Ich
darf nicht dankend," it mixes tonal and atonal elements.[17]

   But Schoenberg did not immediately exploit his discovery of the fruitful
power of George's poetry in the creation of a new musical language. Following
"Ich darf nicht dankend" he next composed the song "In diesen Wintertagen"
(completed on 2 February 1908), using the poem "Winterweihe" by Karl Henckell (whom Schoenberg incorrectly identified as "Georg Henckel").

Winterweihe	Winter Dedication
In diesen Wintertagen,	In these winter days,
Nun sich das Licht verhüllt,	As the light wanes,
Laß uns im Herzen tragen,	Let us carry in our hearts,
Einander traulich sagen,	And speak to each other sadly about,
Was uns mit innerm Licht erfüllt.	That which fills us with inner light.
Was wilde [milde] Glut entzündet,	What smolders with its wild [gentle] glow
Soll brennen fort und fort,	Will burn on and on,
Was Seelen zart verbindet [verbündet]	That which tenderly binds our souls together,
Und Geisterbrükken [-brücken] gründet	Making bridges between our minds,
Sei unser [leises] Losungswort.	Will be our [quiet] motto.

Das Rad der Zeit mag rollen,	The wheel of time may turn,
Wir greifen kaum hinein. [,]	We scarce can slow it down.
Dem Schein der Welt verschollen,	It may well destroy the beauty of the world,
Auf unserm Eiland wollen	But here on our island
Wir Tag und Nacht der seligen Liebe weihn.[18]	Let us devote ourselves day and night to holy love.

The poem shares with "Ich darf nicht dankend" the theme of lovers consoling each other in an alien world, although Henckell's verse has little else in common with the subtlety and richness of George's. Its romantic sentimentality drew from the composer a relatively conservative musical setting—yet another indication that the style of his music at this time corresponded to the tone of the poetry with which he was working. The piece is in C major, although freely so, and it has a clear and straightforward rhythm, development of motives, and ternary form that are more reminiscent of Schoenberg's songs from the preceding decade than of the earlier George setting.

"Ich darf nicht dankend" and "In diesen Wintertagen" were published by Universal Edition in 1920 as Two Songs, Op. 14, although Schoenberg had earlier contemplated a third song, "Am Strande," also for this collection. It was eliminated only in 1920 and left unpublished until 1966. The date of composition of "Am Strande" has long been controversial. At the conclusion of the first full draft, Schoenberg entered the date 8 February 1909; in 1911 or 1912 he made a fair copy of the song, which he marked as "Op. 14, No. 3." At some unspecified later time he returned to the latter manuscript and wrote a note in the margin that suggests that the song was composed considerably earlier, probably in late 1907 or early 1908: "This song was written before the George songs. At the same time as Op. 14: 'In diesen Wintertagen' and 'Ich darf nicht dankend . . .' Could have been published anyway. I didn't bring it out because of its text."[19] Christian Martin Schmidt has put forward considerable evidence that the 1909 date is correct and that Schoenberg's memory was faulty when he returned to the manuscript.[20]

The author of the text of "Am Strande" is unknown. In the 1909 manuscript Schoenberg twice entered the name Rainer Maria Rilke, but the poem is almost certainly not by Rilke, although its freedom of form and highly sophisticated tone suggest the work of an accomplished poet.

Am Strande	On the Beach
Vorüber die Flut. Noch braust es fern.	The flood is past. Still it roars from afar.
Wild Wasser. Und oben Stern an Stern.	Wild water. And above star upon star.
Wer sah es wohl, o selig Land,	Who was witness, O blessed land,
Wie dich die Welle überwand.	When the waves came over you?
Noch braust es fern. Der Nachtwind	Still it roars from afar. The night wind
Bringt Erinnerung	Brings on memories
Und eine Welle verlief im Sand.	And a wave disappears in the sand.

The themes and sentiments of the poem do not conform to those of the other two poems intended for the Op. 14 collection. In the earlier two, selected before the summer of 1908, a man and woman struggle to find meaning in each other in a hostile environment. The song "Am Strande," written after a temporary rupture in the composer's marriage that occurred during that summer, is very different, as the speaker stands alone in utter desolation on the shores of memory, mutely contemplating the aftermath of a great storm that has swept everything away. In his note on the fair copy of the song, Schoenberg recalled that he had struck the work from Op. 14 "because of its text," a remark that has been interpreted as an indication of his uncertainty about its author. The remark may also be taken to mean that he ultimately found the content of the poem inapposite to be placed beside the other two.

Certainly the musical idiom of "Am Strande" is more advanced than in the other songs of Op. 14. By February 1909 Schoenberg had virtually the entire George cycle of Op. 15 behind him, and his greater confidence in atonality as a style that could at last separate itself from the late tonal idiom is apparent in this piece. The mixed idiom of Op. 14 is now almost completely absent. The music has no regular pulse, no regular rhythm or meter, and the lines in the piano and voice are exploded into a mosaic of small, fragmentary figures that do not coalesce into continuous units of thought. There is no key signature, no triadic conclusion, no appearance of familiar chords at structural junctures. The vocal line itself is neither lyrical nor recitational, its anguished words communicated instead by relentless leaps of sevenths, ninths, and tritones. The singer's soliloquy of depair and hopelessness is underscored as well by the utter detachment of the piano part, which depicts a raging distant storm that can take no notice of the poet's distress. The sound of the song is also entirely different from the sound of "Ich darf nicht dankend," since the familiar harmonic residue from tonal music—vagrant and altered chords, triadic tetrachords, and quartal chords—is now fully displaced by a strange and pervasively dissonant harmony.

In a song whose poetic sentiments of despair might well have produced a music of disintegration, Schoenberg looked to the piano part to provide elements of continuity and coherence. These are vested in an economical development of motives, one of which—consisting of a mottolike chord with the tones C E F B—is sustained through all but five measures of the entire work. The sustained motto chord became a familiar structural component in the atonal instrumental music that Schoenberg composed shortly after this song. It is a recurrent feature in the Orchestra Pieces, Op. 16. In a fugal exposition in the first of these, an unceasing dronelike chord (D A C♯) is stated in the bassoons and trombones, and in the third piece, famous for its refinement in timbre, the initial five-note chord returns persistently as a motto. The third of the Three Pieces for Chamber Orchestra (1910) is based likewise upon a sustained six-note chord in the organ. The sustained chord is also apparently related to Schoenberg's great reliance upon ostinato in his instrumental atonal works, the first major instance of which is in the Piano Piece, Op. 11, No. 2, which was begun two weeks after "Am Strande" was completed.

As a referential element, the chord symbolizes the distant storm that "roars from afar," and Schoenberg devised a new sonority on the piano to make it echo all the more realistically. In measures 7–8 the player is instructed to depress silently the four notes of the chord, against which another basic motive, C#–D–G, is played softly, thus causing the upper harmonics of the chord to resonate with an eerie and distant sound. Schoenberg re-created the effect in his Piano Piece, Op. 11, No. 1, which was composed only a few days after he completed "Am Strande," and these were apparently the earliest uses of piano harmonics by a major composer.

"Litanei" and "Entrueckung" from String Quartet No. 2, Op. 10

George's poetry brought Schoenberg not only musical stimulation but also personal comfort in the turbulent year 1908, during which the composer faced the most crucial of decisions concerning his artistic direction and personal life. In March he turned again to George's verse and began to compose songs in which the evolution toward atonality was at last completed by the removal of key signatures and triadic conclusions. Between March and June he finished at least five songs from George's *Book of the Hanging Gardens*, whereupon he left Vienna for a summer retreat on the Traunsee. There he was confronted with a marital crisis during which his wife, Mathilde, left him for the painter Richard Gerstl, after which Schoenberg experienced a great emotional upheaval that forcefully intruded upon his compositional development.

Around 1906 the Schoenbergs were introduced to Gerstl (1883–1908), who stimultated their own budding interest in painting.[21] Eager to associate with musicians, the young artist became virtually a member of Schoenberg's circle, and he acquired an atelier in the Liechtensteinstrasse, no. 20, near the Schoenbergs' apartment at nos. 68/70. He repeatedly painted studies of Schoenberg and his family, concentrating especially on portraits of Mathilde, and a love affair soon erupted between the artist and his model.

Schoenberg was well aware of the liaison before the summer retreat to the Traunsee. According to Gerstl's brother Alois, Schoenberg's daughter had told her father of seeing her mother kiss the painter; Schoenberg then intervened by telling Gerstl that they should not allow a woman to come between them.[22] But the correspondence between Schoenberg and his wife during June of 1908 shows a far deeper level of distrust and cynicism, depicting a marriage that was well on its way to dissolving. In early June, Mathilde, accompanied by her two children and her mother, traveled ahead to Gmunden on the Traunsee to make arrangements for a summer retreat, which would later include Gerstl, the Zemlinskys, and several students. Schoenberg remained behind in Vienna until the end of the month to continue teaching and to complete other projects. During the three weeks of their separation, Mathilde addressed no fewer than twenty letters and cards to her husband, trying to reassure him of her love for him. Although Schoenberg's letters from this time have apparently not survived, her responses show that he was suffering great anxiety and was unconvinced of her good intentions. In a letter of June 21, Mathilde defended herself against his persistent accusations: "Am I really always so disgusting to you? And are you always so good to me? You'd really like to beat me up sometimes (but I would fight back). You're always good and I'm insufferable—that's the way it is and always has been. It really sickens me because I am so very fond of you. But do you believe me? I can't tell you that I do, and you know that I can't!"[23]

Schoenberg arrived in Gmunden on June 26 or 27, at virtually the same moment as Gerstl, whose presence ensured that the atmosphere at the summer retreat would be explosive. Details of the ensuing crisis are known primarily by anecdote. One account has it that Schoenberg caught Mathilde and Gerstl in flagrante delicto, after which she left her husband to live with the painter in Vienna, only to be talked into returning to her family by Webern and other students.[24] Judging from the dates of Mathilde's letters to Schoenberg just after she left him, this upheaval occurred on or about August 27, and it was accompanied by a profound emotional crisis for both Schoenberg and his wife. "In general I am now rather more at peace," she wrote shortly thereafter. "As long as I had hope for an improvement, I cried; now I have none and I am calm. I won't give you my address. . . . If it will put your mind at ease I can tell you that I have a nice room with decent people *not* in Vienna."[25] At times almost incoherent, Mathilde's letters reveal an individual in an extreme state of emotional distress with clearly suicidal impulses. "My dear, dear children. I believe that I won't ever see them again," she exclaimed. "How you must hate me! . . . Now I have literally no one to live for. . . . I have but one hope—that I won't live much longer!"[26] The principal document in which Schoenberg described his own reactions to the crisis is an undated will, a "Testaments-Entwurf," whose contents are highly relevant to the opera *Die glückliche Hand* and will be discussed in chapter 5.

Even as he arrived in Gmunden in late June, Schoenberg was evidently experiencing such anxiety and alienation as to produce a major upheaval in his compositional work. At first this took the form of a stylistic retrenchment, a stepping back from the fully atonal George songs that he had composed earlier that spring and a return to the late tonal style of instrumental composition that he had used in his String Quartet No. 1, Op. 7, and Chamber Symphony No. 1, Op. 9. He did not continue with the George project after arriving in Gmunden but turned instead to the Second String Quartet, a tonal work that he had started during the previous year but left as a fragment with a completed first movement, an incomplete second movement, and a brief sketch of a third. Now he drastically redefined the continuation of the work, discarding the earlier third movement sketch and composing a new third and fourth movement. To these he added a soprano voice to sing texts by George, but his choice of poetry could not have been more different from the selections from *Hanging Gardens* that he had lately been using. In those songs a narrator ever more imperiously demands love; now Schoenberg turned to "Litanei" and "Entrueckung" from George's recently published *Der siebente Ring*, which speak only of death and transfiguration, misery brought by love, and a wish to be dead to the world. A connection between this transformation and the dissolution of his marriage is self-evident.

On 5 July Schoenberg received from his student Karl Horwitz, no doubt at his own request, a handwritten copy of the two poems, and he pasted them into the so-called Sketchbook III on a page following the incomplete draft of the second movement of the Second String Quartet.[27] On the same page he wrote down two new themes using words from "Entrueckung" beside which he wrote: "III[.] Satz Streichquartett." Then he began to compose a new movement using "Litanei," whose music was quickly completed, by 11 July, and situated definitively as the third movement. By 27 July he had also completed the second movement, which he had earlier left as a fragment. There is no extant draft or precise date for the composition of the fourth movement, which uses "Entrueckung" as text and incorporates the themes sketched earlier, although it was almost certainly composed in July or August of 1908. Since he labeled the first sketches for "Entrueckung" as a third movement, it may be that "Litanei" was originally intended as the finale of the quartet. This is the conclusion reached by Christian Martin Schmidt and Walter Frisch, based on plausible evidence.[28] But Schoenberg must have quickly recognized that the two poems made little sense in a reversed order. In "Litanei" the speaker is earthbound and wretched because of love; he wishes only to be with God. In "Entrueckung" he is at last above the clouds and breathing the air of other planets.

The music of "Litanei" represents a volte-face to the final stages of Schoenberg's tonal period, during which he focused upon intensely unified one-movement instrumental works in addition to songs. "Litanei," unlike the first two movements of the quartet, contributes to an intricate cyclic design that is akin to that in Schoenberg's earlier instrumental music. In his "Notes on the Four String Quartets," the composer describes the movement as a freestanding entity that consists of a theme, five variations, coda, and postlude, but its pervasive reuse and extension of thematic material from the first two movements suggest that its role is also that of a development in a single multisectional cycle. The strictness of the variations form, Schoenberg said, was needed to prevent him from becoming too emotional, too dramatic, which must have seemed an imminent danger in music of such deep personal significance.

The theme of the variations (Example 3.2) ends in measure 9, overlapping at that poing with the beginning of the first variation. As Schoenberg noted, the theme is made from four motives that had all appeared in the earlier two movements, thus creating a composite thematic shape akin to one that he would use again in the sketches for *Pierrot lunaire* (see chapter 6). The composer was not specific about the location of the five variations, but, judging from the recurrence of blocks made from the four motives in their original order, these probably begin in measures 9, 17, 25, 34, and 42—divisions that are not especially congruent with the poem's syntax. This pattern of recurrence of the four-motive block is broken after the climatic pause at measure 50, suggesting this as the beginning of the coda. Here the four motives undergo a much freer development than before and lead to a great climax in measure 65, where the voice ascends to a high C as it pleads for God to take love away and to give happiness in-

Example 3.2. Schoenberg, "Litanei" from String Quartet No. 2, Op. 10, measures 1–9

stead. The intensity of this passage goes beyond any music that Schoenberg had composed to this time. So different is it from the George songs from the spring of 1908 or the earlier movements of the quartet that it is hard to imagine that it is not connected with the Gerstl affair, not a vivid musical representation of the composer's own anguished voice.

Schoenberg's effort to retain control of the emotional element in his music through an intricacy of form extends in this movement even more deeply than the presence of a variations design. As in the third movement of the Serenade, Op. 24—the principal variations movement in Schoenberg's atonal oeuvre—two musical designs coexist in "Litanei." In addition to the theme-variations-coda just described, a ternary plan is also evident. A main theme based on motives from the theme of the variations proper is introduced in the voice at measure 14 and recapitulated at measure 59. The contrasting middle section begins at measure 43 with the entrance of a new melodic idea in the violins (Example 3.3a), which, typical of Schoenberg's alliance of themes through the

Example 3.3. Themes from Schoenberg's String Quartet No. 2, Op. 10, movements 3 and 4: (a) "Litanei" (movement 3), measures 43–45 (violin I); (b) "Entrueckung" (movement 4), measures 51–55 (violin I)

process of developing variation, forecasts the principal subsidiary theme of the finale (measures 51–55 of "Entrueckung," shown in Example 3.3b).

In his "Notes on the Four String Quartets," Schoenberg rejects the idea that any movement of this quartet is fully atonal, and his reasons are an important indication of the distinction that he drew between tonal music as it existed in its most attenuated state and atonal music per se, as it already existed in the early songs of Op. 15. He wrote: "The decisive progress toward so-called atonality was not yet carried out. Every one of the four movements ends with a tonic, representing the tonality. Within, one finds many sectional endings on more or less remote relatives of the key."[29] The work, he concludes, documents only a "transition" to atonality, since "key is presented distinctly at all the main dividing points of the formal organization."[30] This generalization is readily apparent in "Litanei," since each of the variations ends with at least a passing reference to an E♭-minor triad, which is also the concluding harmony. But the movement is devoid of any other plainly functional chords—there is no perceptible dominant, no dominant preparations, and no sense of tonal harmonic motion. The E♭ chords are empty vestiges of tonality, having a purely symbolic value and exerting no constructive control over the music that flows between them.

In the finale of the quartet, "Entrueckung," the anguished tone of "Litanei" is replaced by a serenity and freedom that takes its origins from the text and brings the music close to the atmosphere of the George songs from the spring of 1908. As in the songs, the voice is intensely lyrical and the texture less intricate in its counterpoint. There is no key signature, although, as in "Ich darf nicht dankend," several of the structural junctures of the piece are marked by triads relevant to a vestigial tonality, here F♯ major. The coda of the movement, beginning in measure 120, is fully tonal as it moves between tonic and dominant harmonies and leads to a peaceful conclusion on an F♯-major triad.

The text "Entrueckung" is very likely addressed to Mathilde Schoenberg, to whom the quartet was dedicated when it was published in February 1909.

Entrueckung	Enrapture
Ich fühle luft von anderen planeten.	I feel air from other planets.
Mir blassen durch das dunkel die gesichter	The darkness makes pale those faces
Die freundlich eben noch sich zu mir drehten.	That had just turned toward me in friendship.
Und bäum und wege die ich leibte fahlen	And wan the trees and paths that I loved
Dass ich sie kaum mehr kenne und Du lichter	So that I scarcely know them, and You light
Geliebter schatten—rufer meiner qualen—	Beloved shadow—voice of my anguish—
Bist nun erloschen ganz in tiefern gluten	Seem now quite extinguished by the deep embers
Um nach dem taumel streitenden getobes	And after the din of strife and hubbub
mit einem frommen schauer anzumuten.	Reappear with a calm trembling.
Ich löse mich in tönen, kreisend, webend,	I dissolve in tones, circling, interlacing,
Ungründigen danks und unbenamten lobes	With boundless thanks and unspeakable praise,
Dem grossen atem wunschlos mich ergebend.	Yielding involuntarily to the mighty breath.
Mich überfährt ein ungestümes wehen	An impetuous wind sweeps over me
Im rausch der weihe wo inbrünstige schreie	From the fervent cries of pious rapture
In staub geworfner beterinnen flehen:	Rising from the dust where women pray:
Dann seh ich wie sich duftige nebel lüpfen	Then I see as a light mist rises
In einer sonnerfüllten klaren freie	Into a clear expanse filled with sunlight,
Die nur umfängt auf fernsten bergesschlüpfen.	Which stretches to the farthest mountain peaks.
Der boden schüttert weiss und weich wie molke . . .	The ground trembles white and soft as whey . . .
Ich steige über schluchten ungeheur,	I soar above gigantic chasms,
Ich fühle wie ich über lezter wolke	I feel as though I rise beyond the last cloud
In einem meer kristallnen glanzes schwimme—	And swim in a sea of crystal radiance—
Ich bin ein funke nur vom heiligen feuer,	I am but a spark from the holy fire,
Ich bin ein dröhnen nur der heiligen stimme.[31]	I am but an echo of the holy voice.

In his analysis of the movement, Schoenberg cautioned against finding any simple or standard musical design, although he mentions the relevance to sonata form of a recapitulation at measure 100, where the two principal themes from measures 21 and 52 return simultaneously.[32] The primary formal element, he says, is instead the text, which governs the shaping and unfolding of themes as though leitmotives in a Wagner opera. The cyclic element of the work as a whole, at its strongest in the third movement, wanes in the finale as none of the earlier themes reappears, although several distinctive motives from before—including the prominent fifths from the second movement scherzo—return in force.

Schoenberg had almost certainly completed the quartet before he returned to Vienna at the end of August to attempt to salvage his marriage. In September he turned again to George's *Hanging Gardens,* although this project, like the quartet, would now have to take on a new shape that better conformed to the realities of his life following the events in Gmunden.

Fifteen Poems from *Das Buch der hängenden Gärten,* Op. 15

The cycle of George songs, Op. 15, is Schoenberg's first atonal masterpiece, his first monumental work to renounce tonal center and to handle dissonant harmonies as structurally equivalent to consonant ones. By these means the composer acquired an expressive resource that matched the heightened tone of George's poetry and led to a musical style that Schoenberg ultimately made his own, thus redirecting his entire future as a composer.[33]

George's *Hanging Gardens* appeared in 1895 as one of three books of poems collectively titled *Die Bücher der Hirten- und Preisgedichte, der Sagen und Sänge, und der Hängenden Gärten* (The books of eclogues and eulogies, of legends and lays, and the hanging gardens).[34] Schoenberg owned a copy of the third edition, published in 1907. Each book is set in a remote time and place, although George was quick to explain that the poems were not modeled on the popular exotic genre that followed from Goethe's *Der West-östliche Divan.* Instead, as George wrote in a foreword, "they mirror a soul which has temporarily taken refuge in other eras and regions." The third book, *Hanging Gardens,* is placed in a Babylonian paradise, and here George creates a symbolic although clearly autobiographical narrative concerning his own adolescence and the difficulties that he had experienced in establishing his place as an artist in a materialistic society.

The book contains thirty-one poems, spoken—often with a dreamlike disruption of voice and time—both in the first person and by a narrator. Its episodes suggest several narrative subgroupings. The first five poems tell of a king's dreamlike journey back in time to the realm where he was raised, to a kingdom that he had then led to greatness through brave conquests. In poems 6 through 9, the king is again transported back in memory to his childhood, spent in the company of a circle of devoted friends, during which he was occupied with uncovering beautiful gems and creating his own realm close to nature. Finally, he undergoes a spiritual purification to prepare himself for his adult duties. In the tenth poem, "Friedensabend," the adolescent prince rests in a blissful dream that effaces the world. To this point in *Hanging Gardens*, George's narrative is filled with his own personal recollections. As a child he had created a private imaginary realm—he called it Amhara—of which he was king and whose subjects were his childhood friends. In earlier poems, as in "Neuländische Liebesmahle II" from *Hymnen*, he had returned to this imaginary kingdom that still vividly existed in his memory, turning his back resolutely against the real world and the present time.

The next fifteen poems—the ones set to music by Schoenberg in Op. 15—are a lyrical interlude during which the young prince discovers love. In a garden filled with beauty and sadness, the prince falls under the spell of the beloved, from whom he first learns of love. He cries out in torture that he must touch her body or his soul will break apart, although his description of the consummation of his desire is curiously dispassionate, as though uncertainly remembered. Worldly thoughts now intrude upon him—he recalls the danger posed by enemies from outside the garden, and he sees monstrous shadows on its walls. The beloved has become a stranger to him. Finally the garden can only suggest peril, destruction, and inconstancy, as she is about to depart forever. The prince is left behind, doubly trapped by a menacing world outside and a garden that has itself shriveled into a threatening wasteland.

George's garden is indeed the central image of the entire *Buch.* As a literary symbol it resonates with the gardens cultivated by symbolist writers at the turn of the century. It is a place of beauty where "fields of flowers alternate with great halls and gaily colored tiles," a refuge isolated from the ugliness of life and well suited to the languorous ecstasy of love.[35] It recalls for the reader the hedonistic retreats where characters from Verlaine's *Fêtes galantes* whispered amorous thoughts:

Le donneurs de sérénades	The serenaders
Et les belles écouteuses	And the pretty ladies listening
Échangent des propos fades	Exchange their insipid remarks
Sous les ramures chanteuses.[36]	Beneath the singing branches.

But unlike Verlaine's impassive lovers, George's prince transforms the garden into a scene of anguished passion, as he is gripped by an erotic impulse so strong that it imperiously drives him to the edge of self-destruction.

In the final six poems of *Hanging Gardens*, not set to music by Schoenberg, the king tells of the disastrous aftermath of his encounter with love. It has emasculated him, causing him to lose his zest for power, conquest, and duty. He has resigned his throne and become a eunuch who serves a pasha as a mere singer and slave, and, ashamed at his state, he resolves to drown himself in a river. In a concluding poem that virtually re-creates the end of Wilhelm Müller's *Die schöne Müllerin*, the speaker stands at the edge of the river, which speaks to him alluringly as his only possible refuge and consolation.

The chronology of composition of the George songs of Op. 15 can be only partially established, and there also exists a measure of uncertainty about the composer's initial conception of the work. The dating of Schoenberg's music depends largely on the dates that he himself systematically entered into certain of his working manuscripts. Disconnected sketches and incomplete drafts, usually undated, represent the first recorded documents of a new composition. These fragmentary sources exist for songs Nos. 6, 8, 14, and 15 of the George cycle, and, although all are undated, their placement relative to other dated materials within a manuscript can provide a reliable approximation as to when they were set down and when the composition to which they pertain was begun. Schoenberg then moved to the writing of a first draft, which he called the *erste Niederschrift*, which was usually dated at its conclusion and often also at its beginning. Such manuscripts exist for only seven of the songs in Op. 15 (see Table 3.1). Further refinements and a final version were usually set down in a fair copy, which served for early performances and as *Stichvorlagen*, or engraver's copies. Schoenberg produced two undated fair copies of the entire George cycle, one of which was sent in 1914 to Universal Edition as the engraver's copy for the first printing of the cycle as a whole. Two of the songs, Nos. 13 and 14, had already been printed in 1911, in the journals *Der Merker* and *Die Fackel*, respectively, and the complete cycle received its premier performance on 14 January 1910, sung by Martha Winternitz-Dorda.

Table. 3.1 Datable songs in Schoenberg's Op. 15 in chronological order

Manuscript source	Number and title	Page in manuscript	Date at end
Sammelhandschrift 10 (Pierpont Morgan Library, New York)	No. 4, "Da meine Lippen"	3	15 March 1908
	No. 5, "Saget mir"	4	25 March 1908
	No. 3, "Als Neuling trat ich"	2	29 March 1908
	No. 8, "Wenn ich heut nicht deinen Leib" (sketch and draft)	1	13 April 1908
Sammelhandschrift 14 (Arnold Schönberg Center, Vienna)	"Friedensabend" (fragment)	1	no date
	No. 7, "Angst und Hoffen"	2	28 April 1908
	No. 6, "Jedem Werke bin ich fürder tot" (sketch)	4	no date
Sammelhandschrift 22 (Arnold Schönberg Center)	No. 13, "Du lehnest wider eine Silberweide"	1	27 September 1908
	No. 14, "Sprich nicht" (sketch)	2	no date
	No. 15, "Wir bevölkerten" (sketch)	3	no date
Sammelhandschrift 23 (Arnold Schönberg Center)	No. 14, "Sprich nicht" (sketch)	1	no date
	No. 15, "Wir bevölkerten" (draft)	2–4	28 February 1909

The chronology of Op. 15 is documented almost solely by the dates that Schoenberg gave to the seven drafts. He entered these versions, together with a few sketches and fragments, on four different manuscripts—each called a *Sammelhandschrift* by the editors of Schoenberg's *Sämtliche Werke*, since each contains more than one song or composition (see Table 3.1). These dates, the order in which the songs appear in the two earlier *Sammelhandschriften*, and other documentary evidence suggest that Schoenberg at first did not contemplate the fifteen-song cycle that he later created. He had not undertaken a lengthy, poetically unified song cycle since the early stages of *Gurrelieder* in 1899–1900, and this work, transformed into a massive cantata, still remained incomplete in 1908. His tendency since that time was to compose songs as independent entities and only later have them published in collections through which there ran at most a loose affinity of text and musical idiom. Although no firm conclusions can be reached about Schoenberg's initial conception, *Sammelhandschriften* 10 and 14, which he used during March and April 1908, suggest a progressive enlargement from a collection of four songs, as presented in *Sammelhandschrift* 10, to one of six or seven by the addition of the pieces in *Sammelhandschrift* 14. In both cases the songs were written in the two manuscripts in an order that dispels the narrative or cyclic element that George had created. In *Sammelhandschrift* 14 Schoenberg drafted the beginning of "Friedensabend," a poem from *Hanging Gardens* that Schoenberg left as a fragment and subsequently dropped from the cycle. The existence of a blank page in this manuscript (p. 3) reinforces the impression that at the time that the document was in use, beginning in late April, Schoenberg was entering them into the manuscript draft in an intentional, though preliminary, order and that he was not planning to progress continuously through fifteen of George's texts.

A title page found with *Sammelhandschrift* 10 in the Pierpont Morgan Library provides additional evidence that the four songs contained in this manuscript were first intended as a separate collection. On this page Schoenberg wrote, "4 Lieder" and "korrigiert $\overline{16}$," although it is not certain that the title page—which is unbound and different in paper size and sort from the remainder of the manuscript—was meant by the composer to be attached to the four songs of *Sammelhandschrift* 10 or, if so, when it was attached to them or what the meaning of "corrected [19]16" could be.[37] Despite these uncertainties, the annotation "4 Lieder" may indicate that Schoenberg's initial conception of the *Hanging Gardens* was for a short, noncyclic collection of songs, rather on the order of Webern's contemporaneous George settings that Webern later assembled into his Opp. 3 and 4. But Schoenberg would soon transform this apparent indecision concerning overall form into a virtual method for composing a large atonal work. In no major composition of his atonal period did Schoenberg begin to compose with a final form clearly in mind. It was as though he was more confident in relying on his intuition gradually to lead him to a correct large-scale form, which was usually established only when the act of composing per se neared its completion.

Following the summer retreat in Gmunden, Schoenberg returned to *Hanging Gardens*, probably with a new conception that was more attuned to a frame of mind in which love was fleeting and abandonment and despair all too near at hand. The two remaining *Sammelhandschriften* for Op. 15, used in September 1908 and February 1909, contain songs on poetry from the end of George's central fifteen-poem narrative, now exactly duplicating the order given them by George and all the more indicating that Schoenberg by this point had decided upon a large song cycle. It is likely that at least one additional *Sammelhandschrift*, containing the drafts for songs No. 9 through 12, is now lost.

As in many of the great song cycles of the nineteenth century, the unifying element in the George songs is provided almost entirely by its texts. The poetic narrative itself follows an arch shape as it tells of initiation to love, passionate consummation, and ultimate destruction. The keystone of the arch is reached in the outburst of "Wenn ich heut nicht deinen Leib berühre," No. 8. This song has been described by Theodor W. Adorno as the peripeteia of the cycle, the point of division between two large parts after which the songs gradually dissolve. "Just as the first part traces out the drastic rise of passion to the point of naked desire," Adorno writes, "so too the second part intensifies inwardly, out of sight."[38]

Throughout the fifteen songs Schoenberg achieves a great amalgamation of different styles. Traditional elements coexist with the new and unprecedented, thus leaving the listener with quite the opposite impression from the stylistic homogeneity that characterized much of Schoenberg's later atonal and twelve-tone music. In Op. 15, lengthy and fully formed compositions such as "Wir bevölkerten," No. 15, stand beside aphoristic fragments such as "Sprich nicht," No. 14. Songs that strongly suggest late romantic tonality, such as "Das schöne Beet," No. 10, coexist with others like "Unterm Schutz," No. 1, in which there is virtually no residue of key. In some, the voice sings with a lyrical and emotionally laden passion; in others, it intones the text with passive declamation.

The texts of the first two songs, "Unterm Schutz" and "Hain in diesen Paradiesen," form an introduction to the cycle as a whole, as they weave a lushly figurative description of the garden into a poetic tapestry. The garden is a fantastic place where stars drift down like snow, every corner is filled by whispers and soft voices, and all is shrouded in a deeply soothing melancholy. In both songs the vocal line embodies the restrained narrative of the words—somber but with a touch of awe. The voice moves in a recitational melody that closely imitates the sound and rhythm of the words as though spoken, an extreme example of the "musical prose" that Schoenberg had found approvingly in the asymmetrical melodic style of Brahms.[39] Regular rhythm or pulse is not evident. The piano's music enters into a dialogue with this recitative, neither relegated to the role of mere accompaniment nor sharing melodic materials with its partner, but infinitely expressive in depicting every nuance that the words convey.

The next two poems, "Als Neuling trat ich" and "Da meine Lippen," are also linked, here by references to the march of the narrator into the region ruled by the beloved. This is both a land of splendor and a *Gehege*—a wild animal preserve—into which the speaker is lured and then enslaved by a mere distant glance. The musical settings establish a very different tone from the opening pair of songs, now more conventional and songlike, and the sudden stylistic shift at the beginning of the third song makes it all the more plausible that Nos. 1 and 2 were added to the cycle considerably later than Nos. 3 and 4. The voice part in the latter pair is fully lyrical and the rhythm, as at the beginning of "Als Neuling," regular and marchlike, reminiscent of the compulsive march in *Gurrelieder* as Waldemar carries Tove's coffin to the cemetery. Here the piano recedes into accompaniment as the emotional burden of the words is shouldered fully by the voice.

Songs No. 5 through 8 form a third group, characterized by steadily increasing urgency in the narrator's response to the beloved. In No. 5, "Saget mir," he would shower her with gifts and make for her a footstool of his face; in No. 6, "Jedem Werke bin ich fürder tot," he weeps as his nightly visions of her flee with the morning light. He cries out in anguish and shuns all society in No. 7, "Angst und Hoffen"; finally in No. 8, "Wenn ich heut nicht deinen Leib berühre," his distress reaches a climax as his desire for her body stretches his soul to the breaking point. Schoenberg's musical treatment of the four poems places the crescendo of emotion in even sharper profile, as the four songs move progressively faster, from *etwas langsam* to *rasch*, and the voice steadily moves into a higher register. "Saget mir" is uniformly lyrical and restrained. The voice does not exceed the tone F at the top of the staff, and the music proceeds evenly and quietly in simple rhythmic values. Its restraint is stripped away at the very beginning of "Jedem Werke bin ich fürder tot," No. 6, which opens with a petulant outburst, and the lyric element begins to dissolve into a more impassioned speech melody. No. 7 is still more aroused, angular, and speechlike, and the sighs of the beloved are sonorously translated into an accompaniment entirely in the upper register, played solely by the pianist's right hand. The climactic No. 8, "Wenn ich heut nicht deinen Leib berühre," is played at the dynamic level of a "muted forte," in a rash tempo, and the voice is now pushed to a high A.

As noted by Adorno, song No. 9, "Streng ist uns," suggests the beginning of a new cycle that gradually dispels the febrile crescendo of intensity of the first eight songs. Like the first song, No. 9 is slow and melancholy; it opens and closes with passages for the piano alone, and the melodic line is again recitational, closely following the words rather than allowing lyrical melody to supersede them. At the end of the song Schoenberg alerts the listener to the new direction that this half of the cycle will take. The speaker proclaims that his passion still "leaps with renewed ardor," but in the last measure the piano tells us the very opposite, as the line tumbles into the lowest register of the instrument while slowing in tempo and dying away in volume. In the tenth song, "Das schöne Beet," the speaker stares expectantly at the flowers of the garden—symbols for the body of the beloved—which he impassively describes in plainly erotic images. Schoenberg's music is unique in the entire cycle as it makes a startling return to the late romantic style, the post-Tristanesque language of Eros. A lengthy and impassioned piano prelude begins in the key of D major and minor, the key extended to its very limits of perceptibility by free linear motions in multiple parts (Example 3.4). The opening measures adumbrate a D triad, and the introduction concludes in measures 9–10 with a similarly veiled dominant chord in this key. The voice then enters, briefly repeats the piano's opening music, but

Example 3.4. Schoenberg, "Das schöne Beet," Op. 15, No. 10, measures 1–10

then moves effortlessly back into the atonal style. The strongly tonal implications of the work and its reference to the style of *Tristan* were evidently Schoenberg's response to the blatant eroticism of the poem—one of the few such in all of George's verse.

The passionately Tristanesque mood is immediately dispelled in the eleventh song, "Als wir hinter dem beblümten Tore," in which the depressive atmosphere introduced at the end of No. 9 now spreads over all. The speaker can describe his ecstatic encounter only uncertainly, searching in his memory for it. "Did we find that imagined bliss?" he asks rhetorically. The music is low in register and very slow, the voice pure recitation, and the piano confined to a few disjunct reflections upon the words. The gloomy mood intensifies relentlessly in Nos. 12 and 13, "Wenn sich bei heilger Ruh" and "Du lehnest wider eine Silberweide," respectively. The speaker's attention turns to the world outside the garden walls, where white sand is ready to soak up his blood. He boards a skiff, but the beloved refuses to join him, and he silently drifts away from her beneath the sad willows.

The lyrical impulse, so important to the first half of the cycle, is now entirely absent from the voice's line, which is crafted into a lifeless and melancholy recitation only occasionally enlivened by the commentary of the piano.

Just as the progress toward a peak of energy in the first half of the cycle is reached in the eighth song, the abyss of dissolution in the second half is attained in No. 14, "Sprich nicht." The structure of the poem is highly distinctive, made from fourteen fragmentary lines, each having no more than three words. The speaker bitterly forbids the mention of nature, whose creatures he can now only associate with a tortured destruction and inconstancy. The distinctive poetics are matched by Schoenberg's musical setting, which is shortened to a mere eleven measures, thus forecasting the aphoristic style to which he turned in 1910. Adorno also called attention to the importance of the song for future directions: "It is the boldest and most advanced of all," he concluded, "completely devoid of traditional architecture, very abbreviated, dematerialized in composition. Its implications for the future cannot be overestimated: all of Webern comes from it."[40] The voice—almost totally divorced from the piano line—moves in a nonlyrical speech melody, and the piano's motivic elements dwindle to a mosaic of tiny fragments. "Sprich nicht" is very much akin to "Am Strande," which was composed at virtually the same moment.

In the final song, "Wir bevölkerten," the denouement of the tragedy of lost love is finally reached. The speaker now explains that the beloved is leaving, abandoning him to the mercy of a garden that has become his torturer, stabbing him with its sharp points and edges. "The night is overcast and sultry" is his last thought. Schoenberg's setting of this memorable poem is both a personal triumph and an artistic masterpiece. In it the composer looked back wistfully at the romantic and classical periods and, like an intrepid pioneer, boldly faced the future, melding the most intimate personal feelings and reflections with a largeness of utterance that Adorno aptly compared to a great symphonic finale. Its forceful piano prelude could well have as its motto *Der Dichter spricht*, so personal is the mode of expression as the line processes stoically and resolutely from high to low and clearly alludes to the key of D minor, which remained as much Schoenberg's motto in 1909 as it was a decade earlier in *Verklärte Nacht*. After the voice has recited its text, Schoenberg takes us back to his own protest, in a mighty postlude that quotes from the first song at measures 35–36 and 45–46 and ends with the chord D B♭ B E—all musical letters of the composer's name—which are then snuffed out one by one.

In a song cycle with such variety of expressive resources, there are still important common features. One is a sameness of large-scale form. Each of the songs (even the aphoristic "Sprich nicht") reveals a *developmental ternary* plan—similar, in fact, to the design most often encountered in Schoenberg's earlier tonal lieder. The ternary form is developmental in that each of three major sections contains the development of a common group of basic motives, which are first heard at or near the beginning. A contrasting middle section is created by the appearance of themes that are only remotely related to the basic motives, and the contrast is usually heightened by a change of tempo or a new surface rhythmic design. In some of the songs, including "Streng ist uns," No. 9, and

"Als wir hinter dem beblümten Tore," No. 11, there is no clearly articulated beginning to the middle section. Each of the three parts normally coincides with
a unit of thought in the text.

The reprise of the ternary form is handled in many different ways. It is usually shorter than the first section, and the initial motives return with relatively
little variation. In some of the songs the reprise has a freely symmetrical relation to the opening section. In these it begins almost imperceptibly, dovetailing
with the middle section, and only at or near the end do the initial motives clearly
reemerge, there forming a strongly audible link with the beginning.

The sixth song, "Jedem Werke bin ich fürder tot," provides clear examples of
Schoenberg's developmental ternary form and an illustration of the process by
which developing variation produces both newness and unity throughout the
melodic dimension of a work. The first section of the song (measures 1–7) corresponds to the first three lines of poetry; the middle section (measures 8–11) to
lines 4 and 5, and the reprise (measures 12–18) to lines 6 through 8. The basic
motives are introduced in the voice in measures 1–2 (see Example 3.5a). This
phrase immediately leads to a "new melody" in measures 2–5 in the piano right
hand (Example 3.5b), which freely doubles the voice. It introduces new elements, especially whole-tone segments and a new rhythmic profile, but it also
subtly incorporates motivic particles from the beginning and end of the earlier
phrase. The *A* section is rounded off in a contrapuntal texture in which the
piano's main line in measures 5–7 (Example 3.5c) is a relatively simple diminution of the preceding melody. The middle section of the song is reached in measure 8, where it is marked off by a new rhythm and texture and by the appearance of a seemingly new vocal melody (Example 3.5d). On closer inspection, it
is apparent that this line is derived from the head motive of the principal
melodic line from measures 1–2 (the first three notes of both are the same, although changed in order, register, and rhythm). The reprise begins in measure
12 at a change of tempo (*langsamer*), although it is anticipated in the preceding
measure by the voice, which straightforwardly repeats the opening melody. The
melodic events of the first section then return in a freely reversed order during
which they ever more clearly resemble their initial shapes.

The variational process that creates the form of Schoenberg's George songs is
most easily traced among linear figures, but it also exists within the harmonic
dimension. The chords, like motives, are often subjected to a far-reaching transformation through such means as transposition, vertical reordering of tones,
expansion or contraction of certain intervals, and addition or subtraction in the
number of notes. Schoenberg also used strict means of harmonic variation, including the symmetric intervallic inversion of tones that has already been
touched on in regard to "Ich darf nicht dankend." Inversion is used as a variational tool at the beginning of "Angst und Hoffen," No. 7 (Example 3.6). The
piano part begins with a harmonic progression, marked off by a phrasing slur,
that consists of an augmented triad, G♭ B♭ D, then a three-note chord, F♭ B♭ E♭,
and finally two minor thirds. The tones of this progression are linearized in the
vocal melody above. A twice-stated variation of the phrase follows in the piano,
in which the minor thirds precede the two remaining chords. The augmented

Example 3.5. Schoenberg, "Jedem Werke bin ich fürder tot," Op. 15, No. 6: (a) measures 1–2; (b) measures 2–4 (piano); (c) measures 5–7 (piano); (d) measures 8–10 (voice)

triad returns varied only by transposition, but the other three-note chord (A♭ D♭ G in measures 3 and 4) is varied by both transposition and symmetrical inversion—the latter apparent in the reverse order of the fourth and tritone that make up both chords. The atonal style thus offered Schoenberg a new opportunity to create an organism that could be unified by the process of variation in both vertical and horizontal dimensions.

This organic image of musical form also led Schoenberg to new ideas concerning harmonic progression. With the elimination of tonality Schoenberg was left with no established principles for the control and guiding of series of chords. Although he never devised a system in his atonal music for this purpose, he experimented in some of the George songs with the interpenetration of

Example 3.6. Schoenberg, "Angst und Hoffen," Op. 15, No. 7, measures 1–4

chordal successions by motives that functioned as controlling elements, thus increasing the multidimensional unity of these works. The first harmonic progression in the piano part of "Angst und Hoffen" (Example 3.6) contains an example. The opening succession of chords in measures 1–2 is guided by its top line, which states a basic motive, D E♭ C C♭, that is also heard in an ornamented diminution in the voice above. When the underlying harmonic progression is varied in measures 2–4, the top line in the piano simultaneously undergoes a development that isolates and dwells on the descending semitone (C–C♭) of the earlier motive.

A related phenomenon is also seen at the beginning of "Jedem Werke bin ich füder tot" (Example 3.5a). The tones of the opening chord in the piano (G E A♯ D♯), although not destined in their entirety to constitute an important motive in the song, are immediately linearized within the accompaniment to form the top line of the piano part in measures 1–2.[41] Variants of the opening chord recur throughout the song in a development that mirrors the developing variations within the linear dimension. Schoenberg was plainly interested, even in the early atonal style, in finding such ways to integrate the linear and harmonic dimensions of a work—a search that only increased as the twelve-tone idea later crystallized in his thinking. "A melodic line, a voice part, or even a melody derives from horizontal projections of tonal relations," he remarked in "My Evolution" (1949). "A chord results similarly from projections in the vertical direction."[42]

The chords themselves in Op. 15 are predominantly drawn from the mixed palette that Schoenberg brought with him from the late romantic style. Triads and familiar seventh chords continue to appear, although their normative tonal functions are almost entirely absent. These are joined by the families of extended tonal chords that Schoenberg would soon discuss in his *Harmonielehre*—vagrant and altered chords, chords with nonharmonic tones, whole-tone chords, and quartal harmonies—although again dissociated from a tonal context. In his *Harmonielehre* Schoenberg devoted an entire chapter to fourth chords, accounting for them in late tonal music as vagrant harmonies or as "impressionistic" sonorities that expressed certain moods more readily than fulfilling definite harmonic functions. In the atonal context of Op. 15, chords from this family are very prominent, although rarely presented as a simple stacking of notes a fourth apart. The opening three measures of "Wir bevölkerten," No. 15 (Example 3.7), contain two chords from the quartal family. The opening harmony (A E G D) is equivalent to a simple fourth chord whose tones have been shuffled in register (compare the ordering E A D G). Certainly Schoenberg wished this harmony also to allude to the dominant seventh chord in the key of D major or minor, which is hinted at in this opening passage. A three-note fourth chord appears on the downbeat of measure 3 (F♯ C♯ B), its notes again placed in registers that obscure the simple interval of the fourth. There is a close connection between such chords and pentatonic music, since five tones each a fourth apart can be rearranged into a pentatonic scale. Unlike other modernist composers, including Debussy, Ravel, and Bartók, Schoenberg rarely wrote extensive melodic passages based on pentatonic scales, but he was very inclined to use harmonies in his early atonal music from the pentatonic universe, specifically those that contained four of the five notes of a pentatonic scale, as in the first measure of "Wir bevölkerten." They stand out due to their distinctively sweet sound, devoid of intervals of the second, seventh, or tritone.

In his writings on the George cycle and on the early history of atonality, Schoenberg underscored the importance of the text as a formative influence on

Example 3.7. Schoenberg, "Wir bevölkerten," Op. 15, No. 15, measures 1–3 the music. But a precise assessment of the relationship between text and music in Op. 15 is made all the more complex in view of the mixed style of the songs as a whole and the existence in the music of certain "distortive inflections"—a term coined by Harald Krebs to indicate musical gestures that conflict with the sense or metrics of the words.[43] Understandably, the question of how George's poems influenced and shaped Schoenberg's music has been often addressed in specialized writings on the work, although no uniform conclusions have been reached. Adorno drew an analogy between Schoenberg's music in the songs and a literary translation of their poetry, thus deemphasizing the role of motivic variations and large-scale architecture.[44] The expressive demands upon a composer in the genre of song cause him to relinquish some of the formative laws of absolute music and allow new shaping forces to grow into their own. Adorno concluded that the text in Op. 15 was not a substitute for tonality, but a medium that intermingled with music to produce a new expressive language and a form sui generis.

In a pioneering study of the George cycle from 1963, Karl Heinrich Ehrenforth concluded the opposite, that George's poetry was not decisive for musical form in the cycle, which resided instead in a diversified technique of motivic and thematic development.[45] Ehrenforth found the strictness of George's poetics dissolved by Schoenberg's musical prose. These conclusions were strongly opposed by other German writers who came shortly after. Reinhold Brinkmann focused on a variety of complex interactions and relationships between the words and the music in Op. 15.[46] Adopting one of Schoenberg's own ideas, Brinkmann found in the rhythm and meter of the vocal melodies a transformation of George's complex poetics into a free proselike style that lay midway between pure music and speech. His viewpoint was extended into an alliance with modern literary theory by Albrecht Dümling in his 1981 book, *Die fremden Klänge der hängenden Gärten.*[47] Dümling compared Schoenberg's voice as musician in the songs to that of a "lyrical I" that hovers above George's poetry, expressing an aesthetic content distinct from the narrational voice in the foreground of a poem itself.

Schoenberg's own pronouncements on this subject contain a fair measure of ambiguity. In his later years, he often remarked that the text in his early atonal music was a primary formal element that guided the construction of the music, a replacement for tonality. "In the perfect amalgamation of music with a poem," he wrote in 1936, "the form will follow the outline of the text."[48] But in his essays and letters closer to the time of composing the George songs, Schoenberg did not stress a formal connection between text and music so much as the congruence between "tone" (*Ton*) and "sound" (*Klang*) in a poem and similar qualities in its musical setting. In his widely read essay "Relationship to the Text," published in *Der blaue Reiter* (1912), he went so far as claim that he was sometimes even unaware of a poem, other than its very beginning, when setting it to music: "I had composed many of my songs straight through to the end without troubling myself in the slightest about the continuation of the poetic events, without even grasping them in the ecstasy of composing. . . . I had completely understood . . . the poems of Stefan George from their sound alone."[49]

Schoenberg's ambivalence about the role of poetry in his new musical idiom may have lured him away from vocal composition after completing Op. 15 to instrumental pieces in which purely musical values were uncontested and in which the strongly romantic connotations of the song genre were more easily dispelled. Still, George's poetry and Schoenberg's own expressive achievements in Op. 15 were the springboard that vaulted him into a new phase of his atonal experiment.

4

Small Instrumental Works
Opp. 11, 16, and 19 and Three Pieces for Chamber Orchestra

Even before completing the George songs early in 1909, Schoenberg rechanneled his new atonal language into purely instrumental media. He seemed eager to experiment with the adaptability to textless music of the concise and expressive style that George's poetry had inspired—music in which the absence of text would allow for even freer emotional diversity and ever greater motivic unity. The new instrumental works—he called them simply pieces—preserved the brief dimensions and heightened expressivity of song, but with a modestly expanded scale and formal flexibility appropriate to instrumental music. Despite the neutral title, their expressive capacity was intense and flexible, as they were freed from the control of a text and all external programs.

In February 1909 Schoenberg quickly composed two atonal works for piano, later published as Nos. 1 and 2 of Op. 11, and, at about this time, he began several other such compositions that were left as undated fragments.[1] The third and final piece of Op. 11 was added in August, at about the same time that he completed his Five Orchestra Pieces, Op. 16, and just before he composed the one-act opera *Erwartung*. Early in the next year he quickly composed three untitled pieces for chamber orchestra, the last of which was left unfinished. In 1911 he concluded this phase of his atonal period by writing the Six Little Piano Pieces, Op. 19, of which the first five were composed on a single day, 19 February, and the final one on 17 June. The chronology of these works is summarized in Table 4.1.

Schoenberg's new instrumental music was a far cry from his experiences with the orchestra and string quartet only slightly earlier. In those media he had composed in larger classical genres and forms, but such expansiveness was now out of the question. The large sonata or variations forms of the Second String Quartet and the expansive cyclic structure of the Chamber Symphony, Op. 9, were things of the past, like functional tonal progressions, and after Op. 15 these must have seemed only shackles that restrained freedom of the imagination. The experience of the George songs had shown Schoenberg the powerful expression inherent in the atonal style using small forms, each having a concentrated motivic development that made tonality appear all the more unnecessary and restrictive.

Table 4.1. Chronology of Schoenberg's Opp. 11, 16, and 19 and Three Pieces for Chamber Orchestra (from JMS 1: 63–70)

Work	Date of beginning	Date of conclusion
Piano Piece, Op. 11, No. 1		19 February 1909
Piano Piece, Op. 11, No. 2	22 February 1909	
Orchestra Piece, Op. 16, No. 1		23 May 1909
Orchestra Piece, Op. 16, No. 2		before 15 June 1909
Orchestra Piece, Op. 16, No. 3		before 1 July 1909
Orchestra Piece, Op. 16, No. 4		17 July 1909
Piano Piece, Op. 11, No. 3		7 August 1909
Orchestra Piece, Op. 16, No. 5		before 11 August 1909
Three Pieces for Chamber Orchestra, Nos. 1–2		8 February 1910
Three Pieces for Chamber Orchestra, No. 3		after 8 February 1910
Little Piano Pieces, Op. 19, Nos. 1–5		19 February 1911
Little Piano Piece, Op. 19, No. 6		17 June 1911

Three Piano Pieces, Op. 11

Schoenberg's Three Piano Pieces, Op. 11, are not unified as a cycle, either in character or in musical materials. The first two pieces are similar in their introspective mood—Schoenberg called them somber—and in their common formative principles. But the third one, eruptive and virtuosic, represents a significantly new conception of form and character, which Schoenberg devised during the summer of 1909 and reused in the Orchestra Piece, Op. 16, No. 5, and the monodrama *Erwartung*, all composed in August and September of that year.

Composing for the piano was somethingw new for Schoenberg. He had almost entirely avoided this medium during his earlier tonal period; in fact, he had completed no works at all for piano after a group of apprenticeship pieces written under Zemlinsky's eye in 1896. Part of Schoenberg's reticence in writing for piano may have come from his own limited ability as a player and an awareness of the distance that this created between him and the idiomatic treatment of the instrument so apparent in the works of the great pianist-composers of the nineteenth century.

The manuscripts for Op. 11, like those for the George cycle, suggest that Schoenberg's compositional method in the early atonal style relied primarily upon a fluid and momentary inspiration. There is little evidence of the extensive sketching that was so pronounced in his work on the Second String Quartet and Chamber Symphony. There are no independent sketches at all for the Three Piano Pieces, and the manuscripts leave the impression that Schoenberg composed the first full drafts quickly and with few interruptions. He dated the conclusion of the first piece 19 February 1909 and the beginning of the second 22 February 1909; the third was composed months later in Steinakirchen am Forst—its draft is dated 7 August 1909 at the end. There is only one instance of a significant second thought, this in Piece No. 3, in which nine measures near the beginning were eliminated and a shorter alternative added.[2] Evidence compiled by Reinhold Brinkmann suggests that Schoenberg, after deciding to group the three short works into a single collection, wrote out a fair copy that is now lost, probably after being sent to Universal Edition as the *Stichvorlage* for the first edition, which appeared in October 1910. This was Schoenberg's first publication by Universal Edition and also the first publication of any of his atonal music. By then the pieces had already been heard publicly, premiered by Marietta Werndorff in a concert of Vienna's Verein für Kunst und Kultur on 14 January 1910, and Schoenberg had also sent out manuscript copies to other prominent pianists, including Béla Bartók and Ferruccio Busoni, hoping for additional performances.

In revised editions of 1924 and 1942, the composer continued to add refinements to the score, mainly concerning nuances for the performer. In letters to Busoni he emphasized that the works had to be played with pronounced rubato. "I never stay in time!" he wrote. "Never in tempo!"[3] Tempo was indeed a crucial factor in creating the proper effect. Schoenberg urged Edward Steuermann to choose a very slow tempo for the second piece, and he mentioned to Busoni a metronomic rate of 80–90 to the eighth note in this movement.[4] For an American edition in 1942 he added metronome markings for each piece: the quarter note at 66 in No. 1, eighth note at 120 in No. 2 (thus fully 50% faster than the tempo that he had mentioned to Busoni), and eighth note at 132 in No. 3.[5]

The first two pieces dwell on a limited range of sonorities inherent to the piano, and it was on this point that Schoenberg entered in 1909 into a lengthy exchange of letters with Ferruccio Busoni.[6] In this correspondence Schoenberg was for once unguarded in explaining his intentions and working methods; in fact, he lays out his ideas behind the early atonal style with a clarity and detail matched nowhere else in his writings. On 20 July, while vacationing in lower Austria, Schoenberg sent a manuscript copy of the first two pieces of Op. 11 to the great Berlin pianist, hoping that Busoni would play them publicly (which he never did). Busoni, known for his generous assistance to younger composers, wrote back encouragingly but with a mild criticism that the works did not capture the piano's distinctive sound and texture. He told Schoenberg that he had even revised the second piece to add brilliance to it and to remove some of its pianistic infelicities.[7] In the letters that followed in 1909 and 1910, Schoenberg forthrightly explained his conception behind the works, which he defended ever more vigorously, and he was blunt in his critique of Busoni's well-intentioned though certainly tactless alternative version of Piece No. 2. It was his objective, Schoenberg declared, to do away with "piano writing which overstretches the expressive possibilities and mobility of the piano yet is nothing more than a good, or less good, transcription of orchestral music."[8]

In Busoni's alternative version of the second piece, which he excerpted in a letter to Schoenberg in 1909 and then sent to him in toto during the following summer, the brighter sounds of the instrument's upper register are emphasized by transposing certain figures upward; other motives are animated by rhythmic diminutions, and the final cadence is reinforced by the addition of several simple reiterations of the concluding motives.[9] In his response to Busoni, Schoen-

berg pointed to two principal areas in which such changes betrayed his intentions: first, they ran roughshod over his expressive ideas; second, they muddled
the form of the work by introducing motives that had not been properly prepared. On the first point, Schoenberg was quick to observe that no program lay
behind the work, but he left the impression with Busoni that every minute gesture in the piece had a definite expressive meaning. The opening measure, for
example, in which an ostinato pattern weaves above a pedal tone, conveyed the
sense of being "completely immersed in a certain mood." The motive in the right
hand at measures 5–6 is "very expressive: strident, expansive, oboes with cello
portamento." The seventh chord at the reprise at measure 54 is "someone sup-
pressing a tear" (Schoenberg then added tartly that Busoni's rewriting of the
chord could only suggest someone blowing his nose).

The formal principles encountered in the George songs reappear in the first
two pieces of Op. 11, although the differing structural implications of the two
media are also evident. Both piano pieces use a developmental ternary form, but
in each one the main theme is longer and more classically shaped than in the
songs. Basic materials are also more expansively elaborated upon in the piano
works, whose middle sections are considerably longer and subdivided into several distinct parts to provide greater opportunities for changes of mood and a
wider range of expression. The main themes—heard in the first eleven measures in No. 1 and fifteen measures in No. 2—are both examples of what Schoenberg later called small ternary form, a plan often encountered in thematic ex-
positions in classical instrumental music.[10] The main parts are apparent in the
concise main theme of No. 1 (Example 4.1). After the first phrase (measures

Example 4.1. Schoenberg, Piano Piece, Op. 11, No. 1, measures 1–11

1–3), the middle part (measures 4–8) is set off by a new motive that is twice repeated and concluded by a ritard. The third part restates the motives of the first, only slightly varied.

The contrasting middle sections of both pieces follow immediately after the main themes, at measures 12 and 16, respectively. As in the George songs, the middle parts are marked off by a change in tempo, new surface design, and new motive forms at first distant from those of the opening section. Fragmentary and highly varied restatements of the original themes also resurface in these middle sections, but otherwise these passages are very different from the comparable ones in the songs. They are considerably longer, multipartite, and filled with great expressive contrasts. So complex are the middle parts that Brinkmann has described the form of No. 1 not as ternary but as a free alteration of two types of music, the first "thematic," the second "eruptive" due to its greater extremes of register, dynamics, color, and rhythm.

The reprises of the two pieces (at measures 53 and 55, respectively) begin with unmistakable references to the opening motives, after which further development returns. In neither one is there evidence of the retrograded reprise often found in Op. 15, as in "Jedem Werke bin ich fürder tot," in which the greatest similarity with the beginning occurs at the very end of the composition rather than at the point of reprise itself. The end of Piece No. 2 is also unusual in its fragmentation, which creates a sense of dissociation that is enhanced by the ever softer dynamics and continual slowing of tempo from measure 58 to the end. In this haunting codetta, brief motives from both the main theme and the middle section return in a dissolving echo whose effect Schoenberg described to Busoni: "My piece does *not* conclude; it simply stops; one must have the impression that it could still go on for some time—like the hurdy-gurdy in Schubert's 'Leiermann' [from *Winterreise*]."[11]

The harmonic vocabulary in Op. 11, Nos. 1 and 2, also differs subtly from that of many of the George songs in that it greatly reduces the direct use of triads and familiar seventh chords. It also moves cautiously away from the late romantic harmonic palette—altered or vagrant chords, whole-tone harmonies, triadic tetrachords, and pentatonic subsets—that Schoenberg had used repeatedly in the early atonal style of Op. 15. The harmonic language of the Three Piano Pieces begins to show an important change in Schoenberg's thinking about atonal music, as it abandons, however tentatively, the mixed idiom of Op. 15 and adopts a homogeneous, dissonant, and distinctly anti-romantic alternative that had been hinted at in "Sprich nicht" from Op. 15 and in its contemporaneous "Am Strande." This was a new harmonic practice to which Schoenberg referred in 1911 in the *Harmonielehre* when he confessed his

aversion to recalling even remotely the traditional chords. . . . The simple chords of the earlier harmony do not appear successfully in this [new atonal] environment. I believe, however, that there is another reason for their absence here. I believe they would sound too cold, too dry, expressionless. Or, perhaps, what I mentioned on an earlier occasion applies here. Namely, that these simple chords, which are imperfect imitations of nature, seem to us too primitive.[12]

But despite the appearance of new formative ideas in Op. 11, the many residual elements carried over from the romantic style have long attracted the attention of writers who have studied these works. In particular, the possibility that tonality continues to exist in them has greatly influenced the analytic literature, which is one of the largest on any of Schoenberg's compositions. The search for tonality in Op. 11 has stemmed not only from its few tertian harmonies but also from the totality of traditional elements that the works so plainly exhibit, including motivic repetitiveness, familiar overall form, a texture and surface design reminiscent of late romantic piano music, and expressive gestures associated with romantic genres.

The tone for most analyses of Op. 11 was first set by Hugo Leichtentritt in his pioneering discussion of the works in the third edition (1927) of his *Musikalische Formenlehre*. Leichtentritt maintained that organization in the pieces was promoted not only by thematic work but also by a tonality that was still felt despite extensive distortions and inconsistencies. The first piece, for example, was in G major, Leichtentritt wrote, although this key was darkly clouded by polytonality, unresolved alterations of chords, and conflicting tonal implications between melody and accompaniment. Leichtentritt's line of thought was extended into an analytic system by Edwin von der Null in his widely read *Moderne Harmonik* (1932). The new music by Schoenberg, Bartók, Stravinsky, and others from around 1910, Null wrote, used an "expanded tonality" that was still characterized by pitch centers, diatonic scales, and functional harmonic progressions that had been enriched and multiplied, not abandoned. Piece No. 1 from Op. 11, Null concluded, was in the key of "Ee"—E major merged with E minor. Its tonic chord was the four-note collection E G G♯ B apparent in the opening melodic phrase, which was supported by chords whose tonal functions were still evident despite multiple alterations and coloristic effects.

The thinking of Leichtentritt and Null is also apparent in Reinhold Brinkmann's interpretation of the works in his *Arnold Schönberg: Drei Klavierstücke Op. 11. Studien zur frühen Atonalität bei Schönberg* (1969).[13] Brinkmann uncovers a tonality still at work in each of the first two pieces; he interprets the first, for example, as wavering between the keys of E and E♭, thus a recrudescence of Schoenberg's concept of *schwebende Tonalität*. These keys are established mainly in the boundary pitches of lines, Brinkmann says, and also by the frequency of supporting tones a fifth above and below.

But Schoenberg himself was emphatically opposed to theories that found an imperfect expression of key still at work in his music beginning with the George songs. To Busoni on 24 August 1909 he wrote: "My harmony allows no chords or melodies with tonal implications any more."[14] In a marginal note that he added to his copy of Null's treatise he wrote: "This book could just as well have been written 25 years ago. . . . Nothing could be more irrelevant than the contrived argument that the ostensibly '*atonal*' is still '*tonal*.'"[15]

Other important analyses of Op. 11 have rejected the presence of residual tonality and concluded that the music rests on an essentially new conception of form. This is a premise that underlies *set theory*, advanced in the early 1970s by Allen Forte and subsequently used by numerous American and English special ists as a basis for the analysis of atonal music.[16] Forte's theory not only repudiates any pseudotonal interpretations of works such as Op. 11 but also relegates motivic development in them to a superficial level of structure. In fact, Forte's own analytic application of his theory does not build directly upon any existing procedures in the technical literature on Schoenberg, although it is related to the Schenkerian idea that abstract structural archetypes can be deduced from a stylistically interrelated musical repertory and that these shapes control, in a sense, the surface design of the music.

Forte's theory defines relationships among constellations of pitches in a composition by looking at them abstractly and systematically, often on a level that is far removed from the surface of the musical work itself. Specifically, Forte has found that by dividing an entire atonal work into adjacent collections of tones—notes in a chord, in a line, or in a constellation of pitches embedded in a more complex texture—relationships among the intervallic structures in these collections can be established, even though the pitch content of the collections and their motivic contexts may be very different. For example, two collections of tones that differ by transposition, reordering, or symmetrical inversion are so similar in their abstract intervallic structure that Forte defines them as equivalent, even though their modes of presentation may be completely dissimilar. He also postulates secondary relationships, by which one collection of tones can be viewed as distinctly akin to another.

Piece No. 1 has proved to be especially susceptible to analysis by these principles.[17] Forte has shown that the entire work can be divided into groups of four to six tones each, among which his postulates of equivalence and relatedness are strongly apparent. One such relationship is illustrated in Example 4.2, which shows the beginning of a developmental passage in measures 34–36. Clearly enough, this passage contains an elaborate variation upon the head motive of the main theme of the work in measures 1–2 (shown in Example 4.1). This motive returns in measures 34–36 nearly simultaneously in three strata within the right hand alone. But Forte focuses on a more abstract relatedness that arises within an entire two-dimensional texture. He observes that all notes in measure 34 merge into a harmonic entity that is equivalent to the set of notes presented in the line of measures 1–3. The relationship between the two can be

Example 4.2. Schoenberg, Piano Piece, Op. 11, No. 1, measures 34–36

readily observed in the identical succession of intervals that is created when notes of the two collections are placed into a compact scalewise order—E F G G♯ A B (measures 1–3) and F E D D♭ C B♭ (measure 34). This demonstrates an abstract equivalence, to be sure, since it is only partly relevant to the musical context. Since the two collections can be reduced to a similar scalar structure, Forte considers them to be members of a single harmonic family or "set class," as other writers have called it. He has extended the theory to an even more abstract level by precisely defining the relationships that can exist among most or all of the set classes that occur in a large composition, linking an entire work into a unified construct that he calls a set complex. A further discussion of set theory and its relationship to Schoenberg's compositional method will be found later in this chapter.

In the third piece of Op. 11, composed in early August 1909, Schoenberg decisively abandoned the mixed style of early atonality that had existed in Op. 15. The new style, often called *athematic*, was prefigured between May and August of that year in the Five Orchestra Pieces, Op. 16, works that will be discussed momentarily. Piano Piece No. 3 confronts both performer and listener with remarkable innovations and many complex problems. It is dauntingly virtuosic, intricately polyphonic, and highly irregular in its shifting rhythms and constantly changing tempi. Its emotional range is very great—at one moment erupting in impetuous outbursts, the next receding into muted sobs—and its coherence stems from principles of organization and expression that are strikingly different from those in music that Schoenberg composed only a few months before.

Its innovations are especially apparent in its form. Developing variations upon distinctive motives and phrases, heretofore basic to Schoenberg's conception of music as coherent discourse, are almost entirely absent, and the composer has also dispensed with the traditional large-scale formal architecture that closely linked his early atonal works with classical practices. Certainly, Schoenberg did not intend Piece No. 3 to be incoherent. Looking back forty years later, he recalled his daring athematic experiment: "Intoxicated by the enthusiasm of having freed music from the shackles of tonality, I had thought to find further liberty of expression. In fact, I myself and my pupils Anton von Webern and Alban Berg, and even Alois Hába believed that now music could renounce motivic features and remain coherent and comprehensible nevertheless."[18]

But coherence here is entrusted to new formal principles, encountered on both the large and small scale, that exert a far weaker degree of control over the musical materials than ever before. In his atonal instrumental music composed prior to August 1909, Schoenberg used forms unmistakably derived from classical models. These works are subdivided into sections linked together by their expository, developmental, or recapitulatory treatment of a common group of themes, phrases, and motives. As in classical instrumental music, passages introducing thematic material, which is presented in a relatively strict manner, occur at the beginning. Developmental subsections are looser in construction, and recapitulations bring back themes with changes that had been wrought by the intervening developmental processes. Both of the first two pieces of Op. 11 conform to this classical model in their abbreviated *A B A′* shapes.

Piece No. 3 is very different, since traditional thematic development and re-capitulation does not occur. Its coherence relies instead upon broader expressive gestures and shapes. The listener to Piece No. 3 notices, first of all, a succession of brief, clearly contrasted sections, set off from one another by silences, changes in dynamic level and tempo, and sudden shifts in surface rhythm and textural design. Reinhold Brinkmann found in the open form of Piece No. 3 a succession of eighteen free-standing sections (*Satzzonen*), some with a thematic character, others pure texture, but each exhibiting considerable independence.[19] With only a few exceptions, no distinctive materials return to link these sections to-gether, nowhere at all with the clarity of Schoenberg's earlier thematic work. A large-scale coherence that connects the string of sections is achieved instead by a continuous expressive curve. In Piece No. 3 this rhetorical contour takes the shape of a wavelike fluctuation that suggests quickly changing, spontaneous emotions that alternate between the flamboyant and the restrained.

There is no development of motives or developing variation per se, in the sense that Schoenberg used the term *motive* for "a memorable shape or con-tour."[20] But the principle of recurrence is not entirely eliminated. It is relegated instead to a technique, already foreshadowed in "Sprich nicht" from the George cycle, of the free and sporadic return of *motivic particles,* that is, small and usu-ally nondistinctive figures that lack a memorable rhythm or shape. These can be single intervals, minute rhythmic gestures, or even single durations, cells that encompass a few tones, or other minuscule figures that the composer could in-stantaneously call on in a headlong act of composing. In his pedagogical writ-ings Schoenberg recognized the distinction between the motive per se and the motivic particle, although he had no terminology to separate the two, and he was sometimes forced into the confusing definition of a motive as an entity that could be made up of motives. "Every element or feature of a motive or phrase," he wrote, "must be considered to be a motive if it is treated as such, i.e., if it is repeated with or without variation."[21]

The return of motivic particles begins even in the two opening measures of Piece No. 3 (Example 4.3). Among the most prominent of them are two three-note figures that are introduced in the incomplete first measure: the chord C# C E in the right hand and the line A–G#–D in the left. Their tones return in free vari-ants in every measure of the work, but the figures do not retain their original rhythmic profiles or intervallic shapes as in motivic development. For example, the trichord A–G#–D returns in the left-hand line of measure 1 as the succession D–C#–A–G#, reordered and expanded by the additional tone C#; it next reappears verticalized, inverted, and transposed as A D# G# in measure 2 (middle staff). This technique of detaching motivic development from rhythm would prove to be of immense importance in Schoenberg's later development of the atonal style.

Piece No. 3 also eschews a distinctive harmonic profile, as its texture is far more linear and contrapuntal than the earlier two largely homophonic works from the set. The chords that flash by in parallel streams of sound or thunder in massive punctuations tend to be larger than the four-note norm that Schoen-berg used in his earlier atonal style, often expanding now to collections of as

Example 4.3. Schoenberg, Piano Piece, Op. 11, No. 3, measures 1–2

many as ten different tones. This massing of harmony would shortly be used by Schoenberg, especially in *Erwartung* and *Die glückliche Hand,* as a gesture of emphasis, climax, or bravado. Ostinato, so important to Op. 11, No. 2, remains in No. 3 as a flexible structural device that fulfills many purposes. It occurs here near the end (measures 32–33) to prepare the final cadence and to mark a firm completion of thought, which Schoenberg wished to avoid in the earlier two pieces.

The Busoni Manifesto

The athematic style and form of Op. 11, No. 3, represent symptoms of a major change in Schoenberg's thinking about his future direction, and his new objectives are documented in unusually precise detail in his correspondence with Busoni. In the letters from August 1909 Schoenberg speaks of his plan to compose from that time by pure instinct, adding no formal construction and aiming for the utmost diversity in motive, rhythm, and mood. He tells Busoni that Piece No. 3 succeeds most of all due to its colorful diversity of elements (*Buntheit*) and in its novel harmony, which contains "something more slender, more linear."[22] His intention, he says in a letter of mid-August, is to have no intentions, "to place nothing inhibiting in the stream of my unconscious sensations."

In another letter Schoenberg summarized his new aesthetic in the form of a manifesto:

> I strive for: complete liberation from all forms
> from all symbols
> of cohesion and
> of logic.
>   Thus:
> away with "motivic working out."
> Away with harmony as
> cement or bricks of a building.
> Harmony is *expression*
> and nothing else.
>   Then:
> Away with Pathos!
> Away with protracted ten-ton scores, from erected or constructed
>   towers, rocks and other massive claptrap.
> My music must be
> *brief.*
> Concise! In two notes: not built, but "*expressed*"!!
> And the results I wish for:
> no stylized and sterile protracted emotion.
> People are not like that:
> it is *impossible* for a person to have only *one* sensation at a time.
> One has *thousands* simultaneously. And these thousands can no
>   more readily be added together than an apple and a pear. They go
>   their own ways.
> And this variegation, this multifariousness, this *illogicality* which
>   our senses demonstrate, the illogicality presented by their
>   interactions, set forth by some mounting rush of blood, by some
>   reaction of the senses or nerves, this I should like to have in my
>   music.
> It should be an expression of feeling, as our feelings, which bring
>   us in contact with our subconscious, really are, and no false
>   child of feelings and "conscious logic."
> Now I have made my confession and they can burn me.[23]

Two of the objectives that Schoenberg announced in this "confession"— brevity and quickly changing emotional expression—were already apparent in his earlier atonal works from Op. 11, and the spontaneity of composing that he propounds is confirmed in his earlier music by the general absence of sketches. But the rejection of all archetypal musical forms and traditional principles of coherence, including motivic work, represents a renunciation of the classical ideal of form to which he earlier adhered in his music and upon which he insisted in his later writings. "The chief requirements in the creation of a comprehensible form are *logic* and *coherence*," he wrote in the *Fundamentals of Musical Composition.* "The presentation, development, and interconnexion of ideas must be based on [their] relationship."[24] The athematic style thus embodied for Schoenberg a daring and relatively short-lived experiment. It represented a much more revolutionary step into the future of music than did the onset of atonality itself, which had occurred only months before. The early atonal style, with its characteristic mixture of old and new tonal elements, was practiced even at the time by several important progressive musicians, including Aleksandr Scriabin, Béla Bartók, and the Strauss of *Salome* and *Elektra.* If Schoenberg had continued to mine the vein of early atonality, he would probably eventually have earned the public acceptance that he so much desired. This recognition, however, was ruled out by the new athematic manner, which was pure and homogeneous rather than mixed, unified rather than eclectic, and ill at ease in the company of other, even modernistic, approaches to music.

Schoenberg was never successful in explaining the new aesthetic of 1909. In his autobiographical essay "My Evolution," he could only say that he was "intoxicated by enthusiasm" following the removal of key from his music—a rationale that seems scarcely adequate to explain its far-reaching implications.[25] His new attitude may well have been prompted by several external factors, including ideas culled from his readings and discussions, as well as reflections upon recent developments in his personal life. In his remarks to Busoni, Schoenberg repeatedly called attention to the emotions per se—how they exist in the human mind, influence personality, and provoke artistic creativity. It is likely that in the aftermath of the tumultuous Gerstl affair, during which Schoenberg described himself as utterly in the grip of his own emotions, he would be all the more eager to explore emotionality in both a scientific and artistic way. That music should, in its more evolved stages in the twentieth century, be "about" the emotions must have been apparent to him from the ever-increasing expressivity and emotionalism of the late romantic style, and it was an idea buttressed by such admired writers as Schopenhauer, who had described music as a medium of communication beyond intellectual understanding.

Judging from his remarks to Busoni, Schoenberg treated Schopenhauer's ideas with a large dose of modern psychological theory. The emotions, Schoenberg said in the manifesto, exist most purely in the unconscious mind, whose workings can only be distorted and falsified by the rational or conscious faculties. If his music in the future was to stem from and depict the emotions in their genuine and unalloyed state, then it would have to flow directly and by pure instinct in a virtual stream of consciousness, without traditional developmental or architectonic forms that were the products of rational control and calculation. This line of thinking about the human psyche arises repeatedly in Schoenberg's writings from 1909 until about 1912, after which the composer had far less to say on the subject. In the *Harmonielehre*, written in 1910 and 1911, he continued his speculations on the unconscious mind and its relation to the arts:

> The artist's creative activity is instinctive. Consciousness has little influence on it. He feels as if what he does were dictated to him. As if he did it only according to the will of some power or other within him, whose laws he does not know. He is merely the instrument of a will hidden from him, of instinct, of his unconscious. Whether it is new or old, good or bad, beautiful or ugly, he does not know.[26]

In a letter to Wassily Kandinsky of 24 January 1911, he spoke similarly: "Art belongs to the *unconscious!* One must express *oneself!* Express oneself *directly!* Not one's taste, or one's upbringing, or one's intelligence, knowledge or skill. Not all these *acquired* characteristics, but that which is *inborn, instinctive.*"[27]

Schoenberg's references to the unconscious mind point to an awareness of the psychoanalytic theories of Sigmund Freud, which were much discussed at this time by Austrian intellectuals and were of special interest to several members of Schoenberg's circle.[28] But Schoenberg himself appears to have had little direct knowledge of or interest in Freudian theory. In a catalog of his own library that he first made in 1913, no writings by Freud are mentioned,[29] and Schoenberg's essays and correspondence are virtually devoid of any references at all to Freud or to psychoanalysis. Almost certainly Freudian ideas were discussed in Schoenberg's circle, and conversations with Marie Pappenheim, a physician knowledgeable in psychoanalytic theory, during the summer of 1909 may well have stimulated his interest in the unconscious and its relation to emotionalism and artistic creativity.

Another influential source of information for Schoenberg concerning the distinction between intellect and intuition was the writing of Henri Bergson. Schoenberg was apparently an avid reader of Bergson, whose ideas were enjoying a great vogue throughout the world in the decade that preceded World War I. Four books by Bergson were in Schoenberg's library in 1913, and two of them, German translations of *Introduction to Metaphysics* and *Matter and Memory,* may have been read by the composer by the summer of 1909. In the former work Bergson explores the relation between intuitive and intellectual activity. Both, he says, are ways of knowing about the world, but intuition is by far the more immediate and direct. The intellect, by comparison, deals with reality only second hand, through concepts, symbols, and images. Intuition participates directly in the essences of reality and proceeds by spontaneous flashes of insight. Bergson's analysis of the intuitive mind must have reinforced Schoenberg's intention to use music as a means of direct and essential expression.

Five Orchestra Pieces, Op. 16

By midyear 1909 Schoenberg was in the midst of his most fertile and optimistic period as a composer. Inspired by the new musical ideas associated with atonality, his productivity was at its highest level ever. Four major works were composed in a mere seven-month span in 1909. He was enthusiastic about his new music and eager to wield the atonal language in new ways, expanding it into different genres and media and exploring its potential for ever greater expressivity. His letters from this time reveal a self-assured composer, almost exuberant in his belief that recognition of his work was now only a short step away. He sent selections from his new Orchestra Pieces, Op. 16, to Richard Strauss with the utmost confidence. "I have colossally high hopes for them, especially in their sound and atmosphere," Schoenberg confided. The piano pieces of Op. 11 were sent to Busoni with an assurance that they were "distinctive, stylish, and organic" and that they "laid the foundations for a modern piano style."

But his optimism for acceptance—exceedingly important for Schoenberg— soon turned to bitter disillusionment. He certainly anticipated the stormy incomprehension with which contemporary audiences would greet his new music, and he knew well enough that journalists would continue to hurl barbs. But he did not anticipate the reaction that his new music would elicit from the very modernist composers whom he admired. "It would be better for him to shovel snow than to scrawl on music paper," Strauss told Alma Mahler. "I don't know if this kind of thing can be given the name 'music,'" wrote Max Reger about Op. 11. "I don't understand his music," Mahler confided to his wife after hearing the Chamber Symphony, Op. 9.[30] These reactions, of which Schoenberg became all too well aware, were likely the most wounding rejections that he would ever receive. They soon alienated him from most of the leading modernist composers of his day and drove him ever more defiantly into his own sympathetic circle of students.

But in May 1909 his hopes for success were still high, as he turned from the small dimensions of the piano piece to experiment with atonality in music for large orchestra. He had not completed a work for this medium since the tone poem *Pelleas und Melisande* of 1903, and his choice of the large romantic orchestra, not the chamber orchestra that he had used in his two Chamber Symphonies, was probably due to the naive expectation that the new style would be embraced by sympathetic conductors. Richard Strauss, then music director of the Royal Opera in Berlin, may have had a direct influence upon the choice of medium and genre in the works that Schoenberg began in May. Strauss had written to Schoenberg a year before, asking for "a few (not too long) pieces to have a look at," and Schoenberg responded in Op. 16 with a collection of orchestral character pieces (not too long), using the mammoth and diversified orchestra for which Strauss himself was then most famous.[31] The Five Orchestra Pieces, Op. 16, were the outcome of Strauss's "commission." In terms of Schoenberg's own musical development, they brilliantly document his transition from the early atonal style of Op. 11, No. 1, to the new athematic idiom already seen in Op. 11, No. 3. The Five Pieces, in fact, show Schoenberg fully in command of his new style, original at every step, and profoundly inspired in the creation of what must be recognized as one of the great masterpieces for orchestra of the entire twentieth century.

The Five Pieces were probably composed in the order in which they are now known, although Schoenberg's first full drafts, in which he used the short-score format, are dated only at the end of the first (23 May 1909) and fourth pieces (17 July 1909). Hoping for a performance of the works, the composer wasted no time in compiling a fair copy in full score, which he evidently prepared for each piece very shortly after completing its *Particell.* This full score, later used as a *Stichvorlage* by Edition Peters for the first printing in 1912, contains dates at the end of each piece: 9 June, 15 June, 1 July, 18 July, and 11 August 1909 for the five works.[32]

In mid-July, while vacationing in Steinakirchen, Schoenberg sent Strauss a progress report on the pieces, revealing that he was still uncertain about the overall dimensions of the new work:

> They are short orchestra pieces (between 1 and 3 minutes duration) with no cyclic connections. . . . I have already written three, a fourth one can be added in a few days at most and perhaps two or three more will come to life afterwards. . . . There is absolutely nothing symphonic about them, quite the opposite—no architecture, no construction [*Aufbau*]. Purely a diverse [*bunt*], uninterrupted alternation of colors, rhythms, and moods.[33]

On 28 July Schoenberg posted to Strauss a copy of four of the pieces, almost certainly the first four and probably in the same fair-copy manuscript that he later sent to Peters. By this time he had finalized his conception of the collection, which was fixed at five pieces arranged in their current order. The fifth piece, Schoenberg told Strauss, was still unfinished, but it promised to be more cheerful than the "dark" Nos. 1 and 4.

Strauss was quick to respond. A performance of such "daring experiments" in Berlin would not be possible after all, he said, adding that it would prove difficult for Schoenberg to find any conductor who would accept them. Strauss advised Schoenberg to hire an orchestra to read them through, hinting that he would recognize their problems when he heard his experiments realized. Other important figures in Germany's musical life ultimately proved more prescient in their judgment of the new works. Henri Hinrichsen, the director of Edition Peters, described the Five Orchestra Pieces as "epoch making." He wrote to Schoenberg in 1922: "I am myself persuaded that they will someday be a firm cornerstone of the classical repertory," words that Hinrichsen accompanied with an additional honorarium of 3,000 deutsche mark.[34]

Like the Three Pieces for Piano, Schoenberg's Five Orchestra Pieces are diverse character works, not a cyclic composition. Few, if any, distinctive musical materials are shared among movements, and any close analogy with the traditional symphonic cycle is dispelled by the order in which the pieces occur: an impetuous fugue is placed as No. 1, slow and lyrical movements arrive as Nos. 2 and 3, a fast movement returns as No. 4, and a trenchant waltz occupies the finale. In his correspondence with Strauss in 1909, Schoenberg approved of a performance of fewer than all five pieces, and, in their first public performance in Berlin on 4 February 1912, only Nos. 1, 2, and 4 were given, in an eight-hand piano arrangement made by Erwin Stein.

The expressive character of the five works is teasingly suggested by titles that Schoenberg attached to each movement for a performance with the Concertge-

bouw Orchestra of Amsterdam in 1914 and printed with the score beginning
with a revised edition that appeared in 1922. Schoenberg had privately formulated the titles as early as 1912 after receiving a request for them from Hinrichsen. The publisher had then pointedly informed Schoenberg that "compositions
with the title 'Pieces' don't get off the ground," citing examples in recent works
of Christian Sinding and Max Reger.[35] In his diary entry on 28 January of that
year Schoenberg drafted the titles that would appear in 1914 and later, but he
also spoke of his misgivings about Hinrichsen's request:

> Do not altogether like the idea [of titles]. Music is fascinating because you can
> say everything so that the knowledgeable will understand it all, without having
> to give away your secrets, the secrets one does not even admit to oneself. Titles,
> however, give things away. Besides, the music has already said what there is to
> say. Why are words needed? If words were necessary, they would be there.
> Music says more than words. The titles that I may assign will not give anything
> away, partly because they are quite obscure, partly because they refer to tech-
> nical matters. Namely: 1. "Premonitions" (everyone has these); 2. "The Past"
> (everyone has this too); 3. "Chord Colors" (technical); 4. Peripeteia (probably
> general enough); 5. "The Obligatory Recitative" (maybe "fully developed" or
> "endless" would be better).[36]

Although Schoenberg did not give in to Hinrichsen's request in 1912, his
wish to have the music understood at some level ultimately prevailed, and for
the Amsterdam concert two years later the titles were returned, with slight ad-
justments. The second piece was changed from *Vergangenheit* (The past) to *Vergangenes* (Things from the past), and Schoenberg had numerous second thoughts
about the title of the third piece, which was repeatedly renamed. "The Changing Chord," "Colors," "The Changing Chord (Morning on the Traunsee)," "Colors (Summer Morning on the Lake)," and "Summer Morning at a Lake" were all
tried in various concert programs and editions of the work. Schoenberg and his
assistant Richard Hoffmann also formulated English equivalents of the titles for
a revision of the score made in 1949. The terms that they chose—"Premonitions,"
"Yesteryears," "Summer Morning at a Lake," "Peripetia" [*sic*], and "The Obligatory Recitative"—introduce new shades of meaning.

Schoenberg also had second thoughts concerning the use of large orchestra,
especially after Strauss showed so little interest in the work. In addition to a two-
piano reduction made by Anton Webern at the request of Hinrichsen, there are
two published arrangements of Op. 16 for smaller ensembles, one for a "normal-
sized orchestra" made by Schoenberg in 1949 at the same time that he introduced the English subtitles and the other for chamber orchestra (four woodwinds, piano, harmonium, and string quintet) published in 1925 and credited
to Schoenberg's son-in-law, Felix Greissle. The version for chamber orchestra was
based on Schoenberg's own outline, which, though undated, was probably made
early in 1920 for the use of the Verein für Musikalische Privataufführungen
(Society for Private Musical Performances). An arrangement of Op. 16 for chamber orchestra was performed by the Verein at an open rehearsal on 25 February

1920 in Vienna, followed by a performance on 13 March in Prague, but many questions remain concerning its relation to Greissle's 1925 version.

Schoenberg's outline for the chamber orchestra version was entered into a *Handexemplar* of the 1912 full score. In addition to many notes and markings, the composer also tipped in a gathering of manuscript paper on which he had fully written out the third piece in a reduced version. The outline was almost certainly made for the use of the Verein, whose arrangements were often prepared collaboratively by several advanced students, based on instructions from the master. This plan may have been followed with Op. 16, since nowhere in the announcements of the Verein is the identity of an arranger given. After the performance of the chamber version of Op. 16 in Prague in March 1920, its materials were apparently lost in the mail.[37] Greissle's 1925 arrangement, which was also based on Schoenberg's earlier *Handexemplar,* may have reconstructed the 1920 arrangement, or it may have been a new effort on Greissle's part.[38]

The music of the Five Orchestra Pieces again shows Schoenberg boldly extending the new atonal language in multiple directions, some unprecedented in earlier music, others reinterpreting the past. In Piece No. 1, "Premonitions," the earlier style of Op. 11, No. 1, is apparent, but here Schoenberg for the first time experiments with its adaptability to fugue. More than any other strict contrapuntal genre, fugue was closely allied to tonality, whose principles governed not only harmonic motion but also the creation of subjects and answers and patterns of imitation. Given this background, Schoenberg's handling of the traditional fugal form was of necessity free. It preserved the classical division into an imitative exposition, episodes, and a climactic restatement in stretto, but it melds these traditional fugal elements into a pervasive development of motives that is more characteristic of the early atonal style.

The movement begins with a nonfugal introduction (measures 1–25), which contains an exposition of basic motives. The celli in measures 1–3 (see Example 4.4) state the main theme, a figure that outlines an ascending augmented triad and thus introduces whole-tone motion that is ever more apparent as the movement progresses. It is accompanied by an important secondary figure in the bass woodwinds. A persistent development of these and other introductory motives accompanies the fugue that follows, and the main cello theme also recurs as a motto to mark off the principal fugal sections.

A fugal exposition in four voices begins at measure 26, accompanied throughout by recurrences of basic motives from the introduction and by an unceasing dronelike chord (D A C♯) in the bassoons and trombones. The ten-measure subject in the celli has a baroque motoric rhythm, and, although it represents an essentially new thematic element, it is linked to the main theme by prominently outlining an augmented triad near its beginning. The subject is freely answered in measure 38 in the viola, accompanied there by an ostinato countersubject. In measure 49 the third fugal voice enters in violin II, stating the subject form transposed up a fifth, and the fugal exposition is concluded by a final answer at measure 57 in violin I. An episode (measures 63–78) made from a complex and climactic development of earlier motives leads to a tumultuous fugal stretto at 79, and the fugue subsides into a codetta from measure 103.

Example 4.4. Schoenberg, Orchestral Piece, Op. 16, No. 1, measures 1–3 (non-transposing score). © 1952 by Henmar Press Inc. Used by permission.

In a pioneering analysis of this movement published in 1927, Theodor W. Adorno passed over the element of fugue in order to emphasize the relevance of the work to twelve-tone composition.[39] He located this connection in the way that Schoenberg developed motives, not as before in a predominantly linear dimension that was geared to retain rhythmic features, but instead in a multidimensional presentation in which successions of intervals were the sole constants. Specifically, Adorno pointed to two three-note motives in measure 1—the ascending E–F–A in the celli and descending D–C#–G in the bass woodwinds—which he found used as "basic shapes" (*Grundgestalten*), comparable to the use of the initial lines in pre-twelve-tone works such as the Five Piano Pieces, Op. 23. Adorno concluded that in Op. 16 Schoenberg "already composed with rows," and his examples show recurrences of the two basic shapes in transpositions, inversions, and retrogrades, as well as in free forms created by expansion and contraction of intervals.

Piece No. 2, "Yesteryears," contains an unmistakable return to the earliest style of atonality. When he coined the title of the piece in 1912, Schoenberg may have wished to suggest a musical parody, a backward allusion for expressive purposes that would also characterize his *Pierrot lunaire*, a work that he was beginning to contemplate at the very same time. "Yesteryears" is based on the developmental ternary form encountered in Op. 15; it begins with a main theme in small ternary form, as do Op. 11, Nos. 1–2, and it strongly projects a triadically based harmonic vocabulary. Predictably, the central triad or tonality that is alluded to in the outer sections is D minor. The reprise, like those in Op. 11, Nos. 1–2, touches upon fragments of motives from both the opening and the middle sections. The passage from measures 47–56 is especially noteworthy in its orchestration, which emphasizes the clear, sinusoidal tones of celesta, harp, flutes, and solo strings—a distinctively ethereal sound to which Schoenberg re-turned with great expressive power in the opera *Erwartung.*

Piece No. 3 is by far the most famous work in Op. 16, and it is indeed unique in Schoenberg's entire oeuvre in the extent to which changing orchestral tone colors take on direct expressive meaning, even to the extent of diverting atten-tion away from the development of motives. The form of the work is simple enough: It is based on the ternary model, in which the middle section (measures 12–30), while continuing to reuse materials from the opening passage, is made subtly distinct by increasing rhythmic motion, a piling up of motives, a larger harmonic vocabulary, and distinct procedures of orchestration. The first section (measures 1–11) is canonic in five voices, each of which takes its departure from one tone in the opening five-note chord and then follows the slow-moving leading voice in trumpet II on the motive E–F–E♭. Tone color in this section changes in ostinato fashion every quarter note, alternating between two ensem-bles that differ only in the orchestration of the bass line. In the reprise (meas-ures 30–44) the canon returns inverted so that the leading voice has the tones E–D♯–F, and the orchestration is considerably more ramified than before.

The third piece may well have been in Schoenberg's mind two years later, when he wrote the concluding pages of his *Harmonielehre.* There he indulged in what he termed a "futuristic fantasy" concerning what he called tone color melody (*Klangfarbenmelodie*). This, he said, is a melodylike line made from a suc-cession of different timbres.[40] These melodies could be developed and varied and communicate musical thoughts just as traditional themes did, even cap-turing "the illusory stuff of our dreams." But Schoenberg always remained am-bivalent about the expressive role of timbre in atonal music. In his letters to Strauss and Busoni he repeatedly mentions diversity of orchestral color, *Bunt-heit*, as one of the principal objectives of his new music. To Alban Berg in 1914 he again pointed approvingly to the "elegant and refined" sound that he had heard in Op. 16.[41] But the exact role for color in the expression of musical ideas was never settled in his mind, and there was often an element of skepticism about its importance. "I find that when renouncing an *art of form* . . . the little bit of piano sound seems a mere trifle," he told Busoni. "Questions of sonority, whose attraction ranks scarcely so high among the eternal values, are by comparison trivial."[42] Gradually the distrust of color became stronger in Schoenberg's thinking, and by 1941 he could write that colors appealed only to "the childish preference of the primitive ear. . . . More mature minds resist the temptation to become intoxicated by colors and prefer to be coldly convinced by the trans-parency of clear-cut ideas."[43]

Piece No. 4, "Peripeteia," is fast and rash, opening with a fanfare in the wood-winds (see Example 4.5) whose notes restate the chord from the end of the third movement (A C A♭ E B), although transposed and shuffled in register. The move-ment has five sections (beginning at measures 1, 19, 35, 44, and 59), which are laid out as a free rondo in which each section is marked off by a silence, a change of tempo, or other clear means of articulation. The first section (measures 1–18) contains a thematic exposition that takes the form of a chain of motives—nu-merous short, distinct figures presented in quick succession—thus an example of

Example 4.5. Schoenberg, Orchestra Piece, Op. 16, No. 4, measures 1–13. Used by permission of C. F. Peters Corporation.

a common strategy for thematic exposition in Schoenberg's early atonal works. Some of these motives return in the straightforward reprise of the third section and in the climactic, developmental elaboration of the fifth. The intervening episodes contain ideas that are more remotely or sporadically related to the opening ones.

The chords of this movement continue a trend, already apparent in Schoenberg's atonal music to this time, toward expansion from a four-note norm to one in which larger collections of tones are more characteristic. Hexachords are strongly represented in Piece No. 4, and even larger configurations appear at climactic points, as in measure 64. The basic chordal sonority is a sustained hexachord first heard in measure 8 in the horns (see Example 4.5, lower system); it returns in the first reprise in measures 37–39 and, transposed to the fifth, as the last chord of the piece. To the extent that it represents an abstract intervallic structure, this collection of tones is highly characteristic of Schoenberg's atonal music, so much so that it has been interpreted by many writers who use set theory as evidence of a strongly autobiographical subtext that runs through much or even all of Schoenberg's atonal oeuvre. A brief explanation is in order, which must be prefaced by a further discussion of the ideas implicit in set theory.

The basic chord in measure 8 has the pitch content A B♭ C C♯ E F, its notes presented here, for purposes of comparison, in a compact scalewise order. When we use assumptions touched on in the discussion of Op. 11, No. 1, this set of tones can be considered equivalent to those that underlie several other prominent pitch structures near the beginning of the work in that their content of pitches differs only through the variational processes of reordering, transposition, and symmetrical inversion. For example, the bass line of the opening fanfare, whose pitch content similarly disposed is C♯ D E F G♯ A, is related to the basic hexachord in measure 8 by transposition and reordering. The chord stated as a thirty-second-note figure in the trumpets, strings, and woodwinds in measure 6 (A G♯ F♯ F D C♯) is related to it by inversion.

On an abstract intervallic level, a relationship can also be postulated between these hexachords and their *complements*, that is, other hexachords that contain the notes that they themselves do not contain. Consider the thirty-second-note figure, A G♯ F♯ F D C♯, as an example. Its complement contains the tones E♭ C B B♭ E G, those six not present in the initial form. Although the two sets cannot be made identical by any combination of reordering, transposition, or inversion, their tones have the very same capacity to create intervals. This intervallic potential can be measured by pairing off each tone with each of the remaining tones; when applied to the chord A G♯ F♯ F D C♯, exactly three minor seconds, one major second, three minor thirds, four major thirds, three fourths, and one tritone can be created—just the same as can be created by notes of the complementary collection E♭ C B B♭ E G.

The relevance of this computation for the musical usefulness of the chord is certainly open to debate, although total intervallic content is one way of gauging the sound of the chord, and it plainly controls the intervallic profile of any motives that might be spun off from it. A total intervallic content also suggests a structural archetype that can be represented on the surface of a musical work by highly differentiated pitch structures—chords, lines, and textural constellations—all with very different pitch content and motivic shape. The total intervallic content of a collection of tones, for example, is preserved despite the variational process of transposition or inversion enacted upon its tones. All hexachords have an intervallic content that is especially resilient to surface variation, since it is always shared with the complement hexachord. This sameness of intervallic profile among families of atonal chords that are seemingly different in their pitch content and motivic design provides the theoretical basis for an ingenious analytic model that can represent complex harmonic phenomena by a relatively small number of archetypal structures. It allows for an elegant and relatively simple summary of the harmonic content of an entire atonal composition.

In his 1978 article "Schoenberg's Creative Evolution: The Path to Atonality,"[44] Allen Forte proposed that these abstract intervallic archetypes were models not only appropriate to a theory or an analytic system but also central to Schoenberg's compositional method and used by him as expressive symbols and tools. He hypothesized, in effect, that the six musical letters of the name Schönberg—Es C H B E G (or E♭ C B B♭ E G using English note names)—formed an autobiographical symbol that the composer used prominently in virtually every one of his atonal and preatonal works. The signature hexachord itself, Forte wrote, almost never appears but is instead presented covertly in the form of other hexachords that have the same total intervallic content. Forte's hypothesis is vividly illustrated in Piece No. 4. The basic hexachord of measure 8, as well as its equivalent forms just noted, could all be construed as examples of an autobiographical allusion, since they all share the same total intervallic content with the Es C H B E G set, which itself does not appear. The thirty-second-note figure of measure 6 is closest of all to its "source," since it is the complement of the signature set.

Forte's theory concerning autobiographical allusions raises many questions. Certainly Schoenberg relished secret levels of meaning in his music, just as he confided to his diary in the context of the titles for Op. 16. Letter ciphers were used in compositions by others in his circle, most prominently by Berg. Forte's hypothesis also calls attention to the undeniably extraordinary importance of the family of hexachords in Schoenberg's atonal oeuvre of which Es C H B E G is a member. However, the theory of autobiographical allusion rests on an unquestioned assumption that an elegant analytic model offers prima facie evidence of a compositional method—an assumption with which few composers, least of all Schoenberg, would agree. The idea that Schoenberg composed with pitch class sets is entirely plausible in his atonal music written from 1920 to 1923. It is virtually synonymous with what he called composing with tones, a development that will be discussed further in chapter 8. But there is no persuasive evidence that Schoenberg used reordering, transposition, inversion, and complementation as part of a systematic compositional method in the earlier styles of atonality.[45] The hypothesis rests on a viewpoint concerning musical structure that was foreign to Schoenberg's thinking, so far as it can be culled from his own analytic writings on this subject. The remote autobiographical allusions postulated by Forte can only exist if Schoenberg conceived of a musical work as an interaction of structural levels, of which the total intervallic content of the Es C H B E G hexachord is an *Ursatz* and such chords and motives as in measures 1, 6, and 8 its foreground representations. But nowhere in Schoenberg's writings is this hierarchical concept of structure found. Quite the opposite, Schoenberg located the structural basis of any musical composition in the surface of the music itself, usually in the form of motives explicitly stated at or near the beginning.

We return now to the work itself. Op. 16 is closed by a waltz that the composer titled "The Obligatory Recitative," words that are more than a little enigmatic, since the melodic idiom is not at all declamatory. The term was apparently used in Schoenberg's lectures on composition and aesthetics that he gave at the Stern Conservatory in Berlin in fall 1911 and winter 1912, just before he thought of applying it to this movement. In a diary entry for 22 January 1912 he compared recitative to a free form within nature, which is "obligatory" in the sense that only there can the ineffable be represented: "One states the inexpressible in free form. In it one draws close to nature, which is also incomprehensible but in effect all the same."[46] In Schoenberg's mind the image of recitative may also have evoked the impassioned and flexible expressivity of the opera singer, much as Bach used the term for the concluding section of his D-minor Toccata and Fugue, BWV 565. Like Bach's, Schoenberg's piece is an expressive masterpiece, a miniature *Carnaval*, in which our attention darts from one character to the next in a ballroom filled with swirling dancers. Our gaze first lights on the sighing oboe but turns in the very next measure to the clarinet's impetuous harlequin and almost as quickly to the mincing violin in measures 6–7. The dancers surge onward toward a tumultuous climax at measure 109 after which they fall back in exhaustion, as the dance fades into memory.

The piece was completed only days after the Piano Piece, Op. 11, No. 3, with which it shares its open form and linearized texture. But compared to the piano work, the orchestral waltz is far less persistently sectionalized, and motivic recurrences in it are more easily perceived. The form, as in the piano piece, is quite free, shaped more by the expressive arch than by sectional recurrences. Also like the piano piece, the basic recurrent motives, such as the descending semitone figure heard at the very beginning, are abbreviated in stature, made into expressive particles rather than distinctive units of thought. Michael Mäckelmann has aptly described this and the piano piece as Schoenberg's first important compositions to bypass the traditional division of a musical work into sections that have expository, developmental, or recapitulatory functions.[47]

A single leading voice runs throughout the composition, accompanied by a complex web of fleeting subsidiary lines, creating an accompanimental texture that Schoenberg later called "semi-counterpoint."[48] Continuing the maximal coloristic differentiation that characterized the third piece of Op. 16, this "obligatory" line is passed every few notes to a different instrument. To allow the performers to locate the ever elusive main voice, Schoenberg enclosed it in the score in half-brackets, the beginning of a notational system that he used in most later compositions.

Three Pieces for Chamber Orchestra

When Schoenberg completed the Five Orchestra Pieces, Op. 16, in mid-August 1909, he was riding the crest of a great wave of creative energy. Later in the month he turned his attention to yet another genre—opera—continuing his restless and determined expansion of the atonal idiom. The genre of opera had long eluded him; he had already begun no fewer than four operas, each soon abandoned. But now he completed his great atonal opera *Erwartung* in a mere seventeen days and began to work on its companion, *Die glückliche Hand*. Then, for reasons that are not at all clear, his productivity waned. The next completed composition, the diminutive Six Little Piano Pieces, Op. 19, lay almost two years distant. In the interim he wrote his first major theoretical treatise, the *Harmonielehre*, which looked back on tonal composition, perhaps ironically so, since it also contains much information that is relevant to the early atonal style. The *Harmonielehre* occupied him almost entirely from June 1910 until spring or summer of 1911, and he complained to Emil Hertzka, director of Universal Edition, that he had worked on the treatise continually, for up to nine hours daily.

Shortly before writing the *Harmonielehre*, however, Schoenberg began to compose a group of miniature character pieces for chamber orchestra. Two were completed on a single day, 8 February 1910, a third (undated) was left as a fragment, and a manuscript page was prepared for a fourth, although no music was set down. Schoenberg did not return to them later, and they became generally known only in 1959, when they were published in facsimile in Josef Rufer's *Das Werk Arnold Schönbergs*. In their first edition of 1962 they were given the title "Three Pieces for Chamber Orchestra." These works, still among Schoenberg's least known, are pivotal for the broad development of his atonal style. In them he enacted, to the greatest degree ever, the program that he had announced in his manifesto to Busoni. The manuscripts suggest that they were composed directly into a full-score fair copy in a virtual stream of consciousness, and Schoenberg aimed in them for a pure and unreflective outpouring of sounds imbued with emotion and idea. They fully renounce traditional motivic work, and, as a result, they are startlingly brief. "My music must be *brief*. Concise! In two notes: not built, but '*expressed*'!!," he had told Busoni. The two completed pieces last less than one minute each; the second dwindles to a mere seven measures.

Their brevity comes from two technical factors: the radical conciseness of the thematic ideas themselves, which are reduced to figures of only a few notes or rhythmic gestures, and the absence of regular motivic development. On the surface the pieces are utterly fragmented. Short "moments" are laid out one after the other with no clear interconnections by development, rendering the surface of the music with little sense of continuity. Beneath the surface, however, Schoenberg continues to use the technique seen in Op. 11, No. 3, and Op. 16, No. 5, by which highly transformed recurrences of small, little-distinctive motivic particles are notable. Continuity is also promoted throughout Pieces No. 1 and 3 by gestural effects and curves of intensity, often taking on the arch pattern seen in Op. 16, No. 5.

Schoenberg seems to have been driven to this new aphoristic style by a confluence of complex forces that, judging from his later writings, left him quite uncertain about his future direction. In one sense the style represents the outcome of his exuberant experimentation with atonality, his bold and inspired application of its ideas in ever broader contexts and deeper formal patterns. Atonality was never a fixed style or settled compositional method but instead an everchanging mode of musical expression in which exploration and a driving to extremes were always implicit. The aphoristic style of the Three Pieces arose by an intensified extension of tendencies already apparent in the earlier atonal works, some even reaching back to his late tonal period. Schoenberg's earlier avoidance of elaborative ornamentations now produced music with no elaboration at all. Moderate brevity now became extreme brevity; concise melodic ideas became tiny fragments, and Schoenberg's reliance upon inspiration now led him to compose without reflection at all, which ruled out conventional motivic development and left behind minute expressive outbursts as finished works.

Later Schoenberg looked back on his aphoristic pieces with more than a touch of uncertainty. He was able to describe his technical objectives precisely, but he could not vigorously defend the musical results. In an essay known as "A Self-Analysis" (1948), he enumerated the two main constructive features that produced the aphoristic style—motives that were highly abbreviated and the removal of developmental connectives between them: "Soon thereafter I wrote in the extreme short forms. Although I did not dwell very long in this style, it taught me two things: first, to formulate ideas in an aphoristic manner, which did not require continuations out of formal reasons; secondly, to link ideas together without the use of formal connectives, merely by juxtaposition."[49]

Schoenberg's exposure to new ideas in the music of his student Anton Webern, especially in Webern's Five Movements for String Quartet, Op. 5, may also have coaxed him into an experiment with extreme aphoristic brevity. Webern wrote the quartet pieces in the spring of 1909 and, according to his letter to Schoenberg dated 16 June, probably sent them to his teacher at that time.[50] The second, third, and fourth movements are indeed minuscule, each dwindling to only a few measures in length and the quick third movement lasting scarcely more than thirty seconds. Later Alma Mahler recalled Schoenberg's susceptibility to Webern's compelling innovations: "Schoenberg once complained to me and to Werfel how much he was suffering under the dangerous influence of Webern and that he needed all his strength to extricate himself from it."[51] But Webern's pieces still adhere to a technique of developing variation, and they exhibit highly varied sectional recurrences, which make them an unlikely model for Schoenberg's far more radical experiments.

Schoenberg's Three Pieces themselves are each very different in character. The fragmentary third one, only eight measures long, is closest to the style of Op. 16. A six-note chord in the organ (optionally harmonium) runs throughout the entire piece, much as does the bassoon and trombone chord in the fugue of Op. 16, No. 1. Also like this earlier work the sustained chord is soon joined by a twittering ostinato that gradually gathers complexity, leading to a climax, after which the chamber piece breaks off.

Pieces No. 1 and No. 2 use a common form made from a succession of brief but clearly distinct sections, each set off from the next, by changes of tempo in No. 1 and by fermatas in No. 2. There is no sense of development or recapitulation in these sections, although a careful analysis can uncover a free recurrence of submotivic particles from one passage to another, much as occurred in the Piano Piece, Op. 11, No. 3. The pieces do not at all disintegrate into disjunct moments of sound. No. 1 is held together by an overarching expressive contour that gathers intensity and textural complication until measure 8, followed by an ebbing away. Piece No. 2 is, by comparison, somber and spare, its four short sections each ending in a fermata. Adorno likened the work to four verses of a chorale, and he, too, emphasized the recurrence of tiny, undistinctive particles in a generally athematic context.[52]

Six Little Piano Pieces, Op. 19

The Three Pieces for Chamber Orchestra of February 1910 mark the beginning of a great compositional crisis for Schoenberg, the onset of a period during which the composer, by his own admission, felt that he had lost his way, stricken by such self-doubt and artistic confusion that few pieces were begun and even fewer completed. The style of the chamber orchestra pieces must be implicated in this crisis; their incompleteness is an indication that they represented a troubled time in Schoenberg's creative life. The composer often remarked that he could not compose unless inspired to do so, an observation that bears more on the atonal style than any other. It was just this inspiration that must have been undermined by a music—however ingenious and original—that was fragmented, radically abbreviated, and nondevelopmental. The early atonal period had been for Schoenberg a time of exuberant expansion of a new language, during which the composer was perpetually looking ahead for new and untried techniques. But in the elimination of motivic work, of which the extreme aphoristic style was a product, he seems to have overstepped, stumbling into an artistic quandary from which he would need thirteen years to extricate himself fully.

As he neared the completion of the *Harmonielehre* in February 1911, after a year that was completely barren of composing, he made a startling and dramatic move that seemed intended to rekindle his earlier inspiration and resurrect the achievements of his earlier explorations. On the nineteenth of that month, he composed no fewer than five short but complete piano pieces, later to be incorporated in the Six Little Piano Pieces, Op. 19. Here for the first time during his atonal period he does not experiment or extend his idiom; instead he is plainly intent upon consolidation of what had gone before, even returning to styles associated with the earliest atonal compositions. As though chastened by the effect that his manifesto had wrought upon his inspiration, he backed away from it and partially returned to an earlier style that was tried and true. This tendency to look backward as well as forward would continue in a more profound measure in works composed later in 1911 and 1912; indeed, it would continue throughout the remainder of the atonal phase of his career.

The five piano miniatures written on February 19 maintain some of the external features of the manifesto. They are decidedly brief in their overall proportions (the first is the longest, at seventeen measures), some of them avoid motivic development, and all were apparently composed in a headlong manner, with a minimum of reflection. But otherwise they are similar to the earliest instrumental atonal works, that is, Op. 11, Nos. 1–2, and Op. 16, Nos. 1–4. Their themes (especially in Nos. 1, 3, and 4) are comparatively long and classically shaped; Nos. 2 and 4 return explicitly to a developmental ternary form; the harmonic language in every piece reverts to the familiar four- and five-note sets from 1908 and 1909; and the expressive content of the pieces is familiar, ranging from the playful No. 4, to the lyrical No. 3, to the wistful No. 1. Except for their brief dimensions, they have essentially little in common with the doctrinaire and highly experimental atmosphere that hovered above the chamber orchestra pieces.

The first of the Six Little Piano Pieces maintains the outward form of the first two chamber orchestra pieces in its succession of clearly distinct sections, each stating themes that are not developmentally related. But a retardataire element is plain enough in its simple texture, tending toward the homophony of Op. 11, No. 1, and even more in the harmonic vocabulary, which emphasizes the triadic tetrachords of Opp. 11 and 15. The second piece revives the use of ostinato, characteristic of all phases of Schoenberg's atonal music, in the recurrent major third G B, stated in an asymmetrical rhythm. But now there is a hint of ternary form, as the ostinato breaks off in measure 6, returning in a pseudoreprise in measure 7.

The slow and songlike third piece is more conservative still, as it opens with a long, nearly diatonic melody in the left hand, accompanied by triads and triadic tetrachords in the right. Although it does not have a reprise, there is much motivic and harmonic recurrence, as, for example, the return of the opening chord at the very end, where it is transposed down a major third. The scherzo in Piece No. 4 begins with a straightforward melody in period form (antecedent and consequent are each two measures long). Here the developmental ternary form is fully evident as the opening theme returns in a *martellato* diminution in measure 10. The fifth piece returns to the open, sectionalized form of the first.

Following the five piano pieces of February, there are no other datable compositions until June. In the interim Schoenberg revised the Preface of his *Harmonielehre,* and he was no doubt much distracted by the final illness and death of Gustav Mahler on 18 May. Mahler's funeral three days later was attended by Schoenberg, who afterward painted a moving recollection of the event (see Figure 4.1). On 17 June, nearly a month after the funeral, Schoenberg composed another piano miniature, which he added to the five from February to form a collection printed by Universal Edition in 1913 as Op. 19. In his 1921 biography of the composer, Egon Wellesz stated that the sixth piece "came into being as the result of the impression made on him by Mahler's funeral," information that almost certainly came from the composer himself.[53]

The sixth piece is indeed one of Schoenberg's most inspired and expressive compositions ever. Its stark and somber mood, the imperious bell-like chords that run through the work, and the unforgettable ending—dying away "as in a

Figure 4.1. Arnold Schoenberg, *Funeral of Gustav Mahler* (1911), oil on canvas. Collection Lisa Jalowetz Aronson, New York.

breath"—are a tribute to his mastery of a highly recondite idiom and to his ability to turn formal experiment into expressive masterpiece. As in the fourth piece, the sixth returns to a developmental ternary form. The outer sections (measures 1–6 and measure 9) are characterized by reiterations of a six-note chord, whose prominent intervals of the fourth evoke the sound of bells. Minute and interrelated motivic fragments are occasionally heard in muted whispers. Finally, in the middle section, a single plaintive voice utters its tribute, spoken at such an intense level of heartfelt sympathy and devotion that it must dwindle to a mere five tones. By positioning this largeness of utterance within a minuscule form, Schoenberg's sixth piece intimates the "eternity" that Nietzsche found in his own aphorisms. "It is my ambition," he wrote in *Twilight of the Idols*, "to say in ten sentences what everyone else says in a book—what everyone else does *not* say in a book."[54]

Although Schoenberg would soon vehemently reject the brevity and concentration of the aphoristic style, his tribute to Mahler remains a great monument to the power of music to plumb the depths of feeling. It stands beside Bruckner's Seventh Symphony—composed at the time of Wagner's death and as expansive in utterance as Schoenberg's is terse—as one of the greatest funereal tributes in all of modern music.

5

The Operas *Erwartung* and *Die glückliche Hand*

When Schoenberg joined his friends and family at a summer retreat in Steinakirchen am Forst at the end of June 1909, his confidence with the atonal style had reached an exuberant peak. He had proved its adaptability to songs, piano works, and music for large orchestra, and he was still riding on a great wave of creative energy. In Steinakirchen he immediately continued his work on two projects in progress, the Piano Pieces, Op. 11, and Orchestra Pieces, Op. 16, which he completed in a matter of weeks. With virtually no pause he then turned to a new challenge—composing opera. This was the one major genre in which he had no success to that time. He had already made four abortive attempts at writing opera, each in a different genre current at the turn of the century, but each one had failed to inspire him to compose beyond a few fragments.

The first three incomplete operatic projects—Schoenberg wrote text sketches for all three—probably date from around 1901. *Odoakar* was squarely in the heroic Wagnerian vein, *Aberglaube* addressed the conflict between spiritual and physical love, and *Die Schildbürger*, which can be firmly dated from the summer of 1901, was a folk comedy. Shortly after attending the Austrian premiere of Strauss's *Salome* in Graz in May 1906, Schoenberg sketched music for the beginning of a fourth opera, based on Gerhart Hauptmann's new play, *Und Pippa tanzt!* Schoenberg used the beginning of Hauptmann's drama directly as his libretto, experimenting with Strauss's new genre of "literary opera," in which a modern prose play served as a libretto with no intermediary adaptation. The musical fragments that he composed for the beginning of the work also evoke the style of *Salome*, showing that at this time Strauss was still a major musical influence.

Erwartung, Op. 17

Perhaps due to his own unsuccessful efforts in completing an operatic libretto, Schoenberg was ready in 1909 to seek a literary collaborator, someone sympathetic to his literary tastes and to his new interest in the emotions, the unconscious mind, and their close connection to the view of artistic creativity that he expounded to Busoni. He found such a colleague in Marie Pappenheim

(1882–1966), probably a distant relative of the Zemlinskys, who visited the Steinakirchen gathering, whereupon she was introduced to Schoenberg. Born in Preßburg, Pappenheim had moved to Vienna to study medicine. Her efforts as an amateur writer were probably already known to Schoenberg through four poems that had been published under the pseudonym Marie Heim in 1906 in Karl Kraus's *Die Fackel*.

A striking aspect of these poems that must have been noted by the composer was their depiction of intense and highly diverse emotional states. Several were written from Pappenheim's own perspective as a physician who assesses the emotional as well as the physical constitution of a patient. Others dealt specifically with emotional states common to women. In the poem "Prima graviditas," for example, the subject is the jumble of feelings associated with pregnancy, ranging among guilt, nostalgia for maidenhood, and self-contempt. In "Seziersaal" the physician in the autopsy room feels a passionate emotional empathy with the dead.

Seziersaal	Autopsy Room
Ein Weinen klingt in meiner Seele nach—	A crying echoes in my soul—
Ich weiß von jemand, den das Leben brach.	I know of someone broken by life.
Sein Mund ist bleich und seine Augen müd',	His mouth is pale and his eyes weary,
Wie einem, der des Nachts ins Dunkel sieht.	As one who nightly stares into darkness.
Und meine Hand ist schmal und kühl und still,	And my hand is thin and cool and still,
Die er auf seine Augen legen will.	Which he would place over his eyes.
Wie traurig sein Verlangen mich umweht,	How sadly his yearning wafts about me,
Daß mein gequältes Herz sich selbst verrät.	So much that my tortured heart betrays itself.
Dies Herz, das Leben, Taumel, Flammen denkt,	This heart, this life, frenzy, flames think,
Sich einem Müden, Wunden, Kranken schenkt.—	Gives itself to someone weary, sore, sick.—
Die Toten starren steinern und beschwören:	The dead stare petrified and implore:
Zu früh, du Kind, mußt du zu uns gehören.[1]	Too soon, thou child, must you be among us.

In 1963 Pappenheim reminisced to Helmut Kirchmeyer about her meeting with Schoenberg.[2] "Write me an opera text, Fräulein," the composer had commanded. "Write what you want, I need an opera text." Pappenheim then returned to friends in Traunkirchen, where in three weeks she wrote the libretto to *Erwartung*, calling the text a monodrama, since it had only a single role. She had discovered the idea for it, she told Kirchmeyer, during the previous year in Ischl, in her own fearful emotions experienced as she walked at night through a patch of dark woods. She also recalled Schoenberg's reaction:

> I wrote with pencil on large sheets of paper while lying in the grass, didn't keep
> a copy and scarcely read through what I had written, . . . thinking that Schoen-
> berg would read it and propose changes (I didn't know him well then). But I did
> not get the manuscript back; Schoenberg simply told me what he wanted to
> change: Like an "enraptured poet" I had repeatedly used comparisons ("like
> your shadow," for example, plus one or two visual symbols). Schoenberg
> pointed one of these out and calmly said that everything was very lovely, but
> that for composing it was too long—such references should only be used once.
> He seemed to want to compose it just as "headlong fast" as I had written it.[3]

The exact chronology of Schoenberg's collaboration with Pappenheim and the accuracy of her recollections, made at a distance of fifty-four years, remain uncertain. The earliest known text manuscript is a twenty-six-page document handwritten by the author.[4] It contains a considerable number of revisions made by both Schoenberg and Pappenheim, and the different writing imple-ments suggest that the two collaborators went over the text several times. Schoen-berg also entered a few short musical sketches into this manuscript. Pappen-heim typed out a revised version of the text that incorporated most of the changes, although Schoenberg may have already begun to compose the work, using the earlier manuscript as his working text.

The principal musical manuscript is a short-score draft, dated 27 August 1909 at the beginning and 12 September 1909 at the end, thus indicating that the entire complex opera was composed in only seventeen days. Schoenberg then prepared a full-score fair copy, which is dated 4 October 1909 at its con-clusion, and, hoping for a performance, he made his own piano arrangement of the work (which remains unpublished). Edward Steuermann later prepared the piano score that was published by Universal Edition in 1923.

Pappenheim's "lyric poem," the term that she used to describe the text of *Er-wartung* to Kirchmeyer, is divided into four concise scenes, of which the first three are exceedingly brief. On a moonlit night, a Woman appears at the edge of a dark and forbidding forest, looking for her lover. Her thoughts and emotions are in disarray, leaping precipitously from expressions of her fear of the forest to disjointed recollections of the lovers' garden and its flowers. The creatures of nature take on human emotions that mimic her own: a cricket sings a love song, and the moon's pale light transforms her surroundings into phantasms.

In the second scene, the Woman plunges into the forest to continue her quest, although her attacks of anxiety are only increased. She imagines that some crea-ture is touching her, and her recollections of the beauty and solitude of her trysts behind the garden wall are clouded by the admission that her lover did not that evening appear. In fear she begins to run, only to trip over a tree trunk that she at first thinks is a human corpse.

In the third scene, the Woman emerges from the forest into a clearing. Again she is assailed, by hallucinations of a black creature with a hundred hands, then a crawling apparition with large yellow eyes.

The lengthy fourth scene takes place after the Woman, disheveled and bloodied by her dash through the forest, again emerges into a clearing, near a closed-up house amid the moonlit countryside. Everything seems dead and frightful, and she is sure that the strange woman in the house, her rival in love, will not pity her in this condition. As she approaches a bench to sit, her foot touches a corpse, still dripping blood. Unlike the earlier apparitions, it will not disappear.

While trying to pick up the body, she recognizes it as her lover. At first she addresses the corpse, imploring it to speak and to waken. Her thoughts turn again to their bedroom, fragrant with the odor of flowers as she awaits his arrival. But he had not come for three days, and even earlier he had been impatient and preoccupied. Slowly she realizes that he is truly dead, and her pity then turns to resentment and she curses him and kicks his lifeless body. As dawn approaches, she realizes the extent of her plight: her entire world was in him, all of its colors, she says, were in his eyes. Her lot is now to remain alone in darkness. "A thousand people pass by," she says, but he is not to be among them. "I was looking . . . , " is her final broken thought.

As a literary work, Pappenheim's text is an uncanny precursor of the new German theater of the period after 1910, especially in forecasting the style of the "Ich-Drama" later associated with such writers as Reinhard Sorge in his important play *Der Bettler* of 1911. The Woman's fragmented outbursts, her disjointed eruptions of inner thoughts and emotions, the theme of violence as symptom of psychic and social disintegration, the nightmarish atmosphere, treatment of the main character as a symbolic type devoid of proper name, and a pervasive sense of impending doom all make the monodrama an important forerunner of German expressionist playwriting. But Pappenheim's style did not closely conform to any existing school of modern writing, less still to any accepted librettistic model of the turn of the century. She professed an interest among her contemporaries only in the writings of Else Lasker-Schüler, whose plays at this time, such as *Die Wupper* (also written in 1909), are far more in the naturalist-socialist mode than is the grotesque lyricism of *Erwartung.*

Pappenheim's own earlier poetry holds an important key to the interpretation of her nightmarish tale. Just as the poet of "Seziersaal" wrote from the perspective of a physician who explores emotions in a heightened state, Pappenheim in *Erwartung* brings to bear the clinical condition of hysteria as the context for a portrait of emotions out of control. A scientific understanding and treatment of hysteria came into focus only toward the end of the nineteenth century, primarily in the work of the French neurologist Jean-Martin Charcot. He discovered that certain symptoms that lacked pathological causes, such as paralysis of the limbs, could be relieved by inducing the sufferer into a hypnotic state. His work was closely followed by physicians in Vienna, especially Josef Breuer and Sigmund Freud, the latter Charcot's student.

Breuer and Freud extensively developed Charcot's theories in their *Studien über Hysterie* (1895), a work that was widely read by the general public as well as by medical specialists. According to their analysis of hysteric patients that they had treated, the malady was caused by a traumatic event, usually involving sexual factors, whose memory is channeled into the unconscious rather than being coped with by the conscious mind. The trauma persists in the form of physical ailments such as amnesia, hallucinations, and disorders of vision and speech, although their connection to the initial event remains unknown to the patient. The disease most often (although not exclusively) affected women. Breuer and Freud found that the symptoms could be relieved by "catharsis," that is, by coaxing the patient to recall and talk through the initial experience, thus reexposing the trauma to the conscious faculties, where its painful emotions could eventually be worn away.

Pappenheim's interest in the *Studien* must have been especially keen, since one of Breuer's patients analyzed in the book—to whom he gave the pseudonym Anna O.—was actually her kinswoman Bertha Pappenheim.[5] Breuer had treated Bertha Pappenheim beginning in 1880, using a method that marks the first important clinical application of psychoanalysis. Her hysteria had been brought on by the illness and subsequent death of her father and by her attendant anxiety. Her symptoms were especially severe. In addition to paralysis of the limbs and anorexia, she also suffered from visions of snakes, periodic loss of recent memory, and a language defect. "It first became noticeable that she was at a loss to find words," wrote Breuer, "and this difficulty gradually increased. Later she lost her command of grammar and syntax; she no longer conjugated verbs, and eventually she used only infinitives, . . . and she omitted both the definite and indefinite article."[6]

The Woman in *Erwartung* has symptoms that are strikingly close to those of Anna O., suggesting that Breuer's case study was, at least in part, a model used by Pappenheim in writing the libretto. The onset of the Woman's symptoms accompanied the trauma of the loss of her beloved to a rival, a disturbance of a sexual nature that was all the more unbalancing since she had become totally dependent upon him. Like Anna O., the Woman then suffered from amnesia, hallucinations that involved imaginary slithering or crawling animal forms, and a language impediment. The traumatic events of the murder of the beloved were repressed from or "forgotten" by the Woman's conscious mind, although details erupt in fragmentary form during her attacks of anxiety. The hallucinations that she suffers in the second and third scenes seem especially close to Bertha Pappenheim's visions of black snakes. And the Woman's fragmentary exclamations, similar to the later "telegraphic" style of expressionistic writing, have a model that is closer at hand in Bertha Pappenheim's impeded speech.

Breuer held that Anna O. was predisposed to hysteria by an overly protective and monotonous family life, which, he says, led her into the habit of prolonged daydreaming. This was the beginning of a dissociation of her conscious and subconscious faculties and an invitation for traumatic events to be channeled into the latter. An analogy clearly exists with the Woman in *Erwartung*. Her predisposition to hysteria was caused by an excessive reliance upon her partner and a yielding of her own independence to him. "How much I loved you," she says as she drifts into a reverie. "I lived isolated from everything, a stranger to everything. . . . All I knew was you . . . for this whole year since you took my hand for the first time."

Schoenberg's changes in Pappenheim's original text, although relatively few in number and limited almost exclusively to deletions, are important for their effect upon the tone of the work as a whole. Some of these omissions, such as the removal of references to sounds and noises and certain symbolic allusions, do not affect the poem's overall meaning. But the composer also abbreviated the text in a way that makes the Woman's role in the death of the beloved more ambiguous. In Pappenheim's original version it is clear that the Woman was the murderer. In two passages—both omitted by Schoenberg—she blurts out evidence of her guilt amid conflicting denials. Blood is on her hands and she mechanically recollects the events that led to the fatal shot:

> What did they do here? . . . Oh you . . . you . . . I wasn't here. . . . The evening was so peaceful. . . . The rustling leaves against the sky . . . Your hair is bloody . . . your soft brown hair. . . . And blood on my hands . . . and blood on the ground . . . Who did this? . . . Who did this, you? . . . You are the only one here. You must know. . . .
>
> Did you gaze from here over to me? . . . Like this . . . your hand above your eyes . . . here in the shadows. The shadowy caves . . . the robber's nest . . . Here he backed against the tree. . . . And then the shot.[7]

Schoenberg also shortened ghoulishly neurotic passages in the original in which the Woman falls upon her lover's corpse, fondles it, and finally kisses it, actions that may have been a touch too close to Strauss's *Salome*. These lines were eliminated: "(She bends over and kisses him.) Your lips are weary and don't close. . . . Kiss me anyway. . . . Like that . . . and that. . . . (She throws herself upon him.) I love you so much. . . . You are hot . . . hot. . . . Your breath suffocates me."[8]

Schoenberg's elimination of these passages has the effect of making the realistic or clinical context of the poem less apparent and heightening instead its nightmarish tone. Pappenheim herself remarked to Kirchmeyer upon this change of emphasis:

> One of these changes has been for me long disagreeable in concept, namely, deletions in the scene where she sees the dead body. With these deletions, about which I have long forgotten, the mystical or, so to speak, hallucinatory quality is strengthened, while I was not at all sure that it should not be a realistic occurrence. But perhaps it is made stronger the other way in its effect.[9]

Schoenberg's changes suggest that he held a very different interpretation of the libretto from that of its author. In fact, Schoenberg seems to have had little interest in Pappenheim's text as a realistic study of hysteria. His own reading focused directly upon the tangle of emotions that the Woman experiences. In his comments on the opera he repeatedly emphasized that the work was to be interpreted as a study of emotions in a heightened and momentary state of intensity, then slowed so as to be observable in dramatic form. This interpretation was first presented in an article by Egon Wellesz published in November 1920, based almost certainly on information received from the composer: "The poem of the monodrama *Erwartung* sets out to give a dramatic portrayal of the problem of what transpires in a person in a moment of the greatest tension and intensity of feeling. Marie Pappenheim, to whom Schoenberg communicated this idea, attempted to solve the problem in such a way as to disperse the tension throughout a succession of scenes."[10] In notes on his operas written about 1929, Schoenberg himself reiterated this viewpoint concerning *Erwartung:* "The aim is to represent in *slow motion* everything that occurs during a single second of maximum spiritual excitement, stretching it out to half an hour."[11]

Schoenberg's conception of the text also helps to explain an apparent contradiction between Schoenberg and Pappenheim as to who conceived the central idea of the opera. Schoenberg had no doubt that he was its originator: "The librettist (a lady), acting on my suggestions, has conceived and formulated everything just as I envisaged it," he wrote to Busoni just as he began to compose the monodrama.[12] But Pappenheim told a very different story: "I received neither directions nor hints about what I should write, and I would not have accepted them anyway," she informed Kirchmeyer.[13] The contradiction that is apparent in these two accounts is explained by considering the essential differences of interpretation and perspective of the musician and writer. The physician Pappenheim was concerned in *Erwartung* with the Woman as an individual, as a "patient." Her tortured emotions are symptoms of an illness that could have been avoided by her taking possession of her emotional life. For the musician Schoenberg, *Erwartung* dealt with the emotions per se. The individuality and psychology of the Woman were secondary, even arbitrary, matters. Considering the musical language into which Schoenberg translated the poem, a music that, according to the composer, flowed directly from the emotions and depicted their untamed diversity, his interpretation is the more definitive for the opera as a whole.

In a letter to Busoni written during the composing of *Erwartung,* Schoenberg described its music as "something entirely new." Indeed, its musico-dramatic conception had no direct prototype anywhere in operatic literature, although the one-act form and use of violence as a symbol of social and psychological disintegration had a distant echo in *verismo* opera of the late nineteenth century. *Erwartung* is the first important opera to dispense entirely with key and consonant harmony, and its overall structure and principles of dramatic expression essentially diverge from the post-Wagnerian model that still reigned supreme among leading German opera composers such as Richard Strauss. *Erwartung* embodies instead the artistic manifesto that Schoenberg sent in 1909 to Busoni: the work stems from a spontaneous outpouring of expressivity and emotion, it bypasses constructive forms such as thematic development, and its only conscious intention, as the composer also remarked to Busoni, is "to capture the mood of the text." The music is closely related to the athematic style of Op. 11, No. 3, and Op. 16, No. 5, which were composed only weeks before *Erwartung,* although the reintroduction of text added a powerful formative element that distinguishes the work even from these contemporaneous pieces.

As in the Piano Piece, Op. 11, No. 3, the opera's music consists of a succes-

Example 5.1. Schoenberg, *Erwartung*, measures 153–58

sion of disjunct and contrasting sections whose character mimics the rapidly changing emotional states of the Woman. A broad coherence is achieved primarily by the fluctuating expressive curve of her monologue, alternately fearful and reflective. Schoenberg is ever resourceful in plumbing the text to find expressive musical contexts that distinguish one section from another. In some passages (those beginning at measures 197 and 353, for example) the voice moves in a connected line in regular rhythm so as to suggest aria; in others its phrases are utterly angular and disjointed; still others resemble recitation. Ostinatos mark off some passages, especially the brief scene change interludes at measures 91–95 and 114–24. Some sections build steadily to a shrieking climax, while others sustain a static moment of reflection and recollection. The expressive curve of the work, although generally billowing in waves, moves in measure 153 to a great climax at the point where the Woman discovers the corpse, an outburst shortly followed by a general pause (Example 5.1). Writers including Siegfried Mauser and Jan Maegaard have interpreted this as the primary formal division in the structure as a whole, thus a perepeteia similar to the end of the eighth song in the George song cycle.[14]

The sections are not linked together by thematic development or recapitulation, and there are no recurrent or associative motives in the Wagnerian or Straussian manner. Still, the music exhibits many rhetorical means to depict the text. Some passages are onomatopoetic, as in measures 258–60, where an eerie pizzicato in the harp accompanies the line: "Your blood still drips with a soft pulse." The sound of the orchestra follows the Woman's thoughts and the images from nature so carefully and colorfully as to invite a comparison with the lush, decorative art of *Jugendstil.* Pappenheim's many references to the moon, for example, are translated by Schoenberg's use of celesta, solo violin, harp, and solo woodwinds into a shimmering world of fantastic shapes and colors. Just as the Woman expresses herself in disjunct exclamations, so, too, her line is disjoined by its terse phrases and by the constant interpolation of short orchestral interludes. Her moments of greatest anxiety are depicted by a pronounced vocal angularity that suggests a shriek of panic when it reaches the high register. Such moments are often followed by a brief silence, signaling her attempts to restore emotional order. Moments of temporary calm, as in the passages that begin at measures 196 and 353, are reinforced vocally by more placid rhythms and by a vocal style that approximates arioso. The effect of this music is close indeed to Schoenberg's goal of a maximal diversity in musical figures and implicit emotional states.

The coherence of the music apart from the text is promoted by a technique already observed in Opp. 11 and 16, by which small motivic particles recur in free variants without a systematic connection to the dramatic context. H. H. Stuckenschmidt was the first to assess this constructive device in *Erwartung,* in a pioneering article written in 1931 preceding a performance of the monodrama in Essen.[15] Stuckenschmidt first questioned the existing analytic view of this "epochal" work, enunciated by Adorno among others, as an athematic outpouring in which all musical figures and occurrences were essentially unique. Instead Stuckenschmidt found a large amount of recurrence of small and only partially distinctive figures, especially three-note patterns that were constantly recirculated with the freest of changes. The central one of these, he wrote, was the trichord D F C♯. While the opera was not based on motivic work per se, he concluded, Schoenberg relied all the same on a freer technique derived from it.

Stuckenschmidt's hypothesis has importance for the structure of the whole opera as well as for the solution of a special compositional problem with which the composer was faced. Toward the end of her text, Pappenheim inserted a line in the Woman's monologue: "Tausend Menschen ziehn vorüber," which is virtually identical to the first line of John Henry Mackay's poem "Am Wegrand," which Schoenberg had set to music in 1905 and later included in his Eight Songs, Op. 6. It seems unlikely that Pappenheim's use of the line was pure coincidence, especially since the full text of Mackay's poem so precisely captures the Woman's sentiments of abandonment and despair.

The thematic connection of the song to the opera was certainly not lost on Schoenberg. Near the point in the opera where the line occurs (measures 411–12), the composer quotes several themes from the song, which is a tonal composition in the key of D minor.[16] Most prominent is a citation of the song's primary melody, which sets the quoted line by an upward-moving figure that outlines the

Example 5.2. Schoenberg, "Am Wegrand," Op. 6, No. 6, vocal line (text omitted),
measures 3–4

tonic D-minor triad. Thus Schoenberg set for himself the problem of merging
tonal and atonal melodic material, something that always caused him concern.[17]
He overcame the difficulty by gradually preparing the listener for the triadic quotation, subtly asserting the priority of the pitch class D, and increasingly bringing
to the surface of the music a motivic particle contained in the song's principal
melody that the listener could construe as either tonal or atonal.

Example 5.2 shows this opening theme from the song "Am Wegrand," Op. 6,
No. 6. In addition to outlining the D-minor triad, the melody also emphasizes
the lower neighbor tone C♯. The theme contains two prominent statements of
the three-note set C♯ D F, marked in the example by brackets. As Stuckenschmidt
observed, varied forms of this set of three notes reappear throughout *Erwartung*, at first dimly and highly varied, then ever more prominently and explicitly
until they emerge in their pseudotonal context in the song quotation. Statements of the basic trichord are encountered primarily in the linear dimension of
the work and only occasionally (as in the sustained chord in measures 367–68)
as verticalities. The figure rarely functions as an independent motive but instead
functions as a prominently placed fragment (often at the beginning or end of a
line). It is not systematically associated with any recurrent musical theme, dramatic idea, or special orchestrational color.

Example 5.3 shows representative occurrences of the motive and its variants,
from the beginning until the main climax of the opera, when the Woman discovers her lover's body (measure 153). The three-note figure is bracketed in the
example, from which it will be clear that its notes at first are freely reordered, inverted, and transposed. The oboe *Hauptstimme* in measures 1–2 is made from a
concatenation of several of its varied forms, although the specific pitches D F C♯
do not yet occur. Gradually, these three tones emerge, at first with other notes
interpolated between them (measures 12, 15). In the brass line in measure 38
the basic motive finally surfaces in an ascending contour, D–F–C♯. This particular ordering with ascending contour is then increasingly apparent. In the climactic passage at measures 152–53, for example, it is reiterated six times in the
basses in ostinato fashion. Then it is transposed to create the vocal exclamation:
"Das ist er!" (see Example 5.3). In later appearances the basic trichord is sometimes expanded by adding the pitch class A (English horn, measure 222; horn,
measure 227; chord in measure 367; harp, measures 383–84), bringing it all
the closer to the song's main theme and tonic triad. When the song theme is finally quoted beginning in measure 401, its basic materials are already familiar
to the astute listener.

Example 5.3. Schoenberg, *Erwartung*

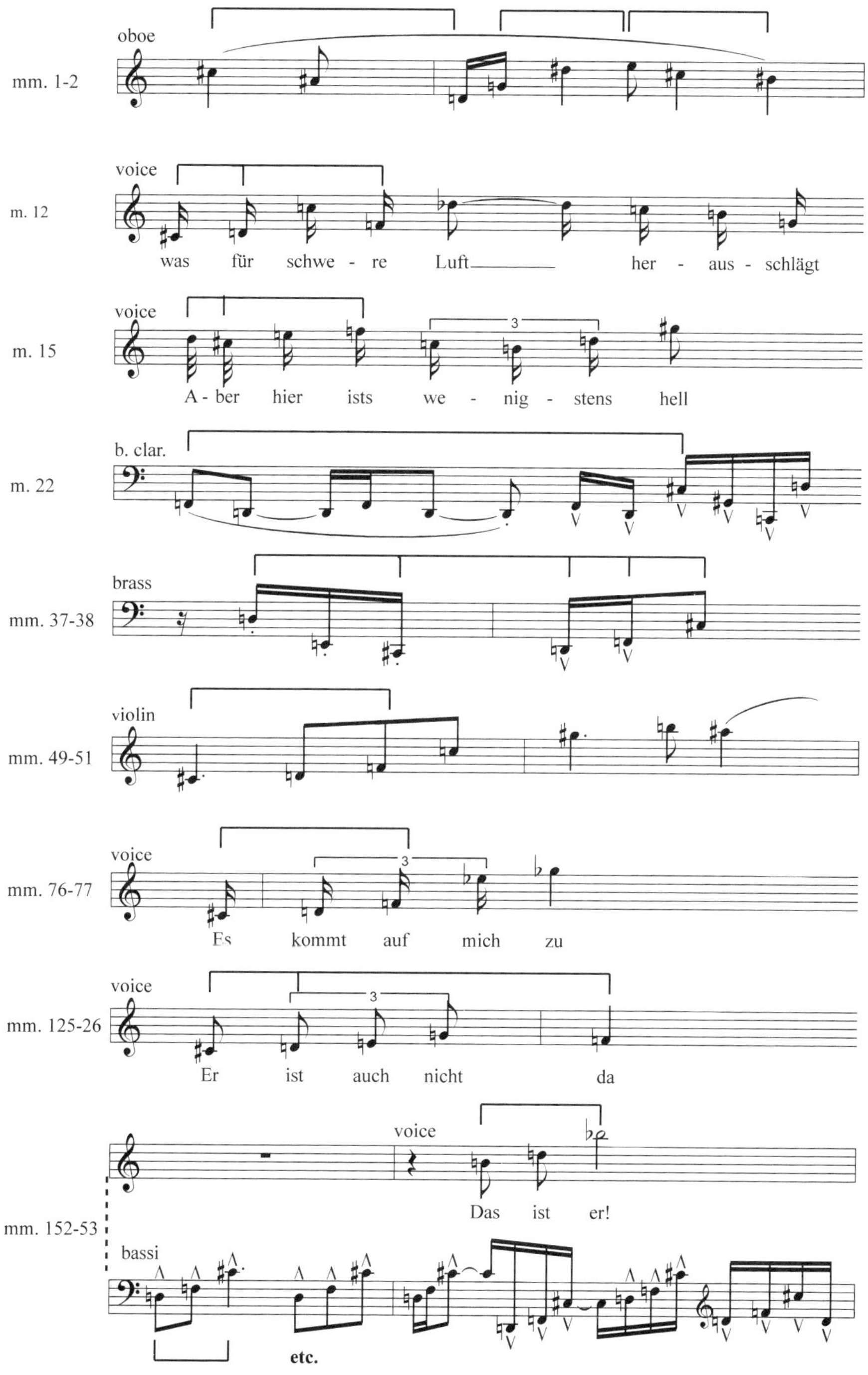

Die glückliche Hand, Op. 18

Even as he worked on *Erwartung* in late August and early September of 1909, Schoenberg probably contemplated a second opera to be the companion of his diminutive monodrama. Pappenheim recalled in her correspondence with Kirchmeyer that the composer had asked her that summer for a second text, which Schoenberg subsequently rejected.[18] In all likelihood she was confusing this with a later commission from Schoenberg, for an oratorio libretto based on Balzac's novel *Séraphita.* In fact, Schoenberg's idea for the new opera was probably hatched even before the summer when *Erwartung* was composed, and it appears to have originated as an artistic interpretation of his most sensitive personal feelings and recent experiences. The new work addressed two related themes concerning the fate of mankind, both of which had universal significance as well as a painful resonance in Schoenberg's own life. The first concerned the true artist, who constantly aspires to a popular success and acceptance that, by the very nature of his artistic achievements, is ever denied him. The second, no doubt triggered by the temporary breakup of Schoenberg's marriage during the summer of 1908, similarly depicts a man caught in a cycle of yearning for love and its inevitable destruction.

For Schoenberg to contemplate making his professional and marital crises the basis for a musical work had by 1909 many precedents. The artwork that takes its origins from its creator's innermost emotional life has roots that go deep into the romantic imagination as well as to early expressionist phenomena. The plays of August Strindberg written shortly before the turn of the century, for example, reflect autobiographically on the writer's marital crises and his battle with nervous disorders. The writings and artworks of Oskar Kokoschka were also compelling models for Schoenberg's self-reflection in artistic form. In 1908, while still a student at Vienna's School of Applied Arts, Kokoschka was invited to exhibit at Vienna's Internationale Kunstschau. Among his contributions was a colored bust of himself, *Self-Portrait as a Warrior* (Figure 5.1), which, in its anguished emotion and concentration upon the artist's own self, was a calculated rebellion against the Secessionist spirit of the exhibition. His 1908 book, *Die träumenden Knaben,* contains a highly original poem, written in the first person in a stream of consciousness, that tells symbolically but clearly autobiographically of an adolescent's growing awareness of sexuality, which is accompanied by violent obsessions. Even in 1909 Schoenberg was strongly attracted to Kokoschka's prodigious talent. Shortly thereafter Schoenberg described him as "the greatest living painter."[19]

Like Strindberg and Kokoschka, Schoenberg soon after the Gerstl affair began to allude to his emotional dilemma through his art—especially in texts that he chose to set to music, as in those selected for Op. 10 and Op. 15, and also in instrumental works that more obliquely embodied his feelings. One such was a fragmentary orchestral composition for which Schoenberg composed two pages of sketches. One page was dated 11 October 1908, and the other, undated but sharing a motive with the former, contains three themes that Schoenberg labeled *Thaten* (actions), *Beschwichtigung* (calming down), and *Schein-Glück* (false hap-

Figure 5.1. Oskar Kokoschka, *Self-Portrait as a Warrior* (1908). Museum of Fine Arts, Boston. Bequest of J. H. and E. A. Payne.

piness). Given the date, these words probably refer to his frame of mind following his wife's departure with Gerstl and echo the sentiments that were soon to reappear in the second opera, although the motives of the fragmentary orchestral work were not reused.[20]

Correspondence from Oskar Kokoschka to Schoenberg in October 1909 suggests that the composer may have sought Kokoschka's advice on the text of the new opera.[21] The two were brought together by a mutual friend, the painter Max Oppenheimer. Mopp, as he was known, had visited the Steinakirchen gathering in the summer of 1909 when he apparently learned of Schoenberg's ideas for a second opera that would deal with a man in the grasp of fate and false happiness. He wrote to Schoenberg on 9 September, saying that he had spoken to Kokoschka regarding Schoenberg's "ideas and plans" and that Kokoschka had found them engaging.[22] In Vienna, where rumors traveled fast, it was immediately assumed that Schoenberg and Kokoschka had begun to collaborate on a new opera. This was mentioned by Marie Pappenheim in an undated letter in which she inquires about further revisions in the *Erwartung* libretto and also confides that "in Vienna it is said that you are writing an opera with Kokoschka. Maybe it will work out better after all? I don't like my monodrama much."[23]

Schoenberg completed the first draft of his new opera text by the end of June 1910. He called it a drama with music, titled *Die glückliche Hand* (The magic touch), and in the fall of that year he made a few musical sketches for it, although its continuation was interrupted by the demands of writing the *Harmonielehre*. Schoenberg later summarized the essential idea of the story of the drama: "A Man, a victim of misfortune, gathers himself up. Fortune again smiles upon him. He is able to complete his work as in the old days. But then again everything proves false, and the brickbats of fate again assail him."[24]

The opera begins with a Man lying in the grasp of a winged monster. A chorus that gazes from behind a curtain laments his repeated efforts to achieve worldly in addition to transcendental success, efforts that are inevitably doomed to fail. But, deaf to their message, he rises, feeling a return of his powers and of his sensual instincts. A Woman enters behind him, whose presence he senses and whose beauty comforts him. He drinks from a goblet that she offers him but does not notice that she has become cold and hostile. She meets an old friend, an elegantly dressed Gentleman, with whom she departs. The Man senses these actions uneasily, without actually seeing them. Immediately, however, she rushes back to him, kneeling and begging for a forgiveness that he willingly gives. But no sooner is this done than she again rushes off, which the Man, as always, fails to notice. As he wrongly thinks that he possesses her forever, his appetite is whetted for creative work. He appears with a bloody sword and the heads of two Saracens tied at his waist and strides confidently into a cave where craftsmen work. Despite their threatening gestures, he grasps a hammer and, with a single stroke, forges a beautiful jewel, at the same time splitting the anvil in half.

But suddenly the Man is possessed by a terrible foreboding. He stands mute as his body seems to exude a crescendo of ever more intensely colored lights, mirroring his own growing anxiety. Then the Woman is seen, lacking part of her dress, which is held out by the Gentleman in a cave above. In great consternation, the Man vainly tries to reach the cave, whereupon the Gentleman indifferently throws him the dress part. The Woman recovers the piece of clothing, and the man now pleads with her to remain. Instead, she leaps to the plateau above and casts down upon him a huge rock, while scornful laughter is heard offstage. The scenery then returns to that of the opening: the rock has changed into the image of the monster, again holding the Man in its clutches. The chorus again asks why the man must ever seek what he can never attain.

The drama intermingles two principal themes, one dealing with art, the other with love. The first of these, an artist spurned by his contemporaries, had long been in Schoenberg's mind as the topic of a dramatic piece. It was the underlying subject of one of his earlier opera libretti, the undated *Odoakar*, in which it was given the outward shape of a heroic tragedy in the vein of Wagnerian opera. Its language was cast in free verse with short irregular lines and much alliteration, and it contained a virtual catalog of Wagnerian themes. The story opens in the dark fortress of Odoakar, the fifth-century Germanic warrior and king of Italy. The hero is asleep, dreaming that he is beset by a band of enemies against whom he defends himself with his horn and his sword. Although the sword is easily shattered by the weakest of his enemies, his horn continues to play, as though by itself.[25] Clearly enough, the sword symbolizes the striving of the hero for success in conquest; the horn, the undying spiritual idea that lies behind his achievements. Odoakar wakens and, reflecting upon his dream, tells his ally Adelrich that the creative works of the hero will inevitably be lost on the world at large, which can only seek superficial sensual pleasure. The hero in *Odoakar* is a prototype for the Man in *Die glückliche Hand.* Both are depicted as creative individuals whose achievements are unappreciated by people around them. Both are presented as artist heroes—idealistic warriors who are ready to take up the sword against their nattering critics.

When Schoenberg returned in *Die glückliche Hand* to the same theme of timeless achievement in the face of mundane failure, he revived in part the Wagnerian apparatus of *Odoakar. Die glückliche Hand* is indeed a *Gesamtkunstwerk* in which visual effects, dialogue, and music cooperate as equals. The Man's cleaving of the anvil and the Woman's offering him a symbolic draught have analogies in *Siegfried* and *Tristan.* The drama is also close to *Parsifal,* as both are filled with magical scenic effects that involve light and color and have a symmetrical overall form. Just as Act 3 of *Parsifal* returns to the setting of Act 1, the fourth scene of *Die glückliche Hand* returns to the same setting as scene 1. The Wagnerian topics shared by *Die glückliche Hand* and *Odoakar* suggest that the origins of the former were in an earlier conception that was close to the Wagnerian heroic genre, only to be transformed by later dramatic and personal circumstances. *Odoakar* documents this earlier stage, in which the Wagnerian prototype is fully evident.

The second major theme in *Die glückliche Hand,* the Man's search for love despite repeated failures, takes its origins in the composer's marital crisis of 1908, which has already been described in chapter 3. In an undated "Testaments-Entwurf," probably written by Schoenberg shortly after the Gerstl affair in the summer of 1908, the composer describes the distance that he felt from his wife, Mathilde: "My wife's soul was so remote from mine that I had neither a truthful nor a false relation with it. We didn't even speak to one another, that is, communicate. We only talked." He continues:

> But it cannot be denied that I was very unhappy over her deception. I cried, acted like one in despair, made up my mind, then changed it, had ideas of suicide and almost carried them out, drifted from one madness to another—in a word, I was entirely torn apart. . . . We never knew each other. I don't even know what she looks like. I can't conjure up her image. Perhaps she doesn't exist at all.[26]

This portrait of Schoenberg's marriage is transferred directly into the opera. Like the composer and his wife, the Man does not speak to the Woman but thinks mistakenly that they trust and understand each other. Nor does the Man look at the Woman, just as in the "Testaments-Entwurf" Schoenberg said that he could not recall his wife's appearance. The Gentleman is Gerstl, who was known as handsome and elegantly attired.[27]

Schoenberg intertwines the themes of love and art, bringing them both to a more timeless than personal level. It is the fate of all creative individuals for their accomplishments to be counterweighted by worldly misfortunes. Like the Man, they will be caught in an eternal cycle of artistic success followed by mundane failure. Like the heroes in Greek tragedy, they are people of superior gifts who can be brought down all too easily by the smallness of those around them. Schoenberg's use of a Greek-type chorus in scenes 1 and 4 underscores the Man's noble pursuits and his entanglement with fate.

In his own interpretations of his drama Schoenberg meticulously avoided any references to his personal situation or frame of mind. The most detailed of these discussions is a lecture on the work that he delivered in Breslau in 1928.[28] His main intention in *Die glückliche Hand,* he says, is solely to "make music with the means of the stage." The emotions and ideas that arise in the plot are to be conveyed by colors, words, sounds, lights, gestures, and music. No one of these takes precedence, and each can bear the same emotional and intellectual content directly to the audience. The work, he concludes, should convey no hidden meaning. In a letter to Alma Mahler written on 7 October 1910, he reiterated his belief that no personal symbolism was at issue in the new opera:

> I do not want to be understood. I want to express myself, but I hope I will be misunderstood. It would be dreadful to me if I could be seen through. . . . I would like to write for a magic theatre. If tones can release feelings when they are heard in whatever sequence, then colors, gestures, movements must be capable of doing this, too. Even if they otherwise have no sense that reason can perceive. Music does not have this either!!—I mean, in short: this is music!—[29]

The chronology of composition of *Die glückliche Hand* is not precisely documented.[30] The main musical manuscript is a score draft that is dated 9 September 1910 at the beginning and 18 November 1913 at the end. Schoenberg completed a fair-copy score only two days after he finished the draft. Unlike his earlier atonal works, most of his second opera is represented by sketches, although none is dated. The chronology compiled by Joseph Auner provides ample evidence that Schoenberg composed little of the opera, other than a few disconnected sketches, before the summer of 1911, at which time he wrote the end of scene 2 and the opening passages of scene 3. The remainder was apparently composed in 1912 and 1913, well after the onset of Schoenberg's compositional crisis at the time of the Three Pieces for Chamber Orchestra and after the completion of *Pierrot lunaire* in July of 1912.

The opera thus represents a musical conception that is several years removed from the athematic style of atonality, which had reached its culmination with the Six Little Piano Pieces, Op. 19. As will be discussed in the next chapter, Schoenberg by 1912 had attempted to extricate himself from the creative dilemma in which he had become mired by fully rejecting the artistic manifesto made earlier to Busoni and by initiating a painstaking process of reconstruction of his entire musical language. The history of *Die glückliche Hand* reveals many symptoms of this new outlook. The opera took more than three years to compose, quite the opposite of the headlong and unreflective composing that had produced *Erwartung.* The presence of extensive sketches suggests a decidedly Apollonian approach to creativity—methodical, reflective, and filled with second thoughts. These changes in method coincide with a more traditional musical style in *Die glückliche Hand,* in which thematic work, traditional architecture, and counterpoint return to favor.

Schoenberg's new compositional philosophy is evident in the overall musical design of *Die glückliche Hand.* The work has a much more traditional operatic form than *Erwartung,* as it is divided into large sections that coincide with major divisions of the text. Each section has its own character, each rests on a traditional musical pattern or formative principle, and the whole is rounded off by a large-scale musical recurrence. The form of the work was almost certainly studied by Berg prior to composing his own opera *Wozzeck,* with which it has many constructive similarities.

The primary musical divisions of *Die glückliche Hand* coincide with the libretto's four scenes, which begin at measures 1, 31, 89, and 203. These are connected by brief but distinct interludes that accompany changes of scenery. The exact extent of the interludes is not clearly marked in the score, although it can be deduced from the staging instructions and musical context. Schoenberg entered the word *Verwandlung* at measures 31, 88, and 200, that is, at or just before each new scene, although the change of scenery before scene 2 begins at measure 23 rather than 31. The first and third interludes, which are virtually identical in music, have a connective role between their framing scenes; the second interlude functions as a musical introduction to scene 3.

Scene 1 is devoted to a single musical idea: an ever-present orchestral ostinato that accompanies a twelve-part mixed chorus. The chorus partly sings and partly whispers in *Sprechmelodie,* roughly the same speechlike style that Schoenberg used for solo voice in *Pierrot lunaire.* Music for the change of scenery at the end of the section introduces two new ideas: a "loud, vulgar, jolly music" heard from the offstage brass, followed by "shrill, scornful laughter" from the offstage chorus.

The second scene is loosely constructed, taking as its formative idea an exposition that corresponds to the appearance of the three protagonists. The Man (the only singing role) is introduced by a short figure in the cello, the Woman appears at measure 35 accompanied by the solo violin (also by flute, celesta, and harp), and the Gentleman arrives at measure 67 amid mocking rhythms in the woodwinds. Although *Die glückliche Hand* does not contain leitmotives in the Wagnerian sense, one recurrent figure, especially prominent in this and in the following scene, suggests an association with the Woman. Its principal appearances and dramatic contexts are summarized in Example 5.4. The figure is always played by the solo violin, and it appears prominently upon the Woman's entrances. By the end of scene 2, the Man—blind to the departure of the Woman and Gentleman—exults in an outburst of false confidence. "Now I possess you forever!" he cries. The orchestra builds to a powerful climax over an eleven-note chord that represents a massing of energy that the Man will convert in the next scene into creativity.

Example 5.4. Schoenberg, *Die glückliche Hand*

The Woman enters and gazes with compassion upon the Man.

mm. 36-37

The Man declares how good and beautiful the Woman is.

mm. 41-42

The Man says that it is good to see and to speak to her.

m. 43

The Woman enters, following the light crescendo.

mm. 153-55

grazioso

The Woman leaps from the cave to the plateau to recover her clothing.

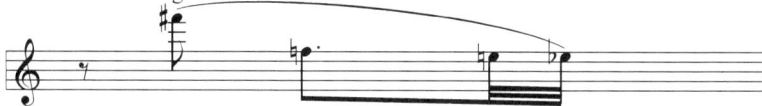

m. 181

The chorus reiterates that wherever the Man may be, something is in and around him.

m. 224

The third scene is strict in construction and generally contrapuntal in premise, both symbolizing the Man's renewed creative activities. The scene is divisi-
ble into four sections: a contrapuntal invention with ostinato episodes (measures
89–124), a "color crescendo" in arch form (measures 125–53), a waltz fragment (measures 154–65), and a final contrapuntal essay that uses a strict developmental ternary design (measures 166–99).

The third section of the scene, the color crescendo, is one of Schoenberg's
most original ideas. Here the Man's presentiment of the liaison between the
Woman and the Gentleman casts him into the grip of emotions so powerful and
unstable that they can only be represented by ever more powerful colors, which
seem to glow from within him. Musically, the passage is based on a free development of a few highly fragmented figures; the sense of form is created by a
great arch of intensity, which moves to a climax at measure 151 and then quickly
dissipates. This expressive curve is underscored by increasing dynamics and by
ever more penetrating colors, chosen with an uncanny similarity to the contemporary color theory of Wassily Kandinsky.[31]

The many sketches for the final passage of scene 3 (measures 166–99) suggest that Schoenberg conceived of it as an inversion canon based on a subject
in the horn.[32] In the final version, the music retains a contrapuntal texture and
foursquare rhythm, but Schoenberg converted it formally into a developmental
ternary form, closely related to similar designs encountered in Op. 11, Nos. 1–2,
and Op. 16, No. 2. The nine-measure main theme in the horn is also strictly presented, laid out as a small ternary form, which then leads to a multisectional contrasting passage in which fragments of the main theme—especially its head
motive—are plainly evident. A strict reprise occurs at measure 187, where the
main theme returns, at first transposed to the fifth but finally returning to the
original pitch level.

The ensuing scene-change music (measures 200–202) exactly repeats the
first *Verwandlung*, a rare but not unprecedented example of an unvaried reprise
in Schoenberg's oeuvre to this time. Its exactness must be understood as a dramatic symbol rather than an element of pure musical construction, since it graphically illustrates the completion of a cycle in the Man's fate of alternating struggle and defeat. Schoenberg himself underscored this interpretation in a way
that also showed the close integration in his mind of the two main topics in his
text: the Man's repeated failures in love and his failures to achieve popular acceptance as an artist. In a marginal note that he made to a review of the opera
by Emil Petschnig following its premiere in Vienna in 1924, the composer discussed the meaning of the musical recurrence at the end: "Can't we assume . . .
that this means that the Man, despite the dejection which he has experienced,
despite his collapse, will immediately return to the fray? Or, stated another way:
that love (Eros) calls him perpetually back to life?"[33]

The final scene continues to recapitulate motives from the first scene, although more highly varied than in the *Verwandlung*. This concluding music is also
considerably extended in length in comparison to the first scene, and it is cast as
a ternary shape rather than having only one part, as earlier. The outer sections
closely resemble the first scene as they reuse the speaking chorus and variants

of the opening motives and ostinato figures. The middle section, measures 224–40, forms a clear contrast by its distinct tempo, normal singing in the chorus rather than speaking voice, and a general absence of motives from the ostinato of scene 1.

This middle passage forms the major climax of the entire opera, the point where the Man's dilemma is finally defined as residing in his recurrent obsession with both the physical as well as the artistic, which drives him through an eternal cycle of dejection and elation, frustration and satisfaction, dormancy and creativity. The passage was repeatedly sketched by the composer, receiving more attention than any other part of the opera. The manuscript that apparently contains the earliest version (archive p. 2439) is for six-voice chorus without orchestra. Schoenberg subsequently tried various orchestral accompaniments, some of which show him experimenting with sets of all twelve pitch classes, which he divides methodically among both voices and instruments to create a unified multidimensional texture.[34] In the final version, the twelve-tone element was removed from the orchestral music, although it was still provocatively maintained in the opening of the choral parts. The first soprano sings a twelve-tone melody, the first such in Schoenberg's oeuvre, whose first half is then imitated by the first tenor in a transposed inversion (Example 5.5). The soprano's twelve-tone line is twice interrupted by an ascending and descending semitonal figure (measures 225, 226–27), which is one of the principal motivic particles that link the entire opera. Given Schoenberg's feelings of kinship with the Man, it may also be relevant that the hexachords in this twelve-tone theme share the same total intervallic content with the Es C H B E G set.

All of this complex structural apparatus was certainly meant to symbolize the words of the chorus, who at this point praise the spiritual gift that is in and around the Man. This suggests a different way of thinking about music for the Schoenberg of 1913 from the composer of 1909. His earlier goal for an intensely poetic musical expression is, in some considerable measure, replaced by concern for spiritual issues that are symbolized by a highly intricate musical structure. This new viewpoint would gradually intensify in Schoenberg's thinking for the remainder of his atonal period.

The musical-dramatic conception of *Die glückliche Hand* is indeed unprecedented in the history of opera. The work is essentially a pantomime—there is relatively little singing—and it does not portray familiar emotions that can be underscored or made poignant by the lyrical voice. Adorno found *Die glückliche Hand* to be closest in genre to the symphony; it reminded him especially of several symphonies by Mahler[35]: "None of his works came closer to the symphonic ideal than this 'drama with music' and this music whose expansive power and striking force Schoenberg hardly ever regained." Its recondite meaning turns on the integration of a complex musical idiom with visual and dramatic images and their direct, abstract contact with the listener's emotions. In order to heighten and make urgent this contact, the composer conceived of a multidimensional drama that touched his own inner emotional life in as direct and truthful a way as possible.

Example 5.5. Schoenberg, *Die glückliche Hand,* measures 224–28 (chorus only)

Plans for Staging

Schoenberg thought of *Erwartung* and *Die glückliche Hand* as companion pieces, intending them to be performed together. He told Albertine Zehme that it was his "burning desire" to hear the two works as a pair.[36] His wish is understandable, since the two works, although outwardly dissimilar in theme, are in many ways complementary: Each contains the interior monologue of a single protagonist who represents not only a gender type but also a viewpoint about what art should be. The Man in *Die glückliche Hand* symbolizes the creative individual, whose other attributes include generosity, naïveté, and persistence in the face of mundane failure and the antagonism of society. The Woman in *Erwartung* is his opposite: She possesses no trace of intellect or creativity, and she is also faithless, weak, and cunning. Her character resonates with the unflattering female image that was common in such turn-of-the-century German literature as Otto Weininger's *Geschlecht und Charakter* and writings by Frank Wedekind, Karl Kraus, and August Strindberg, all of whom Schoenberg admired. On an artistic plane, *Die glückliche Hand* contains a critique of *Erwartung*. One is the opera of a man whose nature is to be creative; the other is the opera of a woman whose nature is to be destructive. Just as Schoenberg by 1913 had turned permanently away from a music that rose spontaneously from the unconscious mind, he shows little sympathy in *Die glückliche Hand* for the Woman, whose emotionality is now depicted as barren, reckless, and manipulative.

Schoenberg's efforts to arrange for performances of the two operas were unflagging, especially in 1913 as *Die glückliche Hand* neared completion.[37] He also corresponded with his editor, Emil Hertzka, about the feasibility of a filmed version of this work. But the outbreak of war in 1914 put all such efforts temporarily to rest. Only in 1924 were the two operas first staged, *Erwartung* in Prague under Zemlinsky's direction and *Die glückliche Hand* at the Vienna Volksoper under Fritz Stiedry. There were few other productions prior to World War II—a complete listing is shown in Table 5.1. These were mostly festival performances with few, if any, repetitions. Although audience enthusiasm was reported after these early hearings, the reviews of the operas were almost uniformly negative, and only in the 1960s did *Erwartung* begin to enter the standard operatic repertory. To this day, performances of *Die glückliche Hand* are rare.

Schoenberg took a keen interest in the staging of his operas, especially in their decor. He strongly opposed the trend toward reinterpretive stagings that had become fashionable by the end of World War I, and he insisted that his basic concept for a mise-en-scène be considered as authoritative as the musical score: "While I was composing I had all the scenic effects in mind, seeing them with the utmost precision."[38] He also conceived of his operas as *Gesamtkunstwerke* that integrated visual and musical dimensions. The decor, he wrote,

Table 5.1. Stagings of *Erwartung* and *Die glückliche Hand* prior to World War II

Beginning date	City, theater	Conductor
Erwartung		
6 June 1924	Prague, Neues Deutsches Theater	Alexander Zemlinsky
22 January 1928	Wiesbaden, Staatstheater	Joseph Rosenstock
7 June 1930	Berlin, Kroll Oper	Alexander Zemlinsky
28 January 1931	Essen, Städtisches Opernhaus	Rudolf Schulz-Dornburg
Die glückliche Hand		
1 October 1924	Vienna, Volksoper	Fritz Stiedry
24 March 1928	Breslau, Stadttheater	Fritz Cortolezis
3 July 1929	Duisburg, Stadttheater	Paul Drach
11 April 1930	Philadelphia, Academy of Music	Leopold Stokowski
22 April 1930	New York, Metropolitan Opera	Leopold Stokowski
7 June 1930	Berlin, Kroll Oper	Otto Klemperer

"must emanate from the music, going through the ears to the eyes."[39] His intentions regarding decor are documented by a series of scene paintings and drawings that he made for both operas.[40] These are undated, but some for *Die glückliche Hand* were exhibited together with other paintings by Schoenberg at Hugo
Heller's Vienna Kunstsalon in October 1910. In Schoenberg's legacy there also
exist miscellaneous sketches and models for scenery, costumes, and stage ma-
chinery for the two works. Some of these were entered into the 1910 text manuscript of *Die glückliche Hand*, and others were apparently made in 1930, prior
to a performance of both works at the Kroll Oper in Berlin.

In Schoenberg's view, the proper degree of realism or abstraction in the decor
of an opera should depend on the underlying idea of the work. In *Erwartung* he
intended an essentially realistic staging. The forest in particular, he said, must
be convincingly fearful. His drawings of scenery for this work seem intent upon
capturing the relationship of the path and the forest trees mentioned in the instructions for the first scene: "The forest is tall and dark; only the first tree trunks
and the beginning of the broad path are lit." Schoenberg's depictions show the
scene realistically, with a narrow path plunging deep into a dense and menacing forest (Figure 5.2). Other pictures show the Woman cowering beneath trees
that seem to threaten her.

Schoenberg had the opposite intention in *Die glückliche Hand:* "The whole
thing should have the effect (not of a dream) but of chords. Of music. It must

Figure 5.2. Arnold Schoenberg, scene drawing for *Erwartung*. Arnold Schoenberg Center, Vienna.

never suggest symbols, or meaning, or thoughts, but simply the play of colors and forms."[41] His scene paintings are more abstract than those for *Erwartung,* although the objects that they depict—the steady gaze of the chorus in scene 1, the bright spring sun of scene 2, the mountains of scene 3—are still fully recognizable.

Schoenberg's prescription for *Die glückliche Hand* as "simply the play of colors and forms" suggests it as an important forerunner of nonnarrative theater. By the end of World War I, drama that bypassed logical action and connected dialogue in favor of suggestive visual and sonorous images had emerged in many European theatrical circles. Schoenberg's conception of *Die glückliche Hand* as purely color and form bears an especially strong resemblance to Wassily Kandinsky's scenario *Der gelbe Klang,* which was published in 1912 in *Der blaue Reiter.* Kandinsky explained the purpose behind this experimental work in his essay "On Stage Composition," also published in *Der blaue Reiter.*[42] *Der gelbe Klang* is an attempt, Kandinsky wrote, to create within the observer an inner effect—a "vibration of the soul"—purely by using musical sounds, dance movements, and colors. The work has virtually no text, no coherent action, and little sense of cooperation among the three basic elements.

Since Schoenberg had conceived of his dramatic idea behind *Die glückliche Hand* by 1910, it is virtually impossible that he was directly influenced by *Der gelbe Klang* or by Kandinsky's color theories. Instead, it is likely that both works sprang from a common spirit of experimentation at the turn of the century in the concept of the total work of art. As was later revealed in their correspondence, both Schoenberg and Kandinsky relied in their experimentation upon creative intuition and internal rather than external experience. Schoenberg was himself quick to note the relationship between the two pieces. In a revealing letter to Kandinsky dated 19 August 1912, he observed that both were representations of inner visions, although he admitted that his opera was conventional in comparison to Kandinsky's drama.[43] Both, he said, took the form of puzzles that attempted to encode the riddles of existence. All such artistic enigmas, he concluded, "are an image of the ungraspable."

6

New Uses of the Voice

Herzgewächse, Pierrot lunaire, and Four Songs, Op. 22

After completing the final number of his Six Little Piano Pieces in mid-June 1911, Schoenberg was still unable to rekindle the zest for composing that he had enjoyed in 1908 and 1909, when the atonal style was still new in his hands. He seemed baffled as much as ever over the causes of his creative inactivity. In his diary for 12 March 1912 he blames the distraction of writing musical theory—"it certainly dries one up," he complained—although by then his *Harmonielehre* had been completed for nearly a year, and he had made little progress on additional treatises that he had contemplated earlier.[1] He confesses in his diary to a sense of rivalry with his students, who, he says, adopt and exaggerate all of his new ideas. He also finds himself questioning the very direction in which his music had taken him, uncertain as to whether he could continue to compose as he had in the past:

> I had already considered the possibility that I might never compose again at all. There seemed to be many reasons for it. The persistence of my students, who are always at my heels trying to outdo what I offer, puts me in danger of becoming their imitator, and it keeps me from calmly building on what I have already attained. They always raise everything to the tenth power. And it works! It is really good. But I don't know whether it is necessary. So I am forced to decide all the more carefully whether I must compose now as before.[2]

Schoenberg also had to contend at this time with many personal distractions, not the least of which was his sudden departure from Vienna in the summer of 1911 and subsequent removal to Berlin in September, a move made urgent by an ugly incident with a neighbor in Vienna.[3] But the roots of Schoenberg's artistic quandary lay primarily with his uncertainty over the atonal style itself and over the state to which it had evolved by 1910—athematic, intuitive, radically abbreviated, and utterly dependent upon flashes of inspiration. After resettling in Berlin in September of 1911, he poured out his self-doubts in correspondence with his friends. On 21 December 1911 he wrote to Berg: "I've lost all interest in my works. I'm not satisfied with anything any more. I see mistakes and inadequacies in everything. Enough of that; I can't begin to tell you how I feel at such times."[4]

"Hergewächse," Op. 20

Less than two weeks before he confided these discouraged thoughts to Berg, Schoenberg hurriedly composed a song, "Herzgewächse," for soprano, harmonium, celesta, and harp. It was a setting of Maurice Maeterlinck's poem "Feuillage du coeur" in a free German translation by K. L. Ammer, and it was written expressly for publication in the art almanac *Der blaue Reiter.* This was edited by Wassily Kandinsky and Franz Marc, and the song appeared there in 1912 together with reproductions of two of Schoenberg's paintings and his essay "Das Verhältnis zum Text."

Kandinsky resided at this time in the Bavarian village of Murnau in the company of other painters, including Gabriele Münter and Franz Marc. Much interested in music himself, Kandinsky wrote to Schoenberg in January 1911, shortly after he heard a concert in Munich at which the Three Piano Pieces, Op. 11, and String Quartet No. 2, Op. 10, were performed. "What we are striving for and our whole manner of thought and feeling," he confided to the composer, "have so much in common that I feel completely justified in expressing my empathy."[5] A lively and valuable exchange of ideas appeared in the letters that subsequently flowed between the two. They first met personally on 31 August 1911, when Kandinsky made the short trip from Murnau to Berg am Starnbergersee to visit with Schoenberg, who was spending the summer in Bavaria.

Almost certainly Kandinsky's visit was prompted by his wish to discuss with Schoenberg the forthcoming *Der blaue Reiter,* on which Kandinsky, Marc, and others in their circle were then hard at work. Kandinsky's plan for the volume relied heavily on contributions from artists in different fields and from different nationalities the world over, by which he hoped to present a summary of modern art as a utopian *Gesamtkunstwerk.* He invited the composer to contribute one or more essays and musical scores for inclusion in the almanac. The day after Kandinsky's visit he wrote to Marc: "Schoenberg *has to* write on German music. . . . Some music should be included, too. Schoenberg, for example, has songs. . . . We just have to show that *everywhere* things are happening."[6]

For his own part, Schoenberg had many reasons to be eager to be represented in Kandinsky's publication. He was no doubt aware that it could lead to publicity for and exhibitions of his paintings, which might promote their sale and provide relief from the uncertainty of his finances. Despite the debacle of the Gerstl affair, he still maintained friendships with painters in Vienna, and he must have been struck by the similarities of his own artistic outlook with that of Kandinsky's circle, similarities of taste that extended to literature as well as music and painting. Like Schoenberg, Kandinsky was much inspired by modern developments in French literature and by writers around the world who had come under the French influence. Kandinsky was a great admirer of the work of Stefan George and, unlike Schoenberg, closely connected with George's personal circle.[7]

The two also shared an enthusiasm for the writing of Maurice Maeterlinck. For Kandinsky, Maeterlinck's symbolist poems and plays opened for the sensitive reader a realm of spirituality, pure feeling, and inner knowledge, which was situated far beyond the trivial materialism of the contemporary world and which offered a fruitful location for development of the artwork of the future.[8] Schoenberg's interest in Maeterlinck was equally keen. After composing his tone poem *Pelleas und Melisande* in 1903, Schoenberg had acquired for his personal library a copy of the thirteen-volume collected works of Maeterlinck, published by Eugen Diederichs, in a German translation by Ammer and Friedrich von Oppeln-Bronikowski. Probably alerted to Kandinsky's great enthusiasm for Maeterlinck, Schoenberg looked in the *Gedichte* volume of this series for a song text that would conform to the highly symbolic and spiritualized tone that Kandinsky and Marc intended for their forthcoming publication.

Schoenberg chose "Herzgewächse" from Maeterlinck's early poetic collection *Serres chaudes* (Hothouses). This was a cycle of thirty-three poems, written squarely in the symbolist manner of Verlaine and Mallarmé. Using an elaborately metaphorical language, Maeterlinck describes a soul shut off from life, trapped alternately in a hothouse, under glass or ice, in a prison or hospital, in a diving bell or aquarium, or in the depths of sleep. All of these isolate the psyche from the external world and from any active involvement with life or nature. But within the walls of the isolated hothouse has grown a richly imaginative vegetation of dreams, memories, feelings, and presentiments of death. Maeterlinck's depiction of the growth within the hothouse is accomplished almost entirely by flamboyant symbols. Hatreds become hyenas; sins, yellow mongrels. Desires are grass that has withered to straw under the glass that traps the soul, tinder that "breaks forth into devouring fires" at the slightest spark of memory.

Herzgewächse	Foliage of the Heart
Meiner müden Schwermut blaues Glas	The blue glass of my tired melancholy
Deckt den alten, unbestimmten Kummer,	Covers my old uncertain sorrow,
Dessen ich genas,	From which I recovered,
Und der nun erstarrt in seinem Schlummer.	And which is now paralyzed in its sleep.
Sinnbildhaft ist seiner Blumen Zier:	The lushness of its flowers is symbolic:
Mancher Freuden düstre Wasserrose,	Gloomy water lilies' many joys,
Palmen der Begier,	Palms' yearning,
Weiche Schlinggewächse, kühle Moose.	Supple vines, cool mosses.
Eine Lilie nur in all dem Flor,	A single lily among all these flowers,
Bleich und starr in ihrer Kränklichkeit,	Pale and rigid in its sickliness,
Richtet sich empor	Rises up
Über all das blattgewordne Leid.	Above all the foliage of grief.
Licht sind ihre Blätter anzuschauen,	Light is seen from its leaves,
Weissen Mondesglanz sie um sich sät.	It sows white moonlight around itself.
Zum Krystall, dem blauen,	Toward the crystal, the blue,
Sendet sie ihr mystisches Gebet.[9]	It sends its mystic prayer.

This is Ammer's text as it appeared in the 1906 *Gedichte*. Compared to the other poems in *Serres chaudes,* it is relatively concrete in its symbolism, and it contains a recapitulation of several of the recurrent images that run throughout the cycle—the blue glass that encloses the poet's soul, the vegetation that symbolizes forgotten and faded passions, and the moonlight that alone can penetrate the sealed-off realm. The central image is the lily, which despite its sickliness rises unremittingly toward the glass that forever separates it from the blue of nature, to which it delivers "its mystic prayer." The image of the lily also recurs throughout the cycle, and, like most of the symbols in Maeterlinck's writings, it has differing connotations in the poet's rich web of allusions. In some poems it suggests the presence of death, in others the purity of prayer. Certainly it has a phallic connotation, the symbol of an erotic desire that can never be fulfilled.

Schoenberg's music for this highly musical poem returns resolutely to the spirit of the Busoni manifesto of August 1909, rather than continuing the tendency toward stylistic retrenchment that was broached in the Six Little Piano Pieces. Like the Five Orchestra Pieces of Op. 16, "Herzgewächse" is a work of brilliant originality in sound and texture, returning to the *Buntheit* of changing colors that characterizes Schoenberg's orchestrational style of 1909. The manuscripts of the work suggest that it was composed in considerable haste. By early December 1911, Kandinsky's final deadline for material for his almanac was very near, and Schoenberg called once again on his proven ability to compose quickly. There are no extant sketches and no draft for the song; like the Three Pieces for Chamber Orchestra, the music was probably first written down as a full score. There are two fair-copy full scores in Schoenberg's hand, one of which was dated 9 December 1911 at its conclusion and sent in early February 1912 to Kandinsky, who printed it in facsimile in *Der blaue Reiter* (the facsimile was reused in 1920 by Universal Edition as the *Stichvorlage* for the work's first engraved edition). The other fair copy was used by Schoenberg to rehearse the song for a performance in Berlin planned for 28 January 1912 and rescheduled for February 4, although "Herzgewächse" was ultimately dropped from the program. Schoenberg's haste is evident in the number of inaccuracies that he made when copying Maeterlinck's poem into the score. These primarily concern capitalization and punctuation, although in the manuscript of the song that he sent to Kandinsky there are also changes of wording made in Ammer's translation. One occurs in the first poetic line, where Schoenberg substituted the word *Sehnsucht* (yearning) for Ammer's word *Schwermut* (melancholy)—perhaps unintentionally, since the original wording is used in the other fair copy.[10]

The form of "Herzgewächse" is based on the constructive model that first appeared in Schoenberg's Piano Piece, Op. 11, No. 3. It consists of several contrasting sections that are bound together into a pronounced expressive contour— here a great rise of intensity that reaches its climax in measure 27, where the voice lights upon a high F, after which the curve then quickly falls back to its final cadence. The song has four sections that are set off from one another by differences in surface design and vocal style. In the first section (measures 1–15), the voice moves in the middle and low registers in a densely chromatic recitative. A succession of melodic fragments arises in the instruments, which creates a thin and sparse texture. In the second section (measures 16–19), on a text that describes the rise of the lily, the voice suddenly shifts into an expressive cantilena, moving in slow, even rhythms and soaring into the upper register. The instruments also change character, playing now with continuity but without a clearly melodic profile. The third section (measures 20–26) contains a flamboyant coloratura for the soprano, which leaps precipitously over its entire range, soaring above the instruments that mass into an ever thicker and busier texture. The final section (measures 26–30) begins with the memorable ascent in the voice up to the high F on the word *mystic,* which is sustained for some eight seconds at the dynamic level of quadruple piano and then tumbles downward to an exhausted conclusion.

There is no conventional motivic recurrence or development in the song, but, as in works beginning with Op. 11, No. 3, a subtle and highly varied return of small, nondistinctive motives may be occasionally heard. The harmonic dimension of the work is also fragmented, with virtually none of the systematically varied recurrences of collections of tones that were so typical of Schoenberg's atonal music before Op. 11, No. 3. Like this Piano Piece, the texture made by the instrumental parts is highly linearized, as the three instruments create streams of chords and fleeting lines that occasionally merge into large harmonies that have little consistency among themselves. The preference for triadic tetrachords apparent in the early atonal style is now almost totally abandoned in favor of larger collections.

Like *Erwartung* and the George songs, "Herzgewächse" is highly innovative in its expressive relationship to its text. A key to this dimension of the song is provided by the essay "Das Verhältnis zum Text," which appeared with the song in *Der blaue Reiter.*[11] This article, one of Schoenberg's most important, may have taken its origins from lectures on composition and aesthetics that he was delivering in 1911 and 1912 at the Stern Conservatory in Berlin, and it also stemmed from the composer's intense interest in the symbolist poetic style, especially as it was represented in works of George and Maeterlinck. Schoenberg's principal thesis in the essay is that a poem and its proper musical setting will reflect each other on an abstract level of meaning, but not necessarily on the superficial level of expressivity that most listeners perceive. Even if there is no apparent expressive correspondence between music and its text, a composition may still achieve the homogeneous unification of elements that is requisite in any genuine artwork, provided that text and music are congruent on a deep level.

It is important to bear in mind regarding "Das Verhältnis zum Text" that Schoenberg does not claim to have eliminated or even diminished the expressivity of his own recent music. In fact, the expressive word painting in "Herzgewächse," especially as the voice soars upward to depict the rise of the lily, could scarcely be more obvious. Schoenberg spoke in the essay only in the abstract about vocal music in which conventional expressivity might be diminished if a deeper relationship between music and poetic tone was established. In his later essay "Gesinnung oder Erkenntnis?" published in the 1926 *Jahrbuch* of Universal Edition, he returned to this issue to clarify his earlier remarks on expressivity, reassuring the reader that his own music from 1909 to 1912 (prior to *Pierrot lunaire*) was still expressive to the fullest measure. "In my essay 'The Relationship to the Text,'" he wrote, "I was perhaps the first to turn away from expressive music—theoretically, for the time being—very soon after my first steps into a new territory where I still used expression to the fullest extent, even if unconsciously."[12]

The theory put forward in "Das Verhältnis zum Text" most directly addresses the multidimensional structure of symbolist poetry, and it has special relevance to Maeterlinck's works, in which the symbolic content invites the reader to uncouple its realistic surface narrative from a more essential subtext created by dissociated images, symbols, and musical sonorities. Schoenberg's encounter with the poetry of George and Maeterlinck directed his attention to this deeper level of meaning and to its implications for music. Especially in "Herzgewächse" and *Pierrot lunaire,* the point of connection between the two arts was sound per se, the distinctive tone of instruments and voices and their varying combinations, which could be made to agree with the underlying sound that the composer intuited from the poem. Schoenberg's insight may well have come into focus when it did through his reading of Oppeln-Bronikowski's postface to Maeterlinck's *Gedichte* as he searched for a song text for Kandinsky's volume. Oppeln-Bronikowski emphasized the musical element in Maeterlinck's verse, quoting Verlaine's famous dictum from his "L'art poétique" concerning the goal of poetry—"de la musique avant toute chose." Equally important for Schoenberg's thoughts was Oppeln-Bronikowski's quotation of a passage from Novalis's *Fragmenten* that speaks to the division of meaning in a poem between a surface level that is dreamlike and incoherent and an underlying level that is essentially musical: "There are tales, like dreams, without coherence but with associations; poems like fragments made from the most diverse of things, purely from melodious and beautiful words, but without any sense and coherence, comprehensible at most in a few strophes. This true poetry can have broadly at most an allegorical sense and, like music, an indirect effect."[13]

This passage from Novalis made a definite impression upon Schoenberg. It underlies his thinking in "Das Verhältnis zum Text," and he also quoted it in the program notes to the premier performance of *Pierrot lunaire,* there in the context of his setting of symbolist poetry by Albert Giraud. In "Das Verhältnis zum Text" Schoenberg asserts the practical relevance for the composer of the music heard by Verlaine and Novalis in poetry, music that for Schoenberg was not just metaphor but also an actual tone or sound that a composer could imitate in the orchestration and harmony of a new work. "Herzgewächse" and *Pierrot lunaire* were his two most immediate applications of the theory, and gradually—in *Pierrot lunaire* and the Four Songs, Op. 22—he also diminished the surface expressivity of the music, leaving the instrumental and vocal sonority as the principal vehicle for expression of the text. The content of his letter of 16 November 1913 to Dehmel, already cited in chapter 3 of this book, comes from the ideas that crystallized in his thinking only in 1911: "I always approached your verse by understanding through sound, and I was thus successful in penetrating it mentally."[14] He returned to this insight often in his later writings about music and poetry. In his 1931 "Self-Analysis," for example, he described his first encounter with a new poem as awakening "an unnameable sense of a sounding and moving space."[15]

The practical effect of Schoenberg's theory upon "Herzgewächse" was in its instrumentation—no longer the piano or conventional orchestra, as in Schoenberg's earlier songs, but instead a small and highly diversified chamber ensemble of celesta, harp, and harmonium. The celesta and harp had appeared prominently in *Erwartung*, especially in the many passages that alluded to the moon. Since the foliage of Maeterlinck's "Herzgewächse" is also drenched in moonlight, Schoenberg may have returned to these two instruments for the same symbolic purposes as in the monodrama. The harmonium, used optionally in Schoenberg's Three Pieces for Chamber Orchestra, was evidently a substitute for the full orchestra, whose instruments it could imitate by its large number of registrations. In later works the composer often used the harmonium for the purpose of representing the essence of an orchestra. It was a distinctive voice in the chamber orchestra that performed in concerts of his Verein für Musikalische Privataufführungen, where arrangements of music originally for large orchestra were a staple of the repertory.

Pierrot lunaire, Op. 21

Shortly after completing "Herzgewächse," Schoenberg began a more monumental application of his theory of musical and poetic sound in *Pierrot lunaire*. His primary inspiration, as in "Herzgewächse," was a translation of modern French poetry. Early in 1912—the exact date is uncertain—he learned that a wealthy Leipzig actress named Albertine Zehme was prepared to offer him a handsome fee to compose melodramas based on poetry from Albert Giraud's anthology *Pierrot lunaire*. In 1892 the fifty poems of this collection had been published in an imaginative German translation by Otto Erich Hartleben (1864–1905, see Figure 6.1).[16] At a *Vortrags-Abend* in Berlin on 4 March 1911, Frau Zehme had already recited a selection of twenty-two of Hartleben's *Pierrot* translations, by adapting songs composed by Otto Vrieslander.[17] Now she wanted Schoenberg to write for her a set of original melodramas that drew upon the same poetic collection but were works that would be more attuned, as she told the composer, to her "distinctive style of performance."

Albertine Zehme (1857–1946) was the ideal Maecenas for the new project. Viennese by birth, she had already established a minor reputation as an actress on various German stages prior to her marriage in 1881 to a wealthy and prominent Leipzig attorney, Felix Zehme.[18] According to H. H. Stuckenschmidt, she had also studied music, being coached in Wagnerian roles by Cosima Wagner, but Edward Steuermann remembered her as "only as musical as the well-bred German ladies of the time."[19] Near the turn of the century, following the example of such prominent actors as Ernst von Possart and Ludwig Wüllner, Frau Zehme attempted to revive her stage career by reciting melodramas. In such pieces a poetic or dramatic reading alternated with or was accompanied by instrumental music. The possibilities in repertory for the aspiring reciter were virtually endless. Effective recitations could be made by joining almost any music to poetry, or the reciter could choose from a large number of original melodra-

Figure 6.1. Moritz Posener, cover drawing for the first edition of Albert Giraud's *Pierrot lunaire,* German translation by Otto Erich Hartleben (1892).

mas, including works by such contemporaries as Richard Strauss (*Enoch Arden* and *Das Schloss am Meere*) and Max von Schillings (*Das Hexenlied,* among other examples).[20] Another alternative, apparently used by Frau Zehme in her 1911 Berlin performance, was to transform lieder into melodramas simply by speaking the voice line or reducing the melody to an expressive singsong.

Expressivity was no doubt her strong suit as a reciter. An impassioned mode of delivery is evident in many anecdotes concerning her later renditions of Schoenberg's *Pierrot lunaire,* in which her emotiveness went far beyond the light tone that Schoenberg intended in the work. Steuermann, for example, remembered her as the "tragic-heroine" type. Her histrionic style is implicit in a note titled "Why I Must Speak These Songs," which she attached to the program of her Berlin performance in March 1911, when she evidently converted Vrieslander's *Pierrot lunaire* songs into recitations:

> The words that we speak should not solely lead to mental concepts, but instead their sounds should allow us to partake of their inner experience. To make

this possible we must have an unconstrained freedom of tone. None of the thousand vibrations should be denied to the expression of feeling. I demand tonal freedom, not thoughts!

The singing voice, that supernatural, chastely controlled instrument, ideally beautiful precisely in its ascetic lack of freedom, is not suited to strong eruptions of feeling—since even one strong breath of air can spoil its incomparable beauty.

Life cannot be exhausted by the beautiful sound alone. The deepest final happiness, the deepest final sorrow dies away unheard, as a silent scream within our breast, which threatens to fly apart or to erupt like a stream of molten lava from our lips. For the expression of these final things it seems to me almost cruel to expect the singing voice to do such a labor, from which it must go forth frayed, splintered, and tattered.

For our poets and composers to communicate, we need both the tones of song as well as those of speech. My unceasing striving in search of the ultimate expressive capabilities for the "artistic experiences in tone" has taught me this fact.[21]

It was predictable that the poetry, not Zehme's expressive speech, would be Schoenberg's muse. The lyric verse in *Pierrot lunaire* flowed from the same robust vein of modern French literature that had already inspired several of Schoenberg's greatest atonal compositions. Its author was a Belgian, Albert Kayenbergh (1860–1929), who wrote under the pseudonym Albert Giraud. *Pierrot lunaire*, published in 1884, was his first important work. Its subject is the lively and fantastic world of Pierrot and the other "insolent clowns" who were his companions on the stage of the commedia dell'arte. Giraud coaxes his readers into their theater in the first poem, in which he hints that the ensuing scenes and adventures came to him in a delicious moonlit dream:

Théâtre	Theater
Je rêve un théâtre de chambre,	I dream of a little theater
Dont Breughel peindrait les volets,	Whose wings Breughel painted,
Shakespeare, les pâles palais,	Shakespeare, the faint palaces
Et Watteau, les fonds couleur d'ambre.	And Watteau the amber-colored backdrop.
Par les frileux soirs de décembre,	On shivering December nights,
En chauffant mes doigts violets,	Rubbing together my purple fingers,
Je rêve un théâtre de chambre,	I dream of a little theater
Dont Breughel peindrait les volets.	Whose wings Breughel painted.
Emoustillés par le gingembre,	Tantalized by ginger,
On y verrait les Crispins laids	The insolent clowns are seen
Ouater leurs décharnés mollets,	Stuffing their bony calves,
Pour Colombine qui se cambre.	For Colombine, who arches her back.
Je rêve un théâtre de chambre.[22]	I dream of a little theater.

The poems that follow are not especially unified in theme or voice. Some depict scenes from nature; others, fantastic visions lit by moonlight, images drawn from poetry and music, grotesque nightmares, or the ludicrous antics of Harlequin, Columbine, and Cassander. The poems that deal directly with Pierrot show him in his many incongruous stage roles—hero and fool, poet and philistine, whoremaster and swain, priest and sinner. In all of his adventures, the moon is his companion. Some of the poems—"La sérénade de Pierrot," "Pierrot cruel," and "Brosseur de lune"—are pure slapstick, as Giraud casts his hero in the traditional guise of buffoon. But Pierrot can take any role, from high priest in the temple of art ("L'église," "Évocation," "Messe rouge," "Les croix") to the homesick vagabond ("Nostalgie," "Parfums de Bergame," "Départ de Pierrot").

In the last poem, "Cristal de Bohême," Pierrot walks to the edge of the stage, removes his mask, and reveals his true identity as the author, Giraud, who then directly addresses the audience:

Cristal de Bohême	Bohemian Crystal
Un rayon de lune enfermé	A ray of moonlight closed up
Dans un beau flacon de Bohême,	In a flask of Bohemian crystal,
Tel est le féerique poème,	That's the magic poem
Que dans ces rondels j'ai rimé.	That I've set into these rondels.
Je suis en Pierrot costumé	I've dressed up as Pierrot
Pour offrir à celle que j'aime	To offer her whom I love
Un rayon de lune enfermé	A ray of moonlight closed up
Dans un beau flacon de Bohême.	In a flask of Bohemian crystal.
Par ce symbole est exprimé	By this symbol is expressed—
O ma très chère, tout moi-même:	O my dear one—everything that I am:
Comme Pierrot, dans son chef blême,	Just like Pierrot, with his floured head,
Je sens, sous mon masque grimé,	I carry under my mask and greasepaint
Un rayon de lune enfermé.[23]	A ray of moonlight closed up.

By donning the costume of Pierrot, Giraud allied his poetry with many other late-nineteenth-century literary adaptations of figures and themes from the commedia dell'arte, a conceit especially beloved of authors who, like Giraud, were associated with the French symbolist or Parnassian movements.[24] Susan Youens has shown that the Pierrot figure among late-nineteenth-century French writers was often a mask behind which stood many self-conscious artists such as Giraud, ready to express the bizarre landscapes of their inner world:

Pierrots were endemic everywhere in late nineteenth/early twentieth century Europe as an archetype of the self-dramatizing artist, who presents to the world a stylized mask both to symbolize and veil artistic ferment, to distinguish the creative artist from the human being. Behind the all-enveloping traditional costume of white blouse, white trousers, and floured face, the Pierrot-character changed with the passage of time, from uncaring prankster to romantic *malheueux* to Dandy, Decadent, and finally, into a brilliant, tormented figure submerged in a bizarre, airless inner world.[25]

Giraud's *Pierrot* also evoked the decadent atmosphere of French writers of the 1880s. As in Karl Huysmans's decadent masterpiece, the novel *À rebours,* the grotesquerie of *Pierrot* is never far removed from a trenchant humor and biting parody. These were the qualities that Schoenberg keenly wanted to preserve in his melodramas, which he described to Fritz and Erika Stiedry as conceived in a "light, ironic-satiric tone."[26] Giraud's imagination was also held in check by applying the strict poetic form of the thirteen-line rondel in every poem. His adaptation of this medieval pattern divides each poem into three strophes—of four, four, and five lines, respectively. The first two lines of each lyric reappear as a refrain in lines 7 and 8 and, reduced to the first line only, in line 13. Typically, the first two strophes paint a fantastic scene, always spun in richly figurative language. This is followed by an action sketched aphoristically in the last line group, in turn fantastic, lurid, or absurd.

After learning of Zehme's commission, Schoenberg scanned Hartleben's translation, which fired his composer's imagination. "Read the foreword, looked at the poems, am enthusiastic," he wrote in his diary on 28 January 1912. "Brilliant idea, just right for me."[27] Shortly before and possibly with the excitement of the new poetic discovery in mind he had written to Berg: "Why aren't you composing anything! You shouldn't let your talent rest so long. Write a few songs, at least. It's a good idea to let poetry lead you back into music."[28] When Schoenberg first read Hartleben's translations in January, he probably looked at a copy of the 1911 edition, which contained a foreword written by Franz Blei as well as an appendix with four of Vrieslander's *Pierrot* songs.[29] Blei drew attention to the character of Pierrot as a modern Everyman, as the "moonstruck cynic who wears a black veil over his red heart, the last grandchild of romantic irony, the supplicant with the most fragile modesty, the most chaste of lechers."[30]

Schoenberg's compositional manuscripts and the letters that he received from Zehme in 1912 paint a reasonably clear picture of the stages through which *Pierrot lunaire* came into existence.[31] Between late January 1912, when he decided to accept her commission, and 12 March, when he completed the first of the melodramas, the composer contemplated a general idea for his new work and negotiated with Zehme on an acceptable contract. But even when he began to compose, he had not settled upon a precise conception of the work as a whole. He was long undecided about the number of pieces that it should contain and their instrumentation, probably even uncertain whether they would form a cycle, like the George songs, or a looser suite of pieces, like Op. 16. Rather than first settling upon an overall plan, he plunged headlong into the work of composing, just as he had done in Opp. 15 and 16, apparently still confident that instinct would ultimately guide him to the correct overall conception.

At first his idea for the melodramas was influenced by Zehme's earlier *Pierrot* performance from March 1911. On that occasion she had selected twenty poems from Giraud's fifty and arranged them into three groups, each with a similar theme. She then framed the entirety by two additional poems, one functioning as an introduction and the other as a conclusion. "In creating my earlier program," she wrote to Schoenberg on 12 March, "I have followed a sort of struc-

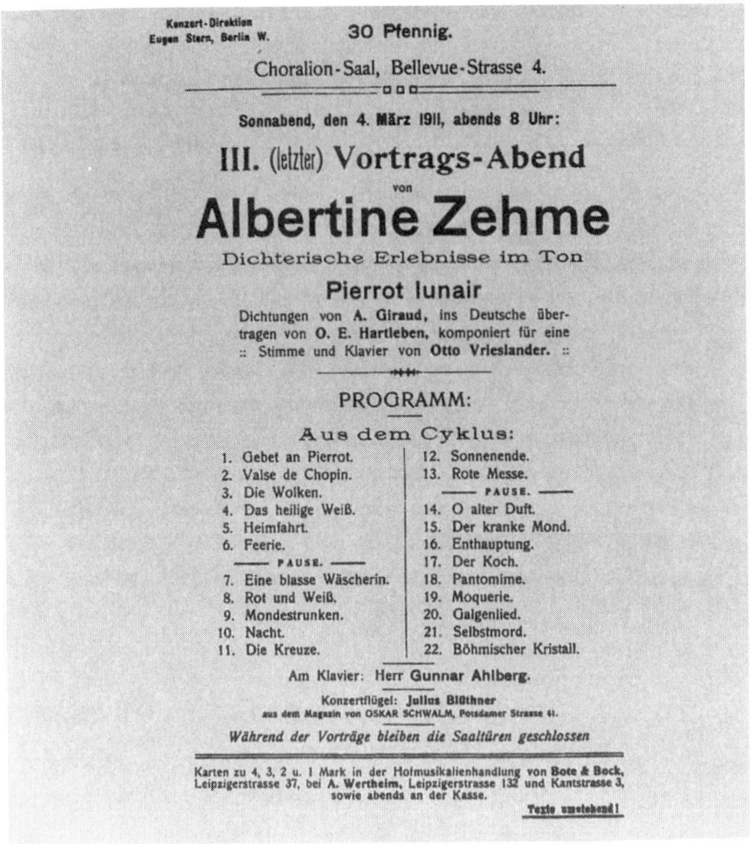

Konzert-Direktion
Eugen Stern, Berlin W.

30 Pfennig.

Choralion-Saal, Bellevue-Strasse 4.

Sonnabend, den 4. März 1911, abends 8 Uhr:

III. (letzter) Vortrags-Abend

von

Albertine Zehme

Dichterische Erlebnisse im Ton

Pierrot lunair

Dichtungen von **A. Giraud**, ins Deutsche übertragen von **O. E. Hartleben**, komponiert für eine :: Stimme und Klavier von **Otto Vrieslander**. ::

PROGRAMM:

Aus dem Cyklus:

1. Gebet an Pierrot.
2. Valse de Chopin.
3. Die Wolken.
4. Das heilige Weiß.
5. Heimfahrt.
6. Feerie.

PAUSE.

7. Eine blasse Wäscherin.
8. Rot und Weiß.
9. Mondestrunken.
10. Nacht.
11. Die Kreuze.
12. Sonnenende.
13. Rote Messe.

PAUSE.

14. O alter Duft.
15. Der kranke Mond.
16. Enthauptung.
17. Der Koch.
18. Pantomime.
19. Moquerie.
20. Galgenlied.
21. Selbstmord.
22. Böhmischer Kristall.

Am Klavier: Herr **Gunnar Ahlberg.**

Konzertflügel: **Julius Blüthner**
aus dem Magazin von OSKAR SCHWALM, Potsdamer Strasse 41.

Während der Vorträge bleiben die Saaltüren geschlossen

Karten zu 4, 3, 2 u. 1 Mark in der Hofmusikalienhandlung von **Bote & Bock**, Leipzigerstrasse 37, bei **A. Wertheim**, Leipzigerstrasse 132 und Kantstrasse 3, sowie abends an der Kasse.

Texte umstehend!

Figure 6.2. From the program brochure for Albertine Zehme's evening of recitations of *Pierrot lunaire*, 4 March 1911.

ture that you will see."[32] Schoenberg subsequently kept Zehme's threefold grouping of texts, although he made them symmetrical with seven poems in each. He also preserved Zehme's notion of crafting a poetic narrative out of Giraud's loosely organized verses, although the cycle that Schoenberg created was distinctively his own.

The poems that Zehme chose for her 1911 evening are shown in Figure 6.2, which is a reproduction of the first page of the printed program for that occasion.[33] In place of Hartleben's first poem ("Eine Bühne"), she substituted "Gebet an Pierrot" for her own introduction, which established a light tone for what was to follow. In this poem the speaker pleads with Pierrot to return her laughter, which has long been lost to her. Zehme kept as her own concluding number Giraud's final poem, "Böhmischer Krystall," in which the author confesses to having dressed up as Pierrot and carried moonlight in his heart and mind. From this text Zehme probably derived the idea of reciting the poetry in Pierrot costume, which she also did when she performed Schoenberg's cycle. This was a practice the composer did not agree with but had to tolerate. His reservations are understandable, since he did not use "Böhmischer Krystall" in his own *Pierrot lunaire* and since most of the poems that he chose are about Pierrot rather than spoken by him. Still, Giraud confirms in "Böhmischer Krystall" that his own voice, disguised as that of Pierrot, is the one that is heard throughout the entire poetic collection, and it is not implausible for the speaker to impersonate the clown.

As Zehme told Schoenberg, the content of each of her three segments had a consistency of theme and tone. Her first part, following the introduction provided by "Gebet an Pierrot," contains five poems in a relatively happy mood. These project images of nature filled with light and color—clouds are colorful flashing fish, the whiteness of the swan and the snow is a symbol of purity, and colorful birds sit like jewels on huge olive branches. In the second part, darkness has descended upon the world, and monstrous images loom up in a series of lurid and erotic nightmares. In the concluding third part, death is the central image and the moon is its agent, alternately a deathbed, an executioner's sword, and the white robe that Pierrot wears as he hangs himself.

Zehme was never able to provide Schoenberg with a published edition of Hartleben's *Pierrot* poetry, which was evidently hard to come by even after a new edition had appeared in 1911. On 5 February, the day after she first met the composer at a matinee concert of his music in Berlin, Zehme sent him one of her 1911 printed programs, in which the full texts of her twenty-two poems were reproduced. To this she added a typescript that contained three additional verses she especially liked. "Here are *all* the texts from Pierrot lunair [*sic*] that are possible," she instructed. "We will need about 22–24 for an evening. You can still leave out this one or that if it doesn't suit you."[34] Later, probably after he had begun to compose the work, Zehme sent the composer a handwritten copy of the complete contents of Hartleben's *Pierrot*, in a manuscript that Schoenberg would then use as his principal textual source for the remainder of the cycle. But the order in which he composed the melodramas was still guided by the contents of Zehme's 1911 presentation. Schoenberg first composed "Gebet an Pierrot," which was also her earlier opening number; next came "Der Dandy," which was not on her 1911 program but one that she specifically requested in a letter to the composer on 12 March and which may well have been included in the typewritten text (now apparently lost) that she had sent him on 5 February. Schoenberg then moved on to "Mondestrunken," "Der kranke Mond," "Eine blasse Wäscherin," and "Rote Messe," all contained in Zehme's earlier program. Only in late April, when he composed "Serenade" and "Gemeinheit," did he definitely depart from her selection and begin to establish his own narrative structure for the cycle as a whole.

In his own arrangement of Hartleben's poems, Schoenberg retained some elements of Zehme's narrative progression from lightness, to darkness, to death, but he transformed them into a personalized narrative of the plight of the artist in society. Into his first part he placed seven poems that describe Pierrot as a poet whose muse is the moon. Moonlight can transform reality, much as art does. In this group Pierrot plays the confident artist, and the moon has become art itself. Pierrot preens in front of a mirror lit by moonlight, he sprinkles the moon's flowers on the hair of his beloved, and he greedily laps up the inspiring wine that the moon pours down upon him.

But in the second group of seven poems, his life as artist has become a ghoulish nightmare. He is a craven grave robber, a demented priest who literally wears his heart upon his sleeve, and art has become his tormentor, before which he cowers in fear. In the final seven poems Pierrot is reduced to the level of a sad-sack buffoon. He tries unsuccessfully to wipe off the spot of moonlight that marks him as an artist, but he finds that fate has permanently cast him in this role. He can only dream nostalgically of a more peaceful time and a return to his happy youth and hope for reconciliation with his fate.

Schoenberg thus reconstituted Giraud's poetry to create a parable concerning the destiny of the artist in a hostile society, an autobiographical narrative, to be sure, and one that was related to the story that he had recently crafted in the drama *Die glückliche Hand.* In a note of December 1916 addressed to Zemlinsky, he explicitly interpreted Pierrot as the modern artist *maudit,* perceived by his fellowmen alternately as a ludicrous clown or as a dangerous pervert, aspiring to respectability but capable of no more in life than chasing after moonbeams:

> It is banal to say that we [artists] are all moonstruck fools; what the poet means is that we are trying our best to wipe off the imaginary moon spots from our clothing at the same time that we worship our crosses. [In Hartleben's "Die Kreuze" poems are said to be the crosses on which the poet is hung to receive the derision of society.] Let us be thankful that we have our wounds [from the cross]: With them we have something that helps us to place a low value on matter. From the scorn for our wounds comes our scorn for our enemies and our power to sacrifice our lives to a moonbeam. One could easily get emotional by thinking about the Pierrot poetry. But for the cuckoo is anything more important than the price of grain?[35]

Even before this autobiographical narrative was firmly in his mind, Schoenberg began to compose. On 10 March he signed a contract with Frau Zehme, agreeing that there would be at least twenty melodramas (she preferred several more) and these would use an accompaniment of piano, with the option of adding two more instruments (Schoenberg was probably thinking of clarinet and flute or piccolo at this point). In a burst of enthusiasm he then composed "Gebet an Pierrot" on 12 March, feeling a return to the powerful instinctive and unconscious creativity that he had not known since the time of the Busoni manifesto in 1909 and 1910. "The sounds here are virtually a direct, animal-like expression of sensual and spiritual movements. Almost as though everything is being transmitted directly," he wrote exuberantly in his diary on 13 March.

His readiness to compose was slightly delayed by a trip to Prague in late March, after which he began to work in earnest. During the months of April and May virtually the entire set of twenty-one melodramas was composed, duplicating the burst of creativity that he had achieved in 1909. The pieces were written down in a first full draft, then immediately recopied and sent piecemeal to Steuermann, who took them to Frau Zehme to be rehearsed and recopied. By the end of May only "Gemeinheit" and "Die Kreuze" still needed to be completed.[36] But even as Schoenberg neared the end of the work, he was still undecided about its exact overall form. This is apparent from a letter that he wrote to Emil Hertzka on 20 June, in which he described the new composition:

> It is called *Pierrot lunair* [*sic*] (after Albert Giraud, translated by Otto Erich Hartleben): *Melodrama Cycle with Accompaniment of Piano, Flute (Picc.), Clar. (Bass Clar.), Violin (Viola) and Cello* (5 players). . . . Every piece has a different instrumentation!!! There are 2 solos (1. piano 2. flute alone!!!), 4 duets, 7 trios, 4 quartets, 5 quintets. 22 pieces in all. (There may be one more yet to come!)[37]

By referring to twenty-two pieces, Schoenberg was apparently counting one or two of the instrumental interludes as separate numbers, and his description of the different ensembles is also difficult to reconcile with the instrumentation of the final version. Despite this indecision, he pressed ahead and on 9 July completed "Die Kreuze," probably the one additional number that he had mentioned to Hertzka. But even as late as 13 July Zehme complained that she had not been informed of the order in which the twenty-one numbers were to be performed. On that day she wrote to Schoenberg: "I very much need the final order. It is important for me inwardly to adapt to the order. I have the draft, but you said that this was not definitive."[38]

Even as Zehme wrote this letter, Schoenberg was finalizing the overall form of the work. He first needed to assemble the numbers into an order that would best convey his statement about the artist in an alien society, no simple matter given the great diversity in theme and tone in the twenty-one texts that he had chosen from Hartleben's collection. Schoenberg also added to the work an element of numerical symbolism based on threes and sevens, which he expressed in the cycle primarily by the organization of the melodramas into three groups of seven each, as well as by other more symbolic gestures.[39] Finally, he reinforced the connectedness of the pieces by increasing the number of interludes. He had already used short linking passages between Nos. 19–20 and 20–21, and shortly after 9 July he added similar connectives between Nos. 5–6, 10–11, 13–14, 15–16, and 17–18.[40] Edward Steuermann later reported that the last music to be composed was the interlude between Nos. 13 and 14, although he did not give it a precise date.[41] On 25 July Schoenberg—residing for the summer in Carlshagen on the Baltic—shipped a manuscript to Zehme that probably contained the final version of *Pierrot,* with the order established and with all of the interludes at last in place. Rehearsals with the full ensemble began in late August and culminated in the premier performance in Berlin on 16 October 1912, followed by a month-long tour of eight German cities. The work was first published by Universal Edition in the summer of 1914.[42]

The cycle opens in "Mondestrunken" with an image of the moon pouring down its intoxicating light upon the poet, an idea that Schoenberg depicts by an ostinato made from a descending motive (shown in Example 6.1a) and by the crystalline sonority of piano, muted violin, and flute. Just at the point where the

Example 6.1. Schoenberg, *Pierrot lunaire*: (a) Central motive (No. 1, measure 1, piano); (b) No. 11, measure 21, piano; (c) No. 12, measure 9, viola; (d) No. 19, measures 25–26, cello

poet is first mentioned (measure 29), the cello, Schoenberg's instrument, enters with a broad and expressive melody. In the second melodrama ("Columbine"), Pierrot sings to Columbine—Harlequin's mistress in the commedia dell'arte— accompanied by a romantically saccharine cadenza in the violin. All of his hopeless yearning, he says, would be assuaged if only he could scatter blooms of moonlight into her hair. His heartache is quickly forgotten in No. 3 ("Der Dandy"), in which he plays the fop, accompanied shrilly in a mock polka by piccolo and clarinet amid brittle mincing in the piano, as he primps before a mirror aglitter with moonlight. In No. 4 ("Eine blasse Wäscherin") the moon itself is the subject. Its pale visage resembles that of a nocturnal washerwoman who is portrayed by hushed and expressionless chords whose placidity is disrupted only in measures 8–11 by a stealthy rhythmic breeze. In No. 5, "Valse de Chopin," the heavy sumptuousness of the waltz becomes overripe and sick with thick "chords of wild lust." An interlude leads directly to No. 6, "Madonna," in which the decadent tones of the Chopin waltz have grown menacing. Now art is the altar of the Pietà, toward which the Madonna approaches carrying the bloodied body of Christ, her even steps measured out in the cello. After she reaches the altar and following a pause, Schoenberg raises his own voice in an instrumental accompaniment that is wrathfully fragmented, its anger directed at the masses who have turned their eyes away from art and refuse even to witness the crimes that they have committed. The composer's rancor is temporarily stilled in the final number of part 1, "Der kranke Mond," as the flute in its breathy lowest register impersonates the moon on its deathbed, swollen and feverish from love, while mankind again pitilessly ignores its distress.

Darkness descends upon the world at the outset of part 2. In No. 8, "Nacht— passacaglia" the bass instruments and piano in its lowest register growl in a menacing and relentless passacaglia, as gigantic butterflies float to earth, blotting out the sun. "Gebet an Pierrot"—No. 9 although the first of the melodramas to be composed—offers a brief respite from the descent into nightmare. On its heels is "Raub," No. 10, in which Pierrot and his drunken comrades tiptoe into a tomb, accompanied by staccato woodwinds and col legno strings, planning to steal gems but quickly fleeing in fear. The centerpiece of the cycle is reached in No. 11, "Rote Messe." To an unearthly piano ostinato and groaning chords in the other instruments, the poet tears out his heart and offers it up as host in a "gruesome Eucharist" to the worship of art. The summit of intensity is reached at the final chord, which encompasses all twelve tones and recalls the similarly dense harmonies that Schoenberg used as climactic markers in *Die glückliche Hand* and *Erwartung.*

The last three poems of part 2 speak of Pierrot's execution. He first will die on the gallows, which has taken the shape of a scrawny whore destined to be his last embrace. Next he is assailed by the moon itself, transformed by Pierrot's febrile and craven imagination into a scimitar. Finally and most ruthlessly he is killed by his own art, which has become a cross on which he is crucified by a vengeful public. The first part of this miniature trilogy, "Galgenlied" (No. 12), is the shortest number in the whole cycle, a whirl of ever-increasing motion ended by an ominous fall in the piccolo as Pierrot drops to his death on the gallows. In "Enthauptung" (No. 13) the music masses into a thicket of sixteenth-note lines as Pierrot cowers in panic anticipating the blow of the moon's fearful blade. In the climactic "Die Kreuze," the last melodrama to be completed, the vile rabble crucifies the artist, although again Schoenberg's own defiant voice is heard in the piano's solo—so bold and complex as to make plain that the composer will not quietly suffer the fate that the people have inflicted upon him.

Part 3 of *Pierrot lunaire* dwells upon ideas of nostalgia and buffoonery, all that is left to the artist after his crucifixion. The seven melodramas in this part return to more traditional formal and expressive principles, manipulating style as he had already done in the Orchestra Piece, Op. 16, No. 2 (*Vergangenes*), and Piano Pieces, Op. 19. Motivic development, which has little importance in the cycle to this point, again becomes prominent; repetitive forms return, and strict counterpoint is revived. Allusions to tonality, almost entirely banished in the first two parts of the cycle, now return in No. 18 (which refers to E$^\flat$ as a central tone) and No. 21 (E is the mock tonic). The orchestration of the third part is also more orchestral than the earlier two parts, tending to use the full ensemble rather than smaller subdivisions.

In "Heimweh," No. 15, Pierrot has become "wooden" and "modishly sentimental." Suddenly he hears the voice of his past, represented by motives in the piano and violin whose insistent return finally unleashes his yearning for his homeland. But before acting upon his nostalgia he still must play out his role as clown. In No. 16 ("Gemeinheit") he indulges in a prank at the expense of Cassander, who for Schoenberg must have represented the music critic. For such people no amount of derision or abuse was too much. Accompanied by a mechanical sixteenth-note motive at first in the cello, Pierrot bores a hole into Cassander's head, fills it with tobacco, and smokes it like a pipe. In No. 17 ("Parodie") an old duenna sits in a bower waiting passionately for the arrival of her lover, Pierrot, while the moon sets the knitting needles in her hair aglitter. Schoenberg's musical parody is exceedingly subtle as he constructs a complex series of canons. In each, a following voice mocks the leading voice by imitating it in inversion, just as the moon derides the old woman's passion. Strict counterpoint is also present in No. 18 ("Der Mondfleck") to accompany another of the moon's pranks. Seeking fortune and adventure, Pierrot has set out wearing his black coat, unaware that the moon has stained it with a spot of light. Finally he turns and sees the spot, but he can only continue on in dismay, trying all the while to rub it off. A canon between the two strings depicts his futile rubbing, and just at the point when he turns to find the spot, the music in both woodwinds and strings turns around and continues to the end in a retrograde of the first half. Schoenberg's parody is broader still in No. 19, "Serenade," as Pierrot practices raucously on his viola, creating music that Schoenberg transforms into an egotistical and maudlin waltz for cello and piano. The music critic Cassander again arrives to complain about the noise, and Pierrot rudely grabs him by the collar and continues his serenade by playing on Cassander's bald head.

In the final two numbers, "Heimfahrt" and "O alter Duft," the memories of Pierrot's Italian homeland awakened in No. 15 now transport him back in time. Although Schoenberg completed "O alter Duft" fully three weeks after "Heimfahrt," he may have conceived of these two as a pair, linked by both a connective interlude and a similar motive made from parallel motion in thirds, the latter plainly representing Pierrot's nostalgia for an earlier time. "O alter Duft" is spoken in the first person, presumably by Pierrot as he finds peace by recalling bygone joys. Schoenberg's own voice, his own nostalgia, is also apparent as the music returns to the early style of atonality—filled with motivic development and reprises that are easily followed, a chordal vocabulary that is based on the triad, even with allusions to a centric triad on E.

Despite this heartfelt conclusion, the score of *Pierrot* is pervaded with irony, sarcasm, and parody, as Schoenberg's music very often comments rather than expresses itself directly. This is a different role for music from the one that it plays in Schoenberg's songs, in which the composer speaks with the same voice as the poet, underscoring his romantic pathos as something genuine, something that can be heightened by music. Here, to the contrary, Pierrot's voice is satirized by that of the composer. The satire is accomplished, first, by moving the burden of expressivity almost fully to the instruments. "Everything of musical importance happens in the instruments," Schoenberg wrote.[43] Their music comments upon the poetry and its recitation, mainly by ironic allusions to existing musical styles and forms. Their tendency to sarcasm is periodically interrupted by the composer's own forthright musical protests, as in Nos. 6 and 14, or confessions, as in No. 21. In his Foreword to the published score (1914) Schoenberg alerted the instrumentalists to their atypical role as commentators rather than impersonators:

> Here the performers never have the duty of shaping the mood and character of the individual pieces from the sense of the words, instead, solely from the music itself. To the extent that the composer considered word painting of feelings and

events in the text to be important, these are found in the music. If the performer notes their absence, he should guard against adding what the composer did not intend. Here he should not give, only take.[44]

An analysis of this ironic element has characterized the recent critical literature on *Pierrot lunaire.* In his 1973 dissertation Alan Lessem set the tone for several later interpretive studies when he held that Schoenberg's music could not be taken at face value since it amounted to a "mimic [of] the play of surface qualities and stylistic mannerisms drawn from the musical traditions of the past, including those that had been taken up in his earlier music." Ultimately *Pierrot* is a parody, Lessem concluded, from which the composer "holds himself aloof."[45] Reinhold Brinkmann considerably extended this line of thought, calling attention to the web of musical allusions.[46] In the score of *Pierrot,* Brinkmann contends, Schoenberg constructed a "historical representation of the problem of the artist in the modern period" by means of a "specific musical speech and specific formal ideas realized musically." The music itself thus wears a theatrical mask, uttering tones that are always modified by the sense of "as though": "In this perspective *Pierrot* is a critical-contemporary statement, not just a piece of music, not just music about music, but music about the past and present at the end of the 19th and the beginning of the 20th centuries: formulated from the modern standpoint."[47]

Perhaps because he spoke with such a mixture of voices in *Pierrot,* Schoenberg was all the more intent upon unifying the work as a cycle. The poetic narrative was his principal tool of consolidation, and, despite piecemeal creation of the melodramas, he also found important musical elements to bind its parts more firmly together. These include instrumental interludes between pieces, certain recurrent motivic shapes, the highly distinctive speaking voice itself, and a resourcefully coherent orchestrational plan. Even in the early stages of composition Schoenberg included preludes, interludes, and postludes within several of the individual numbers, in which they served primarily to clarify the divisions in Giraud's poems. Later in the creation of the work, he decided to link Nos. 19–20 and 20–21 as pairs, which he accomplished by adding instrumental interludes between them and, in the latter pair, by using a common motive made from parallel thirds. These two interludes, as well as interlude No. 17–18, have a similar structure, which firmly connects the two surrounding melodramas by incorporating materials from both. They each contain a first part that extends or recapitulates motives from the earlier number of the pair, then a distinct second part that forecasts a prominent motive in the following number. Most of the other interludes solely extend the melodrama that has just concluded, by continuing or recapitulating its motives.

The function of interlude No. 13–14 is unique in the cycle. Its length of fifteen measures is the greatest of any of these passages, making it the most like a separate number. It is also distinctive in that it overtly brings back passages from earlier in the work—the flute melody and recitation from No. 7 ("Der kranke Mond")—which are recapitulated in an abbreviated and transformed shape. It is far from clear why Schoenberg inserted such a striking recapitulation at just this point in the cycle. The recurrence may be intended to draw attention to similar personifications of the moon in "Der kranke Mond" and "Enthauptung," or it may be Schoenberg's superstitious glance over his shoulder following the thirteenth number. But these reasons are pure speculation.

One of the sketches for *Pierrot lunaire* suggests that Schoenberg may have contemplated an intricate network of motivic recurrences in the interludes, of which only the one in interlude No. 13–14 was left in the final version.[48] This undated sketch contains three measures of music for flute, clarinet, violin, cello, and piano—the same ensemble as in the postlude to No. 14 and interlude No. 20–21–and it may well have been originally intended as one of these passages, later to be discarded. Reinhold Brinkmann has shown that the music in the sketch is built entirely from motives heard elsewhere in the cycle, specifically from Nos. 1, 4, 6, 7, 8, 14, 15, and 16. But in Schoenberg's final version of *Pierrot*, except for the return of the flute melody in interlude No. 13–14, there are virtually no distinctive motivic recurrences that overtly link the different melodramas and interludes.

A sixteenth-note figure presented in ostinato in the piano part at the outset of No. 1 shares its rhythmic profile and contour with numerous other motives throughout the cycle, although it cannot be concluded definitively that the composer intended these relatively undistinctive similarities to constitute significant unifying gestures. When the figure first arises in "Mondestrunken" (Example 6.1a) it depicts the waves of moonlight that, like wine, pour down upon the poet. Selected later appearances of the figure are illustrated in Example 6.1bcd, none of which has exactly this referential context or the strongly whole-tone flavor of the original. Still, the listener easily notes the many recurrences of its rhythmic-metric profile. Jonathan Dunsby has aptly described the figure as a "principal rhythm" to which Schoenberg freely alluded throughout the cycle. "It could be repeated, expanded, contracted, added to, truncated, counterpointed against itself, and—what is most important—set either to repeated pitches or to any number of pitch 'shapes,'" he concludes.[49]

The unity of *Pierrot* is also promoted by the sonorous image of the speaking voice—one of Schoenberg's most original ideas but also one that has posed an enduring and perhaps insoluble interpretive enigma for the performer. Like many other innovations associated with the atonal style, the voice part in *Pierrot lunaire* is based on a late-nineteenth-century idea that Schoenberg transformed in an entirely original way. Near the turn of the twentieth century, several German composers of melodrama experimented with new approaches to recitation, especially by fixing its rhythm and pitch rather than leaving these to a speaker's relatively free delivery. The first important step in this new style of recitation was made in 1897 by Engelbert Humperdinck in his melodrama *Königskinder*. Its voice part, said by Humperdinck to be "controlled" (*gebunden*), was precisely notated in rhythm and pitch, using crosses to replace note heads but otherwise standard in vocal notation.[50] Exactly what Humperdinck intended by this mixed style of delivery is not always clear, although his notation suggests a recitation that was partly singsong and partly sustained or elevated speech. The failure of *Königskinder* in the eyes of the critics cast doubt on the practicalities of Humperdinck's controlled melodrama, and later composers in the genre, such as Strauss and Schillings, returned to freer modes of coordination between voice and accompaniment.

But Schoenberg enthusiastically adopted and extended Humperdinck's concept. Shortly after *Königskinder,* he composed a melodrama that used Humperdinck's notation in part 3 of *Gurrelieder,* in a passage where the speaker describes the impatient quest of the west wind. Schoenberg returned to the style in *Pierrot lunaire* and in the contemporaneous choral music in *Die glückliche Hand,* as well as in numerous later works, although in *Pierrot* Schoenberg's conception of the speaking voice had evolved far beyond the conventional recitation in *Gurrelieder* to become a melodic entity sui generis.

Schoenberg called the new vocal style of *Pierrot* speaking melody (*Sprechmelodie*). Unlike a work such as *Erwartung,* whose singing part Schoenberg said was specifically composed with the voice of Marie Gutheil-Schoder in his ear,[51] *Pierrot lunaire* was probably written with no specific singer or speaker in mind. It was instead an outcome of the experimental spirit of the atonal style—its reaching out into the unknown, extending the idiom into new genres, establishing connections with new ideas of sound and expression. This exploration in sound and expressivity is closely connected to the new mixture of resources that characterizes *Die glückliche Hand,* in which Schoenberg wished to "make music with the elements of the stage."[52] In *Pierrot* he wanted to "make music with words" ("musizieren mit Worten"), to use a description by Steuermann that may well have originated with the composer himself.[53] Alan Lessem has described this phenomenon as the result of the composer's "determination to absorb speech into music."[54]

The element of experimentation present in the recitation of *Pierrot* is apparent in Schoenberg's many conflicting statements about it, especially about its tonal content. In a letter to Berg dated 14 January 1913 and excerpted in Berg's *Gurrelieder Führer* published in the same year, Schoenberg underscored its songlike quality, which made it different from the similarly notated although more recitational melodrama in *Gurrelieder.* "Regarding the melodramas in the *Gurrelieder:* pitch is by no means to be taken as literally here as in the *Pierrot* melodramas," he wrote. "By no means should a similar songlike *Sprechmelodie* be created here."[55] But in the Foreword to the first edition of the score, written about a year after his letter to Berg, he says that a songlike interpretation in *Pierrot* should be avoided above all:

> The melody indicated by notes in the part of the speaker (with certain specially indicated exceptions) is *not* intended to be sung. The performer has the task of transforming it into a *speech melody* by a careful rendition of the indicated pitches. He can do this by
> I. keeping to the rhythm just as precisely as he would when singing, i.e., with no more freedom than he would take in a sung melody;
> II. being quite conscious of the difference between a *sung tone* and a *spoken tone*: the sung tone maintains its pitch without change, the spoken tone touches upon it but then leaves it immediately by descending or ascending. The per-

former must always be on guard against falling into a "singing" manner of speech. That is absolutely not intended. But neither should he aim for a realistic-natural speech. Quite the opposite, there should always be a clear difference between customary speech and speech that contributes to a musical effect. But this should never remind one of song.[56]

Beyond such technical exigencies, Schoenberg attached the greatest importance in the speaker's part to achieving a certain mood and tone—serious to the point of tragedy but still animated, having a certain lightness, and stripped of all pathos. These were the objectives that he wanted accomplished when Erwin Stein led performances of the work in 1921 with the Verein für Musikalische Privataufführungen. Following Stein's thirty-seventh solo rehearsal with the speaker, Erika Stiedry-Wagner, he wrote to Schoenberg: "Above all: what she does is genuine, without sentimentality and pathos and singsong. Perhaps occasionally too elegant, the seriousness not sufficiently cold, the tragedy not overwhelmingly large. But both are there. And when you wrote that everything had to remain 'allegretto' I took it to mean that *these* qualities were not to be overplayed."[57]

An important component in Schoenberg's overall plan for the work was its instrumentation, whose conception developed only gradually as the work progressed. In order to conform to Zehme's wishes, Schoenberg initially thought of using only a piano in the accompaniment, but even before composing the first melodrama he had decided to add two other instruments—probably clarinet and piccolo/flute—and he soon found the need also for violin and cello. In its final form, the instrumental ensemble includes piano (which plays in all but four of the melodramas), flute doubling on piccolo, clarinet doubling on bass clarinet, violin doubling on viola, and cello. No two of the melodramas have exactly the same sound, a diversity accomplished by constant changes in the makeup of the ensembles and by the use of mutes, instrumental doublings, and a brief exchange between A and B♭ clarinet. In four of the melodramas—Nos. 1, 2, 6, and 14—the ensemble is increased in size midway through.

"*Color* is *everything*, the notes mean *absolutely nothing*," Schoenberg told Hertzka.[58] Although he was certainly exaggerating in this statement, Schoenberg wanted to revive in *Pierrot* the coloristic *Buntheit* that he had praised in the Busoni manifesto of 1909. The flexibility of orchestration produced many opportunities for word painting, as when the cello in "Serenade" evokes Pierrot's raucous viola playing, and for parodistic allusions to earlier music, such as the baroque trio sonata texture in "Madonna." The cello is treated in a special manner throughout, suggesting that Schoenberg used it—as he also did in *Die glückliche Hand*—as his personal symbol. His emphasis on variegation also coaxed him to return to certain coloristic experiments from 1909. In Nos. 3, 11, 14, and 15 he revives the piano harmonics that he had used in Op. 11, No. 1, and in the "Valse de Chopin" he returns to the concept of "obbligato recitative"— fragmentary melodic phrases constantly passed from instrument to instrument— that he had used in the Orchestra Piece, Op. 16, No. 5, there, too, in the context of a waltz.

Schoenberg may also have been influenced in the choice of a small heterogeneous ensemble that accompanies speaking voice by the song style of cabaret, although he never mentioned cabaret as influential upon his thinking in the work. Certainly the performance medium of *Pierrot*, the presence of a central figure impersonating a clown, and an ambience rich with *guignol* decadence and satiric masks would have suggested cabaret to its early listeners. The *Sprechgesang* could only have heightened this similarity, to the extent that it evoked the singsong delivery of a cabaret diseuse like Yvette Guilbert or Marya Delvard, the latter almost certainly familiar to Schoenberg from her performances at the Viennese cabarets Fledermaus and Nachtlicht. The ambience of Delvard's cabaret act was especially relevant to early performances of *Pierrot lunaire*, forecasting both its grotesquerie and its distinctive staging. "Marya Delvard sings in the green light of child murder," wrote Alfred Kerr, after hearing her in Berlin in 1904. Her melody, Kerr reported, was "a singsong accompanied by some few instruments. The performer stands separately, in front of a grey cloth."[59] A reviewer for *Musical America* at the first performance of *Pierrot lunaire* paints a similar picture: "At the performance in question a high green screen stretched across the whole front of the stage. A panel in the center of the screen was set back a couple of feet, leaving an opening at one side. The musicians were to be concealed and the reader was to stand upon a small platform in this niche."[60]

Few generalizations are possible concerning the form of individual numbers in *Pierrot lunaire*. In most of the melodramas, Hartleben's rondels provide a loose framework for musical design, governing the placement of changes in tempo, texture, or other surface elements. But the textual refrains in each poem are not accompanied by musical refrains, and in many of the melodramas—Nos. 15 and 16 are examples—the musical divisions and recurrences appear with no apparent relevance to syntactic divisions in the poetry. The cycle is about equally divided into pieces that have motivic development and reprise and others that are athematic and open in form. Those with motivic work and concentric forms are most strongly represented in part 3 of the cycle, where they allude to Pierrot's nostalgia. The athematic model is more pronounced in those numbers that Schoenberg composed first, such as Nos. 1, 2, 4, and 7. These earlier melodramas were written hurriedly, relying on intuition rather than systematic construction, and work on them was supported with little in the way of sketching. Roughly midway through his period of work on the cycle, as he searched for new ways to make the music more subtly parodistic, Schoenberg began to compose in a more deliberate manner, using sketches and in some numbers highly methodical schemes of construction.

Three of the melodramas—"Nacht," "Parodie," and "Der Mondfleck"—fully dispense with the intuitive or unreflective approach to composition that Schoenberg had used since the summer of 1909 and return to a polyphonic organization whose strictness of planning goes far beyond that of his earlier atonal counterpoint, including the fugue in Op. 16, No. 1, and the free canon in Op. 16, No. 3. "Parodie" consists of a succession of canons in which the voice and all instruments except for the piano participate. "Mondfleck" is even stricter in its counterpoint, which makes for an ingenious depiction of the text. The two

stringed instruments play in canon at the octave, the two woodwinds construct
a fugue, and both pairs are laid out as palindromes that meet in the center of
the composition (measure 10), just where Pierrot turns around and notices a
spot of moonlight on his back. The piano works out its own three-voiced fugue,
whose subject duplicates in augmentation that of the woodwind's canon.[61]

For the future direction of form in Schoenberg's oeuvre, No. 8 ("Nacht—passacaglia") is the most important piece in *Pierrot lunaire.* Schoenberg often cited
it as the first step on his path toward twelve-tone composition. Like Nos. 17 and
18, it is a complex contrapuntal invention whose surface motions graphically
portray the text, which in "Nacht" speaks of giant butterflies that sink to earth
and relentlessly blot out the sun:

Nacht—passacaglia	Night—passacaglia
Finstre, schwarze Riesenfalter	Dark, black, giant butterflies
Töteten der Sonne Glanz.	Killed the sunshine.
Ein geschlossnes Zauberbuch,	The horizon rests like
Ruht der Horizont—verschwiegen.	A closed magic book—hidden.
Aus dem Qualm verlorner Tiefen	From the smoke of forgotten depths
Steigt ein Duft, Erinnrung mordend!	Wafts a fragrance, killing the memory!
Finstre, schwarze Riesenfalter	Dark, black, giant butterflies
Töteten der Sonne Glanz.	Killed the sunshine.
Und vom Himmel erdenwärts	And from heaven toward earth
Senken sich mit schweren Schwingen	Sink with heavy swinging
Unsichtbar die Ungetüme	The invisible monsters
Auf die Menschenherzen nieder . . .	Down upon the hearts of mankind . . .
Finstre, schwarze Riesenfalter.[62]	Dark, black, giant butterflies.

The first full draft of "Nacht" is dated 9 May 1912 at its beginning and 21 May
at its conclusion, placing it toward the end of Schoenberg's work on the cycle as
a whole. To judge from its manuscripts, the piece presented the composer with
numerous stumbling blocks, which he overcame only after second thoughts
and with the aid of sketching. One of the sketches, undated and seven measures
in length, contains what appears to be a false start, since it is unrelated to the
music that came later. There are four additional sketches, which show a gradual and hesitating realization of the final conception.[63]

Despite the ingenious and highly witty use of strict polyphony to express its
text, "Nacht" also embodies an abstract musical structure that is not dependent
on or even relevant to its words. It represents an important forerunner of a con-
structivist and antiexpressive outlook that became widespread in the musical
world only in the 1920s. Outwardly, the form of the piece is ternary, with the
three principal sections (beginning at measures 4, 11, and 17) marked off by
changes in tempo and general design and made to coincide with the three strophes of Hartleben's poem. In addition, "Nacht" is framed by an introduction
(measures 1–3, Example 6.2) and a closely related conclusion (measures

Example 6.2. Schoenberg, *Pierrot lunaire*, No. 8 ("Nacht—passacaglia"), measures 1–3

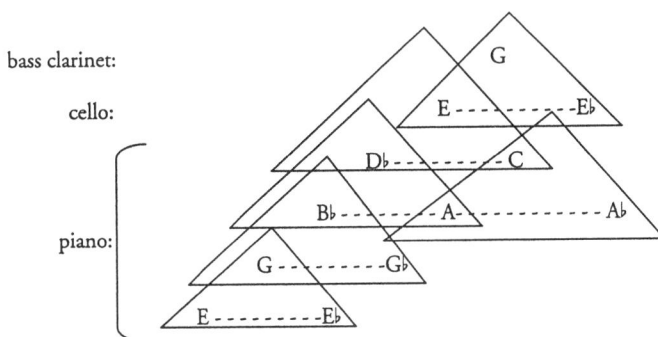

24–26). The contrapuntal structure of the work uses elements of canon, although the canonic sequences are all short-lived and quickly revert to free imitation and freely developing variation. A canon is worked out with reasonable strictness in the *A* section (measures 4–10)—engaging all four instrumental lines—although by measure 8 it begins to dissolve into developmental variations of motives. A second imitative sequence, now in three voices, is begun in measure 12, but this is even briefer and freer than before, and the subsequent imitations are all highly fragmented.[64] In sum, the work embodies a synthesis of strict compositional processes associated with imitative counterpoint and a freer idea of form inherited from Schoenberg's earlier techniques of developing variation. The synthesis that it represents became ever more pronounced in Schoenberg's music as he progressed toward the twelve-tone method of composing.

Schoenberg used the term *passacaglia* in the title of this piece to allude to the presence of continuous variations upon a small motive, first heard in the notes E G E♭ in measure 1. Example 6.2 shows the pattern by which the motive irradiates the texture of the first three measures. Notes are presented in the dia-

Example 6.3. Schoenberg, *Pierrot lunaire*, No. 8, measure 8, bass clarinet in B$^\flat$

gram at the bottom so as to clarify the existence of six superimposed lines, each created by a short, descending chromatic segment. The central three-note motive is deployed in an interlocking sequence of transpositions, each enclosed in the diagram in triangles. This trichord acts, first of all, as a linear figure—a motive—but it also functions as a cell whose proliferation unifies the texture vertically, thus systematically integrating the vertical and horizontal dimensions. Despite its pervasiveness, the central motive still allows for new and distinctive motives to grow from it. The chromatically descending line B$^\flat$–A–A$^\flat$ in the middle of the texture is especially important, as it later underlies the subjects of the canons that begin in measures 4 and 12.

The integration that Schoenberg obtained from this minute shape extended not only to the two-dimensional texture of the work but also to its temporal element. The latter process of integration begins in the bass clarinet part in measure 8 (Example 6.3), the point in the *A* section where the strict canon begins to dissolve. In this measure the clarinet states the basic trichord three times in succession, each at a different transpositional level and each covering the span of a half note. The trichord is also heard over the span of the entire measure, occurring as the first tones of each of the small figures (F$^\sharp$ A F) and also in their peak tones (A C A$^\flat$).

In his lecture "Komposition mit zwölf Tönen," from 1922 or 1923, Schoenberg looked back on "Nacht" as the first step in a new way of thinking about form in atonal music—systematic rather than intuitive, structured rather than free, and coolly objective rather than expressive. He pointed in the lecture especially to the unification of the whole texture of "Nacht" based on the first measure, which can be reduced to the basic motive itself as the crux from which the entire multidimensional work grows by developing variation and counterpoint:

> In the Passacaglia for the first time something was brought to use, even if still unclearly, that would be significant for future developments. . . . The development of the entering voices is derived from the possibilities of their sounding together with the main voice. The first measure is to be understood as the point of origin for all later events and also as a reduction of the whole; the content of this one measure is then deployed in both the vertical and horizontal dimensions. This idea is only fully realizable in twelve-tone composition.[65]

Schoenberg's view of "Nacht" as a forerunner of twelve-tone composition was only one of many considerations that would make *Pierrot lunaire* an important work in his own estimation. Throughout his life he mentioned it with pride, although immediately after he completed it he did not put as much stock in it as he later would. Shortly after he sent the final manuscript off to Albertine Zehme, he described the work to Kandinsky almost slightingly, saying that *Pierrot* achieved "no heartfelt necessity as regards it theme, its content (Giraud's *Pierrot lunaire*), but certainly as regards its form. In any case, remarkable for me as a preparatory study for another work, which I now wish to begin: Balzac's *Seraphita*."[66] But after hearing the work repeatedly on tour later in 1912 and, even more, when the new ideas in modern music of the 1920s began to emerge, Schoenberg's attitude toward *Pierrot lunaire* changed to one of satisfaction and pride. After reading Busoni's *Entwurf einer neuen Ästhetik der Tonkunst* in 1916 or shortly thereafter, he wrote into Busoni's book the entire flute melody of "Der kranke Mond" as an example of pure freedom in music, which could arise without the need for the new scalar systems that Busoni had proposed.[67] Later still, Schoenberg found in *Pierrot* a precursor of Neoclassicism, a style that emerged in the 1920s and quickly dominated modern music worldwide. *Pierrot*'s subtle and witty satire and its diminished expression of the words at their surface level seemed to Schoenberg to prefigure the objective detachment of language that was fashionable among composers of the 1920s. Although Schoenberg had the utmost disdain for Neoclassicism itself, he was plainly delighted by the thought that he was its forerunner. He wrote in 1949 in "This Is My Fault":

> In the preface to *Pierrot lunaire* I had demanded that performers ought not to add illustrations and moods of their own derived from the text. In the epoch after the First World War, it was customary for composers to surpass me radically, even if they did not like my music. Thus when I had asked not to add external expression and illustration, they understood that expression and illustration were out, and that there should be no relation whatsoever to the text.[68]

Four Songs for Voice and Orchestra, Op. 22

With *Pierrot* completed, Schoenberg turned his attention late in the summer of 1912 once again to *Die glückliche Hand,* whose progress remained slow, and also to a new project that foretold an important future direction. This was a "theater piece" based on Honoré de Balzac's novel *Séraphita* (1835), which Schoenberg had read during the preceding summer following an enthusiastic recommendation from Webern.[69] This and other religious works by Balzac had only recently appeared in German, translated by Gisele Etzel in a volume of Balzac's *Philosophische Erzählungen.*[70] By August 1912 Schoenberg's plan for the new work had begun to take shape—it would be a massive drama that consisted of nine scenes drawn from passages throughout the novel, and its music would span three evenings and call for a colossal orchestra and chorus.[71] Schoenberg's interest in Balzac's highly philosophical text marks an important moment in the composer's awakening to religion, a subject that will be discussed further in chapter 7. Musically the grandiose *Seraphita* scarcely got off the ground. On 27 December 1912, immediately after returning from Saint Petersburg, where he had conducted *Pelleas und Melisande,* Schoenberg sketched thirteen measures of the beginning of Seraphita's *Himmelfahrt*, which the composer had planned as the last scene of the third evening. The sketch contains a brief orchestral introduction, then a passage in *Sprechstimme* in which a narrator begins to recount—using Etzel's translation almost verbatim—Balzac's apocalyptic vision of the angel Séraphita's assumption into heaven.[72]

Seraphita progressed no further. Following a retreat on the Baltic in the summer of 1913, Schoenberg returned once again to *Die glückliche Hand*, now redoubling his efforts to complete it. His correspondence of this time is filled with negotiations for a performance of the opera and its companion work, *Erwartung*. But Schoenberg's intensified concentration on *Die glückliche Hand* could not banish *Seraphita* from his mind. On 11 November a letter to Alma Mahler was filled with enthusiasm for Balzac's novel and its potential for a grandiose musical treatment: "This is a work for several years and it will require its own theater. For the 'Himmelfahrt' alone I will need a chorus of at least two thousand singers."[73]

Perhaps to keep the idea of *Seraphita* alive on a more practical scale and also to extend the new structural ideas that he had uncovered while working on *Die glückliche Hand* and *Pierrot lunaire*, Schoenberg composed in September or early October an orchestral song to a poem titled "Seraphita." This was a sonnet by the Englishman Ernest Dowson that had appeared in German in Stefan George's *Zeitgenössische Dichter* in 1905. The poem was an odd choice for a new work. Almost certainly Schoenberg was drawn to it for its title rather than its content, which has virtually nothing to do with Balzac's novel. Dowson's "Seraphita" is a throwback to the composer's earlier literary tastes, not a product of his philosophical and religious frame of mind of 1913. The poem had appeared in Dowson's *Verses* in 1896, one of several in that collection that addresses the topic of the separation of lovers. It is an emotive poem, at times overstated and maudlin, as the speaker bids the memory of his beloved to remain far away—except for one last moment's comfort when he founders in the sea of life.

Seraphita	Seraphita
Come not before me now, O visionary face!	Erscheine jetzt nicht, traumverlornes angesicht.
Me tempest-tost, and borne along life's passionate sea;	Mir windverschlagen auf des lebens wilder see—
Troublous and dark and stormy though my passage be;	Sei meine fahrt auch voll von finster sturm und weh:
Not here and now may we commingle or embrace,	Hier—jetzt—vereinen oder küssen wir uns nicht!
Lest the loud anguish of the waters should efface	Sonst löscht die laute angst der wasser vor der zeit
The bright illumination of thy memory,	Das helle leuchten, deines angedenkens stern
Which dominates the night: rest, far away from me,	Der durch die nächte herrscht—bleib von mir fern
In the serenity of thine abiding-place!	In deines ruhe-ortes heiterkeit!

But when the storm is highest, and the thunders blare,	Doch wenn der sturm am höchsten geht und kracht
And sea and sky are riven, O moon of all my night!	Zerrissen see und himmel, mond in meiner nacht!
Stoop down but once in pity of my great despair,	Dann neige einmal dem verzweifelten dich dar.
And let thine hand, though over late to help, alight	Lass deine hand (wenn auch zu spät nun) hilfbereit
But once upon my pale eyes and my drowning hair,	Noch gleiten auf mein fahles aug und sinkend haar,
Before the great waves conquer in the last vain fight.[74]	Eh grosse woge siegt im letzten leeren streit![75]

The historical circumstances that surround the composition of "Seraphita" contain many uncertainties. It is especially baffling why Schoenberg would have delayed the completion of *Die glückliche Hand* in order to undertake a complex new work, one whose elaborate sketching suggests that it posed many compositional problems. Nothing is known of a prospect for its performance, and there is no evidence that Schoenberg considered it to be part of a larger song cycle or collection at the time that it was composed. Only in 1916 was it joined to three other songs to make up Schoenberg's Four Songs for Voice and Orchestra, Op. 22. Schoenberg almost never mentioned "Seraphita" in his correspondence, and he showed the manuscript only to a few close friends, including Berg.[76] The first full draft of the song is dated 6 October 1913 at its conclusion, and a fair-copy score was made soon thereafter, dated 9 November 1913. Like *Die glückliche Hand,* "Seraphita" is supported by a large number of sketches, which suggest a more methodical and reflective approach to composition than had been the case in Schoenberg's earlier atonal practice.

The theory of expressivity in vocal music that Schoenberg had enunciated in the 1912 essay "Das Verhältnis zum Text" is fully evident in "Seraphita." The vocal line is neither lyrical nor expressive; its rhythm is so mechanical and its contour so undistinctive that the voice could just as well be a part for an accompanying instrument. The music has fewer of the word paintings that appear so prominently in Schoenberg's earlier atonal music for voice. Continuing the tendency begun in "Herzgewächse" to accompany songs with heterogeneous combinations of instruments, he calls in "Seraphita" for a highly unusual orchestra, which consists of violins, celli, and basses, six clarinets, brass, and battery. The expressive element is transferred largely to this distinctive orchestral medium, whose sound must have seemed to Schoenberg congruent with the sound and spirit of the words.

The form of the song contains many important new ideas. This dimension of the work was addressed in a lecture concerning the Four Songs, which Schoenberg wrote in February 1932, prior to the premier performance of the works on Radio Frankfurt.[77] The lecture is especially valuable since it is Schoenberg's only major analysis of an atonal composition, although his outlook on music that was then almost twenty years old is colored by the thinking that characterizes his twelve-tone method. His remarks were addressed to a general audience, not to specialists, and he deals primarily with ways in which motivic development replaces tonality and traditional thematic exposition, development, and reprise. Schoenberg first observes that the songs of Op. 22 embody a style that had advanced beyond the early stages of atonality, especially in their diminished reliance on text to achieve comprehensibility, although this dependence was fully eliminated only later, in his twelve-tone music. In his discussion of "Seraphita," Schoenberg focuses his observations on the melodic dimension of the work, which is based, he says, on continuous variations upon a three-note motivic particle whose tones are separated by a minor second and a minor third and which has no characteristic rhythm. His examples show the figure reappearing in a free and plastic manner within the lines; it is used also as a "fixed motivic unit which occurs most frequently at the beginning of text lines," by which he refers to the particle imbued with a distinctive eighth-note rhythm, thus a motive per se.[78] This motivic form of the figure is first heard as the notes D♯–E–G at the beginning of the first vocal phrase in measure 18. The sketches for "Seraphita" show that this vocal line was the first music to be composed and only later harmonized and preceded by a lengthy instrumental prelude.

The three-note figure can be varied, Schoenberg says, by inverting or changing the order or direction of either interval, by interpolating ornamental tones, or by enlarging one or both of the intervals by a semitone. Perhaps because the central motive is so small and undistinctive, Schoenberg did not mention the concept of developing variation, although his description of the methods of variation of the basic particle in "Seraphita" certainly elucidates this phenomenon, and his discussion also sheds light upon the flexible techniques of deploying the small, malleable cells that have already been encountered in several of Schoenberg's athematic compositions.[79] Even a cursory examination of the lines of the piece shows the ubiquitousness of the basic trichord. It is most densely embedded in the very first phrase of the clarinet line at the opening of the song (Example 6.4), where it or one of its variants appears in overlapping fashion in every contiguous three-note segment, and it also underlies the first accompanying chord (with pitch content G A♭ B). Later in the song the basic particle is more sporadic or veiled, and it is far less in evidence among the jagged lines in the middle of the song, from measures 39 to 53.

In his analysis Schoenberg also describes the general musical design used in the songs of Op. 22, noting that musical sectionalization generally coincides with poetic divisions. This structural congruence between music and poetry in "Seraphita" is reminiscent of pieces such as "Heimweh" and "Serenade" from *Pierrot lunaire*, in which the music is subdivided by changes of tempo and surface design that coincide with divisions in the poem, at which points interludes are also placed. Dowson's sonnet consists of two quatrains and a sestet divided into two three-line groups, and the four corresponding vocal sections (beginning at measures 18, 28, 44, and 54) are all separated by instrumental interludes. The whole work is framed by a lengthy introduction and postlude.

In his analysis Schoenberg also calls attention to the presence of a freely ternary plan. Although there is no recapitulation of themes, a symmetrical ter-

Example 6.4. Schoenberg, "Seraphita," Op. 22, No. 1, measures 1–9 (principal line only)

nary form is created in "Seraphita," as Schoenberg notes, by the insertion of an agitated passage, corresponding to the first half of the sestet, near the middle of the song in measures 39–53. It is plainly set off from the more tranquil outer sections, where the basic trichord is more apparent and where rhythm is more regular. The music of the instrumental passages is differently scored from the vocal ones, the latter more heterogeneous in sound and filigreed in rhythm and the former more homophonic.

"Seraphita" is also characterized by long and full-blown melodic lines, in both the voice and the instruments. The sketches for the work show that the composer's first thoughts were devoted almost entirely to melodic shapes. He first worked out the entire vocal melody by itself, with very few second thoughts, next the long clarinet melody of the introduction. Harmonic ideas came later, and in several important passages their final disposition was established only after extensive revisions.[80]

Schoenberg did not address the harmonic language of "Seraphita" in his analysis, although it is in this dimension that the song is most important for his future direction. Here he continued the tendency toward using ever larger harmonies, of which hexachords now emerge as the most stable and frequent units. At the end of the song, just as at the end of *Die glückliche Hand,* the texture is further thickened by sustained ten-note chords. The harmonic element of the song has many other similarities with the opera. In several passages within the orchestral interludes, Schoenberg continued to experiment with a systematic use of all twelve tones, an experiment that he had begun in the contemporaneous sketches made for passages toward the end of *Die glückliche Hand.* The most striking example of the concern with chromatic completion is found in the orchestral introduction, at measures 14–15 (Example 6.5).[81] In measure 14 the violins sustain a six-note chord, C♯ F A C E G♯, to which the clarinets add an ascending line B–E♭–G–B♭–D–F♯. The latter figure is a transposed linearization of the violin chord and also its complement. The hexachord is thus used to create an *aggregate*, that is, a statement of the twelve pitch classes with none repeated. Like the shape E–G–E♭ in the passacaglia from *Pierrot lunaire,* the hexachord unifies both the horizontal and vertical dimensions of the passage, since it is deployed as both a line and a chord in forms that differ only in level of transposition. In measure 15 Schoenberg repeats the music of measure 14, only more emphatically unifying the two-dimensional space by having the clarinets play divisi a6 so that the notes in each of their lines and each of their six simultaneities duplicate the pitch content of the B E♭ G B♭ D F♯ hexachord, against which the complementary hexachord continues to sound in the violins.

These same pitch materials, used in a somewhat freer manner, return at measures 27–28 (Example 6.6), which is part of the interlude that follows the first quatrain. Here Schoenberg experiments with another way to achieve spatial unification and chromatic completion. In measure 27 the clarinets restate the basic hexachord from measure 14, C♯ F A C E G♯. In the next measure each of five celli plays a fully chromatic scale descending in parallel. The bottom four

Example 6.5. Schoenberg, "Seraphita," Op. 22, No. 1, measures 14–15 (nontransposing score)

Example 6.6. Schoenberg, "Seraphita," Op. 22, No. 1, measures 27–28

tones (E♭ F♯ B D) of their initial five-note chord plus the xylophone's G and B♭ from measure 27 make up the complement of the hexachord in the clarinets.

The hexachord encountered in these measures was plainly fascinating to Schoenberg. In his study of sketch materials for *Die glückliche Hand,* Joseph Auner uncovered evidence that Schoenberg at first considered using a form of this set—reordered and transposed as D F B♭ D♭ G♭ A—as a referential collection that links principal points throughout the opera.[82] When the tones of the violin chord in measure 14 are placed into a compact, scalewise order—for example C C♯ E F G♯ A—it is apparent that the hexachord is symmetrical, its succession of intervals the same read from either left or right.[83] Like all symmetrical sets, it has many special intervallic properties. Its potential for creating aggregates is especially great since there are three transpositions (the major second, tritone, and minor seventh) that will produce the complementary hexachord. Beginning with "Seraphita" and *Die glückliche Hand,* Schoenberg returned again and again to this set, incorporating it into a series of compositions in which its unique structural properties are exploited in ever different ways.

Over a year after "Seraphita" was completed, Schoenberg composed two additional orchestral songs to religious poems by Rainer Maria Rilke (1875–1926). The first, "Alle, welche dich suchen," was begun on 30 November 1914 and finished four days later; the other, "Mach mich zum Wächter deiner Weiten," was completed on New Year's Day 1915, and both scores were then written out in a fair copy. It is not known whether Schoenberg conceived of them at this time as companions for the Dowson song as part of a larger collection. He mentions them in a letter to Zemlinsky of 9 January 1915 only as "2 orchestral songs by Rilke."[84] In his analytic lecture on the Four Songs, Schoenberg found in "Alle, welche dich suchen" a recurrence of the basic three-note cell from "Seraphita," but neither of the new Rilke songs shares any more distinctive musical materials with the earlier piece. In fact, the two new Rilke settings are very dissimilar to the Dowson. Their poetic content is religious rather than secular, and their music is more lyrical and expressive than before, aphoristic and short-

winded in melodic content, and apparently written with none of the construc-
tivist thinking that characterizes "Seraphita."

Schoenberg was an avid reader of poetry by Rilke. In a catalog of his personal
library made in January 1913, he lists nine books by Rilke, mostly in editions
published beginning in 1907. It is not surprising, given his attention to religious
literature during the years just before World War I, that Schoenberg was attracted to Rilke's *Das Stunden-Buch,* which was the poetic source for the two new
works. This collection, first published in 1905, consists of three books—*Vom
mönchischen Leben, Von der Pilgerschaft,* and *Von der Armut und vom Tode*—written
in 1899, 1901, and 1903, respectively. In the first book the speaker of the poems
imagines himself to be a cloistered Russian monk who seeks to know God, using
all of his powers of mind, intuition, and sense. The second book continues to use
the I and Thou dialogues of the first, although a tone of futility and conflict has
now entered into the religious quest. "I have been scattered in pieces, torn by
conflict, mocked by laughter, washed down in drink. In alleyways I sweep myself
up out of garbage and broken glass," the speaker says.[85] Several of the poems in
this part of *Das Stunden-Buch* are strongly pantheistic, suggesting that God is
"the deep one, whose being I trust, for it breaks through the earth into trees, and
rises, when I bow my head, faint as a fragrance from the soil."[86]

In "Alle, welche dich suchen"—the fifteenth poem of the *Book of Pilgrimage*—
the speaker states his intention to know God directly, though nature and intuition, and not by the miracles and images needed by others.

Alle, welche dich suchen, versuchen dich.	All who seek you tempt you.
Und die, so dich finden, binden dich an Bild und Gebärde.	And those who find you thus bind you to image and gesture.
Ich aber will dich begreifen wie dich die Erde begreift; mit meinem Reifen reift dein Reich.	But I will conceive of you as does the earth; with my ripening ripens your realm.
Ich will von dir keine Eitelkeit, die dich beweist. Ich weiß, dass die Zeit anders heisst, als du.	I need from you no arrogant display to prove yourself. I know that time is different from you.
Tu mir kein Wunder zulieb. Gieb deinen Gesetzen recht, die von Geschlecht zu Geschlecht sichtbarer sind.[87]	Perform no miracles for my sake. Be just to your laws, which from generation to generation become ever more apparent.

The third part of *Das Stunden-Buch,* the *Book of Poverty and Death,* was written after Rilke had lived in Paris to research a study of the sculptor Auguste

Rodin, and the disdain for the limited understanding of the common man apparent in "Alle, welche dich suchen" is now replaced by a concern for the plight of the poor, whose suffering Rilke had witnessed firsthand in Paris. A subgroup of poems in this book consists of prayerlike exhortations, asking God for comfort in the face of death, compassion, and enlightenment. "Mach mich zum Wächter deiner Weiten" is one of these, in which the speaker asks God to reveal his presence in the elements of nature. As in poems from the *Book of Monastic Life*, the poet declares his readiness to withdraw from society and to submit unquestioningly to religious authority and rule, represented by the "old blind man" whom he is prepared to follow along an unknown path.

Mach mich zum Wächter deiner Weiten,	Make me the watchman of your expanses,
mach mich zum Horchenden am Stein,	make me the listener at the stone,
gieb mir die Augen auszubreiten	give me eyes to gaze across
auf deiner Meere Einsamsein;	the seclusion of your seas;
laß mich der Flüsse Gang begleiten	let me accompany the rivers' path
aus dem Geschrei zu beiden Seiten	far from the cries along their banks
weit in den Klang der Nacht hinein.	into the sound of the night.
Schick mich in deine leeren Länder,	Send me to your desolate lands,
durch die die weiten Winden gehn,	across those swept by distant winds,
wo große Klöster wie Gewänder	where stand great cloisters like robes
um ungelebte Leben stehn.	over unlived lives.
Dort will ich mich zu Pilger halten,	There I will stay among pilgrims,
von ihren Stimmen und Gestalten	from their voices and shapes
durch keinen Trug mehr abgetrennt,	no longer shut off by delusion,
und hinter einem blinden Alten	and behind an old blind man
des Weges gehn, den keiner kennt.[88]	walk the path that no one knows.

The music of the two Rilke songs is closely related. Both use a heterogeneous chamber orchestra made primarily from woodwinds and solo strings. Both, according to Schoenberg's own analysis, use a ternary design, created not by overt thematic processes so much as by changes in character and subtle motivic transformations. The main features of this form are seen most clearly in "Mach mich zum Wächter." The middle passage begins at measure 15, where the instrumental music becomes more active rhythmically and far more contrapuntal than earlier in the song, thus capturing the sense of words that speak of the din and hubbub of life. Gradually this activity subsides, leading to a pseudoreprise at measures 27–28. Here the character of the first section returns, as does a highly transformed reference to the first vocal phrase from measures 4–5. At this point a definite thematic relationship with "Alle, welche dich suchen" becomes apparent. The interrelated principal themes of the outer sections of "Mach mich zum Wächter" are themselves transformations of the main theme from the earlier song: all rest upon a similar shape created by the tones D♭–C–F–B–C/C♯ (see Example 6.7abc).

Example 6.7. Schoenberg, Four Songs for Voice and Orchestra, Op. 22, Nos. 2–3: (a) "Alle welche dich suchen" (Op. 22, No. 2), measures 1–2, (voice); (b) "Mach mich zum Wächter" (Op. 22, No. 3), measures 4–5, (voice); (c) Mach mich zum Wächter," measures 27–29 (voice)

The concern in "Seraphita" for a systematic unification of musical space and chromatic completion is not evident in the two Rilke songs, which represent a return to the rapid and unreflective approach to composing of the period before *Die glückliche Hand.* There is only one fleeting exception—at the entrance of the voice in measure 4 of "Mach mich zum Wächter"—where complementary forms of the symmetric hexachord from the Dowson song (A C♯ A♭ C F E and B D♯ G B♭ G♭ D) return side by side to form an aggregate (Example 6.8). Unlike "Seraphita," however, their overlapping presentation and the nonconsistent registral placement of tones suggest that their effect was not carefully preplanned, as it was in the earlier piece. The harmonies, furthermore, have little consistency in themselves in either song, even returning in the aphoristic "Alle, welche dich suchen" to the four- and five-note norm of 1909.

In late July 1916, during or just after his first period of military service in the Austrian army, Schoenberg composed a third Rilke song, "Vorgefühl," whose text came from Rilke's *Das Buch der Bilder:*

Vorgefühl	Presentiment
Ich bin wie eine Fahne von Fernen umgeben.	I am like a flag surrounded by distances.
Ich ahne die Winde, die kommen, und muß sie leben,	I sense the winds, which come, and must live them
während die Dinge unten sich noch nicht rühren:	while things below still do not stir:
die Türen schließen noch sanft, und in den Kaminen ist Stille;	the doors close softly, and the chimneys are still;

Example 6.8. Schoenberg, "Mach mich zum Wächter," Op. 22, No. 3, measure 4

die Fenster zittern noch nicht, und der Staub ist noch schwer.	the windows do not yet clatter, and the dust is heavy.
Da weiß ich die Stürme schon und bin erregt wie das Meer.	Here I already know the storms and I am whipped up like the sea.
Und breite mich aus und falle in mich hinein	And I unfurl and fall into myself
und werfe mich ab und bin ganz allein	and I throw myself off and am entirely alone
in dem großen Sturm.[89]	in the great storm.

As in his own drama *Die glückliche Hand,* Schoenberg found in Rilke's poem a statement concerning his personal artistic destiny—the precursor who bears the brunt of the storm—which he then used as a topic for a musical work. This was a self-conscious gesture that he would duplicate in numerous later compositions, including *Moses und Aron,* Four Pieces for Mixed Chorus, Op. 27, and Three Satires for Mixed Chorus, Op. 28. His choice of Rilke's poem may also have been prompted by its image of a violent storm buffeting the speaker, which parallels a theme in Dowson's "Seraphita." The similarity of the two poems suggests that when "Vorgefühl" was composed, Schoenberg at last had in mind using the song in a collection that would be framed by the secular "Seraphita" and "Vorgefühl" and whose middle would be occupied by Rilke's two religious lyrics.

The music of "Vorgefühl," like its text, has certain parallels with "Seraphita." The orchestra again includes brass instruments, in addition to woodwinds and strings, and the voice part begins with two consecutive statements (E♭–D–F and F–D♭–C) of the basic three-note particle of "Seraphita." The image of the storm common to the two poems is suggested in the voice by angular leaps and in the instruments by a windswept ostinato (at measures 65–68 in "Seraphita" and 13–14 in "Vorgefühl"). But the differences between the two pieces are also considerable. "Vorgefühl" is aphoristic and athematic, having little motivic or harmonic consistency. Its form is similarly free and open, consisting of only two parts divided at measure 15.

The three Rilke songs and Dowson's "Seraphita" were published as Four Songs for Voice and Orchestra, Op. 22, in 1917, whereupon they appeared in a highly original short-score format that Schoenberg called a "simplified study and conducting score."[90] In his Foreword to the 1917 publication, he explained its relevance to his working methods:

> I have long written the first draft of my orchestral works on two to six or eight staves and I usually immediately enter the complete instrumentation. After receiving a few revisions and small changes this first draft will serve together with the fair-copy full score (which I make as always in the old way; but with a different purpose: purely for the copying of parts!) in the production of the simplified study and conducting score, which I will publish from now on.[91]

The new format was evidently not the practical success that Schoenberg had hoped for, and it was abandoned after this one essay. The songs of Op. 22 remained unperformed until 1932, when they were broadcast by the Frankfurt radio orchestra, led by Hans Rosbaud. In part because of their unusual orchestration, they remain among Schoenberg's least-known major compositions.

The vocal compositions from 1911 to 1916 reveal Schoenberg's atonal style at middle age: nostalgic for its youth and ready to leap back into its former self but also compelled to face a future where the passions of youth had faded and where more cautious and carefully planned steps were inevitable. The works do not portray a unified direction, but for the future they point unmistakably to Schoenberg's next stage of development, characterized by an attachment to philosophical and religious ideas, a return to pieces of greater length created by thematic development and traditional formal patterns, and a preparing for the future of music not by unprecedented experiment but by building new structures upon the foundations of the past.

7

On the Road from Earth to Heaven

Symphony and *Die Jakobsleiter*

Schoenberg was still thoroughly engrossed in Balzac's *Séraphita* after he completed *Die glückliche Hand* in November 1913. "It is the most splendid book
that exists," he exclaimed to Alma Mahler.[1] Although one of Balzac's least popular novels, *Séraphita* had many characteristics that were sure to appeal to the
composer. Its lengthy discourses on the ideas of Emanuel Swedenborg would
have reminded him of writings by August Strindberg, long one of Schoenberg's
favorite authors. Balzac's novel also had much to say on ideas that echoed
Schoenberg's outlook on art, including evolutionism, the continual progress of
mankind toward higher forms of understanding, and the role of the genius as a
prophet who could link the past and present with the future. The composer's
burgeoning religious consciousness was fired by the final chapters of the novel,
in which Balzac's angel, Séraphita, reveals the ultimate destiny of mankind: Life,
the angel says, is lived on a road that connects earth to heaven. It has stations
through which man must pass, beginning with the mundane and illusory, pro-
ceeding through death, then undergoing cycles of reincarnations that lead to
ever higher levels of existence. Advancement along this path is furthered by
prayer, which can bring mortals to the very frontier of heaven. In Balzac's apocalyptic final chapter, Séraphita is assumed into heaven, accompanied by a melt-
ing away of all material reality and a mystical unification of the senses and faculties of mind. For Schoenberg these topics and images were so portentous that
they would inspire his musical imagination for nearly a decade.

"Religion Perceived with the Artistic Senses"

Schoenberg's initial encounter in the summer of 1911 with Balzac's novel
marked the beginning of a period when he intensely explored his capacity for
spirituality. In a letter to Richard Dehmel from 13 December 1912, Schoenberg
invited the poet to write a text for an oratorio about the religious aspirations of
"modern man," and his description almost certainly summarizes his personal
religious history to that time:

> For a long time I have been wanting to write an oratorio on the following sub-
> ject: modern man, having passed through materialism, socialism, and anarchy

151

and, despite having been an atheist, still having in him some residue of ancient faith (in the form of superstition), wrestles with God (see also Strindberg's *Jacob Wrestling*) and finally succeeds in finding God and becoming religious. Learning to pray! It is *not* through any action, any blows of fate, least of all through any love of woman, that this change of heart is to come about.[2]

The struggle toward orthodox forms of religion that is suggested by this note has little resonance in the texts that Schoenberg had chosen for his music earlier. Until 1912 these were highly secular, and when religious ideas appeared the spiritual element was usually swallowed up by the worldly. An example is Jens Peter Jacobsen's *Gurrelieder*, a poem from the 1860s that is frankly atheistic. Waldemar, the leading character, lives for passionate love, and he refuses to be defeated by the harsh fate that he must endure. Following the death of his beloved Tove, he curses God and finally triumphs over fate by regaining Tove's essence within nature. Jacobsen's theme of love as the supreme divinity reappeared at an explosive level of intensity in Richard Dehmel's poem "Jesus bettelt," which Schoenberg set to music in 1899 and published in his Four Songs, Op. 2. In this controversial work, Jesus begs Mary Magdalen for sex. It and other poems in Dehmel's *Weib und Welt* were found so objectionable that the author was brought before a Prussian court on charges of blasphemy and lewdness, although the controversy did not prevent Schoenberg from including the song among his earliest publications. In the symbolist and decadent literature that Schoenberg preferred beginning in 1908, art becomes a partner with Eros as the object of sacred devotion. This characteristic is strongly apparent in *Pierrot lunaire*, which caused many early listeners to find the religious references in the work offensive. Marya Freund reported such objections after a performance of *Pierrot* in Paris in 1922, and Schoenberg's response could only be described as disingenuous. He wrote back:

> At no time in my life have I been antireligious or even unreligious. I interpreted these poems ["Madonna," "Rote Messe," and "Die Kreuze"] apparently in a much more naive way than do most people, and I'm still not convinced that this is entirely unjustified. All the same, I am not responsible for what people want to read into the text. If they were musical they wouldn't care about the text.[3]

But after *Pierrot* Schoenberg was ready to use music to express his newly intensified religiosity, just as his romantic forebears, including Liszt, Wagner, and Mahler, had done. In August 1912 Schoenberg told Kandinsky about his intention in the Balzac theater piece that he then contemplated. "Philosophy, religion perceived with the artistic senses," he explained.[4] Between that year and 1917 he initiated three new and interrelated projects—Rudolf Stephan has aptly described them as *Weltanschauungsmusik*—that were based on quasi-religious texts. Each of the three is massive in scale and destined to remain incomplete. The earliest is the theater piece *Seraphita*, already mentioned in chapter 6, for which only a few measures of music were composed. When this project was abandoned, probably early in 1914, it was followed by a grandiose Symphony, akin to Mahler's symphonies in its enlarged scale, use of voices, and overt treatment of a meta-physical topic. By the summer of 1915 Schoenberg had lost interest in this work, too, and, following military service during World War I, he turned his attention to an oratorio based on his own philosophical text, *Die Jakobsleiter,* which he had earlier contemplated as the finale of the Symphony. *Die Jakobsleiter,* the most fully developed of the three monumental fragments, occupied Schoenberg until 1922, when the advancement of his twelve-tone method led him back to purely musical issues and to predominantly instrumental composition.

The texts of these fragmentary compositions reflect the composer's new literary tastes. The underlying model for all three is Balzac's *Séraphita,* which Schoenberg fleshed out with ideas culled from the Bible and probably from Illuminist writings, to which he also added original material on the role of the artist. The texts document the composer's own religious beliefs, which were still highly eclectic and nondoctrinaire and mixed together with his ideas concerning art and his own historical role as musician. They sweep across several religious traditions, as though the composer was grasped during these years by an intense, though undirected, spiritual struggle. This was the frame of mind that led Schoenberg to almost completely reconstruct the atonal style and to reformulate his ideal for music of the future. Although it is pure conjecture to suggest a connection between Schoenberg's growing religiosity and his preliminary experiments with twelve-tone composition, it is reasonable to say that an intensely methodical process of probing and seeking underlies both developments.

During the decade when he planned and sketched these major works, he also began numerous smaller compositions, of which only the Four Songs, Op. 22, were completed. Most of these fragments are for solo voice and orchestra, on texts from the Psalms and from philosophical poetry by Rilke and Rabindranath Tagore, thus suggesting a relation to the major compositions but conceived on a more manageable scale. Schoenberg also sketched the beginnings of a few chamber or orchestral pieces during the same period, although instrumental music seemed secondary at this time to his expansive and intensely programmatic musical interests.

Symphony (1914–15)

The first mention of a symphony with voices on a religious theme occurs in Schoenberg's correspondence with Dehmel from December 1912. Although he could not accommodate the composer in his request for an oratorio text (see the letter cited previously), Dehmel sent Schoenberg a short poem titled "Schöpfungsfeier: *Oratorium natale,*" which he would soon publish in his collection *Schöne wilde Welt.* "I will certainly compose it," Schoenberg wrote back enthusiastically, "although in a different way from what you suspect. Specifically, I see it as the middle movement, perhaps the finale, of a symphony. I already have ideas for one and definitely hope to get something done on it during vacation (in summer)."[5] But Schoenberg first intended to work on his Balzac theater piece, although the lack of a usable libretto remained a stumbling block. As *Die glückliche Hand* neared completion in the fall of 1913, he turned to Marie Pappenheim for an adaptation of Balzac's novel. Judging from their partially undated correspondence, Pappenheim accepted Schoenberg's invitation and worked from November 1913 to February 1914 on a text based on the novel.[6] Schoenberg did not write any music for her libretto, and he soon abandoned the idea of *Seraphita* altogether, although many of its literary themes would reappear in his text for *Die Jakobsleiter.* The whereabouts of Pappenheim's libretto are unknown.

In the spring of 1914 the composer refocused his attention on the Symphony. Although it is impossible to reconstruct a firm chronology of the stages through which it evolved, Schoenberg apparently began the new work much as he had done with *Pierrot lunaire,* sketching and composing even before an overall plan was firmly settled. On an undated folio of music paper on which there are also musical sketches, he wrote down a general plan for the composition, outlining a tentative form, giving titles for each movement, and enumerating the texts that he planned to use, and he also added a few explanatory and orchestrational notes.[7] The original plan encompassed six movements. The first was to be titled "Lebenswende" (Life's turning point), to which Schoenberg added as an annotation: "Look backward, glimpse into the future; gloomy, defiant, repressed. All motives later having importance appear here." His description points to a movement that would contain a presentiment of the whole work viewed from the point at which the artist protagonist takes stock of his life and assesses the dissatisfaction that it has produced. The second movement, called "Lebenslust" (Lust for life), would have two parts, the first a scherzo with two trios, the second a reprise with a voice singing Dehmel's poems "Freudenruf," "Götterhochzeit," and "Äonische Stunde" from *Schöne wilde Welt.* Each of these three texts speaks optimistically about life and the joys and ecstasies that outnumber its passing sadnesses. The movement was apparently intended to give a flashback into the protagonist's past, recalling his happy and carefree youth.

The third movement, Allegretto, is titled "Der bürgerliche Gott" (The bourgeois God), and it would use Dehmel's "Schöpfungsfeier" as its text and an orchestra of flutes, clarinets, violas, and harps. Dehmel's poem, the one that he sent to the composer in advance of its publication, continues the optimistic tone that runs throughout *Schöne wilde Welt.* It takes the form of a mock libretto and contains conversations among God (the "father spirit"), Nature (the "mother soul"), and their mortal children, who live in joy and love.[8] In the fourth movement, an interlude, Dehmel's optimism and the consolation provided by conventional religion ("the bourgeois God") have crumbled in the face of death. The movement was to have two parts, the first titled "Unbefriedigt" (Unfulfilled), "the bourgeois God does not suffice," and the second bringing in a quartet of solo voices to sing four poems (Nos. 86, 88, 92, and 100) from Rabindranath Tagore's *Gitanjali* (*Song Offerings*). Each of these prose poems concerns death, the idea of which has seized the helpless protagonist and rendered him desolate and despondent. The fifth movement is called "Psalm" ("based on Bible texts"). On separate pages Schoenberg wrote out or identified the biblical passages from which he apparently planned to choose his texts for this movement—Jeremiah 10:14–15; 17:1, 5; 23:23–24; Romans 2:1–3, 19–23; 3:20; 8:10, 18–25, 29–30, 38–39;

9:17; 10:20; and Psalms 22 and 88. In the lower right margin of the general plan he also cited Isaiah 58 and 66 and Jeremiah 7 and 17, although the movement to which these texts pertain is unclear. Schoenberg's biblical selections are far too numerous to allow any single theme to emerge, but in the two psalms an anguished cry to God arises from the suffering individual, who is abused, friendless, and alienated.

The sixth and final movement was to be called "Totentanz der Prinzipien" (Death dance of principles), and it would have four sections—funeral, funeral oration, death dance, and a concluding prayer. Between the funeral oration and dance of death, Schoenberg also alluded in the plan to a "short sketch of the events lying between, with distant orchestra from 'Freudenruf.'" As a text, only one poem by Tagore (No. 88 from *Gitanjali*) is cited—also among those listed for the third movement. This is Tagore's "Deity of the Ruined Temple!," a solemn and desolate lamentation that describes a world that had become utterly oblivious of God. The Symphony thus ends with a pessimistic vision of man's destiny, by which death has triumphed over all. Only in the very last section, the prayer, is there cause for optimism, given the importance accorded to prayer in Balzac's novel and also in Schoenberg's statement to Dehmel, to whom it was held out as the means by which mankind, bereft of spiritual values, could regain contact with God. Schoenberg later wrote his own text for the "Totentanz" movement, although he may not have had this poem in mind when he drafted the original plan for the Symphony's finale.

Although the programmatic conception of the Symphony was a composite made from Schoenberg's personal religious history and various literary sources, it has an uncanny similarity to the early and similarly autobiographical symphonies of Gustav Mahler, especially his Symphony No. 2 in C Minor. When Schoenberg mentioned the idea for a programmatic symphony to Dehmel in December 1912, Mahler was much in his thoughts. Only weeks before, Schoenberg had given a major lecture on Mahler in Vienna (he had also presented it in Prague and Berlin earlier in 1912).[9] In his talk he recalled the effect that Mahler's Second Symphony had on him when he first heard it. "I was overwhelmed; completely overwhelmed," he said. "I was seized, especially in certain passages, with an excitement which expressed itself even physically, in the violent throbbing of my heart."[10] The similarities between the two works are numerous, and they extend to both programmatic and formal ideas. Although Mahler was always skeptical of the value of programs for his symphonies, he wrote out a description of the expressive content of the C-Minor Symphony for use at a performance in Dresden in December 1901, also sending a copy to his fiancée, Alma Schindler, "for whom it is actually intended."[11] According to these notes, the program that underlies his symphony virtually duplicates the one later used by Schoenberg. Mahler's artist protagonist is provoked in the first movement to take stock of his life and to question its meaning and his own destiny. In a series of interludes in the middle movements he thinks back to his happy and innocent youth, then to his gathering despair and disgust with life. Finally he hears the inner voice of simple faith and, after a terrifying apocalpytic dance of death in the opening of the finale, gazes upon the eternal realm of heavenly love.

The musical form that Schoenberg at first contemplated for his Symphony also has many similarities with Mahler's Symphony No. 2. Both have an expanded overall shape and orchestration—Schoenberg contemplated an orchestra of more than two hundred for his new work. Both have interludelike middle movements, also a scherzo with two trios (a Mahler trademark), and both use voices and songlike passages. Schoenberg's intention to introduce all of the work's main themes in the first movement is true in part to Mahler's formal model for the symphony, by which the outer movements are expressly linked by common themes. Certainly the episode that Schoenberg had intended for the finale, in which an offstage orchestra was to quote from an earlier movement that had depicted the joys of earthly life, would have reminded his listeners of the finale of Mahler's Second Symhony. Just before the entrance to heaven in the latter work (at rehearsal no. 29), Mahler inserted a memorable interlude for offstage brass, amid which the flute and piccolo imitate birdsong—"a last tremulous echo of earthly life," he wrote in the notes for Dresden.

Schoenberg subsequently transformed the Mahleresque conception upon which his Symphony at first rested into a new shape that was more closely related to *Séraphita,* and he eventually arrived at such an extensive revision of the original idea as to make further work on the Symphony impossible and necessitate an entirely new composition, *Die Jakobsleiter.* Probably late in 1914—the date is uncertain—Schoenberg returned to his original formal plan and made extensive changes. He crossed out the fourth and fifth movements, grouped the first three into a "Part I," and made up a "Part II" from the "Totentanz" and a new fifth movement, which was to express "Der Glaube des 'Desillusionierten'" (The faith of the "disillusioned man"), which he explained as "the joining of a sober, skeptical realism with faith. The mystical resides in the simplest things." The two parts would thus depict a consciousness before and after death. Despite his earlier reluctance to write his own texts for such a complex project, he decided to base all or most of part 2 of the Symphony on his own words, creating his own distinctive interpretation of the Balzacian afterlife.

A draft of his poem for the "Totentanz," now the fourth movement, was completed on 15 January 1915, and it contains a description of the protagonist's first impressions of the realm of death, just after his funeral.[12] The "principles" involved in the death dance are those of earthly life—cause and effect, matter and logic, feeling and form—all of which are now topsy-turvy. The distinctions of the real world have disappeared: darkness is light, spirit is sense, reasons are effects. Schoenberg's vision of the afterlife was plainly indebted to Balzac's apocalypse. An existence in the realm of death, the novelist wrote, was a "life that gave no hold to the senses. . . . It shed fragrance without odour, and melody without the help of sound; . . . there were neither surfaces, nor angles, nor atmosphere."[13] The protagonist of Schoenberg's "Totentanz" struggles to adjust—"Unbearable!" he cries out—and all that he can retain of his earlier reality is a vague sense of remorse. Given this pessimistic introduction to the spiritual realm, Schoenberg probably felt the need for more than a simple prayer to conclude.

His new idea for a finale—a movement that expressed "the joining of sober, skeptical realism with faith"—suggests models from Strindberg's autobiographical writings, especially *Inferno* and *Legends*, the last part of which is *Jacob Wrestling*, mentioned by the composer admiringly to Dehmel in 1912. These were all works heavy with Swedenborgian mysticism, occultism, and superstition, qualities that made them appeal all the more to Schoenberg. In the postscript to *Jacob Wrestling*, Strindberg tells of his own return to faith, which was accomplished, just as for Schoenberg's protagonist, by a simple decision to believe in God, all the while maintaining the attitude of an enlightened realist:

> All efforts to approach religion by the way of reasoning lead to absurdities. The cause for this must be that religion like science begins with certain axioms, and axioms do not need to be proved and *cannot* be proved. . . . When the author in 1894 abandoned as a matter of principle his skeptical attitude, which threatened to make havoc of all intellectual life, and began, as a kind of experiment, to adopt the point of view of a believer, there opened before him a new spiritual life.[14]

But the Strindbergian finale also proved short-lived. As he was writing the "Totentanz" poem, Schoenberg apparently abandoned "Der Glaube des 'Desillusionierten'" and hatched a third plan for a finale, one that was truer to Balzac's conception and a more vivid depiction of the afterlife introduced darkly in the "Totentanz." This was the part that eventually led to the text of the oratorio *Die Jakobsleiter.* Its chronology and development while still associated with the Symphony cannot be firmly known, since the texts that Schoenberg wrote for it were later absorbed into those for the oratorio.[15] Still, a few existing documents allow for a plausible hypothesis concerning its poetic content. Among the text sketches for *Die Jakobsleiter* is an outline with the heading "fourth movement" next to a crossed-out "fifth."[16] The page evidently contains a plan for the finale of the Symphony, made just at the time that Schoenberg had decided to shorten the work to four movements, a change that occurred prior to 18 January 1915. According to this outline, the new finale would have two main sections, "Revue (Rundschau)" (Review [look around]) and "Erleuchtung" (Enlightenment), and then a "Schluss—Gebet" (Conclusion—prayer). In the Review the prayers and confessions of three levels of souls would be heard. First are those of a mass of voices from the "lower level," speaking of worldly joys, sufferings, and aspirations. Next come the prayers of the "middle level," consisting of individuals who had made some degree of spiritual advancement in earlier lives. They are identified only as a Called One (*ein Berufener*), a Chosen One (*ein Auserwählter*), a Monk (*ein Mönch*), a Struggler (*ein Ringender*), and a Dying One (*ein Sterbender*). Finally, the upper level appears, consisting of a Soul (*eine Seele*) and a choir of angels. No explanation is given about the concluding "Enlightenment" or "Prayer."

After he made this outline, Schoenberg wrote out a nineteen-page draft for the text of part or all of the new finale. This draft is now apparently lost,[17] although Josef Rufer and Jan Maegaard, who examined it earlier, noted that it had the heading "fourth movement" and was dated 18 January 1915 at its beginning. One page from it that contained the speech of the Struggler mentioned in the outline was reproduced in facsimile in the *Festschrift* for Schoenberg's fiftieth birthday.[18] Its length of nineteen pages and other evidence suggest that it corresponded in content only to the first half of what became the libretto for *Die Jakobsleiter.* Nothing is known of a text for the Enlightenment and Prayer sections of the finale, although these rubrics may have guided the composer later as he wrote the second half of the poem for *Die Jakobsleiter.*

Although Schoenberg composed a large amount of music for the Symphony, he did not leave behind enough material to allow any part of the work to be assessed as a completed composition.[19] All the same, the sketches for the work are among the most important in Schoenberg's legacy, since they document a major turning point in his compositional development. Most significant, they record the first important preliminary stage that led to twelve-tone composition. While a few hints of dodecaphonic and serial thinking are evident in earlier works—examples include the end of *Die glückliche Hand,* the opening of the song "Seraphita," and the passacaglia from *Pierrot lunaire*—the music for the Symphony suddenly reveals elements of the method in an amazingly advanced state. The Symphony fragments also document a more general rethinking of the atonal style, in which the brevity, athematicism, and formal freedom that had been its hallmarks since 1909 are abandoned in favor of a return to more traditional thematic structures and formal archetypes. Schoenberg was well aware that the Symphony represented a new direction in his oeuvre, one that looked both forward and backward. In a letter to Zemlinsky dated 9 January 1915 he called attention to the new work as a return to an earlier stage in his compositional development: "Once again it will be a 'worked out' composition," he said, "the opposite of the many purely impressionistic things from my recent past."[20] In his later correspondence, he also alluded to the Symphony as a leap into the future, his first important application of the twelve-tone principle.[21] Schoenberg never explained why he began to experiment with such fundamental changes in his musical outlook just at this time, although it seems likely that the difficulties in composing that he had experienced since 1910 were important factors. His taste of success at the 1913 premiere of *Gurrelieder* may also have been a consideration in his attempt in the Symphony to reshape the atonal style in a more familiar mold and give it a more epic scope.

The Symphony fragments show Schoenberg engaged in a way of composing very different from his earlier atonal practices. In these earlier works there are usually few sketches, if any, and these most often concern disconnected passages where the composer evidently tried to solve a specific compositional problem. Normally in the atonal works Schoenberg quickly drafted a continuous matrix of musical ideas in which one or more principal lines were fleetly given a harmonic-contrapuntal accompaniment. If a composition did not flow rapidly from his pen, he usually discontinued it, leaving behind only a brief opening fragment. The sketches for the Symphony reveal a very different method of work. They cover no fewer than twenty-seven pages, and they occupied Schoenberg sporadically for at least a year. Work on the Symphony led the composer to revive the practice of keeping a sketchbook, which he had not done since the days of his late tonal music. The sketches for the Symphony are laid out in the format of an enlarged short score, although the space is filled slenderly and almost entirely by lines. Beginning composing by drafting a principal melodic line was typical of Schoenberg's working method—recall the first sketch for the song "Seraphita"—but it is significant that he did not quickly advance beyond this stage, especially during such a long period of work. The curiously incomplete texture in the sketches suggests that Schoenberg was preoccupied with the creation of new ways by which the lines could be interrelated.

The musical fragments of the Symphony were entered on loose sheets and folios of music paper and on five pages at the beginning of a sketchbook that Schoenberg dated 4 May 1915.[22] The only other date entered on the manuscripts is 27 May 1914, at the opening of a partial draft of the beginning of the scherzo movement. Most of the existing music concerns this second movement. The dated four-page draft (archive pp. U395–98) contains 102 measures of the beginning of the movement,[23] although for several stretches only a single line was written down (all of these main themes were also worked out in separate sketches). An additional page of short score (U391) was probably intended to continue the draft of the scherzo, since it begins with a duplication of a melody that ended the longer segment. The music contained in the draft was then extensively revised and abbreviated in the sketchbook. Later parts of the scherzo—containing settings of Dehmel's "Freudenruf" and "Äonische Stunde"—were also drafted, and, as Schoenberg noted in the general plan, these bring back melodic materials from earlier in the movement. The only fragments that can be conclusively assigned to a movement other than the second are found on page U394, which has the heading "3. Satz Kinder Gavotte" (3rd movement children gavotte).[24]

Despite its incomplete texture, the draft of the beginning of the scherzo (pp. U395–98 plus 391)[25] reveals a musical composition that is based on a new conception of theme and thematic variation. The music contains two strikingly new ideas: the principal theme is made from all twelve tones with none repeated, and it is subsequently varied, at least in part, by serial procedures that keep the twelve tones together as an integral unit, a tone row. These ideas would be of the utmost importance for the remainder of Schoenberg's atonal period and prefigure virtually all of his later music.

The main theme of the movement (Example 7.1) is presented at the outset as a sustained ostinato, which continues with gradual changes throughout the opening section (measures 1–42). A succession of short melodic figures derived in a complex manner from the opening ostinato is also introduced. A new tempo in measure 43 (*feurig*) marks the beginning of a contrasting or middle section, in which the ostinato disappears, to be replaced by a succession of ideas that have at most a distant relation to the ostinato figure. At measure 96 the first tempo returns, and at measure 99 a reprise is marked by the recapitulation of the basic ostinato figure, reformulated as a melody for cello. Variants of this theme are brought in until measure 121, where the draft breaks off.

By 1914 themes made from twelve different notes were not new. The opening lines in Liszt's *Faust* Symphony and in the "Von der Wissenschaft" section of Richard Strauss's *Also sprach Zarathustra* use all twelve tones with only minor

Example 7.1. Schoenberg, Symphony, measure 1 (ostinato theme)

repetitions. Schoenberg himself had already composed such a theme for the concluding chorus of *Die glückliche Hand* (first sopranos, measures 224–28), although he later pointed to the ostinato theme of this scherzo as his first true twelve-tone melody.[26] But the variational processes that he applied to the theme had no precedent in 1914. Some of the melodic ideas are freely derived from the main theme, resembling it only in rhythm or contour; others are generated systematically in a provocative forecast of twelve-tone techniques. Heretofore, Schoenberg had varied themes primarily by working with their motives or motivic particles, continuously transforming these small rhythmic-intervallic building blocks so that seemingly new themes grew up in an organic manner. Now he experimented with a concept of variation that approached an entire theme or phrase as an indivisible entity. Some of the new lines in the scherzo are derived from the opening ostinato phrase by transforming its entire row of tones so that the identity of the row itself is retained. This was done by transposing the row so as to produce a new theme—it appears a fourth higher in the line at measure 12 and a fourth lower at measure 23—and by inverting it (measure 11 of p. U391). These new methods of working with a theme will henceforth be called *serialized variations,* since the order of intervals in the original melody is retained in the later variant. Nowhere in the scherzo draft is a theme made from a full retrograde of the basic row or a retrograde of its inversion, as in the later twelve-tone method, although retrogrades occur plainly in the sketches on page U380.

In other variations the basic row is treated more freely—it is shortened, lengthened by interpolating foreign tones, and partially reordered to create new lines. In an especially provocative sketch on page U380, Schoenberg placed the basic line above its inversion, making it apparent that tones 6 through 9 in both forms had the same content of pitches (E F B C, reversed in the inversional form). He bracketed these four notes and used them in several special ways—isolating them to create new lines, as in measures 33–35 and 73–80, or removing them from the basic phrase to create a new eight-note variant of the ostinato figure. This eight-note row is presented in measures 32–37 in an intricate canonic ostinato, against which the four missing tones are brought in as a line in the mallet instruments to complete the aggregate.

Schoenberg also derives chords from the twelve-tone line so as to unify the two dimensions of the musical space. Although this is not a new practice, the systematic thinking by which he achieves an integration of the total musical texture forecasts later twelve-tone techniques. As in the mature twelve-tone

Example 7.2. Schoenberg, Symphony, measures 14–16 (U391)

method, chords in the scherzo sometimes consist of notes from a segment of a row. An example in the draft occurs at measures 14–16 on page U391, where two five-note chords are heard in succession (Example 7.2). The first has the pitch content E♭ A♭ B♭ E A, and the second G D♭ G♭ C F, that is, notes 1 through 5 and 6 through 10 of the twelve-tone row transposed down a major seventh (shown at the bottom of Example 7.2). With the exception of a single note (G), the registers in which these chordal tones are placed are the same as in the transposed tone row. As the twelve-tone idea later matured, Schoenberg would exercise considerably more freedom in departing from the original linear shape when he chose registers in which to place the tones of a chord. Following the two chords in measure 15 of the draft, the operative twelve-tone row is completed by the motive D–B.

Schoenberg may have chosen just these two segments of the row to make into chords because of a structural similarity that exists between their total content of tones. When the two groups of five notes occur in the basic line, they are not especially similar in their intervals or in their motivic contour, but the two sets of pitches still share an important relationship, since they are transpositionally equivalent. This can be readily seen when their tones are rearranged in a compact scalewise order: the first scale of tones (A♭ A B♭ E♭ E) transposed down a minor third duplicates the pitches of the second (F G♭ G C D♭). These are the only five-note segments of the row whose pitches are transpositionally equivalent. The association of chords on the basis of a relationship in their pitch content had long been a feature of Schoenberg's atonal harmonic practice, but it was now joined to a greater attention to the intervallic shape of lines. This new perspective allowed Schoenberg to bring in a powerful element of unity between the horizontal and vertical dimensions of his music, building much more broadly upon the device for unifying texture that he had discovered in the passacaglia from *Pierrot lunaire.*

Another example of the interpenetration of intervallic resources shared by lines and chords is encountered in the beginning and middle parts of the draft.

Example 7.3. Schoenberg, Symphony, scherzo, interconnected pitch structures

Two rapidly alternating four-note chords (F♯ A C♯ G and E♭ B♭ D A♭) arise in measures 35–39 and again in measures 71–77 (shown in Example 7.3c). From evidence within the sketches, Fusako Hamao has reconstructed the steps through which Schoenberg derived the chords from the basic twelve-tone theme, a process that is summarized in Example 7.3abc.[27] First, the row that underlies the theme (Example 7.3a) was pared down to eight tones (Example 7.3b) by removing the E–F–B–C tetrachord and by slightly changing the order of the last three notes; then this new row was used to create an ostinato canon in measures 32–39. Finally, the two four-note chords (Example 7.3c) were each made by extracting every other tone from the eight-note row. Schoenberg may again have been guided in this highly artificial process by his awareness of the close relationship that exists in the pitch content of the two tetrachords and tetrachordal segments of the row. The pitch content of the last tetrachord of the theme (C–G♭–D♭–B♭) is equivalent by inversion and transposition to the notes of the first chord in Example 7.3c; similarly, the content of the first tetrachord of the theme (D–G–E♭–A) is equivalent to that of the second chord. As in the earlier example, Schoenberg was apparently experimenting with ways by which his older "impressionistic" composing could be folded into a newly "worked out" procedure, and he was especially keen to find new methods by which to integrate an entire texture, in both the vertical and horizontal directions.

From the Symphony to *Die Jakobsleiter*

By summer of 1915 the many changes in Schoenberg's original conception for the Symphony had dampened his enthusiasm for the entire project. He wrote to Zemlinsky on 29 July:

> I don't know how this Symphony will finally look. For the last two movements I have put together some text myself (when I have a chance I would like to show it to you) and now I think I will also write something for the 1st and 2d move-

ment, since this will suit me better than the Dehmel poems that were originally intended. But I have already sketched a lot of music for the first idea, so I really can't make up my mind.[28]

His indecision about the future of the Symphony was further prolonged by his service in the Austrian military during World War I. During the first two years of the war he composed little—the only completed work was "Vorgefühl," written hurriedly in July 1916 to round out the Four Songs of Op. 22. Following his release from the army on 20 October 1916,[29] he had apparently abandoned any idea of returning to the Symphony and his thoughts moved instead to other incomplete projects. He first returned to his Chamber Symphony No. 2, a tonal composition that he had begun in 1906 but now reconceived as a work for full orchestra.[30] Beginning in early December he made numerous sketches for its continuation, although he was still unsuccessful in bringing it to a conclusion. At this time he may also have considered transforming the Chamber Symphony into a melodrama on a short text that he had written, called "Wendepunkt," although the exact date of this plan is uncertain, and Schoenberg apparently composed no music for such an idea.[31]

Realizing that he had lost the thread of the Chamber Symphony, he returned to the libretto of the Symphony finale, which he then revised as the text for an oratorio. In February 1917 he drafted the second part of the poem, apparently fleshing out the Enlightenment and Prayer sections that he had noted down in the earlier outline. He reported on the advancement of this part of the project in a letter to Zemlinsky of 21 February: "Finally, I've worked once again on the text of my choral work that I began 2 years ago, now I've also finished roughing out the 2d part. When I have revised it I will send you a copy."[32] The long and complex libretto occupied him until 26 May, the date that he entered at the end of a fair copy of the entire text.

But six days earlier, just as he was completing this copy, he began another Rilke song, "Liebeslied" from Rilke's *Neue Gedichte*, for alto voice, violin, viola, cello, and harmonium. Schoenberg drafted the entire voice line of thirty-four measures and part of the instrumental accompaniment up to measures 20–21, where it dwindled off. He also made a fair copy of the first nineteen measures, in which he revised the opening passage.[33] While Rilke's love poem has no relation to the philosophical content of *Die Jakobsleiter*, the music may have been intended as an exercise in the new methods of thematic variation that he had broached in the Symphony and that would prepare him for his impending work on the oratorio. Rilke's text itself has a provocative parallel with the composer's contemporaneous experiments in finding a deeper relation among the lines of a musical composition. The poem is based upon a metaphor by which a pair of lovers are described as strings on an instrument that vibrate sympathetically to produce a single tone. In a similar way the lines of the "Liebeslied" resonate with each other, not only by the traditional process of growth associated with developing or motivic variation but also by the new variational process introduced in the Symphony by which the row of tones that underlies a theme is manipulated as a whole.

Example 7.4. Schoenberg, "Liebeslied": (a) violin, measures 1–7 (draft); (b) harmonium, measures 5–8 (draft); (c) viola, measures 4–6 (fair copy)

This process of serialized variation had quickly become a basic tool in Schoenberg's compositional workshop. It can be illustrated by a few examples from the beginning of the song. The basic thematic element that will undergo variation is stated in the violin in measures 1–2 (Example 7.4a). It is longer than a motive, more akin to what Schoenberg in his teaching called a phrase or a "shape." In the variations that follow, its rhythm is not of primary importance, unlike developing variation upon motives, in which a rhythmic idea is usually reshaped in a continual and plastic manner. Instead, its ordered succession of intervals—created by a row of tones that are fixed in their placement relative to one another—is extracted, transformed as a unit, and replanted into seemingly new melodic shapes. The intervals are not, in general, subject to the slight expansions and contractions that are present in motivic variation.

The opening violin line in the draft (Example 7.4a) is made from a chain of serialized variants of the opening shape by which its underlying five-note row is transposed successively to three different levels. The voice part, which enters in measure 3, also begins with another transposition of the five-tone row, and still other transpositions resurface within the instrumental lines throughout the song.[34] The row also returns transformed by retrograde motion and inversion. The former is heard in the left hand of the harmonium in measures 5–8 (Example 7.4b), which begins with two interlocking statements of the row in retrograde. The viola in measures 4–5 of the fair-copy version plays an inversion of the row followed by an incomplete statement of the original (or "prime") form transposed to begin on the tone B♭ (Example 7.4c).

This sharing of a common series of intervals among several themes not only allowed Schoenberg to achieve a more intense unity in the linear dimension of his music but also initiated a whole new outlook on the variational process. The composer was able to relinquish rhythm as a distinctive feature of a phrase or motive and still preserve its identity as it grew into other figures. This elimination of rhythm as an indispensable element of variation can be seen by comparing the opening violin shape in measures 1–2 to the beginning of the line in the viola in measures 4–6 (Examples 7.4a and c). The two are variationally related, but they share no distinctive similarities in rhythm or phrasing, normally requisite in motivic variation. But Schoenberg was still feeling his way toward a new concept of coherence, apparently not wanting to go too far too fast. Although he diminishes the importance of rhythm in the variational process, he cautiously maintains the profile of a melodic figure in its later serialized variants. For example, all transpositionally related statements of the tone row in "Liebeslied" have the same steadily descending shape; the inversional and retrograded statements all steadily ascend. As in the Symphony sketches, Schoenberg was not yet prepared to use pitch registers as variables that could introduce an added measure of variety, contrast, and newness to the developmental method.

Die Jakobsleiter

By early June 1917, apparently satisfied with the potential for unity that his new variational tool could produce, Schoenberg discontinued the song and returned to the oratorio. Its title, *Die Jakobsleiter,* was decided upon only as the libretto neared completion. Predictably, the name given to the new work was contained in Balzac's *Séraphita,* which once again became the primary inspiration and literary source for the entire composition. At the beginning of chapter 5, "The Farewell," Balzac laments the fate of the common man, who plods through life unaware of higher spiritual realities. "None but the loftier spirits open to faith can discern Jacob's mystical ladder," he concludes.[35] According to the story in Genesis 28:10–22, Jacob paused to sleep during a journey, using a stone for a pillow. During the night, "he dreamt that he saw a ladder, which rested on the ground with its top reaching to heaven, and angels of God were going up and down upon it" (*The New English Bible with the Apocrypha,* 1970). The story of Jacob's ladder does not directly figure in the libretto or in Balzac's novel—the title was almost certainly an afterthought for Schoenberg—but it neatly locates the connection between earth and heaven, which is the setting for the oratorio.

In its final form the libretto has two parts that were to be linked by a symphonic interlude. The first closely follows the Review that Schoenberg had outlined for the Symphony finale. A few characters are added, the most important of whom is the archangel Gabriel, who acts as a moderator, embodying an angelic voice that urges mankind ever onward and dispenses guidance and criticism after failed experiences. The addition of Gabriel's part was again suggested by Balzac's novel, in which Séraphita asks her mortal friends, "Do you not

plainly hear the voice that cries to you, 'On! On!'"³⁶ By adding a central and recurrent role for Gabriel, Schoenberg made the text conform to the traditional
librettistic model of the oratorio, especially as it appears in a work such as Bach's
Christmas Oratorio and Haydn's *The Creation.* In Bach's oratorio, the central recurrent role is that of the Evangelist, who narrates the Christmas story in a
melodious recitative that is comparable to Gabriel's speaking voice. In the text
of Haydn's *The Creation* the narrative function is divided among three arch-
angels, one of whom is Gabriel, whose role in this work certainly must have
been in Schoenberg's mind when he was constructing his own libretto. Schoenberg's use of allegorical personages has a history in the German baroque oratorio, and associations with the musical traditions of the genre will be discussed
shortly.

After an introductory exhortation by Gabriel, Schoenberg's tale begins with
a chorus made from souls who speak in a jumble about their many objectives
and interests, all highly mundane. Another group articulates more precise attitudes about their former lives—rejoicing, doubting, dissatisfaction, indifference, and resignation—but all agree that they would prefer to return to earth
as they were before. Their lowly aspirations are described by Balzac. "Alas! Most
men doubt, lack faith, will, and perseverance," says Séraphita. "Though some
set out on the road, they presently look back and return. Few are they who
know how to choose between these two extremes—to go or to stay, heaven or
the muck-heap."³⁷

Gabriel then summons any of the souls who think that their lives have
brought them to a higher level. Six step forward, essentially the same group that
occupied the "middle level" in the Review. A Called One (*ein Berufener*) tells of
his search for beauty, which made life joyful. Gabriel tells him that he has no vision. A Protester (*ein Aufrührerischer*) complains that his instincts conflict with
God's commandments, but Gabriel tells him that the two can coexist. A Struggler (*ein Ringender*) describes his good intentions to follow commandments, only
to find them lacking in crucial situations. Guidance for him, Gabriel says, should
come from the Chosen One (*der Auserwählte*), who then reluctantly approaches.

Both in the second half of the libretto and in sketches for the first, Schoenberg
refers to the Chosen One also as the "Genius." His relation to his fellowmen, the
composer says, is that of a variation upon a theme: the genius has the same
essence as other men, but he is more advanced, driven to be new, to enunciate
the future. Foretelling Schoenberg's later distinction between style and idea, the
Chosen One tells his fellowmen that he can only uplift them through his words,
which change with the passage of time; his form, on the contrary, is imperish-
able, staying permanently with him. These ideas are again from Balzac: Séraphita
relates that the normal human mind can only cope with ideas about the past,
not the future, which is the special property of the genius. "The mind alone pre-
serves a tradition of former states," says the angel. "This unbroken legacy of the
past to the present, and of the present to the future, is the secret of human genius. . . . Yes, whoever possesses one of these gifts, touches the infinite at one
spot."³⁸

The Monk (*der Mönch*) is the next to speak. Since he never allowed himself to be tempted, his sacrifices and spiritual advancement are hollow. Gabriel tells him to go forth and suffer, to be a prophet and a martyr. Finally, the Dying One (*der Sterbender*) steps forward and tells of his thousand previous lives and his joy at the prospect of being released from the cycle of reincarnation. The first half ends, as it did in the early outline, with a duet and chorus that mingle the voices of angels, the vocalise of a Soul (the same voice as the Dying One), and Gabriel's command that the souls must return to earth for yet another reincarnation.

The second half of the libretto covers much of the same ground as the first, although its events are laid out in a reversed order and it ends by pointing to heaven, whereas the first half ended looking back to earth. Gabriel's first speech takes up the thread from the end of the first part—the souls that are to be sent back to earth, he says, will mostly forget their spiritual origins and return to lives that are as imperfect as before. As they depart, they engage in a repartee with heavenly beings (demons, genies, stars, gods, and angels), who will continue to represent them before the Highest. Some of the individuals from the middle level in the first part—now simply "voices"—continue their pleading. The "fifth voice" is the Chosen One, who still cannot understand his rightful place in the world. Schoenberg's personal voice is now heard clearly in the words of the Chosen One. This character's dilemma is quite the same as that of the Man in *Die glückliche Hand*—he is driven to seek acceptance but forever feels abandoned and betrayed. He watches as the great procession of souls returns to earth, all of whom speak out revealing their state of imperfection. A god tells the Chosen One that he is akin to all of them since he has an earthly burden, just as they do. But his task is more specific—to uplift them, to be an "image of the future"— and he should have pity rather than disdain for them.

Now Gabriel intercedes with a long and occasionally murky discourse on meta-physical subjects—spirit, matter, free will, infinity, space, and time, among others—finally coming to the central issue of prayer, which, he says, can expiate sin and reach directly to God. The topic of prayer is treated in *Die Jakobsleiter* much as it is in *Séraphita*. In the sixth chapter of the novel, the angel points to prayer as the principal link between the individual and God: "He who is on the frontier of the divine worlds prays, and his prayer is expression, meditation, and action all in one! Yes, his prayer contains everything, includes everything; it completes your nature by showing you the Spirit and the Way. Prayer is the fair and radiant daughter of all the human virtues, the arch connecting heaven and earth."[39]

The libretto is then concluded by a grandiose passage for three choruses, which represent voices from the three levels of spirits. The souls from the lower level echo many of the same thoughts from the opening of the first part, but the ending of the oratorio is more optimistic, as the earthly souls finally join in a prayer that the higher choruses eagerly take up:

Herrgott im Himmel,	Lord God in heaven,
Hör unser Flehn,	Hear our plea,
Verzeih unsre Sünden,	Forgive our sins,
Hab Gnade für uns,	Have mercy upon us,

Gewähr unsre Bitten,	Grant us our request,
Erfüll unsre Wünsche,	Fulfill our wishes,
Gib statt unsern Klagen,	Grant us our petition,
Schenk uns die ewige Liebe und Seligkeit.[40]	Give us eternal love and salvation.

Balzac's novel is the central literary model for the work, although Schoenberg enunciates in it a large and complex network of ideas that may also reflect other sources. Jean Christensen has argued that the Sermon on the Mount is an important prototype.[41] Karl Wörner and Michael Mäckelmann have written that Schoenberg's text was also influenced by the theosophical writings of Madame Blavatsky and Rudolf Steiner, although there is no evidence that the composer was directly influenced by such ideas.[42] The text, in fact, addresses several different themes, some quite mundane despite the theological garb. As in *Die glückliche Hand*, Schoenberg deals in several parts of the libretto with long-standing views concerning the role of the artist, ideas that are especially evident in the songs of the first five individuals. Several of these characters reflect the composer's own self-image. The Chosen One is the genius who is driven to wrestle with the future of art, and, like the composer himself, he is conflicted in his relationship with his contemporaries. Schoenberg must also have seen his former self in the Chosen One, who abandons all in the pursuit of beauty, and in the Protester, who would follow instinct rather than law. The Struggler and the Monk represent lesser artists. The Struggler is the epigone who cannot see into the future and who, as Gabriel tells him, must rely on the Genius for a proper direction. The Monk is the artist who has settled for a shallow and temporary success, since he lacks the courage to walk on the rocky path of necessity.

Although the music of *Die Jakobsleiter* is one of Schoenberg's finest achievements, the text has proved a barrier to the work's greater acceptance. Wörner's assessment of it is typical when he describes it as "a vacillation between operatic libretto, sermon, contemplation and theological exegesis—an unfortunate misjudgment of Schoenberg's that sheds light on some problematical traits in his character."[43] Many ideas crowd together, and the language of the libretto is often cryptic, so abbreviated as to leave crucial matters unexplained. For a listener without an acquaintance with Balzac's *Séraphita* or Schoenberg's earlier writings, his libretto is sometimes impenetrable.

At about the time that he put aside the Rilke song "Liebeslied" and made his final revisions of the libretto on 7 June 1917, Schoenberg began an intensely concentrated period of composing the new oratorio. In the little more than three months before he was called back to the Austrian army on 19 September, he had composed 603 measures of a complex work for large orchestra, choruses, and solo voices, arriving just at the beginning of the central symphonic interlude when his work was interrupted. His composing during this period was exceedingly methodical. He began by extensive sketching, entering the most important ideas into a primary sketchbook and placing first thoughts or difficult passages into other papers or smaller sketchbooks. Jean Christensen has shown that the principal sketchbook[44] contains two nearly simultaneous streams of work, one consisting of disjunct preliminaries, the other of a continuous and more complete draft. At about the same time that this continuous draft was prepared, Schoenberg transferred and refined its contents into a more expansive short score, making relatively few significant changes or additions. None of the work is represented by a full score or fair copy.

Schoenberg's astonishingly rapid composing was disrupted by his recall on 19 September, an intrusion that caused him permanently to lose the thread of the composition. From that day forward he could only sporadically continue his work on *Die Jakobsleiter*. After his demobilization less than two months later, he made several false starts on its continuation, but even by 1922 he was able to extend the short score only to measure 702, still within the central symphonic interlude. This was as far as he would bring the continuous music for the work, although numerous fragmentary sketches were also made for its second half. *Die Jakobsleiter* sporadically occupied Schoenberg's thoughts for the remainder of his life.[45] He began a major revision in 1944 but made little headway on it. Only weeks before his death in 1951 he wrote to his former pupil Karl Rankl, inviting him to prepare a score of the first part of the oratorio plus the central interlude, which Schoenberg hoped to finish composing shortly.[46] After the composer's death, Rankl informed his widow, Gertrud, that he could not undertake the project in Schoenberg's absence.[47] In 1955 she turned instead to Winfried Zillig (1905–63), another former student, who accepted the challenge of preparing a version of the 702-measure fragment, which he would base primarily on the materials in the short score and the principal sketchbook.

Zillig's main task was to realize the orchestration of the oratorio fragment, no simple matter, since the composer had never settled on the size of orchestra that he had in mind and since the short score poses many complex questions concerning the doubling and distribution of lines. Zillig also had to flesh out passages in the short score that were unfinished and to find a best reading in areas where the sources conflicted. His reconstruction was a mixed success, praiseworthy in general but prepared without full knowledge of the sketches and questionable in many details.[48] His version of the first half of the oratorio was first performed in Vienna in 1961 and published, with minor revisions, in a piano-vocal score (1974) and orchestral score (1981), the latter revised by Rudolf Stephan and reissued with additional minor changes in 1985 in the Schoenberg *Sämtliche Werke*.[49]

The music of *Die Jakobsleiter*, although a fragment, achieves the originality and sweeping vision that are characteristic of Schoenberg's greatest atonal compositions. The work is based upon the formal archetype of the traditional oratorio, which consists of discrete sections or movements devoted to chorus, solo voices, vocal ensembles, and orchestral music. The traditional distinction in the oratorio between aria and recitative is retained by the contrast between singing and speaking voice, the latter of which is used in both soloistic and choral passages.

Four large, connected parts are evident in the existing music (summarized in Table 7.1). The work opens with a brief orchestral introduction wherein basic musical materials are clearly presented. It is followed by the first lines for Gabriel, who uses a melodious speaking voice. His music, both sung and spoken,

Table 7.1. Overall form of *Die Jakobsleiter*, measures 1–700

I.   Introduction and Choruses (measures 1–174)
   a. Introduction (1–19)
   b. Choruses of souls (19–174)
     1. Full chorus (19–98)
     2. Doubters, Dissatisfied, Rejoicers (98–128)
     3. The Indifferent and Meek (129–174)

II. Solos (175–564)
   a. Called One (175–255)
   b. Protester (256–287)
   c. Struggler (288–331)
   d. Chosen One (332–446)
   e. Monk (446–514)
   f. Dying One (515–564)

III. Duet (Soul and Gabriel) and Chorus (565–601)

IV. "Great symphonic interlude" (602–700, incomplete)

recurs periodically throughout the oratorio, mainly taking the form of preludes, interludes, and postludes. The remainder of the first main part of the oratorio is loose in construction. It consists of numerous subsections, some set apart by orchestral interludes. An intense thematic development is present, primarily in the orchestra although occasionally reaching into the lines of the chorus. It is typical of *Die Jakobsleiter* that important musical themes often appear in the speaking voices, which in this work have a far greater thematic involvement than in *Pierrot lunaire.* The development of a theme normally concludes at the end of a major section, but a few themes span larger units. An example is the "süßes Behagen" ("sweet contentment") motive in the chorus in measures 59–60, which returns at "O wie schön!" (measures 158–59 and the following interlude) and also in the song of the Called One (at "Mein Leben war von heller Freude erfüllt," from measure 215). Given the similar texts in these passages, this is a rare instance in *Die Jakobsleiter* of a line used unmistakably as a leitmotive.

The six songs that make up the second large part of the oratorio contain some of the most expressive music in the work, as Schoenberg creates intimate musical portraits of the six individuals. The first song, for the Called One, is a great aria for *Heldentenor.* His credo is beauty above all, which is embodied in music that imitates the late romantic style—impetuous, overstated, and in its treatment of the tenor voice more than a touch reminiscent of Mahler. Returning to the parodic stance of *Pierrot lunaire,* Schoenberg writes triadic harmonies in measures 205–6, even alluding to a tonal cadence in A major. But the heroic vein is suddenly dispelled by the shrill whining of the Protester—accompanied by pointed rhythms and metallic woodwinds—who complains about his difficulty in facing up to things necessary in life. His plaint is followed by that of the

Struggler, who speaks of the need for guidance, in music that seems intentionally plodding.

The song of the Chosen One is framed by two long, lyrical passages for Gabriel, in which the archangel for the first time sings rather than speaks. Fusako Hamao has shown that the Chosen One's song itself contains significant twelve-tone and serialized features.[50] Given Schoenberg's apparent feelings of kinship with the Chosen One, he makes this music conform most closely to his current thinking about coherence and structure. Next comes the anguished confession of the Monk, who has never exposed himself to happiness and would have no willpower to resist its temptations. The music follows his growing unease, finally breaking down into an emotional avowal of his weakness. Finally, the Dying One sings of his approach to heaven, accompanied by music that at first hesitates in fragments and finally reaches an ecstatic glissade on the syllable "Oh!" The trumpet in measures 563–64 then accompanies him upward as he ascends to heaven.

The voice of the Dying One becomes that of the Soul in the next major part (measures 565–601), where it is called upon to perform a monumentally difficult vocalise placed within a duet with Gabriel and supported by chorus. A great melisma begins with a variant of a motive that Schoenberg had sketched for Dehmel's "Äonische Stunde" in the Symphony, a rare example of his transferring material from one work to another. The singing resurrects the vocal style of *Herzgewächse* in its rich coloratura, which moves over the entire range of the soprano voice. As in the earlier song, the Soul begins with a steady and deliberate motion that finally blossoms into a flamboyant cadenza and soars to a sustained high F, then falls back to a cadence in a lower register.

The last of the four existing parts (measures 602–700) is a long orchestral interlude. Although it is incomplete, the composer's later remarks suggest that there was little more music to be added to it. In the published text of *Die Jakobsleiter*, Schoenberg described it as a "great symphonic interlude that expresses the tableaux and scenes that follow in the place of words."[51] But in a note tipped into the main sketchbook, he outlined a different plan by which the interlude was to consist of an introduction that suggests heaven, a development of themes from the first part that depict the transformation of the earthly characters, and a climactic conclusion in which "music streams into the entire hall from all sides."[52] The music that exists for the symphonic interlude is not closely related to either plan. Motives from the passage beginning at measure 565 are brought back (compare this measure to measures 608, 653, and 685), but otherwise the interlude consists of a far-reaching symphonic development of two new themes, the first introduced in the violin at measure 602 and the other in the cello at measure 615. The latter passages of the interlude, from measure 640 onward, were composed in 1922, and in these (especially measures 675–84) the development of themes is carried out by inversional and retrograded forms of tone rows in addition to traditional variations upon rhythm and shape. Finally, the voice of the soul echoes from two positions offstage, as it again takes up the great melisma from measure 565. On the soprano's ethereal high C, the music breaks off.

The composer never settled on a definitive medium for the oratorio. His earliest plan was to continue the larger-than-life scale that he envisaged in the Symphony and *Seraphita* projects. On a page tipped into the main sketchbook for *Die Jakobsleiter,* he specifies an orchestra and chorus of roughly one thousand performers. In later notes, this number was gradually whittled down, and Zillig—generally following the revision of 1944—calls only for a moderately large orchestra, twelve-part mixed chorus, and eight solo voices. In the central symphonic interlude, Schoenberg wrote for four offstage ensembles, two placed at a distance and two higher up, although he again gave different information about their makeup. Zillig calls for harmonium and six violins in each, plus varying numbers of voices, woodwinds, and brass. The highly dramatic spatial effects created by the offstage ensembles are probably indebted to Mahler's Symphony No. 2, where they similarly bring the audience directly into a vision of the apocalypse.

After his experiments in the Symphony and "Liebeslied" with strict thematic work, Schoenberg was ready in *Die Jakobsleiter* to brandish his new variational arsenal more boldly than at any time before. In April 1917, less than two months before he began to compose the oratorio, he outlined a treatise on composition, titled "Zusammenhang, Kontrapunkt, Instrumentation, Formenlehre," in which the topic of integration and unity among thematic materials is placed front and center.[53] But as is typical of Schoenberg's pedagogical writings, he touches in this outline solely on traditional variational practices inherited from the tonal period, not on his current methods for using themes, which were still highly guarded. In this outline he for the first time discusses the notion of "developing variation," which he defines as a process of change applied to motives within a theme, "allowing new ideas to arise."[54] A motive, he explains, is a small "sounding, rhythmicized phenomenon," and the examples of developing variation that he gives show progressive changes in the rhythms, intervals, and contour of such motives that eventually lead to new themes.[55] This traditional type of variation is still evident in *Die Jakobsleiter.* The Struggler's song, a passage that is especially strict in form and thematic usage, provides examples. The beginning of the main theme of the song is shown in Example 7.5a, the second theme in 7.5b. The first theme is economically constructed from variations upon its initial motive—a rhythmic-intervallic shape that is first stated in the downward leap on the tones D♭–F, then repeated with minor variations as E–G♯, G–A, and E♭–G. This variational process is then continued in the second theme, which begins with rhythmic alterations and a concatenation of the D♭–F and E–G♯ pairs, continues upward with F–A, and finally inverts the figure as F♯–A♯, F–B, and E–D. The variational process, as Schoenberg said, allowed an apparently new theme to arise.

Die Jakobsleiter also returns to the technique of serialized variation that Schoenberg developed in the "Liebeslied." This type of thematic work does not deal with motives or with their distinctive rhythms, as does developing variation, but it applies instead to longer phrases and whole themes. An example is found in the opening measures of the song of the Struggler. The bass line of measures 291–94 (Example 7.6) is a serialized variant of the first theme, which

Example 7.5. Schoenberg, *Die Jakobsleiter,* song of the Struggler: (a) first theme, measures 288–90; (b) second theme, measures 300–303

immediately precedes it in measures 288–90 (Example 7.5a), even though the two share no rhythmic or gestural ideas. The intervals of the bass line are an exact inversion of those of the earlier theme. Another way to view their relationship is to consider the earlier melodic phrase to embody the tone row D♭–F–D–E–G♯–G–A–G♭–E♭–G, which is inverted and transposed up four semitones to form the row of the line in 291–94, F–D♭–E–D–B♭–B–A–C–E♭–B. As in the inversional variations sketched in the Symphony and "Liebeslied," Schoenberg places the tones of the inversion in this passage from *Die Jakobsleiter* in registers that retain and mirror the registers of the opening phrase. Still at this time Schoenberg felt it necessary to retain the shape of an intial theme or phrase in a later serialized variant; only later did he aim for a more remote degree of serialized variation by a free treatment of registers through which the constancy of a shape was dispelled.

In *Die Jakobsleiter* Schoenberg also experimented with yet another technique of thematic variation that was intended to link and integrate themes throughout the entire work. It takes its origin from the cello figure at the very opening (Example 7.7). As with the basic figures that begin *Pierrot lunaire* and the Symphony scherzo, this line is presented in ostinato, which was now Schoenberg's way of highlighting an important structural element of a work at its very outset. But unlike any of Schoenberg's earlier compositions, the basic element here

Example 7.6. Schoenberg, *Die Jakobsleiter,* song of the Struggler, measures 291–94

Example 7.7. Schoenberg, *Die Jakobsleiter,* measures 1–8

is not the shape, motive, or interval succession per se, instead solely a collection of six pitch classes, C♯ D F E G♯ G, which have no prototypal ordering, registral placement, or rhythmic characteristics. When the notes of the hexachord reappear, they are freely rearranged, placed into different registers and rhythmic configurations, shadowed by their complement, transposed, extended by additional tones following or within, shortened to incomplete forms, verticalized into chords, or subjected to a combination of these techniques. This method of varying a theme, which in this book will be called *permutational variation,* was regularly used by Schoenberg from the time of *Die Jakobsleiter* in 1917 to that of the "Dance Scene" from the Serenade, Op. 24, in 1923. It was then dropped, only to be revived in the 1940s in works such as *Ode to Napoleon Buonaparte* and *A Survivor from Warsaw.*

In *Die Jakobsleiter* a permutational variant of the basic hexachord is most typically encountered at the beginning of a new theme, whose continuation is then guided by developing variation. The first theme of the Struggler's song (Example 7.5a) provides an example of this mode of occurrence: The first six notes of the theme (D♭–F–D–E–G♯–G) state the content of the basic hexachord, and the remaining ones are the outcome of a freer process of motivic development. When the tones of the basic hexachord are rearranged into a compact scalewise order, C♯ D E F G G♯, it is apparent that they form a symmetrical set, having the same succession of intervals read from either left or right and thus a musical allusion to Gabriel's first words in measures 11–12: "Whether to the right or left . . . you must go on." The themes and chords that contain the central hexachord or its variants occur sporadically throughout the composition, in virtually any musical or dramatic context, but they appear most prominently at the beginnings and endings of structural units, as though Schoenberg thought of the hexachord as a replacement for a tonic harmony in earlier music.

The strictness of thematic work that Schoenberg envisioned for *Die Jakobsleiter* is accompanied by a revival of the use of conventional forms, designs that rest on patterns created by thematic exposition, development, contrast, and reprise. The song of the Struggler again provides a typical example of Schoenberg's revival of traditional forms, as it does his experimentation with new thematic practices. The structure of the text is a primary formative element.[56] The music and its text reach cadences or formal junctures at the same points, although the music does not intimately mirror the expressive content of the words, which tends to be narrative and philosophical. The musical plan itself is close to the ternary model. An exposition (measures 288–303) contains the two basic themes already illustrated in Examples 7.5a and b; they are developed in measures 306 to 317 and recapitulated at measures 317 and 321, respectively, after which a coda (measures 326–31) concludes the song. Gabriel's interjection of a line in the middle of the Struggler's speech is treated as an episode, lodged between the exposition and development, which does not share in the thematic material that surrounds it. All of the important themes throughout the song occur in the orchestra rather than in the voice.

The main theme is strictly presented as a small ternary form. Its first phrase, shown in Example 7.5a, is contained in a brief orchestral introduction. The middle section of the small ternary form (measures 291–96) contains the Struggler's first utterance. Although it contrasts on the surface with the first part, it rests, as has been shown, on a bass line that is a serialized variant of the opening melody. The end of the small ternary form (measures 296–98), corresponding to the Struggler's second sentence, brings back the first phrase only slightly varied. The second main theme (Example 7.5b) seems new, but it is again developmentally related to the opening phrase and shares its accompanimental materials. The development section proper has three subsections—the first (from measure 306) deals with the codetta figure from measure 291, the second (from measure 308) with the second theme, and the last (from measure 314) with the first phrase, to which an entirely new theme is added by the viola. The recapitulation of the song is strict; the two main themes return intact while the music is varied primarily by a more enriched texture than in the exposition.

The creation of aggregates and the reinforcement of multidimensional unity that concerned Schoenberg in the Symphony are again taken up in the orchestral introduction to *Die Jakobsleiter*. As the celli continue their ostinato in measures 2–6 (see Example 7.7), the brass and woodwinds gradually pile up a six-note chord made from notes of the complement of the basic hexachord, thus creating by measure 6 an aggregate of the twelve tones. Schoenberg had already tried this way of forming an aggregate in measures 14–15 of the song "Seraphita," but he must certainly have been aware that the aggregate in *Die Jakobsleiter* would be less unified than the one in the Dowson song, in which the complementary hexachords were also transpositions of one another. The second hexachord in *Die Jakobsleiter* cannot be derived from the basic hexachord by any combination of reordering of tones, transposition, and inversion. This difference between the two may well have led Schoenberg to deemphasize the creation of aggregates later in *Die Jakobsleiter*. They are, in fact, rare, although in a few passages (see measures 92 and 675) Schoenberg returns to the opening idea of accompanying a line made from the basic hexachord with its complement lodged elsewhere in the texture. Many of the long themes throughout the work contain all twelve tones, but almost never as true aggregates in which no tone is repeated before all twelve have been brought in.

In measures 6–9 of the introduction, Schoenberg extends the aggregate by constructing a brief six-voice canon that replaces the initial ostinato (Example 7.7). In this canon, similar to the one in measures 32–34 of the Symphony scherzo, the vertical and horizontal dimensions are integrated by sharing the same pitch content. Each voice of the canon states the basic hexachord, either fully or incomplete, and, when all voices of the canon have finally entered in measure 8, each fleeting verticality contains a complete statement of its six tones. From measure 9 the strictness in use of materials quickly dissolves into freer forms, leading to the entrance of Gabriel in measure 11. His introductory passage in speaking voice is relatively free from the basic hexachord, except in measures 15–16, where the opening aggregate is briefly resurrected to mark the end of his first sentence of text.

Schoenberg admitted that his search for coherence in *Die Jakobsleiter* was also stimulated by his study of the works of other modern composers, which is surprising only in that he almost never confessed to the influence of a contemporary musician. He remarked that the idea of embedding permutations and variants of a six-note set of tones in themes and chords throughout the work came to him after reading the article "*Prometheus* von Skrjabin" by Leonid Sabaneyev, which was published in Kandinsky's German translation in *Der blaue Reiter* in 1912.[57] Prior to its publication Kandinsky had asked Schoenberg to edit his German version of the article for correct musical terminology, although given its many linguistic infelicities it is uncertain whether Schoenberg actually helped with it. In the article Sabaneyev asserts that Scriabin systematically used a central "mystic" chord of six tones throughout *Prometheus;* most typically the basic harmony is presented with its notes separated by perfect, diminished, and augmented fourths (e.g., C F♯ B♭ E A D), but the notes are also found transposed, stated in incomplete forms, and linearized in melodic ideas. "All melodic parts," wrote Sabanayev, "are built upon the sounds of the accompanying harmony, and all counterpoints are submitted to this same principle."[58] The author then reproduces principal themes from *Prometheus* with their accompanying harmonies. The mystic chord or its subsets appear in each, its notes freely re-ordered, transposed, and presented equally in lines as well as chords.

Die Jakobsleiter thus contains a great synopsis of Schoenberg's recent compositional experiments in thematic formation, which he merges with traditional ideas concerning genre, form, and development. The oratorio was a major step forward in his great quest for new variational and developmental resources in music, new methods for achieving a deep integration and organic coherence among pitch structures throughout a composition that can still be filled with contrast and the influx of new ideas. His experiments with ever more systematic variational techniques pushed the intuitive program for composition embodied in the 1909 Busoni manifesto far into the background, and they turned his attention ever more clearly toward a new Apollonian conception of music for the future.

Composing with Tones

Five Piano Pieces, Op. 23, and Serenade, Op. 24

By the time that Schoenberg had completed the first half of *Die Jakobsleiter* in the fall of 1917, his reconstruction of the atonal style had progressed well beyond the mixed and sporadic experiments apparent in *Pierrot lunaire* and the Four Orchestral Songs, Op. 22. The composer was now driven by a desire to regain full control over the compositional process and to write music methodically and coherently, leaving behind his earlier reliance on intuition, momentary inspiration, and free self-expression. This older frame of mind was now dismissed as a mere dream, from which he had at last awakened to confront the "laws" of nature and thought as they pertained to music. In 1941 he looked back and attempted to explain his change of outlook:

> The desire for a conscious control of the new means and forms will arise in every artist's mind; and he will wish to know *consciously* the laws and rules which govern the forms which he has conceived "as in a dream." Strongly convincing as this dream may have been, the conviction that these new sounds obey the laws of nature and of our manner of thinking—the conviction that order, logic, comprehensibility and form cannot be present without obedience to such laws— forces the composer along the road of exploration. He must find, if not laws or rules, at least ways to justify the dissonant character of these harmonies and their successions.[1]

New Perspectives, 1917–1923

Schoenberg conducted his search for logic and form on three separate fronts: thematic development, integration of musical space, and deployment of the full spectrum of chromatic tones. All of these built upon styles that he had found in the great music of the past, and according to his strictly evolutionist philosophy these paths would have to lead to the future of music. On the issue of thematic work, he was ready to continue his older practice of motivic variation, in which progressive changes in small rhythmic-intervallic figures led to new themes, and he added to this technique the outcome of his experiments in the Symphony, "Liebeslied," and *Die Jakobsleiter* with serialized and permutational variation of themes. These new methods of development promised to open the way toward an ever deeper level of unity in the linear dimension of a composition, and, at the same time, they could unify the musical space when a specific collection of tones returned not only horizontally but also vertically or distributed throughout a contrapuntal texture. Only later was the twelve-tone element to develop fully in Schoenberg's thinking, although he had already found ways to control the full chromatic gamut by writing twelve-tone themes, constructing densely chromatic fields (especially at the beginning or climax of a work), and joining complementary collections of pitches in different strata of a musical texture to form aggregates. His experiments in these three areas continued after 1917, whereupon his larger objective seems to have been the location of a single and integrated system that could accomplish all three simultaneously and take effect throughout an entire composition while still allowing for the degree of variety and contrast that was necessary in any engaging musical work.

In order to enunciate his new compositional practices, Schoenberg coined two new terms—*basic shape* (*Grundgestalt*) and *composing with tones.* Despite their importance to his evolving artistic outlook, he gave in his own published writings no detailed explanation of either one. The concept of basic shape can be reconstructed from the recollections of students such as Erwin Stein and Josef Rufer.[2] Schoenberg mentions "composing with tones" or "composing with tones of a motive" in several writings from the 1930s and 1940s, but this phrase is not mentioned by his students, and it may well have been a private compositional idea, probably closely linked to the notion of basic shape. The first published discussion of basic shape is contained in Erwin Stein's important article "Neue Formprinzipien," which appeared in 1924 in a special Schoenberg issue of the *Musikblätter des Anbruch.* In the summer of 1920, after earlier studies with Schoenberg, Stein returned to Vienna from Darmstadt to become a *Vortragsmeister* in the Verein für Musikalische Privataufführungen. He soon joined Webern, Berg, and Rufer as a member of the composer's innermost circle, to which Schoenberg periodically imparted highly confidential technical information about his new works. Such discussions and lectures took in ever larger numbers until February 1923, when Schoenberg called all his students together to spell out the workings and goals of his new method. Stein's 1924 article is a detailed and insightful conflation of ideas that came directly from Schoenberg himself on these occasions.

Stein first reflects upon Schoenberg's quest for form in atonal music, but his main intention is to describe the composer's practice of serialized variation as it had evolved in Schoenberg's music to 1923. He does not mention the technique of permutational variation that the composer also used at this time. Schoenberg's recent works, Stein says, are based upon a central "melodic" motive—a linear shape created solely by a row of pitches that form a fixed ordering of intervals. The succession of intervals replaces rhythm as the most basic thematic characteristic, the one most persistently retained in later variants: "Formal cohesion and connection are attained, in the first place, by motivic work. Only, the rhythmic motive is now of less importance than the melodic line. Melody is mostly formed, not as before by melodic variation of rhythmic motives, but by rhythmic variation of melodic motives."[3]

The prototypal "melodic motive" is what Schoenberg—according to Stein—called the basic shape of a work, "basic" in that it is the original form from which later variants derive their intervallic order or content and a "shape" in that it is an abstract entity, an unrhythmicized succession of intervals. Stein wrote:

> The most significant feature of the new method is the introduction of a succession of notes, a *basic shape,* as Schoenberg calls it, which carries the form of a piece. . . . The basic shape consists of several notes whose melodic structure (i.e., the relation between whose intervals) is binding upon the entire piece. The rhythm, however, is free. . . . Three typical mirror forms of the melodic motive [basic shape] play a fundamental role: inversion, retrograde motion, and retrograde inversion. They greatly change the physiognomy of the motive but retain its structure.[4]

Schoenberg's concept of "composing with tones" was apparently synonymous with composing with basic shapes, although it may also have admitted the device of permutational variation, in which there could be no systematic preservation of shape. His fullest description of the idea occurs in a letter from 1937 to Nicolas Slonimsky:

> I arrived [in the Piano Pieces, Op. 23] at a technique which I called (for myself) "composing with tones," a very vague term, but it meant something to me. Namely: in contrast to the ordinary way of using a motive, I used it already almost in the manner of a "basic set of twelve tones." I built other motives and themes from it, and also accompaniments and other chords—but the theme did not consist of twelve tones.[5]

A more detailed outline of composing with tones (although the term itself is not used) occurs in Stein's account of how Schoenberg applied a basic shape in works composed just prior to the maturation of the twelve-tone method. A basic shape may have fewer than all twelve pitch classes, he says, and some tones may be repeated, although this redundancy should be minimized. Some pieces will have several basic shapes, and these will usually appear at the beginning of a work, rhythmicized as phrases within the principal themes. The tones of a basic shape will reappear subsequently in the work embodied in new lines, chords, or both; they can also be partitioned into several simultaneous lines, split into smaller parts or extended by the interpolation of foreign notes, and transformed by transposition, inversion, retrogression, or a combination of these. By 1923 Schoenberg had begun to apply the concept of basic shape more pervasively than before, and he then dispensed with the notion of composing with tones. From this date a work was governed by a single twelve-tone basic shape. Writing in 1939 about the evolution of his variational practices, Schoenberg said: "Earlier I [spoke] of 'new motives,' but since then I have come to believe in the availability of just one motive."[6]

Schoenberg's new outlook on composing with basic shapes did not immediately stimulate his creativity. Between the time of his discharge from the army in December 1917 and the summer of 1922, he composed exceedingly little, as his attention was redirected into teaching and practical musicianship. His main activity during these years was the founding and oversight of the Verein für Musikalische Privataufführungen. Although valuable as an interlude that allowed him to ponder the future of his music, it was the most fallow extended period in his entire career as a composer. The few works from these years—all short pieces or fragments—continued the experimentation that would bring him closer to the twelve-tone idea.

On 9 March 1918—about three weeks before he moved from Vienna to the suburb of Mödling—he began to compose both a piano piece and a string septet.[7] The former was left after only ten measures; the latter, after thirty-four measures. Despite its brevity, the piano piece is a revealing forerunner of the piano character pieces of Opp. 23 and 25 and an indication that Schoenberg was turning away from the *Weltanschauungsmusik* of the preceding six years in favor of instrumental works of strict construction.[8] The two structural issues that are most evident in the fragment are serialized variation and integration of musical texture. A system for chromatic completion—the "twelve-tone" element—seems to have occupied the composer considerably less at this time than it did in the Symphony or in the opening of *Die Jakobsleiter.* Throughout the piano piece Schoenberg is intent upon finding ways in which serial variants of lines and small figures can be brought back, not just as additional lines but also as con-figurations that were spread throughout the texture—partly chordal, contra-puntal, and linear. In this way serialized variation could become the instrument of a more intense multidimensional unity in the musical space. The first three measures of the piano fragment contain several short figures—lines, chords, or a combination of both—that return later in serialized variants that are spatially reconfigured.[9] This discussion will be limited to the most important of them, an impetuous seven-note line first heard in the left hand prior to measure 1 (Example 8.1a). It recurs in several serialized variants later in the fragment, and these begin to show an important new freedom. This is clearly evident in the line in the right hand of measure 9 (Example 8.1b). The tone row of the origi-nal line returns almost exactly, but not its shape, since the tones are assigned to differing registers. The freeing of registers of tones in a row, as Fusako Hamao has noted, shows the composer "working with pitch classes" rather than with pitches per se.[10] Other recurrences of the opening figure are more covert, since they are reconfigured texturally rather than kept as simple lines. In measure 6, beats 2–3, for example, the tones of the opening figure return in the left hand as an accompaniment that is primarily chordal (Example 8.1c). Here the origi-nal order of notes is preserved, but there is no rhythmic or textural relationship with the opening line. Several occurrences in measure 1 (Example 8.1a) use in-versional and retrograded forms of the seven-note row. For example, the top part of the first two chords in the right hand of this measure, A G B D♯, then F B♭ E, amounts to a serialized variant of the basic figure inverted and transposed up seven semitones (A–G–B–D♯–E–F–B♭). Ethan Haimo has noted that this in-versional form plus the basic form (with which it is juxtaposed) cover all of the twelve pitch classes. It was typical of Schoenberg's music of this time to begin a

Example 8.1. Schoenberg, Piano Piece (1918): (a) measure 1; (b) measure 9;
(c) measure 6

work with a fully chromatic field, but given the duplication of two notes (E and G), there is no systematically formed aggregate. Schoenberg would later be skeptical of the value of such redundant twelve-tone fields, since the duplicated tones might be construed as tonics and thus "awaken false expectations."[11]

More than a year passed before Schoenberg again composed. In March 1919 he began a song accompanied by chamber orchestra on poetry by Tagore, "Ich fühle, daß alle Sterne in mir scheinen"—and probably also a second, undated Tagore song, "Lausche, mein Herz"—but both were soon discontinued. Neither fragment reveals a clear continuation of the structural thinking characteristic of his recent music. "I absolutely can't work," he exclaimed to Zemlinsky in August. "I can't clear my head. I worry over making a living, over political conditions and security; and even now during vacation I am still giving 15 lessons per

Example 8.2 Schoenberg, Passacaglia for Orchestra (1920): (a) draft (manuscript p. U275): (b) diplomatic transcription

Example 8.2 *continued*

Passacaglia für Orchester

—*continued*

Example 8.2 (b) *continued*

week."[12] Still another year slipped by with no new compositions. On 5 March 1920 he began a Passacaglia for Orchestra in which he returned to a strategy for chromatic completion and multidimensional integration that was by then tried and true. The eleven-measure fragment (Example 8.2a and b) begins with an ostinato in which the violins and clarinets gradually amass the tones B C D♯ E G A♭, much as the brass instruments built up their chord at the opening of *Die Jakobsleiter.* In measure 7 the lower strings take over the ostinato, now using the complementary hexachord C♯ D F G♭ A B♭, above which fragments of the first os-tinato return to complete the chromatic set. The two hexachords themselves (forms of set class 6–20) are equivalent by transposition to the ones that he had used similarly to create an aggregate in measures 14–15 of "Seraphita," Op. 22, No. 1.

The special structural properties of this hexachord, already touched upon in the preceding chapter, coaxed Schoenberg later to return to the Passacaglia to explore more completely its capacity to form aggregates. As with *Die Jakobsleiter,* he may have returned to the work several times over a period of years, although exact dates cannot be firmly established, since all drafts, sketches, and charts other than the one page from 1920 are undated. Some of these later materials and their contents resemble those for the Suite, Op. 29, composed in 1924, and others are similar to documents known to have originated in 1926.[13] Some of the later manuscripts almost certainly date from March 1926, since Schoenberg mentioned the piece to several correspondents in that month.[14] In these later materials Schoenberg revised the opening, sketched additional passages using a mature twelve-tone technique, and constructed row tables that plainly show a later maturation of his method than exists in the 1920 fragment.

Shortly after the orchestral essay, in the summer of 1920, Schoenberg's prolonged silence as a composer eased somewhat. In July and August he started on new works in the same genres that he had begun in March 1918—the piano character piece and the septet—but at last he was able to bring several of them to completion and to focus his new methods of composing. In June or July he started at least three piano pieces. Two of them (later designated as Op. 23, Nos. 1–2) were quickly finished, and the third was taken up again in 1923, whereupon it was completed and designated Op. 23, No. 4. Two other undated piano pieces were probably also begun in the summer of 1920, although they were permanently left incomplete. Jan Maegaard has named them Op. 23A and Op. 23B, given the similarity of their manuscripts and musical contents to the first two of the Op. 23 group.[15] Several movements from the new septet, later to become the Serenade, Op. 24, were also begun, and one of them (later placed as the third movement) was nearly brought to completion.

But after the promising revival during the summer of 1920, Schoenberg's muse again deserted him. During most of the 1920–21 season he lived in Holland, primarily in Zandvoort, where he taught and oversaw performances of his works, but he did not compose at all. In the summer of 1921, during a sojourn in Traunkirchen that lasted until the end of October, he again took up the thread of his works from the previous summer, and he was able to complete the first movement of the Serenade and a new piano piece that would later become the Prelude of his Suite, Op. 25. But the 1921–22 season was again almost totally devoid of composing.

The seamless transition from tonal to atonal composition that he had achieved in 1907 and 1908 and the burst of creativity that the new style had then provoked totally eluded Schoenberg as he approached the twelve-tone method. Evidently he needed some additional stimulus to refire his inspiration, something that went beyond a theory of musical form, however ingenious, to jolt him back into a vigorous career as a composer. This incentive came to him at last during 1921 and 1922, when he became aware of the Neoclassical style that was just then beginning to emerge among composers living in France. It would soon make Schoenberg snap out of his creative doldrums.

Prior to the end of World War I the notion of modernism in European music was associated mainly with a generation of composers—Gustav Mahler, Max Reger, Richard Strauss, Claude Debussy, Aleksandr Scriabin, and Schoenberg, among others—who had grown out of the romantic style. By 1920 all except Schoenberg and Strauss were dead, and even Strauss had returned to his romantic roots following *Elektra*, essentially rejecting modernism. Schoenberg was left virtually alone as a leader of the modern movement in music. Given his position in the musical world, he bore the brunt of the rebellion embodied in the

Neoclassical style. This "new music" of the 1920s represented a vigorous attack upon the older notion of modernism that Schoenberg represented. Its composers forcefully rejected the late romantic ethos of expressivity and complexity. Their music was lifelike where the older modernism was larger than life; their approach was eclectic in style rather than uniform, cool and detached rather than hotly expressive, popular in flavor rather than elitist. Its leaders were not German masters but young Frenchmen and the Russian Igor Stravinsky.

Schoenberg's first direct encounter with the Neoclassical style was in the concerts of his own Verein für Musikalische Privataufführungen, which generally emphasized the older type of modernism. An important event was the concert on 8 June 1921, at which Edward Steuermann performed Stravinsky's *Piano-Rag-Music* (1919). The work made a strong impression on the audience through a style that foretold the new taste of the 1920s.[16] It was unpretentious music, intended to be heard with the eyes wide open. It stirred together the seemingly incongruous—high art and *Kleinkunst*, consonance and dissonance, tonality and atonality, regular rhythm and irregular meter. It was witty, cool, with none of the wrenching angst that was well known to audiences of the Society. For Schoenberg such music amounted to an aesthetic misdirection, although one that could not be ignored. His public response to the new style soon became hostile, but he immediately began to make concessions to the idiom in his own works. In the March from his Serenade, Op. 24, composed in September and October of 1921, he refashioned his compositional experiments in a style filled with broad allusions to traditional music. This was what Stravinsky had done in his *Piano-Rag-Music,* but Schoenberg leaves behind enough grotesquerie to make it plain that his essay in "new music" was in large part a critique of the new taste, not just an imitation of it. Always ready to meet a new challenge, Schoenberg could no longer afford to remain compositionally silent, to experiment privately in unpublished pieces and fragments. He would instead have to match the productivity and innovativeness of his younger rivals in order to protect his hard-won accomplishments and reputation. "While composing for me had been a pleasure, now it became a duty. I knew I had to fulfil a task: I had to express what was necessary to be expressed and I knew I had the duty of developing my ideas for the sake of progress in music, whether I liked it or not," he concluded.[17]

Probably pondering his role in the future of the new music movement, Schoenberg returned in July 1922 to his vacation retreat in Traunkirchen and devoted himself mainly to *Die Jakobsleiter,* sketching ideas for the final chorus and extending the central symphonic interlude. Oddly, he showed little interest in the music that had occupied him for the previous two summers—the two series of piano pieces that would later become Opp. 23 and 25 and the Serenade—although he began the Sonnet movement of this last work, which brings in voice on a poem by Petrarch. But when Schoenberg admitted to having lost the thread of the oratorio, he quickly returned to these fragmentary instrumental compositions, determined to complete them and see them published and performed. During a trip to Copenhagen in January 1923 he entered into a contract with the Copenhagen publisher Wilhelm Hansen that would force him to complete four new compositions in the near future, two for Hansen and two for Universal Edition. "I ought to get something finished again at long last after so many disturbances," he explained to Zemlinsky.[18]

Five Piano Pieces, Op. 23

The first to be completed was the Five Piano Pieces, Op. 23, which had been started in the summer of 1920, probably for use in concerts of the Society, where Nos. 1 and 2 were premiered by Edward Steuermann on 9 October. The set of five was hurriedly completed in February 1923 and sent for publication to Hansen. In the atonal style, the piano character piece was Schoenberg's laboratory for trying out new ideas. The Three Pieces, Op. 11, were composed near the beginning of his atonal period, and in them he experimented with piano harmonics, ostinati, and the free forms of athematicism. The Six Little Piano Pieces, Op. 19, were the crucible in which the aphoristic style was forged. Now with the dawning of the twelve-tone method, Schoenberg returned almost predictably to the resources of the instrument.

When he composed the first piece in July 1920, it is unlikely that he foresaw the collection of five works that later appeared as Op. 23. These were instead free-standing studies, each addressing a different compositional issue, expressive gesture, and formal problem. Josef Rufer described Op. 23 as a "series of experiments" in which the composer used the piano since it was "in performability, composition, and tonal scope the most practical medium."[19] Unlike the Suite, Op. 25, there is no thread that runs throughout Op. 23, no common materials, not even a central compositional principle. All the same, the series of the five pieces and the order in which Schoenberg arranged them has a distant echo in the Five Orchestra Pieces, Op. 16. Both consist of a suite of five essentially independent works of different character, both end with a waltz, and both include a fugue (Piece No. 3 in Op. 23 and Piece No. 1 in Op. 16).

Schoenberg recorded the date 9 July 1920 at the end of Piece No. 1, and it was probably begun shortly before. The draft has a note at the top calling it a "Preludium" for "Suite No. 1," although these labels appear to have been entered later than the music itself, presumably in February or March 1923, when Schoenberg was thinking of two "series" or "suites" of piano pieces, one loosely connected (Op. 23) and one sharing a common tone row (Op. 25). The preliminary title "suite" for Op. 23—used definitively for Op. 25—may well have been a concession to the burgeoning Neoclassical taste, an effort to make the pieces more performable in the new atmosphere of the 1920s. But the retardataire title has no strong relevance to the works themselves. Piece No. 1 has no introductory or dancelike character, as it is slow and wistful and roughly the same length as the other pieces in Op. 23, although its relative simplicity and traditional form may have made the composer think of it as a prelude to the more complex studies that follow.

In form, the work is based on the ternary model. The opening section (measures 1–12) is divided into two equal parts; the first introduces basic thematic

Example 8.3. Schoenberg, Piano Piece, Op. 23, No. 1, measures 1–5

materials, and the second continues with new lines that incorporate motives from the opening. The texture of this opening section is strictly divided into three contrapuntal though interrelated strata—Stein aptly described it as "three-part invention."[20] The similarity of the three lines is most evident at the beginning (Example 8.3), where each voice alternates intervals equivalent to the minor third and minor second. In the middle section (measures 13–22) the three lines begin to dissolve into a freer texture, and there is a new rhythmic design, a slower tempo, and seemingly new motivic and harmonic ideas. Two themes from the opening then intercede—in measures 16–18 (right hand) the top line from the opening reappears, its original span of a fourth now splayed out to four octaves plus a fourth. It is echoed expressively in measures 19–20 by the return of the lowest line from the opening. The original tempo is regained in measure 21, although the reprise does not properly begin until measure 23, at which point the three lines of the exposition fully return in varied diminutions. From measure 26 to the end, the opening ideas continue to recirculate in a highly varied and fragmented state in which rhythmic and harmonic ideas from the middle section are also present.

The piece is primarily a study in developing and serialized variation upon themes and motives—the creation of aggregates and integration of texture are not directly or extensively addressed. The more traditional process of developing variation can be observed in the lowest line in measures 1–5 (Example 8.3) and in its relation to the main idea of the middle section that begins in measure 13 (Example 8.4). The basic motive, bracketed in the first example, consists of an ascending minor third followed by a descending minor second in a short-long-long rhythm. Interlocking with the first statement of this motive is another that is moved up sequentially and changed in rhythm. In measures 4–5 the motive is enlarged to four tones with more extensive changes. The first interval is expanded to a major third (C–E), and the minor second is split off as the tones B♭–A; elements of the initial rhythm are still retained. The developmental process

Example 8.4. Schoenberg, Piano Piece, Op. 23, No. 1, measures 13–15

then continues in measure 13 in the context of a seemingly new idea (Example 8.4). The major third and minor second from measures 4–5 are now reconfigured vertically as a major third (G B) and major seventh (D C♯). The rhythmic context may seem entirely different, although it, too, picks up a rhythmic figure already introduced in the lowest line in measures 8–9. The variational process on a small rhythmic-intervallic motive is thus a "developing variation"; as Schoenberg wrote, it allows for and leads to a new idea.

Serialized variation also plays a role in Piece No. 1, although in a comparatively simplified form. The tone rows of each of the three lines in measures 1–6 are brought back later in the work, but mainly in simple repetitions rather than in transposed, inverted, or retrograded variants. Especially from measure 26 to the end, only small fragments of the interval successions that underlie the initial lines are reproduced, and in one instance (in the left hand from measure 30 to measure 32) the first six tones of the top line reappear in retrograde. Schoenberg is also conservative in retaining the initial registers of tones, although segments of the themes are sometimes shifted into different octaves.

Following the muted first piece, No. 2 seems to explode and to vent a fury that breaks free from the symmetry of its forerunner. George Perle has aptly described Piece No. 2 as a "work of concentrated power and logic and one of the most effective of Schoenberg's creations."[21] It has none of the balance or roundedness of its predecessor. After its eruptive opening nine measures, it proceeds through a string of subsections, each of a distinct character and each progressively slower, until the music finally dissolves into a state of depletion in the depths of the instrument. Formally, the work consists of a free succession of variations upon two ideas: an upward moving line in measure 1 (Example 8.5a) and an angry dialogue in measures 5–6 between a jagged line in the left hand and chords in the right. This second idea returns freely varied in measures 8–9, 13, and 16–17 with hardly a trace of Schoenberg's serial thinking, but the first theme embodies a basic shape that reappears in numerous serialized variants. An example is in the improvisatory arpeggio in measure 7 (Example 8.5b) where the nine-note row of pitch classes returns directly. As in the piano fragment from 1918, the shape of the original figure is not retained, as the tones of the row are freely assigned to new registers. The end of the arpeggio is made from freely chosen tones, which are then verticalized a minor ninth higher in the chord

Example 8.5. Schoenberg, Piano Piece, op. 23, No. 2: (a) measure 1; (b) measure 7

under the fermata. The nine-note row then undergoes a series of motivic, rhythmic, and expressive reformulations that vividly reveal the power of the new method to produce a diversity of character. It appears in a succession of different transpositions in measures 10–14 and in three simultaneous inverted forms in 18–19.[22] As the music dwindles away in its last measure, a final statement of the row is presented, completely unlike the first statement in rhythm, contour, division between the hands, and character.

Piece No. 4 was begun on 26 July 1920, just as No. 2 was being completed, but was interrupted at the end of measure 14 and only resumed and completed in February 1923. The compositional premises that it embodies show again that Schoenberg was not pursuing a straight or even coherent line of development in his compositions during the summer of 1920, but experimenting instead with new ideas and combining them freely with older ones. No. 4 has a capricious, almost improvisatory character; it is generally thin in texture and moves lightly and quickly through numerous short subsections that establish different moods. Like No. 1, the form is ternary. The first section (measures 1–13) contains several related ideas and ends with a restatement of the main theme from measure 1. The middle section (measures 14–23) contrasts mainly in character and a greater degree of expressive complexity, and the recapitulation (measures 24–28) brings back the whole matrix of pitch classes from the first six measures, although these tones are totally reconfigured into new lines and chords. A coda (measures 29–35) dwells upon "tonic chords"—Erwin Stein's description of the return of opening materials at their original level of transposition—and the work ends with a final reference to the main theme.

One of the many remarkable features of Piece No. 4 is its minimalization of basic pitch materials. Recurrences of tones from three hexachords in the first measure can plausibly account for every note throughout the work. There are no free passages as in Nos. 1 and 2. These three basic hexachords are shown in Example 8.6a, where they are labeled *A*, *B*, and *C*. The main theme is contained in *A*, which is related to the other two hexachordal shapes since the notes in all three are generally paired off to form major thirds (sometimes minor thirds) or their inversions. As in the beginnings of other pieces composed at this time, the first measure of Piece No. 4 is saturated with the twelve tones, several of which are freely repeated.

Example 8.6. Schoenberg, Piano Piece, Op. 23, No. 4 (a) measures 1–3. Subscript numbers that follow *A* and *C* indicate the transposition in number of semitones relative to the original occurrence; the complement of set *C* is abbreviated "comp"; (b) measures 24–26

The three hexachords are only rarely used as basic shapes. More often they reappear in the form of permutational variations, as Schoenberg resurrects in this piece the principal compositional device that he was still using in *Die Jakobsleiter.* As in the oratorio, pitches in the central hexachords are freely reordered, transposed, echoed by their complements, and reconfigured into an endless variety of new lines, chords, and textural shapes that have little, if any, connection in rhythm or motive to their models from measure 1. Example 8.6a shows the process of permutational variation at work from the very outset of the composition, as hexachords *A, B,* and *C* begin to recirculate immediately after the first measure. Occasionally the order of intervals of the figures from measure 1 is retained to create a serialized variant, as in the transposed statement of *A* in measure 2, but more often the tones are shuffled in order, as in the return of *C* in measure 2 and *A* at the end of measure 3. Sometimes the rhythm and contour of a small part of a shape are preserved in later variants, thus suggesting a developing variation. An example is found in measure 3 in the strettolike recurrences E–G–A, E♭–G–B♭, and B–D–E in the middle and lower lines, where these figures develop the motive B–D–E from the main theme. But more often the variations totally dispense with the rhythm and phrasing of their models, to which they relate solely by a total pitch content that is transformed primarily through transposition, complementation, and inversion.

The recapitulation (measures 24–28) is created by the nearly exact return of the matrix of pitch classes from the opening six measures, although the registers of these tones and their precise order, rhythm, and deployment in lines and chords are so extensively changed that there is virtually no reference to the opening outside of total pitch class content. Example 8.6b shows the first three measures of the reprise, in which this new concept of recapitulation can be readily observed by comparing the music to that in Example 8.6a. "How different it looks from the opening," exclaimed Stein, "although we meet exactly the same notes!"[23]

The draft manuscript for measures 1–14 of Piece No. 4 (Example 8.7) contains provocative analytic annotations, which were entered by Schoenberg himself and are unique among his compositional manuscripts. These consist of circles placed around three groups of tones in the first two measures and labels attached to subgroups of tones within the circles. A_1 indicates the single note D♯ from the main theme; A_2, the remainder of the theme (B–B♭–D–E–G). Other labels are connected to these tone groups:

B_1 = C♯–A
B_2 = C–A♭
B_3 = G–B
C_1 = D–B♭ and A–D♭
C_2 = C–F
D_1 = A♭–C and G♭–B♭
D_2 = A–F.

The pseudomathematical appearance of these annotations is similar to the markings that Schoenberg sometimes used in his theoretical writings to indi-

Example 8.7. Schoenberg, Piano Piece, Op. 23, No. 4, measures 1–14 (first draft)

cate small motives or motivic particles.[24] In the manuscript of Piece No. 4 he uses the labels similarly, to designate minute figures, mainly dyads whose tones are separated by a major third or its inversion. When these small tone-groups recur in the fourteen-measure fragment—usually at their original pitch or sometimes transposed—they are given the appropriate labels. Schoenberg also makes note of certain equivalences among these dyads. In the left margin under the date of 26 July 1920, he writes: "$B_1 + B_2 = C_1$," that is, the tones $C^{\sharp}$–A plus C–A$^{\flat}$ are equivalent (by transposition and reordering) to D–B$^{\flat}$ and A–D$^{\flat}$.

It is most likely that Schoenberg made his annotations in the summer of 1920 to help him to overcome a problem that he had encountered in measure 14. It is certain that he had no intention of producing a general analysis or even assessing the work's most basic pitch structures, which are the larger hexachordal collections. In the original version of measure 14 (shown at the end of Example 8.7), the three basic hexachords return at their original level of transposition, although extensively reconfigured in surface design. The closeness of this version of measure 14 to measure 1 is reflected in the large number of labels that Schoenberg entered before he crossed out the entire measure. He then made no fewer than seven additional sketches for this measure,[25] apparently wanting to retain a reference to the three basic hexachords but without so many simple repetitions in pitch. He arrived at a final version that is similar to the first one except that the tones are transposed up a minor third and the initial motives are better hidden.

The final two pieces of Op. 23—Nos. 3 and 5—were begun and quickly completed in February 1923. In the intervening two and a half years, Schoenberg had composed his first full-fledged twelve-tone compositions: the Prelude of the Suite, Op. 25, and the Sonnet from the Serenade, although the latter was still incomplete. He had also begun several other movements from these two works in addition to a few other short fragments and arrangements. During these years he had refined and extended his experiments with serialized variation and chromatic completion, but he had still not decided upon any one compositional method to carry into the future. When he resurrected Op. 23 in February of 1923, he continued to sample different structural ideas, some old and others new. Just as he had revived the permutational approach to variation from *Die Jakobsleiter* in Piece No. 4, Schoenberg looked again to the oratorio for other ideas to bring to Piece No. 3, which he then joined to an ever stricter application of the serial principle.

Piece No. 3 was begun on 6 February 1923 and completed three days later. The work is by far the longest in Op. 23, and its complex structure poses a challenge to the technical and interpretive skills of the performer. It begins in the manner of a stolid fugue, although the strictness of counterpoint quickly dissolves into a succession of virtuosic gestures. The form of Piece No. 3 resembles that of Piece No. 2 in its open chain of subsections, each having a different character. There is no definitive reprise, although the pitch materials of the opening return several times (see measures 9, 12, 20, 26, and 30), albeit in motivic forms that are remote from the first measures.

The structure of the work takes its origin from a five-note basic shape heard in the right hand at the outset (Example 8.8). The pitch content of this figure resembles that of the opening hexachord of *Die Jakobsleiter* since both are segments of an octatonic scale; also like the oratorio, its notes sometimes return freely reordered, in addition to their reappearance as serialized variants. These strict variants, which almost always preserve the contour of the opening statement, sometimes recur contrapuntally, as at the end of measure 8, where sev-

Example 8.8. Schoenberg, Piano Piece, Op. 23, No. 3

eral different row forms are stated simultaneously in different strands of the texture. Often (see measures 9–10, 12–13, 20–21, and 26–29) they are presented as "acrostics," to use Stein's description, by which the notes of the basic shape are heard in long values around and between which other pitches intervene.

Given the ever greater importance of serialized variation in Schoenberg's music from 1923, it will be useful at this point to introduce abbreviations to designate transformations of tone rows. Schoenberg himself used such abbreviations. In his sketches beginning in 1920, he often labels the tones of a basic shape with the letter *T* for *Thema*, *U* (*Umkehrung*) for its inversion, *K* (*Krebs*) for its retrograde, or a combination of these. Somewhat later he began to attach numbers to these labels to show the interval of transposition of the underlying row. Although there is still no widely standardized system for such abbreviations, the discussion that follows will use the letter *P* (prime form) for the row of pitch classes within a basic shape and a subscript number beside it to indicate transposition, that is, the number of semitones above the original statement at which the row form is placed. For example, the initial statement of a basic shape in a work will, by definition, embody the row form P_0. The letter *I* will indicate an inversion of that shape, *R* the retrograde of a prime form, and *RI* the retrograde of an inversion, with subscript numbers used as with the prime form.

These abbreviations will facilitate an assessment of an important interpretive disagreement among specialists who have written on Piece No. 3. Does the pitch structure of the entire piece derive from the basic shape by serialized and permutational variations, or, as in Pieces No. 1 and 2, do such variants appear only sporadically amid passages that are freely constructed? Ethan Haimo and George Perle have taken the latter position, but others—including Erwin Stein, Hans Oesch, Martha M. Hyde, and Martina Sichardt—have concluded that virtually the entire composition is unified by transformations of the tones of the central pentad, sometimes presented serially but more often freely reordered, spread covertly into the texture, or transformed into other related pitch collections. The uncertainty of the matter is evident in the first three measures, which are shown schematically at the bottom of Example 8.8. For the sake of clarity, the notes are shown solely as pitch classes, aligned so as to reflect registers and linear connections within the texture. The only straightforward serialized variation of the basic shape in these measures is the fuguelike answer in the left hand in measures 2–3, which contains a statement of P_7 (F–A–B–F♯–G♯). But given the chromatic pitch content of the basic shape itself and given Schoenberg's saturation of the passage with chromatic tones, it is possible to adduce many other reordered occurrences. The analytic interpretation in Example 8.8 shows every note as a member of a constellation made from the tones of some row form, although the segmentation of these tones does not necessarily reflect the musical structure. As the piece progresses, dividing the entire texture into variants of the initial shape becomes ever more difficult and requires analytic strategies that fully bypass the musical context and, in all likelihood, the composer's intentions.

Martha M. Hyde, for example, has called attention to an abstract notion of complementation of the basic shape. In her analysis of the work she interprets, for example, the series of pitches in the right-hand line in measures 2 and 3—C♯–E–F–E♭–G♭–A–D–E♭–C—as a distinct structural entity, since it embodies the complement of the basic shape at P_9.[26] An analyst less inclined to find systematic unity in the piece would object that this succession of tones does not coincide with any single theme or phrase and that its five-note complement is nowhere nearby. However, complement relations unquestionably play a role in Schoenberg's sketches for the piece, as in the music of the codalike passage from measure 30 to be discussed momentarily. Hans Oesch and Martina Sichardt use an analytic strategy that Sichardt calls interlacing (*Verschachtelung*) to derive irregular pitch structures from the basic shape.[27] According to this procedure, notes in many noncontiguous locations within the musical texture are identified as members of row forms, thus bringing together tones that have at most a remote proximity and no distinct musical identity. There can be no firm conclusion as to which of these two analytic interpretations is correct. But it is relevant that the search for a systematic theory that can account for any and all aspects of pitch structure in Schoenberg's atonal and twelve-tone music much more strongly characterized technical writings on his music since the 1950s than it did the composer's own writings or those of his circle.

Far more than in Pieces No. 1, 2, and 4, Schoenberg experimented in Piece No. 3 with the systematic formation of aggregates. On a page of sketches,[28] he extracted various pairs of row forms from a single chromatic scale, apparently looking for those that did not intersect in pitch content. Finally he hit upon P_0 and I_{11}, which share no tones and together need only the notes G and C to complete the chromatic set. Beneath this sketch he wrote: "This [sketch] is after the fact!! [It was] constructed and came to mind in the 2d measure: the form, which I painstakingly looked for here, occurred to me right in the second measure."[29] Since measure 2 does not involve the row form I_{11}, Schoenberg was probably referring to his intention in the fuguelike exposition of measures 1–2 to juxtapose row forms that do not intersect in pitch content. But his ultimate choice of a row form for the answer, P_7, was evidently governed by an allusion to the traditional fugue, in which a subject is answered at the fifth, and it does not fulfill his intention of avoiding pitch duplications, since the row forms P_0 and P_7 share the note B. Still, the nearly complementary relation of the two rows was then planted in his mind and worked out in the sketches as the piece neared completion. The juxtaposition of P_0 and I_{11} occurs at the end of the work, in the codalike passage in measures 30–35, which closely relates to the sketch. At the marking *tempo* in measure 30, a verticalized statement of P_0 is placed next to a statement of I_{11}, similarly disposed, beneath which the pedal tones C and G complete the aggregate. The two pedal tones are then sustained to the end of the piece—another parody of the fugue—and the row forms alternate among P_0, P_7, I_4, and I_{11}, forms that Schoenberg apparently thought of as fulfilling a "tonic" function.

Piece No. 5, titled "Waltz," followed on the heels of No. 3; it was completed on 17 February and begun a few days before.[30] In this work more than anywhere else in Op. 23, concessions to the Neoclassical style are evident. Such allusions had already been made in movements from the Serenade, which will be discussed shortly. The Waltz is playful, light in texture, and relatively regular in rhythm and meter, and its form is filled with repetitions and symmetries. Its overall plan is ternary. The first section (measures 1–28) is expanded by developing variations upon the rhythmic figures of the opening measure (see Example 8.9). The middle section (measures 29–73) begins with a new melody that parodies traditional period form (Example 8.10), and the section then dwells on motives that are reasonably remote from the opening passage. The reprise (measures 74–99) brings back the rhythmic motives of the opening, although the choice of pitches is changed. Recalling the end of the waltz in Op. 16, No. 5, the dance finally dies away in a coda (measures 100–113) amid echoes of the main theme.

The Waltz of Op. 23 is a true twelve-tone composition, the third such in Schoenberg's oeuvre, following only the Prelude from Op. 25 (1921) and the still-fragmentary Sonnet from Op. 24. By placing the Waltz last in the Five Piano Pieces, the composer may have intended to signal that his long period of exploration into new compositional methods was now over. He had sorted through his experiments from the preceding nine years and selected those that he would

Example 8.9. Schoenberg, Piano Piece, Op. 23, No. 5, measures 1–4

bring with him into the future—the systematic exploitation of the complete chromatic set, minimalization of pitch resources, strictness of serialized variations upon a basic shape, and the deployment of these variants throughout the two-dimensional musical space. These would constitute the unified and coherent approach to composing that he had long sought and which he would soon name the "method of composition with twelve tones related only one to another."

The entire contrapuntal and harmonic content of Piece No. 5 is derived from a single twelve-tone row that is constantly recirculated with only a few deviations or liberties. The prototypal shape is introduced in the main theme in measures 1–4 in the right hand (Example 8.9), and it is based on the tone row C♯–A–B–G–A♭–F♯–A♯–D–E–E♭–C–F. Schoenberg further minimalizes the pitch resources at his disposal by using solely this one row form throughout the entire piece, except for a brief appearance of R_0 in measures 104–10. This limitation posed a challenging and complex problem. How could the composer create a diversified work, filled with development, newness, and contrast, while confining himself to the recirculation of a single tone row?

The answers that he found were highly influential upon the later development of the twelve-tone method. To begin with, he freed the notes of the row almost entirely from the registers that they occupied in the initial statement of the shape. Even in Piece No. 3, the contour of the basic shape tended to be retained within a serialized variant, but in the Waltz he treats the tones of the basic shape as pitch classes that can be repositioned in any register. For this reason, the expression "basic shape"—a term that suggests a fixed contour—becomes a misnomer, and Schoenberg was later inclined to replace it with *basic set* or *basic row* to designate the prototypal structure of a twelve-tone composition.

Next, he revived the structural principle of developing variation, which had been less evident in his music governed by serialized variations. Developing vari-

Example 8.10. Schoenberg, Piano Piece, Op. 23, No. 5, measures 29–34

ation—that is, progressive changes carried out on small rhythmic-intervallic motives—is evident, for example, in the relationship between the main theme (Example 8.9) and the second theme in measures 29–34 (Example 8.10). The latter is based on a concatenation of two small intervallic-rhythmic ideas from the main theme: the descending fifth from the end of measure 4 (C–F) and the rhythm of measure 1. The theme in Example 8.10 also contains an important example of how Schoenberg could construct a new theme that has such developmental features while still adhering to the original row. The melody is made by extracting tones 1, 6, 11, 12, 7, 12, 5, and 6 from three consecutive statements of P_0, while the intervening tones of these three statements are shunted into the accompaniment in the left hand. This way of distributing notes of a row form into a contrapuntal texture, often called *partitioning*, would become Schoenberg's standard practice in his later twelve-tone pieces. A simple linear statement of a row form is used only at a structural juncture—in this work, only at the very beginning. In the first four measures Schoenberg accompanies the melody by a statement in the left hand of P_0 that has been rotated to begin with its sixth tone and conclude with its fifth. A multidimensional presentation of aggregates results. Both the left hand and the right hand of measures 1–4 contain linearized statements of the twelve tones, and aggregates are also present vertically in measures 1–2 and 2–4 by the juxtaposition of a melodic phrase and its accompaniment. Increasingly in his twelve-tone music Schoenberg would find ever more subtle and ingenious ways to unify a two-dimensional texture by such interlocking aggregates.

But why were the twelve tones desirable at all? Schoenberg later stated that a basic shape made from twelve tones, with none omitted and none repeated, was an essential that he had discovered late in his period of experimentation, probably only in 1923, thus transforming "composition with tones" into twelve-tone composition per se. He could certainly have continued composing with nondo-decaphonic basic shapes and probably continued to achieve such satisfying results as he did in Piece No. 2 from Op. 23. In fact, Schoenberg was never able to give a convincing reason why his music had to be twelve-tone. His often-repeated explanation was curiously antiquated, drawn from an observation about the early atonal style that he had made in the *Harmonielehre.* There he recommended avoiding octave doublings. "I have noticed that tone doublings, octaves, seldom appear," he wrote. "The explanation for that is, perhaps, that the tone doubled would acquire a predominance over the others and would thereby turn into a kind of root, which it should scarcely be."[31] Now he returned to this thinking to explain why basic shapes had to have twelve tones:

> The construction of a basic set of twelve tones derives from the intention to postpone the repetition of every tone as long as possible. I have stated in my *Harmonielehre* that the emphasis given to a tone by a premature repetition is capable of heightening it to the rank of a tonic. But the regular application of a set of twelve tones emphasises all the other tones in the same manner, thus depriving one single tone of the privilege of supremacy. It seemed in the first stages immensely important to avoid a similarity with tonality.[32]

This strangely inadequate explanation can only be understood in light of extraneous factors. The first was Schoenberg's self-conscious reluctance to discuss technical or constructive aspects of twelve-tone rows. These were secrets that he guarded with the utmost caution. Although Schoenberg never wrote about the structural advantages of twelve-tone rows compared to non-twelve-tone rows, these were almost certainly factors in the ultimate formulation of his twelve-tone method. One such is the elegance of relations that exists between complementary hexachords. The two halves of a row invariably share the same total intervallic content, although their pitch-class content is interrelated in several different and compositionally provocative ways—sometimes by transposition, by inversion, or by neither of these. Schoenberg was well aware of the often-enigmatic relations among complementary hexachords through his experiments going back as far as "Seraphita," Op. 22, No. 1.

Another crucial factor in Schoenberg's decision to compose with twelve-tone rows was his bitter rivalry with other progressive composers—including such outsiders as Josef Matthias Hauer and even his own students Webern and Fritz Heinrich Klein—all of whom were experimenting with systematic applications of the chromatic scale at the same time as Schoenberg. The ideas of Hauer were especially unsettling to Schoenberg in their relation to his own more fragmented experiments. Even by 1919 Hauer had advanced a competing twelve-tone outlook on composing. In his 1920 treatise *Vom Wesen des Musikalischen,* he announced a "law" of atonal melody: "Within a given succession of tones," Hauer wrote, "no note [may be] repeated and none may be omitted."[33] Schoenberg's extensive marginalia in his personal copy of this treatise, as well as in several of Hauer's articles and musical compositions, show that he carefully studied Hauer's ideas during the summers of 1921 and 1922. Although Schoenberg felt no challenge from Hauer as a composer, the originality of Hauer's concept for the use of the chromatic set must surely have been a spur for him to expand his own incipient method to embrace chromaticism in a comparably universal manner. [34] But before Schoenberg was permanently to settle on twelve-tone composition, one major atonal work, the Serenade, Op. 24, still lay incomplete on his workbench.

Serenade, Op. 24

The Serenade marks the end of Schoenberg's atonal period of composition, the end of a fifteen-year experiment with the capacity of music to absorb new ideas and to extend its means of expression. As much as any work, the Serenade demonstrates that Schoenberg's atonal period does not contain music that is stylistically or structurally homogeneous. In Schoenberg's hands atonality amounted to a liberated outlook on artistic expression, one that was infinitely adaptable to new perspectives on how music could be coherent and communicative. The Serenade builds upon the compositional methods that Schoenberg had developed since the Symphony in 1914, but in style and overall form it has no predecessor or model anywhere in his oeuvre. The irony and parody that were subtly present in *Pierrot lunaire* are here made so blatant that they seem to collide with the composer's long-standing aesthetic principles. The overall form of the work, for example, is governed by large and exact sectional repetitions, apparently repudiating Schoenberg's belief that modern music should not use literal repetition, that an idea once stated did not need to be heard a second time. The Serenade overtly refers its listeners to existing though highly disparate music by other composers, primarily Mozart and Stravinsky, and in doing so it seems to disagree with Schoenberg's insistence that music had to move forward coherently into the future. The work is written in a mixed style, which Schoenberg only three years later dismissed as something ludicrous, like "painting a marble slab with lacquer."[35]

The antinomies embodied by the Serenade were baffling to many of Schoenberg's supporters. Adorno, for example, had to rummage deep in his bag of dialectic in order to explain them. The Serenade, he opined, contained an expression of pure irony that was born of a conflict between form and formlessness, between the outer object and the inner subject:

> Faced with the experience that form no longer exists, in which [art] wafts up from the abyss of subjective inwardness, he [the composer] encounters the exact opposite experience: that inwardness cannot live here and achieve permanence as aesthetic image, so it must find objective footholds outside itself. The dialectic of these contrary experiences—experiences that arise from a developing essence rather than psychological records, achieved in the purest material immanence—is at the root of Schoenberg's irony.[36]

The history and interpretation of the Serenade are among the most complex and uncertain for any of Schoenberg's major compositions. The stages in its creation are obscured by its long period of gestation, which covered nearly three years and coincided with the final steps toward the twelve-tone method and with the emergence of the Neoclassical style, both of which exerted a strong influence upon the language that Schoenberg adopted. There are many sketches and drafts for each movement, but since these are not consistently dated there remains uncertainty about the chronology of composition, the relation of the Serenade to other works from the years 1920–23, and the steps through which the final conception came into existence. An analysis of the music itself is made all the more complex since Schoenberg adopts a new compositional method in every movement, and these are far more unpredictable and, in many cases, more recondite than the mature twelve-tone method itself.

Continuing a pattern that characterizes all of the major works from the atonal period, Schoenberg began to compose the Serenade well before he had settled on its overall form, which gradually evolved in his mind and was finalized only at the very end of the compositional process. The earliest dated sketches come from early August 1920, shortly after his first period of composing the Five Piano Pieces, Op. 23. At this time Schoenberg began at least four separate movements for an unusual combination of seven instruments: clarinet, bass clarinet, mandolin, guitar, violin, viola, and cello. These augment the body of chamber pieces that he had begun in the years from 1918 to 1922—works in which he continually experimented with new compositional procedures but which he evidently felt no need to complete. The four fragments from 1920 suggest a collection of character pieces, just as diverse as in the piano pieces that he was composing earlier that summer. They include a theme and variations in a slow tempo that Schoenberg would later position as the third movement of Op. 24 and title "Variations"; another fragment, in a lively triple meter, became the fifth movement, later titled "Dance Scene." A forty-measure dancelike fragment in a "Tempo zwischen langsamem Walzer u. Polacca" (tempo between a slow waltz and polacca) was eventually dropped from the Serenade and left incomplete, as was a shorter sketch for solo bass clarinet.[37] In these fragments from 1920 there is little to suggest the final conception of the Serenade as a parody of the Mozartean genre and a critique of the Neoclassical style, both of which ultimately became central premises of the work. But in the next summer (1921), as Neoclassical compositions began to appear on the programs of European modern music festivals, Schoenberg returned to his character pieces and added movements to them in which allusions to both Mozart and Stravinsky are unmistakable. During this summer Schoenberg completed a "March" using the distinctive Serenade instrumentation of the previous year—it would later occupy the first movement of Op. 24—and he also began a Minuet that would become its second movement. The ultimate though still general conception of the work was apparently in the composer's mind from this time, but the details of its realization were still far from settled.

During the summer of 1922, which was devoted primarily to *Die Jakobsleiter*, he added the beginning of a vocal movement on a Petrarchan sonnet, with the Serenade ensemble in accompaniment. Beginning in February of 1923—then ready to take on the Neoclassicists and pressured to fulfill his contract with Hansen—Schoenberg quickly finished all of his major fragmentary works begun

since 1920. First he returned to the Five Piano Pieces, Op. 23, completing the
remaining ones between 9 and 17 February; next he addressed the Suite, Op.
25, finishing it off between 23 February and 8 March. Then he returned to the
Serenade. In a letter to Zemlinsky dated 12 February 1923 he described the
state in which it then existed, showing that even at this point he was undecided
about how many movements it would have and what these movements would
be. In his letter he mentions "6–7 movements of which 3 are almost finished and
3 sketched out, or rather, begun."[38] The three movements "almost finished"
were certainly the Variations and March and probably also the Minuet, which
lacked only about thirty measures of its final form. The three movements only
begun were the Dance Scene, Sonnet, and slow waltz (Op. 24A). Between 8 and
30 March he hurriedly completed the Variations, Minuet, Sonnet, and Dance
Scene, whereupon he decided to drop Op. 24A and to add two additional movements, a "Song (without Words)" and a recapitulatory Finale, which were composed in two weeks' time.

His final structural plan for the work had a symmetry that was also apparent
in *Pierrot lunaire*. The seven movements of the Serenade are arranged into an
arch. The last movement essentially restates the first, which is a trenchant parody of the "new music" of the 1920s. Movements 2 and 6 (Minuet and Song
[without Words]) are lyrical interludes, and movements 3 and 5 (Variations and
Dance Scene) epitomize the timeless musical genres of variation and dance. The
Sonnet—the movement most unlike the others and the least related to either
the instrumental serenade or the spirit of Neoclassicism—is placed as the keystone of the arch. Here Schoenberg removes the ironic mask that he wears elsewhere in the work and permits his own unalloyed voice finally to be heard, to
words by Petrarch that speak as directly and humanely to the twentieth century
as to the Middle Ages.

The whole work was complete by 14 April, whereupon Schoenberg continued the making of clean scores.[39] Even as the full score was being prepared for
delivery to Hansen, Schoenberg's son-in-law, Felix Greissle, was at work fashioning arrangements. Versions for piano four hands; for piano, violin, and cello;
and a piano-vocal score of the Sonnet alone were published by Hansen in 1924
and 1925, and Greissle also arranged the work for orchestra, although this version remains unpublished.[40] A curious addendum to the history of the Serenade was made in a remark by Schoenberg in a letter to Hansen dated 31 December 1929, in which he proposed replacing the Sonnet movement with a
new "concert scene, something virtuoso (perhaps even several pieces)" in order
to promote more performances.[41]

One of Schoenberg's manuscripts for the Serenade, archive page 861, is especially problematic in its relevance to the work's early history and conception.[42] The sheet contains the main themes from the March, Minuet, Sonnet,
and Dance Scene, each labeled as to the movement from which the music comes.
The themes are related in rhythm and contour to their counterparts in the final
version of the work, but their pitches are changed and made to adopt notes from
the tone row used in the Variations movement. Jan Maegaard interpreted the
page, which he called "sheet 19," as "a quite early general outline of the Sere-

nade," made prior to 6 August 1920, when the Dance Scene was first sketched as a separate unit.[43] His theory concerning this document has proved very influential on the subsequent literature about the work, suggesting as it does that Schoenberg conceived of the Serenade in advance of early August 1920 and, from the very beginning, foresaw a cyclic composition that had at least the four movements March, Minuet, Sonnet, and Dance Scene. As later in Op. 25, each of these movements was to share a common tone row. But Maegaard's dating of 861 is almost certainly erroneous, as is the theory of the original conception of the work based upon it. Martina Sichardt has given persuasive evidence that the page originated near the end of Schoenberg's work on the Serenade, probably in early April 1923, when the composer was planning a Finale that would begin with citations of themes from earlier movements reinterpreted so as to take on the notes of the tone row from the Variations.[44] A cyclic conception of the work, by which themes from several movements use a common tone row drawn from the Variations, was probably in Schoenberg's mind well before April 1923, since evidence of it also appears in other undated sketches and drafts, especially for the Dance Scene. But there is no convincing evidence that it extends back to the time of very origins of the work in 1920.

The evolution of language and idea in the Serenade can be most expeditiously unraveled by looking first at the three movements nearly completed in 1920 and 1921—the Variations, March, and Minuet—then moving to those only begun in those two years, the Dance Scene and Sonnet, and ending with a discussion of the last two movements: Song (without Words) and Finale, which were composed entirely in 1923. The earliest of all was the third movement, called *Variationen*. Its chronology is especially complex, although it was very likely begun and completed, except for its coda, during late summer of 1920. On the numerous drafts and sketches for the piece only two dates appear: 3 August 1920 on archive page 836, which contains, in addition to sketchlike passages, the basic shape for the movement in its prime and inverted forms plus their retrogrades, and 11 March 1923 on a page of a sketchbook at the end of the final draft of the coda.[45] Schoenberg himself later recalled that the movement was "composed no later than 1920, so . . . it may have been conceived in 1919," although there is no concrete evidence to suggest a date earlier than 1920.[46]

Schoenberg had not worked with the strict form of theme and variations since 1908, in the third movement of his String Quartet No. 2, although he had applied the freer variations principle associated with passacaglia several times. As his conception of the new work later crystallized around the model of the Mozartean serenade, the theme-and-variations movement that he had begun in 1920 was still apposite, since the form appeared in movements of several of Mozart's divertimenti and serenades (see K. 253, 287, 334, and 361).[47] In *Fundamentals of Musical Composition* Schoenberg reviewed the classical theme-and-variations form, in effect underscoring the close relation of this movement to the classical prototype. The variations genre, Schoenberg says, can be divided into "formal" or "character" types, although these two can also be combined. In a 1931 lecture on his Variations for Orchestra, Op. 31, he explained the two categories: "The variations that follow [in Op. 31] are so-called 'formal' or 'developing' variations inasmuch as everything develops from the theme and its individual features. . . . But they are also 'character' variations, in that each of them at the same time develops some particular 'character.'"[48]

In *Fundamentals* Schoenberg elaborated upon the role of developing variation in the "formal" type by identifying a unifying feature—a "motive of variation"—that characterizes the thematic element in each variation of such a work. A motive of variation—which can be shared by several individual variations within a piece—takes its origin from an underlying structural feature of the theme. In formal variations, the different motives of variation and the theme itself are linked together by the process of developing variation. The theme, Schoenberg continues, should exhibit a strict design, such as a binary or ternary form, and its proportions and structural relations should then be retained in the variations that follow.

The Variations movement from Op. 24 closely adheres to Schoenberg's description of the classical prototype. As with the Orchestral Variations, Op. 31, it combines both the formal and character subgenres. The movement consists of a theme, five variations, and coda. Each of the variations establishes its own distinct character by virtue of its tempo, meter, and surface design, and these range among the delicate and filigreed texture of Variation 1, the mock-romantic lyricism of Variation 4, and the aggressive posturing in Variation 5. Each of five variations has its own distinctive motivic content—its own "motive of variation"—each derived from the theme and interconnected among themselves by motivic development. The theme itself (Example 8.11) is a strictly symmetrical binary or period structure, consisting of an antecedent phrase that embodies the basic shape (measures 1–6) and a consequent phrase (measures 6–11) based on the retrograde of the row that underlies the basic shape. The pitch row of the basic shape has fourteen tones, including all of the pitch classes except B. Every note in the variations and coda that follow can be traced back to it—the first time in Schoenberg's oeuvre that an entire movement is generated by pervasive references to a single tone row.

As in the variations movement of the Second String Quartet, the variations of the Serenade are arranged in a developmental ternary plan, *A B A'*. Variations 1 and 2 constitute the *A* section, in which the theme or its fragments are still dimly perceptible within the lines and where the underlying basic shape is deployed in a primarily linear fashion. Variations 3 and 4 create the contrasting middle section, whose motives and phrases have no direct resemblance to the theme and where Schoenberg experiments with new ways of distributing the tones of the basic shape among several simultaneous strands within the musical space. A reference to the theme then recurs in the fifth variation, marking a reprise, although fragments from the middle part also reappear. The coda begins with a recapitulation of the motive of Variation 3 and continues with a reprise of compositional ideas from the entire movement.

The two-part structure of the theme and its length of eleven measures are retained, at least outwardly, in each of the five variations and coda that follow. The variations and coda are marked off in the score in regular eleven-measure

Example 8.11. Schoenberg, Serenade, Op. 24, movement 3, measures 1–11

units, and each is divided into two parts by changes of tempo or by divisions that occur between musical phrases. In this way the composer projects a rigid numerical symbolism that was apparently a premise in the work, and he also retains the "proportions and structural relations of the theme" that he referred to in *Fundamentals of Musical Composition*. But the music in several variations proceeds differently from this external or notational pattern. Variation 2, for example, is actually twelve measures in length (measures 23–34), and within this extended space it creates a small ternary rather than binary form, one that mirrors the design of the entire movement, as contrasting thematic material enters at measure 27 and the motive of the variation (clearly representing the theme) returns at measure 29.

Schoenberg's application of the row contains many new ideas, as he experiments with ways to achieve variety and contrast in a work that is pervasively governed by only four row forms—the basic prime form, its inversion, and their retrogrades (all untransposed). In Variations 1 and 2 these row forms appear mainly in lines, although in many instances foreign or ornamental tones are interpolated and incomplete forms are also used. Chords in the strings in measures 23–24 are formed by verticalizing three-note segments of the retrograded row. The top line of these chords in the violin, F–E–F♯–G♯–A, thus comes from every third note of this row, a method of partitioning a row that is used extensively in the contrasting third and fourth variations. For example, the main melody in Variation 4 (in the clarinet) begins with the same five notes as in the violin in measures 23–24, and it then continues with the "every-third-note" partition, applied in turn to P, I, and RI. The melody that results seems entirely different from the theme, although the four basic row forms are still operative within the texture at large.

As is typical of his music composed in 1920, Schoenberg does not emphasize the formation of aggregates so much as he does the possibilities of serialized variation to unify the two-dimensional texture. Still, he continues his earlier practice of informally saturating many passages of the movement with all twelve tones, and he continues to use the process of complementation to promote that objective. In Variation 1 and in the coda, the notes B or A—those lacking in the prime form of the row and its inversion, respectively—are ever-present as pedal tones. Swirling around them are motives and phrases made from the other eleven notes as they occur in P and I, thus permeating the texture with all twelve pitch classes.

Schoenberg returned to the Serenade in the summer of 1921, at which time he apparently settled upon a general idea for the work. It would recreate the Mozartean serenade in a way that would also remind listeners of the emerging Neoclassical style, but it would improve on the Neoclassicists' eclecticism, which Schoenberg believed to be misguided. Late in this summer, after first devoting himself to movements of the Suite, Op. 25, he added to the Serenade a March and the beginning of a Minuet, both of which were traditional components of the eighteenth-century serenade or divertimento. Mozart composed marches for most or all of his Salzburg serenades. A march was played by the musicians as they walked toward the site where they were to perform, and it was repeated to accompany their departure. In Mozart's works the march is always an uncomplicated and repetitive piece, usually in D major, and cast into simple or rounded binary form.[49]

Schoenberg began to compose his own March movement, according to a date on the manuscript draft, on 27 September 1921. He entered the same date at the end of the draft, although it is questionable that a long and complex movement, supported by many sketches, was composed in a single day. The end of the fair copy of the short score is dated 6 October 1921, and this may be closer to the actual point at which the movement was finished. The March is the first of Schoenberg's many compositions written under the bittersweet influence of the Neoclassical style. Although formally related to Mozart's marches, the music sounds like Stravinsky, especially like the Soldier's March or the Little Concerto from Stravinsky's *L'histoire du soldat* (1918). The music of both has a regular, incisive beat that coexists with irregular and changing meters. Both pieces allude to key, but both are essentially atonal; both contain exact sectional repetitions—for Schoenberg the first such in his entire atonal oeuvre—and both establish a tone that is detached, objective, and witty—in fact, nearly Ivesian in the parody of a popular idiom. If, as Adorno claimed, Stravinsky's early Neoclassical works are music about music, then Schoenberg's March is music about music about music. His intention was in part practical—he wanted his works to be performed and to be successful in the new environment for modern music of the 1920s—but it was also didactic, showing the Neoclassicists how they could be retrospective and eclectic and still continue on a path that led to the future.

The March itself is made from three sections of nearly identical length. The first (measures 1–48) is an exposition. The viola and guitar begin with an eight-measure introduction, which dissolves in its last two measures into a mock drumroll. Next comes the seven-measure main theme, played by the clarinet (supported by the bass clarinet and violin) in a 5/4 meter that is subdivided into 2s and 3s that are constantly reversed. As the main theme is sounded, the viola's introductory line is made into an accompaniment that is subdivided between viola and cello such that the cello plays marchlike fourths. After another drumroll in measure 16, the lines of the first sixteen measures are all repeated in symmetrical inversions pivoted around the tone D, which, perhaps honoring the Mozartean model, is the mock tonic of the entire movement.[50] The exposition is rounded out by an exact repeat of measures 9–16 and 25–32.

The second main section (measures 49–95) is also exactly repeated. It has some characteristics of the contrasting trio of a march, but it more resembles a development section concerned with both the main and introductory themes, which are paraphrased repeatedly and freely recapitulated beginning in measure 80. The final section (measures 96–145) resembles a Beethoven coda, as it contains a second development and a second reprise, the latter entering at measure 122.

As Jan Maegaard has shown in his analysis of the work, serialized variations upon fragments of the two opening themes (especially the introductory one in the viola) recur sporadically in various inversions and transpositions throughout.[51] But the basic shapes in this movement are far more closely identified with the themes that embody them than they are abstractable successions of intervals or tone rows. The process of inversion, for example, is applied less to a series of pitch classes represented by the shape than to an entire formal unit, as occurs in measures 17–33 and 41–49. Otherwise the basic themes are subject to free motivic and thematic development, only partially guided by serialized variations. The idea of applying inversion and retrograde to a complete two-dimensional formal unit was plainly influential on Alban Berg, who uses a similar principle in his Chamber Concerto (1925).

Only two days after he had finished recopying the score of the March on 6 October 1921, Schoenberg began to compose the Minuet of the Serenade. Its chronology—unlike other movements of the Serenade—is reasonably uncomplicated. There are relatively few sketches and none of the extensive experiments with and manipulations of tone rows that characterize such movements as the Variations and Dance Scene. Schoenberg was apparently able to move quickly to a full draft, which he began on 8 October and brought to measure 88 before returning to Vienna from his summer retreat in Traunkirchen at the end of that month, whereupon he put the movement aside. He returned to it in 1923, probably just after completing the March on 11 March, and by 16 March he finished the remaining twenty-one measures of the trio and the nine-measure coda.

Minuets, like marches, were fixtures of the Mozartean genre of the serenade, in which they are usually songful and relatively uncomplicated, as is Schoenberg's new movement. The standard plan in Mozart's minuet begins with the minuet proper, cast as a rounded binary form in triple meter and played in a moderate tempo. This is followed by a second minuet, called a trio, which contrasts in character and often in orchestration, although it is usually identical with the foregoing in form. The first minuet is then repeated to create a large ternary form. An alternative form that was especially congenial to Mozart in his serenades and divertimenti (as in K. 131, 185, 250, 320, 334, 361, and 563) is the minuet with two or three trios, which alternate in rondolike fashion with the minuet.

The form of Schoenberg's Minuet follows the Mozartean model in its large ternary plan but not in smaller details. It consists of a minuet (measures 1–44), a trio (measures 45–109), an exact repeat of the minuet, and a coda (measures 110–18). Within the two major sections, however, there is no overt use of a simple or rounded binary form, as in the classical prototype. The movement begins, all the same, with classical strictness, as the main theme in the clarinet and violin is presented as a sixteen-measure period. The remainder of the minuet is developmental, made partly from free motivic variation and partly from serialized variants upon small fragments of the main theme and the opening accompanimental lines. The trio is similarly formed. After a four-measure introduction based on a viola ostinato, the main theme is stated in the cello in measures 49–52 and a subsidiary idea is presented in the bass clarinet in measure 53. These figures are then expanded, primarily by developing variation, for the remainder of the section. Serialized variants of the main motives also appear, but usually shortened to small fragments. The coda brings back reminiscences of motives from both sections, which gradually dwindle away.

The earliest of the three movements of the Serenade that had only been "sketched out, or rather, begun" when Schoenberg returned to the work in 1923 was the Dance Scene, which would later be situated as the fifth movement. According to the few dates on the manuscripts, it was begun in August 1920 and revised and completed between 30 March and 7 April 1923. Like the Variations movement, how much of the Dance Scene was composed in 1920 and how much in 1923 cannot be precisely determined,[52] although it is likely that Schoenberg's conception of it in 1920 was almost totally different from the one that he would later develop, the two sharing only the initial thematic materials. The composer said as much himself. When he composed the full draft of the final version in 1923, he referred to it as a *Bearbeitung* (a reworking or arrangement) of what went before, not a simple continuation. The earlier portion of the piece was recorded on a manuscript draft located at the former Deutsche Staatsbibliothek in Berlin, dated 6 August 1920 at the beginning. Its contents were recopied and slightly revised, probably at about the same time that the draft was composed, on a clean two-page score (archive pp. 873–74). This source has twenty-nine measures of music and is roughly equivalent in thematic content to the first major section (measures 1–58) of the final version, although its materials are far more concise in their working out. The themes and motives of the fragment are developed freely, with little evidence of serialized variation or aggregate formation. The music is lively in tempo and in a triple meter that suggests a quick waltz, but it has no distinctive relevance to the eighteenth-century serenade or Neoclassical style—features that would emerge prominently in the 1923 revision.

The manuscripts also contain several provocative hints that Schoenberg may have briefly returned to the work between 1920 and 1923. In a datebook that covers the period from September 1921 through December 1922, the composer jotted down a version of the main theme of the movement that was extended so as to embody a twelve-tone row, although the theme in this form was not used in the final version of the piece.[53] In several other unused sketches Schoenberg experiments with different ways of bringing together the main theme of the Dance Scene with the tone row of the Variations, thus suggesting a partially cyclic composition. As already mentioned in regard to manuscript page 861, there is no reason to think that this interconnection of movements was in the composer's mind in 1920, although the idea may have arisen in 1921, as an outgrowth of his work then on the first two movements of the Suite, Op. 25, which share a common tone row. After experimenting with several different ways to integrate the Variations row with the themes of the Dance Scene, Schoenberg apparently decided to confine the idea to the recapitulatory Finale.

At the end of March 1923, just after finishing the Sonnet movement of Op. 24, Schoenberg returned to the Dance Scene, which he completed as a composite of several traditional dance genres that could be adapted to the mock Neoclassicism that he had by then chosen for the work as a whole. The quick waltz from 1920 was expanded in length, in part by adding repeat signs around measures 1–33, and it was then grafted to a slower triolike *Ländler* and rounded off by a lengthy recapitulation of both waltz and *Ländler*. The movement took on a highly witty tone, full of the humor and parody that Schoenberg had already used in 1921 in the March movement. The material that he newly composed in 1923—roughly measures 59 to the end of the movement in measure 200—is constructed in a systematic fashion that uses permutational variations and aggregates formed by the conjunction of complementary hexachords, similar to the methods that he had used in the opening of *Die Jakobsleiter* and in the Piano Piece, Op. 23, No. 4.

The Dance Scene has a strictly symmetrical ternary form within which the number of exact sectional repetitions even outstrips the eighteenth-century dance. The first section (measures 1–58) is an expansion of the 1920 fragment. It begins with three principal ideas (Example 8.12): the first occurs in the mandolin in measures 1–2 (call this phrase *A*), the next in the same part in measures 3–5, and the last in the clarinet in measures 6–7. Prior to the repeat sign at measure 33, these ideas are freely varied and placed amid several other loosely related or contrasting motives. The first section is then rounded out in measures 35–58 by new motives and phrases—Stein found them to be transitional in character—which are carried along by an ostinato in the mandolin. The very end of the first section (measures 56–58), probably composed in 1923, forecasts the basic constructive method used for the remainder of the movement. Here the ostinato in the mandolin (sounding the tones C♯–D) and guitar (G–A♭) and the harmonics in the strings in measure 58 (B F) duplicate the six notes at the beginning of phrase *A*—G–D–F–C♯–B–G♯—although in a different order. The texture is filled out in measures 56–57 by the strings, whose harmonics sound the complementary hexachord B♭ C F♯ E♭ A E. An aggregate is formed, just as in the beginning of *Die Jakobsleiter* or the Passacaglia of 1920, which integrates the two-dimensional space by a systematic manipulation of the pitch content of the opening basic shape.

In the second major section (measures 59–111) the tempo slows to that of the *Ländler,* and the music is laid out in a rondolike succession of six short subsections, most repeated. The *Ländler* theme from measures 63–70 returns, changed only in accompanimental texture, at measures 81 and 105, and these recurrent passages are separated by distinct although related episodes. The final section (measures 112–200) of the Dance Scene is a synoptic recapitulation that re-

Example 8.12. Schoenberg, Serenade, Op. 24, movement 5, measures 1–7 (non-transposing score)

verses the order of events in the opening section. It begins with the ostinato figures from measures 36–55 and then recapitulates variants of the motives from
the first section. The *Ländler* theme reappears as well (measures 157–76) .

The 1923 portions of the Dance Scene contained Schoenberg's last important application of the principle of permutational variation during his atonal
period, although the technique was revived in later works such as the *Ode to
Napoleon Buonaparte* (1942). The permutations take their departure from
phrase *A* in measures 1–2. This phrase originated in 1920 as a component of a
normal atonal theme. It was characterized by its shape as well as by a distinctive rhythm and articulation, all of which were then the basis for developing
variations in measures 1–33. But after 1920 Schoenberg must have noted that
the first six tones of the motive—G–D–F–C♯–B–G♯—had nearly the same symmetry that he had found so useful in the central hexachord of *Die Jakobsleiter,* although this characteristic was obscured by the order in which he had placed the
notes in the phrase itself. Rearranged into the compact scalewise order
F–G–G♯–B–C♯–D, it is apparent that the hexachord lacks only the tone B♭ to be a
seven-note segment of a symmetrical octatonic scale. When he reworked the
piece beginning in 1923, he divorced the collection of six pitch classes from the
order that characterized the basic shape of phrase *A* and proceeded to explore
its compositional use as a reorderable set of tones that could create new lines or
chords or both. As he had done at the beginning of the oratorio or in the Passacaglia of 1920, Schoenberg further integrated the musical space by restating
the hexachord in one strand of the texture and the complementary hexachord
in another, thus forming a series of aggregates. The degree of integration within
the musical space was all the greater since the complement in this case is an inversional form of the original.

These structural features are most plainly realized in the middle section of the
Dance Scene, which is strictly based on the conjunction of the two constantly
reordered complementary hexachords. The tones of the *Ländler* theme itself—
A–E–F♯–B♭–C–E♭ (measures 63–70 in the clarinet)—are the complement of the
original hexachord from phrase *A,* whose notes appear in the accompaniment
in these measures. The conjunction of the two hexachords continues throughout the middle section and sporadically in the reprise, where it produces a
stream of new expressive ideas and figures.

The Sonnet of Op. 24, begun in October 1922 and completed in March 1923,
stands as the centerpiece of the work as a whole. In it the personal voice of the
composer is most clearly heard and the element of musical parody is at its faintest.
Vocal movements were not part of the eighteenth-century instrumental serenade, although the term may also have suggested to Schoenberg the traditional
love song performed by a swain beneath his lady's window—the type of music
parodied in Don Giovanni's "Deh vieni alla finestra." In drawing his text from a
Petrarchan sonnet, however, Schoenberg made a thoroughly un-Mozartean
choice. These were works of the utmost intensity and artificiality, more akin in
high rhetoric and psychological exploration to the poetry of Maeterlinck and
George than to the earthiness of Da Ponte.

Schoenberg was long attracted to Petrarch's sonnets as musical texts. He had used three of them in 1904 in his Orchestral Songs, Op. 8. For the Serenade he chose "Far potess'io vendetta di colei," using a translation made early in the nineteenth century by the poet Karl August Förster.

CCXVII	Sonnet 217 [256]
O könnt' ich je der Rach' an ihr genesen,	Oh, that I might find relief from that resentment against her,
Die mich durch Blick und Rede gleich zerstöret,	Who assails me by glance and speech alike,
Und dann zu grösserm Leid sich von mir kehret,	And, causing greater suffering still, turns away,
Die Augen bergend mir, die süssen, bösen!	And hides from me her sweet and evil eyes.
So meiner Geister matt bekümmert Wesen	Thus she gradually consumes and saps
Sauget mir aus allmählig und verzehret	The feeble, fretful essence of myself,
Und brüllend, wie ein Leu, an's Herz mir fähret	And like a lion bellows at my heart
Die Nacht, die ich zur Ruhe mir erlesen!	At night, which I would rather have for rest.
Die Seele, die sonst nur der Tod verdränget,	My soul, which should take flight only at death,
Trennt sich von mir, und, ihrer Haft entkommen,	Leaves me and, escaping its imprisonment,
Fliegt sie zu ihr, die drohend sie empfänget.	Flies off to her, who receives it threateningly.
Wohl hat es manchmal Wunde mich genommen,	I oft have wondered,
Wenn die nun spricht und weint und sie umfänget,	When it speaks and cries and embraces her,
Dass fort sie schläft, wenn solches sie vernommen.[54]	How she sleeps on, if she is listening.

It is scarcely imaginable that Schoenberg would have chosen a poem that speaks in such an intensely personal tone if the words did not also resonate in his private life. His years around 1921 and 1922 were burdened by the many emotional problems that rose from his perpetual indigence and inability to compose, exacerbated by anti-Semitic incidents that had recently been directed at him and his family. These may well have brought on a return of his feelings of resentment toward his wife, Mathilde, which had apparently simmered since the Gerstl affair in 1908. Coping with bitterness and feelings of vengeance is the pretext for Petrarch's poem, which brings into focus for the poet—presumably also for the musician—a division of his psyche. The speaker of the poem is the mediator; his resentment awakens a lower component of his being, which is counterbalanced by his highest faculty, his soul, which he has already bequeathed to the beloved. But she has received it with indifference and remains all too insensitive to its importance.

The relevance of Petrarch's sonnet to Schoenberg's emotional frame of mind in 1922 is underscored by a poetic "Requiem" that the composer had written shortly before and considered setting to music before publishing it as a purely literary piece.[55] The poem is full of scarcely containable emotion and self-pity. It begins: "Pain, rage yourself to a standstill, / grief, lament till you are weary!" Almost certainly it was directed at Mathilde, who is addressed near the end: "Hopeless: perhaps we pass each other by, / perhaps forever, / and never meet again."[56] Ironically, the Requiem was left as a fragment until Mathilde's untimely death in 1923, whereupon Schoenberg finished it in a definitely conciliatory tone.

The vocal line of the Sonnet and the beginning of the accompaniment were composed in a preliminary form in October 1922, after Schoenberg had again given up on *Die Jakobsleiter.* The sketches show that from the very beginning it was to be a twelve-tone work, second in time of origin only to the twelve-tone Prelude and Intermezzo from Op. 25, begun the previous summer. Typical of long-standing working methods in music for solo voice, Schoenberg first composed the entire voice part, which reiterates a single twelve-tone row, and then sketched in an instrumental introduction that more freely embodies the same series. His sketches also show him experimenting with systems for extracting chords of different intervallic content from this one row, as in the Variations movement seeking a maximal diversity in the materials that can be deduced from highly limited intervallic resources. When he returned to the piece on 16 March 1923, he changed the order of tones in the row—probably, as Martina Sichardt has asserted, to allow for greater intervallic variety—and then quickly drafted the remainder of the movement, finishing it by 29 March.[57]

The form of the Sonnet is governed by its text, which is divided into two quatrains and two tercets in which each line contains eleven syllables. At the beginning and end and between each of these line groups, a short instrumental passage is inserted. Otherwise the piece is through-composed, so unlike the parodic repetitiveness of the other movements. An intense motivic development coexists with strict twelve-tone serialization, and Schoenberg's treatment of the text returns to the style of the Orchestral Songs, Op. 22, in which surface expressivity is limited to only the most pregnant of verbal images.

The use of the twelve-tone row in the Sonnet is strict although "primitive," Schoenberg's own characterization of it. The basic row of pitch classes is repeated over and over in the voice, and the instruments also repeatedly distribute notes from the same row into a two-dimensional space, just as Schoenberg would do later in the Waltz from Op. 23. It has often been noted that the composer achieves intervallic variety in the voice line by superimposing the recurrent tone row over poetic-musical lines that consistently have eleven notes, thus mechanically rotating the row in the music of each successive line. This way of using a twelve-tone row may have arisen in discussions between Schoenberg and Berg during the previous year, stimulated by the music and theories of Fritz Heinrich Klein, one of Berg's students. Klein had used a similar procedure in his *Die Maschine*, a work for chamber orchestra that was the winning entry in a competition for new works in this medium sponsored by the Verein für Musikalische Privataufführungen in 1921, and it was later published in a version for piano four hands.[58] The work is filled with mechanistic combinations of pedal points, rhythmic ostinati, a twelve-tone theme (Klein called it a *Modellthema*), a theme with twelve different intervals, and other structures that later had a considerable influence on Berg's own twelve-tone music.[59] One of Klein's ideas in the piece (seen at measures 4–16 and 45–62) was to superimpose the reiterated twelve-tone theme over an eleven-note ostinato, which produced, as in Schoenberg's Sonnet, a succession of rotations of the underlying row. Klein, who considered himself one of the discoverers of the twelve-tone principle and made little secret of a "personal antipathy" toward Schoenberg, no doubt took an impish delight in sending Schoenberg a copy of the piano score of *Die Maschine* when it was published. Amid fulsome declarations of admiration, Klein wrote on the score: "This is the same machine which was in your dear hands (as a score for chamber orchestra) in the summer of 1921 (on the occasion of the competition of the Society f. P. M. P)." Schoenberg got the message. Beneath Klein's words he wrote:

> Not correct. In Webern's [*recte* Berg's] hands, who told me about it but was not able to interest me in it. I doubt if I had this in my hands, even more that I looked at it, and least of all that I knew what it contained. In any case, he has fundamentally nothing in common with 12-tone composition: a compositional means that had its distinct precursor in "working with tones," which I used for 2 or 3 years (before discovering the ultimate necessity of the twelve).[60]

By the end of March 1923 Schoenberg was at work on the Serenade with an intensity that he had not experienced since composing *Die Jakobsleiter.* By then he had evidently decided on the final shape—as a seven-movement work—and by 30 March he had completed the first four. On that day he returned to the Dance Scene, began to recompose its fragment from 1920, and, on the same day, interrupted this work and composed the sixth movement, "Song (without Words)," in its entirety. The need for a slow, lyrical movement was plain enough—it would balance the *gesangvoll* second movement and provide the counterpart to the slow movement of the typical Mozartean serenade or divertimento. Often for Mozart, especially in his divertimenti, the slow movement was an adagio, as in Schoenberg's new movement. The form was usually rounded binary, a model that Schoenberg changed only by removing the repeat signs, making his own adagio a concise and simple ternary form with coda.

The Song is the simplest movement of the Serenade and the least relevant to twelve-tone thinking. Its brevity suggests an interlude before the rollicking Finale. The first section (measures 1–7) is made from a peaceful and muted violin melody, accompanied by chords in the guitar and a steady bass line in the bass clarinet. In the contrasting middle section (measures 8–15) the violin's tune blooms into a sonorous arabesque, and the opening melody then returns at measure 16 in the cello, changed only slightly in contour and rhythm. The music dies away in the coda (measures 23–26), echoing the opening.

The lyric interlude in the Song is soon swept aside by the high-spirited Finale. Here Schoenberg again follows the model of the Mozartean serenade, in which the opening march was normally repeated to accompany the players' departure.[61] Schoenberg's Finale contains an exact repeat of the first movement, beginning in the thirty-third measure of the March and continuing to the end. An introduction (measures 1–44) and a slow episode (measures 149–54) are added. In the introduction, thematic materials from the March are freely developed and restated. But inserted into this framework are references to themes from earlier movements, specifically, to those from the Sonnet (measures 8–9), Minuet and Trio (measures 10–17), and *Ländler* (measures 23–26 and 33–35). These thematic allusions, however, are far from straightforward, since some of them are fitted with the tones of the row of the Variations movement (including its prime, inverted, and retrograded forms), and even their rhythms are sometimes varied by augmentation and diminution. In one allusion to the *Ländler* melody (measures 23–26), notes from the Song are substituted, and even the March themes themselves periodically succumb to the invasion of the foreign tones, as in measures 18–22, where the main March theme turns up whistling the row of the Variations. Erwin Stein told of Schoenberg's own explanation of the introduction: it was "a conference," he said, "of the instruments on the question of what actually ought to be played at the end of the Serenade."[62] There is no reason to question or add to the simplicity of these thoughts.

At measure 149, just before the return of the final coda of the March, Schoenberg inserts a six-measure episode in the slow tempo of the Song, whose opening materials are brought back only slightly varied and into which the clarinet puckishly inserts the *Ländler* tune. The work then ends with ruffles and flourishes, all as lighthearted as a potpourri (a term that Schoenberg used for the movement in one of the sketches) and much in the spirit of the quodlibet from the end of Bach's *Goldberg* Variations.

WITH THE CHEERFUL CONCLUSION of the Serenade, Schoenberg's explorations in the atonal style came to an end. Even before completing the Finale, he had decided to cease his decade-long experimentation in alternative methods of composition and to adopt a more unfied and coherent outlook, thus the twelve-tone method that he would use to compose most of his remaining works. Its first mature application had already been made—in the Prelude from the Suite for Piano, Op. 25, composed in 1921—and its basic features had even earlier been tried out in the Symphony and *Die Jakobsleiter.*

Schoenberg's twelve-tone period of composition differed from his atonal period not only by establishing a new body of technical, structural, and stylistic features but even more by the acceptance of a new viewpoint concerning music, one that valued the known over the unknown, discovery rather than continual exploration, and restriction rather than total freedom. By 1923 the atonal style for Schoenberg had completed its life cycle. It was born from the chaotic aftermath of the romantic period, grew to maturity under the tutelage of modernist movements in all of the fine arts, and entered its old age following World War I, when an insistence on control, order, and limitation spread throughout art and society. Schoenberg—always sensitive to the necessities of history—was certainly aware of the exhaustion of the older order and the need for a new one. But at no time did he consider his atonal oeuvre to be imperfect or transitional, as did many commentators in the 1950s and 1960s. He revised none of his atonal works in light of the twelve-tone method and maintained a lifelong satisfaction with them.

Near the end of his life Schoenberg looked back on his astonishingly revolutionary and diverse oeuvre and embraced it all, finding its phases not so different from each other since they all came from his own highly individualized perspective. "To me stylistic differences of this nature are not of special importance," he wrote. "I do not know which of my compositions are better; I like them all, because I liked them when I wrote them."[63]

Glossary

AGGREGATE A contiguous presentation of the twelve pitch classes with none omitted and none repeated except in an immediate context. Aggregates usually result from a systematic method of choosing tones.

APHORISTIC STYLE A musical style marked by unusual brevity that results from curtailment in the length of thematic ideas and the absence of conventional development.

ATHEMATIC STYLE Related to the aphoristic style, a musical style in which themes or motives are generally not developed or recapitulated.

ATONALITY A phenomenon in twentieth-century music characterized by the absence of tonal, functional harmonic progressions. Atonal music is normally characterized by dissonant harmonies, which are prominent and stable units (structurally equivalent to consonant or triadic harmonies), and the twelve pitch classes appear in it equivalently and nonhierarchically.

BASIC SHAPE A phraselike succession of pitches at the beginning of a tonal, atonal, or twelve-tone work that subsequently underlies its primary melodic, harmonic, and textural pitch structures.

COMPLEMENTATION A relation between two pitch sets by which the pitch class content of one set is identical to the pitch classes absent in the other set.

COMPOSING WITH TONES (*Komponieren mit Tönen*) Schoenberg's term for a compositional technique that preceded the twelve-tone method, by which all or most pitch structures throughout a composition are derived (by transposition, inversion, or retrograde arrangement) from an initial basic shape of fewer than twelve tones.

DEVELOPING VARIATION (*entwickelnde Variation*) Schoenberg's term for traditional motivic variation, by which motives (distinctive intervallic-rhythmic figures) return with progressively greater changes, eventually producing new melodic ideas.

INVERSION (sometimes abbreviated *I*) In atonal and twelve-tone music, a means of varying the pitch content of a set or tone row, by which the notes of the inverted collection exhibit intervals that are the inversions of those that separate the analogous tones of the original form.

PARTITIONING The distribution of notes in a tone row into two or more strands of a texture.

PERMUTATIONAL VARIATION A means of varying the pitch content of a figure by reordering its notes, optionally followed by transposition, inversion, or both.

PITCH CLASS A representation of all tones of the same letter name and their enharmonic equivalents. There are twelve pitch classes in traditonal music.

PITCH-CLASS SET A collection of pitch classes normally encountered in a musical work as a contiguous entity—notes in a line, a chord, or a textural field.

PRIME FORM (sometimes abbreviated *P*) The uninverted, unretrograded form of a tone row encountered at the beginning of a serialized work or one of its transpositions.

SERIALIZED VARIATION A means of variation by which the order of intervals that underlie a basic shape is maintained in its later appearances, either directly, inverted, or arranged in retrograde.

SPEECH MELODY (*Sprechmelodie, Sprechgesang*) Schoenberg's terms for a partly recitational vocal style in which a notated rhythm is strictly maintained and pitch is approximated.

SUSPENDED TONALITY (*aufgehobene Tonalität*) Schoenberg's term for a development in music of the late nineteenth and early twentieth centuries by which key is temporarily set aside by the pervasive use of vagrant chords.

TONE COLOR MELODY (*Klangfarbenmelodie*) Schoenberg's term for a melodic entity made from diverse tone colors.

TRIADIC TETRACHORD A pitch class set that has four tones of which three create a major or minor triad.

VAGRANT CHORD (*vagierender Akkord*) Schoenberg's term for a harmony that has a functional value in two or more keys simultaneously.

VARIATION See developing variation, permutational variation, serialized variation.

WAVERING TONALITY (*schwebende Tonalität*) Schoenberg's term for a phenomenon in music of the late nineteenth and early twentieth centuries by which functional harmonic references to two keys exist simultaneously.

Notes

Preface

1. Arnold Schoenberg, "Analysis of the Four Orchestral Songs Opus 22," translated by Claudio Spies, *Perspectives of New Music* 3 (1964–65): 10.

Chapter 1

1. Arnold Schoenberg, letter of 13 July 1909, BSL 382.
2. Ibid, 382.
3. "How One Becomes Lonely" (1937), SI 50.
4. "Composition with Twelve Tones" (1941), SI 217.
5. Kurt Westphal, *Die moderne Musik* (Leipzig: B. G. Teubner, 1928): 39.
6. "Es [war] das Problem einer ganzen Generation, das er durchkämpfte. Überall, in ganz Europa wurde dieser Kampf von den Jungen, Vorstoßenden, Kühnen aufgenommen. Es wurden Parteien gebildet, Schlagworte formuliert, Absagen ausgesprochen, Programme aufgestellt. Die Musik trat in das Stadium der Revolution, zu deren geistigem Führer Schönberg geworden war." Hans Mersmann, "Neue Musik" (1927), reprinted in *Melos* 37 (1970): 266.
7. "Neue Musik," in "Neunzehn Beiträge über neue Musik" (ca. 1946), in AGS 18 (1984): 80.
8. Ernst Krenek, "Atonality," translated by Barthold Fles in Krenek, *Music Here and Now* (New York: Norton, 1939): 165.
9. HL 416.
10. English translation by Dika Newlin ("The Relationship to the Text"), SI 141–45.
11. Alexander L. Ringer, *Arnold Schoenberg: The Composer as Jew* (Oxford: Clarendon, 1990): 29.
12. Ibid., 33.
13. Allen Forte, *The Structure of Atonal Music* (New Haven: Yale University Press, 1973): ix.
14. George Perle, *Serial Composition and Atonality: An Introduction to the Music of Schoenberg, Berg, and Webern,* 3d. ed., revised and enlarged (Berkeley: University of California Press, 1972): 9. See also Robert P. Morgan, "Secret Languages: The Roots of Musical Modernism," *Critical Inquiry* 10 (1984); and Ethan Haimo, *Schoenberg's Serial Odyssey: The Evolution of His Twelve-Tone Method, 1914–1928* (Oxford: Clarendon, 1990).

Chapter 2

1. Untitled program notes for a concert in Vienna on 14 January 1910, in Willi Reich, *Schoenberg: A Critical Biography,* translated by Leo Black (New York: Praeger, 1971): 49.

2. Arnold Schoenberg, "Self-Analysis" (1931), in ibid., 241.

3. Martin Thrun, *Neue Musik im deutschen Musikleben bis 1933,* vol. 1 (Bonn: Orpheus, 1995): 210.

4. "Sie sind atonal und heben den Begriff der Dissonanz auf." Egon Wellesz, "Arnold Schönberg," *Zeitschrift der internationalen Musikgesellschaft* 12 (1911): 347. All translations are the work of the author, unless otherwise indicated.

5. Egon Wellesz, "Schönberg and Beyond," *Musical Quarterly* 2 (1916): 76–95.

6. Thrun, *Neue Musik im deutschen Musikleben bis 1933,* 1:205–14.

7. "In der atonalen Musik gibt es keine Toniken, Dominanten, Subdominanten, Stufen, Auflösungen, Konsonanzen, Dissonanzen mehr, sondern nur die 12 Intervalle der gleichschwebenden Temperatur; ihre 'Tonleiter' besteht also aus den 12 temperierten Halbtönen. In der atonalen Melodie ist sowohl das rein Physische, Sinnliche, als auch das Triviale und Sentimentale soweit wie nur möglich ausgeschaltet und ihr 'Gesetz,' ihr 'Nomos' besteht darin, dass innerhalb einer gewissen Tonreihe sich kein Ton wiederholen und keiner ausgelassen werden darf." Josef Matthias Hauer, *Vom Wesen des Musikalischen* (Leipzig: Waldheim-Eberle, 1920): 53.

8. Eberhard Freitag has compiled several of Schoenberg's statements about the term in *Arnold Schönberg in Selbstzeugnissen und Bilddokumenten,* Rowohlts Monographien (N.p.: Rowohlt, 1973): 51–52.

9. "Der Ausdruck 'atonale Musik' ist unsinnig. Tonal ist, was dem Ton *gemäss* ist; Tonalität wird bereits im Sinne einer begrenzenden Spezialisierung des Begriffes angewendet; indem hier verlangt wird, dass in einem Tonstück alles auf einen Ton (die Tonika) rückbeziehbar sei, macht man sich einer bedeutenden sprachlichen Ungenauigkeit schuldig. Ein solches Stück müsste *monotonal* heissen. Atonal aber kann etwas, in dem Tönen vorkommen nicht sein, weil was dem Ton nicht gemäss ist, sich mit ihm nicht verbindet. Aber auch im Sinn, wie man Tonalität gebraucht, lässt sich atonal nicht anwenden, da eine Folge von Tönen, die sich nicht in irgendeinerweise auf einander Beziehen [*sic*] keine Folge wäre. Man könnte vielleicht *polytonal* sagen. Jedenfalls aber: der Ausdruck atonal wurde vor meiner Musik bereits auf Reger, Mahler und Strauss angewendet, weil die Beziehung auf eine einzige Tonika nicht nachweisbar ist. Ebenso falsch! Ich habe den Ausdruck immer abgelehnt." Transcribed by Anita Luginbühl, archives of the Arnold Schönberg Center, Vienna.

10. HL 432.

11. Schoenberg spoke to his students about twelve-tone composition on several occasions in the early 1920s. Josef Polnauer recalled one such discussion held in February 1923, and in a draft of a letter to Hauer dated 25 July 1922 Schoenberg mentioned "a few lectures given to my students several months ago" concerning the method. For the complete text of this letter see Bryan R. Simms, "Who First Composed Twelve-Tone Music, Schoenberg or Hauer?" JASI 10 (1987): 122.

12. "Mit dem Eintritt in die Zwölftonkomposition war man plötzlich vis-à-vis du rien gestellt, das Alte wurde abgelehnt, eine neue Form war noch nicht gefunden. Zunächst hat man nach dem Gefühl komponiert. Aber das Suchen nach einer bewußten Spitze des Formgefühls konnte nicht aufgegeben werden, sondern war eine Notwendigkeit. Diese ersten Versuche haben etwas ergeben, was ebenfalls eine Notwendigkeit war: die Kürze. Wenn Motivwiederholung und Motiventwicklung wegfallen, dann war es auch unmöglich lange Kompositionen zu schrieben." Transcribed by Rudolf Stephan in "Ein frühes Dokument zur Entstehung der Zwölftonkompo-

sition," in *Festschrift Arno Forchert zum 60. Geburtstag am 29. Dezember 1985*, edited by Gerhard Allroggen and Detlef Altenburg (Kassel: Bärenreiter, 1986): 297. Another transcription of the document with English translation is found in Arved Mark Ashby, "The Development of Berg's Twelve-Tone Aesthetic As Seen in the *Lyric Suite* and Its Sources" (Ph.D. diss., Yale University, 1995): 223–33.

13. HL 432.

14. HL 27.

15. HL 28.

16. "Problems of Harmony," SI 279–80.

17. SFH 99. The second chord in measure 1, shown as II with a slash that indicates alteration, is presumably a misprint for an altered VI.

18. HL 258.

19. Concerning vagrant chords, see SFH 44–50 and HL 238–67.

20. "Problems of Harmony," SI 274.

21. SFH 81–82.

22. The relevance of this limitation in Schoenberg's tonal theory for the emergence of atonality is discussed by Ethan Haimo in "Schoenberg and the Origins of Atonality," in *Constructive Dissonance: Arnold Schoenberg and the Transformations of Twentieth-Century Culture*, edited by Christopher Hailey and Juliane Brand (Berkeley: University of California Press, 1997): 71–86.

23. "Composition with Twelve Tones" (1941), SI 216.

24. A sensitive analysis of tonality in Debussy's music is found in Adele T. Katz, *Challenge to Musical Tradition: A New Concept of Tonality* (London: Putnam, 1945): 248–93.

25. SFH 35–43.

26. HL 247.

27. Béla Bartók, "Das Problem der neuen Musik," *Melos* 1 (1920): 108. Translated by Bryan R. Simms in *Composers on Modern Musical Culture: An Anthology of Readings on Twentieth-Century Music* (New York: Schirmer Books, 1999): 46.

28. "Composition with Twelve Tones," SI 216.

29. Robert Falck, "Emancipation of the Dissonance," JASI 6 (1982): 106–7. The Louis book was owned by Schoenberg.

30. HL 323.

31. "Composition with Twelve Tones," SI 217.

32. Chapters 17, 20, and 21 in HL. The first edition of the *Harmonielehre* did not use numbered chapters.

33. HL 70.

34. HL 309–44.

35. HL 309.

36. See Heinrich Schenker's response to it, "Further Consideration of the Urlinie: II" (1926), translated by John Rothgeb, in Schenker, *The Masterwork in Music*, vol. 2 (Cambridge: Cambridge University Press, 1996): 12–17; also see the critique in Katz, *Challenge to Musical Tradition*, 350–97.

37. This tetrachord forms members of set class 4–19 (0, 1, 4, 8).

38. See especially HL 365–66.

39. Here and elsewhere in this book, notes sounded simultaneously in a chord will be stated from lowest to highest in pitch; the notes of a linear figure or tone row will be separated by dashes.

40. HL 324–25.

41. HL 365. Schoenberg uses the chord in this context in his song "Verlassen," Op. 6, No. 4, at the cadence of the first stanza of text in measures 16–17, where a tonic E♭-minor triad rests on the pedal tone D.

42. An overview of Schoenberg's theoretical writings is given in Arnold Schoenberg, *Coherence, Counterpoint, Instrumentation, Instruction in Form*, edited by Severine Neff, translated by Charlotte M. Cross and Severine Neff (Lincoln and London: University of Nebraska Press, 1994): xxxiv–xli.

43. HL 420.

44. HL 421.

45. SFH 76.

46. Schoenberg, "Self-Analysis," 238.

47. See the analyses by Walter Frisch in *The Early Works of Arnold Schoenberg, 1893–1908* (Berkeley: University of California Press, 1993): 92–98; Frisch, "Schoenberg and the Poetry of Richard Dehmel," JASI 9 (1986): 137–79; and Edward T. Cone, "Sound and Syntax: An Introduction to Schoenberg's Harmony," *Perspectives of New Music* 13 (1974–75): 28–30.

48. HL 383–84.

49. HL 359.

50. Frisch, *The Early Works of Arnold Schoenberg*, 97.

51. HL 128; SFH 111.

52. HL 128.

53. The songs "Lockung" and "Der Wanderer" from Op. 6 and "Voll jener Süße" from Op. 8 are analyzed in SFH 110–13 and in HL 383–84.

54. Cone, "Sound and Syntax," 21–40.

55. SFH 110–11.

Chapter 3

1. Arnold Schoenberg, "Self-Analysis" (1931), in Willi Reich, *Schoenberg: A Critical Biography*, translated by Leo Black (New York: Praeger, 1971): 241.

2. "How One Becomes Lonely" (1937), SI 49–50.

3. Translated by Olga Marx and Ernst Morwitz, in *The Works of Stefan George*, 2nd ed. (Chapel Hill: University of North Carolina Press, 1974): 109.

4. Albrecht Dümling, *Die fremden Klänge der hängenden Gärten: Die öffentliche Einsamkeit der neuen Musik am Beispiel von Arnold Schönberg und Stefan George* (Munich: Kindler, 1981): 172.

5. The original text is in Joachim Birke, "Richard Dehmel und Arnold Schönberg: Ein Briefwechsel," *Die Musikforschung* 11 (1958): 285

6. Cited in Hellmut Federhofer, "Heinrich Schenkers Verhältnis zu Arnold Schönberg," *Mitteilungen der Kommission für Musikforschung*, No. 33 (Vienna: Österreichischen Akademie der Wissenschaften, 1981): 380.

7. Schmidt, Christian Martin ed., *Kritischer Bericht*, SSW, section 1, series B, vol. 1/2, part 1: 51.

8. Quoted in *Arnold Schönberg, 1874–1951: Lebensgeschichte in Begegnungen*, edited by Nuria Nono-Schoenberg (Klagenfurt: Ritter, 1992): 54.

9. ". . . indem sie zu überbieten trachten, was ich biete, bringt mich in Gefahr, ihr Nachahmer zu werden. . . ." Arnold Schoenberg, *Berliner Tagebuch*, edited by Josef Rufer (Frankfurt: Propyläen, 1974): 34.

10. Stefan George, *Das Jahr der Seele* (Berlin: Georg Bondi, 1908): 27.

11. SI 86.

12. Concerning the symbolism of the tonality D in Schoenberg's work, see Bryan R. Simms, "Alban Berg's Four Songs, Op. 2: A Tribute to Schoenberg," in *Musical Humanism and Its Legacy: Essays in Honor of Claude V. Palisca*, edited by Nancy Kovaleff Baker and Barbara Russano Hanning, Festschrift Series, 11 (Stuyvesant, NY: Pendragon, 1992): 487–501.

13. FMC 8.

14. Arnold Schoenberg, *Coherence, Counterpoint, Instrumentation, Instruction in Form*, edited by Severine Neff, translated by Charlotte M. Cross and Severine Neff (Lincoln: University of Nebraska Press, 1994): 39. Concerning developing variations also see David Epstein, *Beyond Orpheus: Studies in Musical Structure* (Cambridge: MIT Press, 1979): 207–10; and Walter Frisch, *Brahms and the Principle of Developing Variation* (Berkeley: University of California Press, 1984): 1–34.

15. "Es soll ja ein Held, der sich im 3ten Akt erschießen wird, wohl schon im ersten Akt so gezeichnet sein, daß ein Ahnungsreicher das Schicksal vorherwissen könnte. Aber man darf ihn doch nicht im ersten Akt schon 'erschossen' auf die Bühne bringen—Ich meine: erst das Ei, dann das Huhn." Quoted in Reinhold Brinkmann, "Ausdruck und Spiel: Zwei Ansichten eines Stückes," in *Bericht über den 2. Kongreß der Internationalen Schönberg-Gesellschaft: "Die Wiener Schule in der Musikgeschichte des 20. Jahrhunderts,"* edited by Rudolf Stephan and Sigrid Wiesmann (Vienna: Elisabeth Lafite, 1984): 35. Schoenberg's analogy between motives and dramatic personae may have been inspired by his reading of Heinrich Schenker's *Harmonielehre* (1906). See Schenker, *Harmony*, edited and annotated by Oswald Jonas, translated by Elisabeth Mann Borgese (Chicago: University of Chicago Press, 1954): 13.

16. David Lewin, "Inversional Balance as an Organizing Force in Schoenberg's Music and Thought," *Perspectives of New Music* 6 (1967–68): 1–21.

17. The fragment is transcribed in SSW, section 1, series B, vol. 1/2, part 1: 384.

18. Karl Henckell, *Gesammelte Werke*, vol. 3 (Munich: J. Michael Müller, 1923): 139. The text is given as it appeared in the 1920 first edition of Schoenberg's song; variant readings from Henckell's original text are placed in brackets.

19. "Dieses Lied ist vor den George Liedern geschrieben. Gleichzeitig mit Op. 14: 'In diesen Wintertagen' und 'Ich darf nicht dankend . . .' Hätte immerhin veröffentlicht werden können. Ich habe es wegen des Textes nicht herausgegeben." SSW, section 1, series B, vol. 1/2, part 1: 49.

20. Schmidt, *Kritischer Bericht*, 49–50.

21. Concerning Gerstl and his relation with the Schoenbergs, see Otto Breicha, *Gerstl und Schönberg: Eine Beziehung* (Salzburg: Galerie Welz, 1993); Jane Kallir, *Richard Gerstl, Oskar Kokoschka* (New York: Galerie St. Etinne, 1992); Otto Kallir, "Richard Gerstl (1883–1908): Beiträge zur Dokumentation seines Lebens und Werkes," *Mitteilungen der Österreichischen Galerie*, vol. 17, no. 64 (1974): 125–93; and Arnold Schoenberg, "Malerische Einflüsse" (1938), trans. Gertrud Zeisl ("Painting Influences") JASI 2 (1978): 233–39.

22. Breicha, *Gerstl und Schönberg*, 14.

23. "Bin ich wirklich immer so ekelhaft zu Dir? Und Du bist immer immer gut zu mir. Du solltest mich vielleicht wirklich manchmal prügeln (ich würde aber zurückhauen). Du bist eben gut, und ich unausstehlich. So ist es und bleibt es. Ich kränk' mich eigentlich riesig darüber, denn ich hab' Dich so riesig lieb. Aber weisst Du? Sagen kann ich das nicht, und eigentlich solltest Du's wissen, dass ich das nicht kann." Letter, Library of Congress.

24. Jane Kallir, *Richard Gerstl, Oskar Kokoschka*, 11–12.

25. "Ich bin im Ganzen jetzt etwas ruhiger. Solange ich Hoffnung gehabt habe auf Besserung, habe ich geweint. Nun hab' ich keine mehr und bin ruhig. Meine Adresse werde ich Dir nicht sagen . . . . Wenn es Dich beruhigt will, ich Dir nur sagen, dass ich ein nettes Zimmer bei anständigen Leuten *nicht* in Wein habe." Undated letter, Library of Congress.

26. "Meine lieben, lieben Kinder. Ich glaube, ich werde sie nie wiedersehen. . . . Und wie Du mir hassen musst! . . . Ich habe nur noch eine Hoffnung, dass ich nicht längst mehr leben werde." Undated letter, Library of Congress.

27. Christian Martin Schmidt, ed., *Kritischer Bericht,* SSW, section 6, series B, vol. 20: 170.

28. Ibid., 193; Walter Frisch, *The Early Works of Arnold Schoenberg, 1893–1908* (Berkeley: University of California Press, 1993): 267.

29. Arnold Schoenberg, "Notes on the Four String Quartets," in *The String Quartets: A Documentary Study,* edited by Ursula von Rauchhaupt, liner notes to the recording *Neue Wiener Schule: Schönberg, Berg, Webern* Deutsche Grammophon no. 419 994–2 (1987): 42.

30. "My Evolution" (1949), SI 86.

31. Stefan George, *Der siebente Ring,* in *Gesamt-Ausgabe der Werke, endgültige Fassung,* vols. 6–7 (Berlin: Georg Bondi, 1931): 122–23.

32. Schoenberg, "Notes on the Four String Quartets," 50.

33. A survey of writings on Op. 15 is found in the bibliography.

34. See the contemporaneous review by Hugo von Hofmannsthal, "Gedichte von Stefan George," reprinted in Hofmannsthal, *Ausgewählte Werke,* edited by Rudolf Hirsch, vol. 2 (Frankfurt: Fischer, 1957), 306–13. Other recommended sources of information about George are: H. R. Klieneberger, *George, Rilke, Hofmannsthal and the Romantic Tradition* (Stuttgart: H. D. Heinz, 1991); Michael M. Metzger and Erika A. Metzger, *Stefan George,* Twayne's World Authors Series, 182 (New York: Twayne, 1972). Among the many personal reminiscences of the poet and of others in his circle see Edgar Salin, *Um Stefan George: Erinnerung und Zeugnis,* 2nd ed. (Munich: Küpper-Bondi, 1954).

35. Concerning the changing meaning of the garden in modern art and literature, see Carl E. Schorske, *Fin-de-siècle Vienna: Politics and Culture* (New York: Knopf, 1980): 279–366.

36. Paul Verlaine, "Mandoline," *Fêtes galantes,* edited by Yvel-Gérard Le Dantec (Paris: Cluny, 1939): 30.

37. Maegaard considers the title page to be connected with four earlier songs whose manuscripts are also in the Morgan Library. See JMS 1: 156.

38. Theodor W. Adorno, "Zu den Georgeliedern," in *Arnold Schönberg: Fünfzehn Gedichte aus "Das Buch der hängenden Gärten" von Stefan George* (Wiesbaden: Insel-Verlag, 1959): 80, in AGS 18:411–17.

39. See "Brahms the Progressive" (1947), SI 398–441; Carl Dahlhaus, "Musical Prose" (1964), in *Schoenberg and the New Music: Essays by Carl Dahlhaus,* translated by Derrick Puffett and Alfred Clayton (Cambridge: Cambridge University Press, 1987): 105–19; and Hermann Danuser, *Musikalische Prosa,* Studien zur Musikgeschichte des 19. Jahrhunderts, 46 (Regensburg: Gustav Bosse, 1975).

40. "Es ist von allen das kühnste und avancierteste, vollends ohne herkömmliche Architektur, ganz verkürzt, im Satz immaterialisiert. Seine Tragweite für die Folge läßt sich nicht überschätzen: von ihm stammt der gesamte Webern her." Adorno, "Zu den Georgeliedern," 82.

41. See Allen Forte, "Concepts of Linearity in Schoenberg's Atonal Music: A Study of the Opus 15 Song Cycle," *Journal of Music Theory* 36 (1992): 288.

42. SI 87.

43. Harald Krebs, "Three Versions of Schoenberg's Op. 15 No. 14: Obvious Differences and Hidden Similarities," JASI 8 (1984): 131–40.

44. Adorno, "Zu den Georgeliedern," 76.

45. Karl Heinrich Ehrenforth, *Ausdruck und Form: Schönbergs Durchbruch zur Atonalität in den George-Liedern Op. 15* (Bonn: Bouvier, 1963).

46. Reinhold Brinkmann, "Schönberg und George: Interpretation eines Liedes [Op. 15, No. 14]," *Archiv für Musikwissenschaft* 26 (1969): 1–28.

47. Dümling, *Die fremden Klänge der hängenden Gärten,* 172.

48. Schoenberg, "Notes on the Four String Quartets," 50.

49. SI 144.

Chapter 4

1. In a letter to Ferruccio Busoni dated 13 July 1909, Schoenberg wrote: "I have two piano pieces (several others have been started, but their completion was interrupted by another work [presumably the Five Orchestra Pieces, Op. 16])." BSL 382. The existing fragmentary piano works are found in SSW, section 2, series B, vol. 4: 114–20.

2. Transcribed in SSW, section 2, series B, vol. 4: 53–54.

3. BSL 395.

4. BSL 404; Gunther Schuller, "A Conversation with Steuermann," *Perspectives of New Music* 3/1 (1964–65): 27.

5. Arnold Schoenberg, *Three Piano Pieces* (*Drei Klavierstücke*), *Op. 11*, rev. ed. (New York: Universal Edition, Associated Music Publishers, 1942).

6. Translated in toto in BSL 381–423.

7. Following revisions, Busoni's version was published as *Klavierstück: Op. 11, No. 2 von Arnold Schönberg. Konzertmäßige Interpretation von Ferruccio Busoni* (Vienna: Universal Edition, 1910).

8. BSL 387.

9. Concerning Schoenberg's critique of Busoni's transcription, see BSL 384–409; Reinhold Brinkmann, "Ausdruck und Spiel: Zwei Ansichten eines Stückes," in *Bericht über den 2. Kongreß der Internationalen Schönberg-Gesellschaft: "Die Wiener Schule in der Musikgeschichte des 20. Jahrhunderts,"* 31–41, edited by Rudolf Stephan and Sigrid Wiesmann (Vienna: Elisabeth Lafite, 1984): 31–41; and Daniel M. Raessler, "Schoenberg and Busoni: Aspects of Their Relationship," JASI 7 (1983): 7–28.

10. FMC 119–36.

11. "Mein Stück schließt *nicht;* es hört nur auf; man müßte die Vorstellung haben, daß es eigentlich noch lange so weitergeht—wie der 'Leierkasten' von Schuberts 'Leiermann.'" Quoted by Brinkmann in "Ausdruck und Spiel," 31.

12. HL 420.

13. Reinhold Brinkmann, *Arnold Schönberg: Drei Klavierstücke Op. 11. Studien zur frühen Atonalität bei Schönberg* (Wiesbaden: Franz Steiner, 1969).

14. BSL 395.

15. "Dieses Buch könnte ebensogut vor 25 Jahren geschrieben sein. . . . Nichts könnte unwesentlicher sein, als der gezwungene Beweis, daß angeblich 'Atonales' dennoch 'tonal' ist." Archives of the Arnold Schönberg Center, Vienna.

16. See Allen Forte, *The Structure of Atonal Music* (New Haven: Yale University Press, 1973).

17. See Allen Forte, "The Magical Kaleidoscope," JASI 5 (1981): 127–68; and Gary Wittlich, "Interval Set Structure in Schoenberg's Op. 11, No. 1," *Perspectives of New Music* 13 (1974–75): 41–55.

18. From "My Evolution" (1949), SI 88.

19. Brinkmann, *Arnold Schönberg: Drei Klavierstücke Op. 11*, 60–96.

20. FMC 8.

21. FMC 9. Schoenberg also discusses the use of motivic particles in his lecture "Analysis of the Four Orchestral Songs Opus 22" (1932), translated by Claudio Spies, *Perspectives of New Music* 3 (1964–65): 1–21.

22. BSL 396.

23. BSL 389.

24. FMC 1.

25. SI 88.

26. HL 416.

27. In *Arnold Schoenberg, Wassily Kandinsky: Letters, Pictures and Documents*, edited by Jelena Hahl-Koch, translated by John C. Crawford (London: Faber and Faber, 1984): 23.

28. See Lewis Wickes, "Schoenberg, *Erwartung*, and the Reception of Psychoanalysis in Musical Circles in Vienna until 1910/1911," *Studies in Music* 23 (1989): 88–106.

29. Clara Steuermann, "From the Archives: Schoenberg's Library Catalogue," JASI 3 (1979): 203–18.

30. Schoenberg quoted Strauss's remark in a letter of 22 April 1914, ASL 50; Reger's was written in a letter of 31 December 1910 to August Stradal (quoted in BSL 409); Mahler's was recounted in Alma Mahler, *Gustav Mahler: Memories and Letters*, 3d ed., edited by Donald Mitchell, translated by Basil Creighton (Seattle: University of Washington Press, 1973): 112.

31. Strauss's correspondence with Schoenberg is excerpted in H. H. Stuckenschmidt, *Schoenberg: His Life, World and Work*, translated by Humphrey Searle (New York: Schirmer, 1977): 68 and passim.

32. See SSW, section 4, series B, vol. 12: 5.

33. The letter is excerpted in ibid., xiii.

34. Eberhardt Klemm, "Der Briefwechsel zwischen Arnold Schönberg und dem Verlag C. F. Peters," *Deutsches Jahrbuch der Musikwissenschaft* 14 (1970): 41.

35. Ibid., 18–19.

36. Arnold Schoenberg, "Attempt at a Diary," translated by Anita M. Luginbühl (with minor editorial alterations), JASI 9 (1986): 14.

37. See the letter from Schoenberg to Zemlinsky dated 16 February 1923 in AZB 248.

38. Concerning the arrangement, see Wulf Konold, "Struktur und Klangfarbe: Bemerkungen zu Original und Bearbeitung von Schöbergs *Fünf Orchesterstücken* op. 16," in *Schönbergs Verein für musikalische Privataufführungen*, edited by Heinz-Klaus Metzger and Rainer Riehn, Musik-Konzepte, vol. 36 (Munich: Edition text + kritik, 1984): 43–64.

39. "Schönberg: Fünf Orchesterstücke, Op. 16," *Pult und Taktstock* 4 (1927): 36–43, in AGS 18:335–44.

40. HL 421–22.

41. Letter dated 18 January 1914, BSC 203.

42. BSL 393.

43. "Composition with Twelve Tones" (1941), SI 235.

44. Allen Forte, "Schoenberg's Creative Evolution: The Path to Atonality," *Musical Quarterly* 64 (1978): 133–76.

45. Concerning this issue see Ethan Haimo, "Atonality, Analysis, and the Intentional Fallacy," *Music Theory Spectrum* 18 (1996): 167–99.

46. "Das Unaussprechliche sagt man in der freien Form. In der nähert es sich der Natur, die auch unfaßbar und trotzdem wirksam ist." In Arnold Schoenberg, *Berliner Tagebuch*, edited by Josef Rufer (Frankfurt: Propyläen, 1974): 11.

47. Michael Mäckelmann, *Arnold Schönberg: Fünf Orchesterstücke Op. 16* (Munich: Wilhelm Fink, 1987): 15.

48. FMC 85

49. SI 78.

50. Quoted in Hans Moldenhauer and Rosaleen Moldenhauer, *Anton von Webern: A Chronicle of His Life and Work* (New York: Knopf, 1979): 123.

51. Alma Mahler-Werfel, *Mein Leben* (Frankfurt: Fischer, 1960): 77.

52. "Über einige Arbeiten Arnold Schönbergs" (1963), in AGS 17: 327–44.

53. Egon Wellesz, *Arnold Schoenberg*, translated by W. H. Kerridge (London: Dent, 1925): 31.

54. Translated by Walter Kaufmann in *The Portable Nietzsche* (New York: Penguin Books, 1976): 556.

Chapter 5

1. Marie Heim [Marie Pappenheim], "Seziersaal," *Die Fackel* 202 (1906): 23.

2. Helmut Kirchmeyer, liner notes to the recording *Erwartung,* Wergo 50 001 (1963).

3. "Ich schrieb im Gras liegend mit Bleistift auf großen Bogen Papier, hatte keine Kopie, las das Geschriebene kaum durch, . . . und glaubte, Schönberg werde es lesen, ändern, Vorschläge machen (ich kannte ihn damals noch nicht sehr gut). Dann bekam ich das Manuskript überhaupt nicht mehr zurück, Schönberg sagte mir nur, was er ändern wolle: Ich hatte wie jeder 'verzückte Dichter' überall mehrere Gleichnisse geschrieben (etwa 'wie dein Schatten' etc., dabei war noch ein oder zwei Erinnerungsbild). Schönberg zeigte mir eines, sagte beruhigend, alles sei sehr schön, aber in der Komposition zu lang—er werde überall nur eine solche Stelle stehen lassen. Er schien es eben so 'rasendschnell' komponieren zu wollen wie ich es geschrieben hatte." Letter dated 15 June 1963 from Marie Pappenheim to Helmut Kirchmeyer, transcribed in Peter Naumann, "Untersuchungen zum Wort-Ton-Verhältnis in den Einaktern Arnold Schönbergs," vol. 2 (Ph.D. diss., Universität zu Köln, 1988): 1–3.

4. All of the manuscripts are located in the archives of the Arnold Schönberg Center, Vienna.

5. Concerning the kinship of Bertha and Marie Pappenheim, see Diane Holloway Penney, "Schoenberg's Janus-Work *Erwartung*: Its Musico-Dramatic Structure and Relationship to the Melodrama and Lied Traditions" (Ph.D. diss., University of North Texas, 1989): 94.

6. Josef Breuer, "Case l: Fräulein Anna O.," in *Studies on Hysteria* by Josef Breuer and Sigmund Freud, *The Standard Edition of the Complete Psychological Works of Sigmund Freud*, translated and edited by James Strachey, et al., vol. 2 (London: Hogarth Press, Institute of Psycho-Analysis, 1955): 25.

7. "Was haben sie dir getan? . . . Oh du . . . du . . . ich war nicht hier. . . . Der Abend war so friedlich. . . . Die zitternden Blätter vor dem Himmel . . . dein Haar is blutig . . . dein weiches braunes Haar. . . . Und Blut an meinen Händen . . . und Blut auf dem Boden. . . . Wer hat das getan? . . . Wer hat das getan, du? . . . Du bist das Einzige hier. Du musst es wissen. . . .

Hast du von hier [aus] zu mir hinübergespäht? . . . So . . . die Hand über den Augen . . . hier im Schatten. Die Schattenhöhlen . . . das Räubernest . . . Hier drückte er sich an den Stamm. . . . Und dann der Schuß." Pappenheim's complete original text is transcribed in José Maria Garcia Laborda, *Studien zu Schönbergs Monodram "Erwartung" op. 17* (Laaber: Laaber, 1981): 122–41. The passages quoted here are found on pp. 134–35.

8. "(Über ihn gebeugt, küßt ihn.) Deine Lippen sind matt und schliessen sich nicht. . . . Küß mich doch. . . . So . . . so. . . . (Sie wirft sich ganz über ihn.) Ich liebe dich so sehr. . . . Du bist heiss . . . heiss. . . . Dein Atem erstickt mich." Ibid., 133.

9. "Eine dieser Änderungen war mir in Gedanken noch lange Zeit unangenehm, nämlich Striche in der Szene da sie den toten Körper sieht. Durch diese Striche, die ich längst nicht mehr weiss, wurde das Mystische, oder sagen wir Halluzinatorische

verstärkt, während ich gar nicht so sicher war, dass es nicht eine wahre Begebenheit sei. Vielleicht ist es aber wirklich dadurch in der Wirkung stärker geworden." Naumann, "Untersuchungen zum Wort-Ton-Verhältnis," 2:2–3.

10. Egon Wellesz, "Arnold Schönbergs Bühnenwerke," *Musikblätter des Anbruch* 2 (1920): 604.

11. "New Music: My Music," SI 105.

12. BSL 399.

13. Naumann, "Untersuchungen zum Wort-Ton-Verhältnis," 2: 3.

14. JMS 2: 454 and passim; Siegfried Mauser, *Das expressionistische Musiktheater der Wiener Schule* (Regensburg: Gustav Bosse, 1982): 21.

15. H. H. Stuckenschmidt, "Arnold Schönbergs 'Erwartung,'" *Der Scheinwerfer* (Essen) 4/9 (January 1931): 1–4.

16. The quotation was noted by several early writers on the work, including Stuckenschmidt, (ibid.). Also see Herbert H. Buchanan, "A Key to Schoenberg's *Erwartung* (Op. 17)," *Journal of the American Musicological Society* 20 (1967): 434–49.

17. In the *Harmonielehre* he admitted to an instinctive "aversion to recalling even remotely the traditional chords." HL 420.

18. See Naumann, "Untersuchungen zum Wort-Ton-Verhältnis," 2: 4.

19. Letter from Schoenberg to Karl Hagemann, 14 February 1910, Arnold Schoenberg Collection, Library of Congress, Washington, D.C.

20. Another view is given by Harald Krebs, "New Light on the Source Materials of Schoenberg's *Die glückliche Hand*," JASI 11 (1988): 131.

21. See the two letters from Kokoschka to Schoenberg in *Oskar Kokoschka. Briefe I: 1905–1919* (Düsseldorf: Claasen, 1984): 10.

22. The letter is excerpted in Jane Kallir, *Arnold Schoenberg's Vienna* (New York: Galerie St. Etienne/Rizzoli, 1984): 90.

23. "In Wien kursiert, daß Sie mit Kokoschka eine Oper schreiben. Vielleicht wär's doch besser gewesen? Mein Monodr. gefällt mir wenig." Arnold Schoenberg Collection, Library of Congress, Washington, D.C.

24. "Ein von Unglück geschlagener Mann rafft sich auf. Das Glück lächelt ihm wieder. Er vermag Leistungen zu vollbringen wie in früheren Zeiten. Doch abermals erweist sich alles als trügerisch, und von neuen Schicksalsschlägen getroffen, bricht er zusammen." Erwin Stein, "Schönbergs 'Glückliche Hand,'" *Die Oper: Blätter des Breslauer Stadttheaters*, No. 16 (1927–28): 4.

25. Schoenberg reused this idea in an outline (1926) for his play *Der biblische Weg.* See Moshe Lazar, "Arnold Schoenberg and His Doubles: A Psychodramatic Journey to His Roots," JASI 17 (1994): 65.

26. "Nun ist aber doch nicht zu leugnen, dass ich über ihren Treubruch äusserst unglücklich bin. Ich habe geweint, habe mich wie ein Verzweifelter gebärdet, habe Entschlüsse gefasst und wieder verworfen, habe Selbstmordideen gehabt und beinahe ausgeführt, habe mich von einer Tollheit in die andere gestürzt—mit einem Wort ich bin ganz zerrissen. . . . Wir haben einander nie gekannt. Ich weiss auch gar nicht wie sie aussieht. Ich kann mir gar kein Bild von ihr machen. Vielleicht existiert sie überhaupt nicht." "Testaments-Entwurf," archives of the Arnold Schönberg Center, Vienna.

27. See Otto Kallir, "Richard Gerstl (1883–1908): Beiträge zur Dokumentation seines Lebens und Werkes," *Mitteilungen der Österreichischen Galerie* 17 (1974): 64.

28. Arnold Schoenberg, "Breslau Lecture on *Die glückliche Hand*," in *Arnold Schoenberg, Wassily Kandinsky: Letters, Pictures and Documents,* edited by Jelena Hahl-Koch, translated by John C. Crawford (London: Faber and Faber, 1984): 102–7.

29. Quoted in *Arnold Schoenberg: Paintings and Drawings,* edited by Thomas Zaunschirm, translated by Alfred M. Fischer (Klagenfurt: Ritter, 1991): 437.

30. For an extensive reconstruction of this chronology, see Joseph Auner, "Schoenberg's Compositional and Aesthetic Transformations, 1910–1913" (Ph.D. diss., University of Chicago, 1991): 36–149.

31. On this point see John C. Crawford, "*Die glückliche Hand:* Schoenberg's *Gesamtkunstwerk,*" *Musical Quarterly* 60 (1974): 583–601; Reinhard Gerlach, "Farbklang—Klangfarbe, Rausch und Konstruktion," *Neue Zeitschrift für Musik* 134/1 (1973): 10–19; Philip Truman, "Synaesthesia and *Die glückliche Hand,*" *Interface* 12 (1983): 481–503; and Frits C. Weiland, "'Der gelbe Klang,'" *Interface* 10 (1981): 1–13. Concerning the sketches and musical structure of the passage see Harald Krebs, "The 'Color Crescendo' from *Die glückliche Hand:* A Comparison of Sketch and Final Version," JASI 12 (1989): 61–67.

32. See the facsimile and discussion of a sketch for this passage given by Joseph Auner, "'Heart and Brain in Music': The Genesis of Schoenberg's *Die glückliche Hand,*" in *Constructive Dissonance: Arnold Schoenberg and the Transformations of Twentieth-Century Culture,* edited by Christopher Hailey and Juliane Brand (Berkeley: University of California Press, 1997): 122–23.

33. "Entnimmt man daraus nicht . . . dass sich der Mann, trotz der Niederlage die er erlebt hat, so zusammengebrochen er zunächst ist, sofort wieder zum Kampf stellt? Oder, anders gesehen: dass die Liebe (Eros) ihn immer wieder zum Leben zurückruft?" Archives of the Arnold Schönberg Center, Vienna. For more information on Petschnig's review and Schoenberg's commentary, see Ena Steiner, "The 'Happy Hand': Genius and Interpretation of Schoenberg's *Monumentalkunstwerk,*" *Music Review* 41 (1980): 207–22.

34. Discussed in Joseph Auner, "In Schoenberg's Workshop: Aggregates and Referential Collections in *Die glückliche Hand,*" *Music Theory Spectrum* 18 (1996): 77–105.

35. "Die Musik zur 'Glückliche Hand,'" *Die Tribüne* (Cologne) 24/18 (May 1955), AGS 18 (1984): 408–10.

36. "Es ist mein 'heißer' Wunsch (verbrennen Sie sich nicht daran) es mit dem Monodram zusammen aufgeführt zu bekommen." Letter from Schoenberg to Albertine Zehme, 13 September 1913, Arnold Schoenberg Collection, Library of Congress, Washington, D.C.

37. See his correspondence with Emil Hertzka of Universal Edition, which is excerpted in Michael Wurstbauer, "Uraufführung der *Erwartung*—Erwartung der Uraufführung: Von der Entstehung bis zur Uraufführung des Monodrams *Erwartung* op. 17," in *40.000 Musikerbriefe auf Knopfdruck,* edited by Ernst Hilmar (Tutzing: Hans Schneider, 1989): 75–96.

38. Letter of 14 April 1930 to Ernst Legal, ASL 139.

39. "Sie muß ja von der Musik ausgehen, über die Ohren zu den Augen." Letter to Rudolf Schulz-Dornburg, Arnold Schoenberg Collection, Library of Congress, Washington, D.C.

40. Reproduced in Zaunschirm, *Arnold Schoenberg,* 308–25.

41. Letter to Emil Hertzka, Autumn 1913, in ASL 43.

42. Translated by John C. Crawford in Hahl-Koch, *Arnold Schoenberg, Wassily Kandinsky,* 111–25.

43. Ibid., 53–55.

Chapter 6

1. For more information on Schoenberg's plan for a cycle of treatises, see Bryan R. Simms, "Commentary on *Theory of Harmony,* by Arnold Schoenberg, translated by Roy E. Carter," *Music Theory Spectrum* 4 (1982): 156–57.

2. "Ich hatte schon an die Möglichkeit gedacht, daß ich überhaupt nie wieder komponiere. Es schien viele Gründe dafür zu geben. Die Hartnäckigkeit, mit der mir meine Schüler auf den Fersen sind, indem sie zu überbieten trachten, was ich biete, bringt mich in Gefahr, ihr Nachahmer zu werden, und hindert mich, dort ruhig auszubauen, wo ich eben stehe. Sie bringen gleich alles zur zehnten Potenz erhoben. Und es stimmt! Es ist wirklich gut. Aber ich weiß nicht, ob es nötig ist. Ich bin deshalb jetzt gezwungen, noch sorgfältiger zu unterscheiden, ob ich schreiben muß, als früher." Arnold Schoenberg, *Berliner Tagebuch,* edited by Josef Rufer (Frankfurt: Propyläen, 1974): 33–34.

3. Concerning this incident, see BSC 11n.

4. Ibid., 60.

5. The complete letter exchange between the two is found in *Arnold Schoenberg, Wassily Kandinsky: Letters, Pictures and Documents,* edited by Jelena Hahl-Koch, translated by John C. Crawford (London: Faber and Faber, 1984): 21–85.

6. "Schönberg *muß* über deutsche Musik schreiben. . . . Etwas Noten sollen auch drin sein. Schönberg hat ja z. B. Lieder. . . . Wir müssen eben zeigen, daß *überall* was vorkommt." *Wassily Kandinsky, Franz Marc, Briefwechsel,* edited by Klaus Lankeit (Munich: R. Piper, 1983): 54–55.

7. See Peg Weiss, *Kandinsky in Munich: The Formative Jugendstil Years* (Princeton: Princeton University Press, 1979): 81–91.

8. See Wassily Kandinsky, *Concerning the Spiritual in Art,* translated by M. T. H. Sadler (1914; reprinted New York: Dover, 1977): 14–15.

9. Maurice Maeterlinck, *Gedichte,* translated into German by K. L. Ammer and Friedrich von Oppeln-Bronikowski (Jena: Eugen Diederichs, 1906): 11. English translation by the author.

10. A facsimile of the first page of this manuscript is given in Bonny Hough, "Schoenberg's *Herzgewächse* and the *Blaue Reiter* Almanac," JASI 7 (1983): 198. Reinhold Brinkmann has postulated the existence of an earlier first draft that is now lost, and he considers the version in *Der blaue Reiter* to be a more definitive reworking of the version in the other fair copy. See Brinkmann, ed., *Kritischer Bericht,* SSW, section 6, series B, vol. 24/2: 1–18.

11. Translated by Dika Newlin as "The Relationship to the Text," SI 141–45.

12. "Opinion or Insight?" (1926), SI 260.

13. "Es lassen sich Erzählungen ohne Zusammenhang, jedoch mit Assoziationen, wie Träume, denken; Gedichte, die bloss wohlklingend und voll schöner Worte sind, aber auch ohne allen Sinn und Zusammenhang, höchstens einige Strophen verständlich, wie Bruchstücke aus den verschiedenartigsten Dingen. Diese wahre Poesie kann höchstens einen allegorischen Sinn im Grossen und eine indirekte Wirkung wie Musik haben." Quoted in Maeterlinck, *Gedichte,* 68.

14. Joachim Birke, "Richard Dehmel und Arnold Schönberg: Ein Briefwechsel," *Die Musikforschung* 11 (1958): 285.

15. Cited in Willi Reich, *Schoenberg: A Critical Biography,* translated by Leo Black (New York: Praeger, 1971): 238.

16. Albert Giraud, *Pierrot lunaire: Rondels. Deutsch von Otto Erich Hartleben* (Berlin: n.p., 1892). There were three later editions: in 1893 (Berlin: Deutscher Phantasten), 1895 (Berlin: Deutsche Schriftsteller-Genossenschaft), and 1911 (Munich: Georg Müller).

17. Otto Vrieslander, *Pierrot lunaire für eine Singstimme mit Pianoforte* (Munich: Lewy, 1905).

18. Concerning Albertine Zehme, see H. H. Stuckenschmidt, *Schoenberg: His Life, World and Work,* translated by Humphrey Searle (New York: Schirmer, 1977): 195–218.

19. Edward Steuermann, *"Pierrot lunaire* in Retrospect," *Juilliard News Bulletin* (1963), JASI 2 (1977): 50.

20. See Edward F. Kravitt, "The Joining of Words and Music in Late Romantic Melodrama," *Musical Quarterly* 62 (1976): 571–90.

21. "Die Worte, die wir sprechen, sollen nicht allein dem Sinne nach Begriffe werden, sondern sollen uns auch als Klang Anteil am inneren Erlebnis gestatten. Um das zu ermöglichen, müssen wir aber uneingeschränkte Tonfreiheit haben. Keine der tausend Schwingungen zum Gefühlsausdruck zu benutzen darf verwehrt sein. Ich fordre nicht Gedanken-, sondern Tonfreiheit!

"Die Singstimme, dieses überirdisch keusch gebundene, gerade in seiner asketischen Unfreiheit so ideal schöne Instrument—schon ein starker Lufthauch trübt seine unnahbare Schönheit—eignet sich nicht zu starkem Gefühlsausbruch.

"Das Leben ist nun aber mit dem schönen Klang allein nicht auszuschöpfen. Das tiefste letzte Glück, das tiefste letzte Leid verklingt als lautloser Schrei ungehört in unsrer Brust, die zu zerspringen droht, oder es bricht sich, wie ein Strom glühender Lava, die Bahn über unsre Lippen. Für den Ausdruck dieser letzten Dinge scheint es mir fast grausam, die Singstimme naturalistische Frohndienste verrichten zu lassen, aus denen sie nur zerweht, zerfasert, zerbrochen hervor gehen muss.

"Um unsere Dichter, um unsere Komponisten mitzuteilen, brauchen wir Beides, den Gesangs- wie auch den Sprachton. Die unablässige Arbeit nach dem Suchen der letzten Ausdrucks-Möglichkeiten für die "künstlerischen Erlebnisse im Ton" hat mich diese Notwendigkeit gelehrt." Quoted in Reinhold Brinkmann, *Kritischer Bericht (Pierrot lunaire)*, SSW, section 6, series B, vol. 24/1: 307. Albertine Zehme was also the author of a treatise on recitation, *Die Grundlagen des künstlerischen Sprechens und Singens* (Leipzig: Carl Merseburger, 1920).

22. Albert Giraud, *Héros et Pierrots* (Brussels: La Vie Intellectuelle, 1928): 55.

23. Ibid., 104.

24. Concerning the appearance of figures from traditional comedy in the arts of this period, see Martin Green and John Swan, *The Triumph of Pierrot: The Commedia dell'Arte and the Modern Imagination* (New York: Macmillan, 1986).

25. Susan Youens, "Excavating an Allegory: The Texts of *Pierrot lunaire*," JASI 8 (1984): 96.

26. From a letter dated 31 August 1940, quoted in Brinkmann, *Kritischer Bericht (Pierrot lunaire)*, 302.

27. "Habe Vorwort gelesen, Gedichte angeschaut, bin begeistert. Glänzende Idee, ganz in meinem Sinn." Schoenberg, *Berliner Tagebuch*, 13.

28. Arnold Schoenberg, letter dated 13 January 1912 in BSC 65.

29. Albert Giraud and Otto Erich Hartleben, *Pierrot lunaire: Mit vier Musikstücken von Otto Vrieslander* (Munich: Georg Müller, 1911).

30. " . . . diesen mondsüchtigen Cyniker mit dem schwarzen Flor über dem roten Herzen, der romantischen Ironie letzten Enkel, den Adoranten mit der verletzlichsten Scham, den keuschesten Wüstling." In Giraud and Hartleben, *Pierrot lunaire*, "Einleitung" (unpaginated).

31. See the exhaustive compilation of documents in Brinkmann, *Kritischer Bericht (Pierrot lunaire)*.

32. Ibid., 228.

33. Ibid., 306.

34. "Hier sind *alle* die Texte, die aus dem Pierrot lunair in Frage kommen. Etwa 22–24 brauchen wir für einen Abend. Sie können also immer noch dies und das ausscheiden, wenn Ihnen etwas nicht liegt." Quoted in ibid., 225.

35. "Est ist banal zu sagen, daß wir alle solche mondsüchtigen Wursteln sind; das meint ja der Dichter, daß wir eingebildete Mondflecke von unseren Kleidern

abzuwischen uns bemühen und aber unsere Kreuze anbeten. Seien wir froh daß wir Wunden haben: Wir haben damit etwas, was uns hilft die Materie gering zu schät-zen. Von der Verachtung für unsere Wunden stammt die Verachtung für unsere Feinde, stammt unsere Kraft, unsere Leben einem Mondstrahl zu opfern. Man wird leicht pathetisch, wenn man an die Pierrot-Dichtung denkt. Aber zum Kuckuck, gibt es denn nur mehr Getreidepreise?" AZB 161. The note was written by Schoenberg in a copy of the *Pierrot* score that was given to Zemlinsky as a Christmas gift in 1916.

36. For a precise chronology of composition, see Brinkmann, *Kritischer Bericht (Pierrot lunaire)*, 178–83 and passim.

37. "Es heißt: *Pierrot lunair* (nach Albert Giraud übersetzt von Otto Erich Hartle-ben): *Melodramen-Cyklus mit Begleitung von Klavier Flöte (Picc) Clar (Bass Clar) Geige (Bratsche) und Vcell* (5 Spieler). . . . Jedes Stück hat eine andere Besetzung!!! Es kom-men vor 2 Soli (1. Klavier 2. Flöte allein!!!) 4 Duos, 7 Trios, 4 Quartette, 5 Quintette. Insgesamt 22 Stücke. (Vielleicht kommt noch eines dazu!)." Quoted in ibid., 230–31.

38. "Ich bitte sehr um die endgültige Reihenfolge. Est ist wichtig, mich innerlich schon auf die Reihenfolge einzustellen. Den Entwurf habe ich, Sie meinten aber, der sei nicht bindend." Quoted in ibid., 235.

39. Reinhold Brinkmann has speculated that Schoenberg may have been influ-enced in this number symbolism by a comparable scheme in Stefan George's poetic anthology *Der siebente Ring*. Also see Colin C. Sterne, "Pythagoras and Pierrot: An Approach to Schoenberg's Use of Numerology in the Construction of 'Pierrot lu-naire,'" *Perpectives of New Music* 21 (1982–83): 506–34.

40. Evidence for this chronology is put forward by Brinkmann, *Kritischer Bericht (Pierrot lunaire)*, 215 and passim, based on an analysis of the manuscripts.

41. Steuermann, "*Pierrot lunaire* in Retrospect," 50.

42. Arnold Schoenberg, *Dreimal sieben Gedichte aus Albert Girauds "Pierrot lu-naire" Op. 21*, score (Vienna: Universal Edition no. 5336, 1914). The history of early performances is recounted in H. H. Stuckenschmidt, *Schoenberg: His Life, World and Work*, 202–17, and in Brinkmann, *Kritischer Bericht (Pierrot lunaire)*, 246–90.

43. Letter of 15 February 1949 to Hans Rosbaud, quoted in Brinkmann, *Kritis-cher Bericht (Pierrot lunaire)*, 304.

44. "Niemals haben die Ausführenden hier die Aufgabe, aus dem Sinn der Worte die Stimmung und den Charakter der einzelnen Stücke zu gestalten, sondern stets lediglich aus der Musik. Soweit dem Autor die tonmalerische Darstellung der im Text gegebenen Vorgänge und Gefühle wichtig war, findet sie sich ohnedies in der Musik. Wo der Ausführende sie vermißt, verzichte er darauf, etwas zu geben, was der Autor nicht gewollt hat. Er würde hier nicht geben, sondern nehmen." Schoenberg, *Dreimal sieben Gedichte aus Albert Girauds "Pierrot lunaire*," Foreword.

45. Alan Philip Lessem, *Music and Text in the Works of Arnold Schoenberg: The Crit-ical Years, 1908–1922*, Studies in Musicology, No. 8 (Ann Arbor: UMI Research Press, 1979): 126 and passim.

46. See especially Brinkmann, *Kritischer Bericht (Pierrot lunaire)*, 212–14.

47. "In dieser Perspektive ist der *Pierrot* eine aktuell-kritische Stellungnahme, nicht mehr nur Musik, nicht mehr allein Musik über Musik, sondern Musik über Geschichte und Gegenwart des endenden 19. und anbrechenden 20. Jahrhunderts, allerdings: formuliert vom Standpunkt der Moderne." Ibid., 213.

48. A diplomatic transcription and discussion is given in ibid., 215.

49. Jonathan Dunsby, *Schoenberg: "Pierrot lunaire*," Cambridge Music Handbooks (Cambridge: Cambridge University Press, 1992): 28.

50. See Rudolf Stephan, "Zur jüngsten Geschichte des Melodrams," *Archiv für Musikwissenschaft* 17 (1960): 183–92.

51. ASL 40.

52. See Arnold Schoenberg, "Breslau Lecture on *Die glückliche Hand*," in Hahl-Koch, *Arnold Schoenberg, Wassily Kandinsky*, 102–7.

53. In Gunther Schuller, "A Conversation with Steuermann," *Perspectives of New Music* 3 (1964–65): 25.

54. Lessem, *Music and Text in the Works of Arnold Schoenberg*, 136.

55. BSC 143.

56. "Die in der Sprechstimme durch Noten angegebene Melodie ist (bis auf einzelne besonders bezeichnete Ausnahmen) *nicht* zum Singen bestimmt. Der Ausführende hat die Aufgabe, sie unter guter Berücksichtigung der vorgezeichneten Tonhöhen in eine *Sprechmelodie* umzuwandeln. Das geschieht, indem er

    I. den Rhythmus haarscharf so einhält, als ob er sänge, d.h. mit nicht mehr Freiheit, als er sich bei einer Gesangsmelodie gestatten dürfte;

    II. sich des Unterschiedes zwischen *Gesangston* und *Sprechton* genau bewußt wird: der Gesangston hält die Tonhöhe unabänderlich fest, der Sprechton gibt sie zwar an, verläßt sie aber durch Fallen oder Steigen sofort wieder. Der Ausführende muß sich aber sehr davor hüten, in eine 'singende' Sprechweise zu verfallen. Das ist absolut nicht gemeint. Es wird zwar keineswegs ein realistisch-natürliches Sprechen angestrebt. Im Gegenteil, der Unterschied zwischen gewöhnlichem und einem Sprechen, das in einer musikalischen Form mitwirkt, soll deutlich werden. Aber es darf auch nie an Gesang erinnern." In Schoenberg, *Dreimal sieben Gedichte aus Albert Girauds "Pierrot lunaire,"* Foreword.

57. "Vor allem: was sie bringt ist echt, ohne Sentimentalität und Pathos und Singsang. Vielleicht mitunter zu vornehm, der Ernst nicht kalt genug, die Tragik nicht überwältigend groß. Aber da ist beides. Und ich glaubte Sie so zu verstehen, daß *das* nicht allzuviel ausmacht, als Sie schrieben, daß alles "Allegretto" bleiben müßte." Letter from 28 February 1921, Vienna, archives of the Arnold Schoenberg Center. Quoted in Bryan R. Simms, "The Society for Private Musical Performances: Resources and Documents in Schoenberg's Legacy," JASI 3 (1979): 141. The location of the letter by Schoenberg to which Stein refers is unknown.

58. "Die *Farbe alles*, die Noten *gar nichts* bedeuten." Letter from Schoenberg to Emil Hertzka dated 5 July 1912, quoted in Brinkmann, *Kritischer Bericht (Pierrot lunaire)*, 233.

59. Alfred Kerr, *Gesammelte Schriften*, vol. 4 (Berlin: Fischer, 1917): 345.

60. *Musical America*, 16 November 1912, in *Dossier de presse de "Pierrot lunaire" d'Arnold Schönberg*, edited by François Lesure (Geneva: Editions Minkoff, 1985): 14.

61. These two movements, also No. 8, are analyzed in detail by Kathryn Bailey, "Formal Organization and Structural Imagery in Schoenberg's Pierrot lunaire," *Studies in Music from the University of Western Ontario* 2 (1977): 93–107. See also Claus Raab, "Der Fleck im 'Mondfleck': Zu den Takten 8 bis 12 der Nr. 18 in Arnold Schönbergs 'Pierrot lunaire' op. 21," *Die Musikforschung* 46 (1993): 411–16.

62. Giraud and Hartleben, *Pierrot lunaire*, 19.

63. Reproduced in Brinkmann, *Kritischer Bericht (Pierrot lunaire)*, 195–98.

64. A careful analysis is given in Bailey, "Formal Organization and Structural Imagery in Schoenberg's Pierrot lunaire," 101–7; see also Joseph N. Straus, *Introduction to Post-Tonal Theory* (Englewood Cliffs: Prentice Hall, 1990): 22–25.

65. "Aber in der Passacaglia ist zum erstenmal etwas in Anwendung gebracht worden, wenn auch noch in unklarer Weise, was für die Weiterentwicklung von Bedeutung ist. . . . Die Entwicklung der hinzutretenden Stimmen wird abgeleitet aus den Möglichkeiten des Zusammenklangs mit der Hauptstimme. Der erste Takt ist aufzufassen als Ausgangspunkt von allem weiteren Geschehen und als Reduktion

des Ganzen; der Inhalt des einen Taktes ist in der Vertikalen und Horizontalen ausgebreitet. Auch das ist erst durch die Zwölftonkomposition möglich geworden." In Rudolf Stephan, "Ein frühes Dokument zur Entstehung der Zwölftonkomposition," in *Festschrift Arno Forchert zum 60. Geburtstag zum 29. Dezember 1985,* edited by Gerhard Allroggen and Detlef Altenburg (Kassel: Bärenreiter, 1986): 298.

66. Letter of 19 August 1912, quoted in Hahl-Koch, *Arnold Schoenberg, Wassily Kandinsky,* p. 54.

67. See Ferruccio Busoni, *Entwurf einer neuen Ästhetik der Tonkunst: Mit Anmerkungen von Arnold Schönberg,* edited by H. H. Stuckenschmidt (Frankfurt: Suhrkamp, 1974): 73–75. Schoenberg's marginal note is undated.

68. SI 145–46.

69. See Matthias Hansen, *Arnold Schönberg: Ein Konzept der Moderne* (Kassel: Bärenreiter, 1993): 144.

70. Honoré de Balzac, *Philosophische Erzählungen* (Leipzig: Insel-Verlag, 1910).

71. An outline of the work, undated although probably made at this time, is reproduced in *Arnold Schönberg, 1874–1951: Lebensgeschichte in Begegnungen,* edited by Nuria Nono Schoenberg (Klagenfurt: Ritter, 1992): 125.

72. A facsimile of part of this sketch is reproduced in Joseph Auner, "Schoenberg's Compositional and Aesthetic Transformations, 1910–1913: The Genesis of *Die glückliche Hand*" (Ph.D. diss., University of Chicago, 1991): 127.

73. "Das ist eine Arbeit für einige Jahre und wird ein eigenes Theater nötig haben. Ich brauche für die 'Himmelfahrt' allein einen Chor von wenigstens zweitausend Sängern." Quoted in Nono-Schoenberg, *Arnold Schönberg, 1874– 1951,* 125.

74. Ernest Dowson, *Verses* (London: Chiswick Press, 1896): no. 41.

75. Stefan George, trans., *Zeitgenössische Dichter,* vol. 1 (Berlin: Georg Bondi, 1905): 48.

76. See Berg's letter to Schoenberg dated 8 October 1914 in BSC 220.

77. "Analyse der 4 Orchesterlieder op. 22," in *Stil und Gedanke: Aufsätze zur Musik,* edited by Ivan Vojtěch, Arnold Schönberg Gesammelte Schriften, 1 (N.p.: Fischer, 1976): 286–300. Translated by Claudio Spies ("Analysis of the Four Orchestral Songs Opus 22"), *Perspectives of New Music* 3 (1964–65): 1–21.

78. Schoenberg, "Analysis of the Four Orchestral Songs Opus 22," 7.

79. See Jack Boss, "Schoenberg's Op. 22 Radio Talk and Developing Variation in Atonal Music," *Music Theory Spectrum* 14 (1992): 125–49.

80. The sketches are transcribed by Christian Martin Schmidt in SSW, section 1, series B, vol. 3: 196–200. An analytic interpretation of them is given in Bryan R. Simms, "Line and Harmony in the Sketches of Schoenberg's 'Seraphita,' Op. 22, No. 1," *Journal of Music Theory* 26 (1982): 291–312.

81. See the analysis of this passage in Allen Forte, "Sets and Nonsets in Schoenberg's Atonal Music," *Perspectives of New Music* 11 (1972–73): 53–54.

82. Joseph Auner, "In Schoenberg's Workshop: Aggregates and Referential Collections in *Die glückliche Hand,*" *Music Theory Spectrum* 18 (1996): 85–87.

83. The hexachord is a member of set class 6–20 (0, 1, 4, 5, 8, 9).

84. AZB 132.

85. Translated by Anita Barrows and Joanna Macy in *Rilke's Book of Hours: Love Poems to God* (New York: Riverhead, 1996): 97.

86. Ibid., 101.

87. Rainer Maria Rilke, *Werke in drei Bänden,* vol. 1 (N.p.: Insel-Verlag, 1991): 75–76. English translation by the author.

88. Ibid., 100–101.

89. Rilke, *Werke in drei Bänden,* 1: 158–59.

90. Arnold Schoenberg, *Vier Lieder, Op. 22, für Gesang und Orchester: Vereinfachte Studier- und Dirigierpartitur* (Vienna: Universal Edition no. 6060, 1917).

91. "Ich schreibe seit langem die erste Niederschrift meiner Orchesterwerke in zwei bis sechs oder acht Zeilen auf und vermerke gewöhnlich gleich die vollständige Instrumentation. Durch etwas Nacharbeiten und Eintragung kleiner Veränderungen dient diese erste Niederschrift im Verein mit der Reinpartitur (welche ich nach wie vor in der alten Weise anfertige; aber zu anderem Zweck: bloß zum Stimmenausschreiben!) als Grundlage für die Herstellung der vereinfachten Studier-und Dirigierpartitur, die ich von nun an herausgebe." Ibid., 2.

Chapter 7

1. Letter of 11 November 1913, transcribed in *Arnold Schönberg, 1874–1951: Lebensgeschichte in Begegnungen,* edited by Nuria Nono-Schoenberg (Klagenfurt: Ritter, 1992): 125.

2. ASL 35.

3. "Ich [war] zu keiner Zeit meines Lebens antireligiös, ja auch eigentlich nie unreligiös. Ich habe diese Gedichte scheinbar überhaupt viel naiver aufgefaßt als die meisten Menschen und bin noch nicht ganz ungewiß, ob das so durchaus unberechtigt ist. Jedenfalls bin ich für das, was die Leute aus dem Text herauslesen wollen, nicht verantwortlich. Wären sie musikalisch, so würde sich um den Text kein Mensch scheren." Quoted in Reinhold Brinkman, ed., *Kritischer Bericht (Pierrot lunaire),* SSW, section 6, series B, vol. 24/1: 300.

4. Letter of 19 August 1912, quoted in *Arnold Schoenberg, Wassily Kandinsky: Letters, Pictures and Documents,* edited by Jelena Hahl-Koch, translated by John C. Crawford (London: Faber and Faber, 1984): 54.

5. "Das werde ich unbedingt, wenn auch in anderer Weise, als Sie annehmen, komponieren. Und zwar denke ich es mir als Mittelsatz, vielleicht als Schlußsatz einer Symphonie. Ich habe bereits Ideen dafür und hoffe bestimmt, in den Ferien (im Sommer) was zustande zu bringen." Quoted in Joachim Birke, "Richard Dehmel und Arnold Schönberg: Ein Briefwechsel," *Die Musikforschung* 11 (1958): 284.

6. See the outline of Schoenberg's correspondence (mainly at the Library of Congress in Washington, D.C.) in "Preliminary Inventory of Schoenberg Correspondence," JASI 18–19 (1995–96).

7. Vienna, Arnold Schönberg Center, archive page U393. The page that contains the general plan is transcribed and translated in Walter B. Bailey, *Programmatic Elements in the Works of Schoenberg,* Studies in Musicology, 74 (Ann Arbor: UMI Research Press, 1984): 85; and in Josef Rufer, *The Works of Arnold Schoenberg,* translated by Dika Newlin (London: Faber and Faber, 1962): 115–16; it is also transcribed in JMS 1: 81.

8. Dehmel provided Schoenberg with his own interpretation of the poem: "It represents not a struggle with God but the triumphant peace in God which elevates us above the human struggles of life or death." See his letters of 15 and 29 December 1912 in Birke, "Richard Dehmel und Arnold Schönberg," 283–84.

9. For a revised version of this text, see SI 449–72.

10. Ibid., 450.

11. Its text is given in toto in Alma Mahler, *Gustav Mahler: Memories and Letters,* 3rd ed., edited by Donald Mitchell, translated by Basil Creighton (Seattle: University of Washington Press, 1975): 213–14.

12. The text is given in Arnold Schoenberg *Texte: Die glückliche Hand, Totentanz der Prinzipien, Requiem, Die Jakobsleiter* (Vienna: Univeral Edition, 1926): 21–28; an English translation is provided by Bailey in *Programmatic Elements,* 100.

13. Honoré de Balzac, *Séraphita (and Louis Lambert and The Exiles),* translated by Clara Bell (New York: Hippocrene, 1989): 147.

14. August Strindberg, *Inferno, Alone and Other Writings,* translated by Evert Sprinchorn (Garden City: Anchor Books, 1968): 345.

15. The text sketches and fragments are transcribed in Jean Christensen, "Arnold Schoenberg's Oratorio *Die Jakobsleiter,*" vol. 2 (Ph.D. diss., University of California, Los Angeles, 1979).

16. See ibid., 58.

17. Ibid., 72–73.

18. *Musikblätter des Anbruch* (special issue "Arnold Schönberg zum fünfzigsten Geburtstage") 6/8–9 (1924): opposite p. 282.

19. The musical fragments for the Symphony have not yet been published in their entirety, either transcribed or in facsimile. The largest number of facsimiles is available in Bailey, *Programmatic Elements,* where all the drafts of the scherzo movement are shown (pp. 107–17 and 121) in addition to other pages of sketches. Other facsimiles are included in Martina Sichardt, *Die Entstehung der Zwölftonmethode Arnold Schönbergs* (Mainz: Schott, 1990): 35, 37–38; Ethan Haimo, *Schoenberg's Serial Odyssey: The Evolution of his Twelve-Tone Method, 1914–1928* (Oxford: Clarendon, 1990): 49, 51–52, 55, 57–59; and JMS 3: facsimile no. 4.

20. "Das wird wieder ein 'gearbeitetes' Werk, im Gegensatz zu den vielen rein impressionistischen meiner letzten Zeit." AZB 132.

21. See the letter of 3 June 1937 to Nicolas Slonimsky, printed in Slonimsky, *Music since 1900,* 5th ed. (New York: Schirmer, 1994): 1029–30.

22. Called Sketchbook IV by Rufer in *The Works of Arnold Schoenberg,* 127–28; Jan Maegaard refers to the same sketchbook as "Sk15–22" in JMS 1: 21–22.

23. Measure numbers in this draft are approximate, since Schoenberg added a partial measure at the end of measure 34; this partial measure is not counted in the measure numbers given in this discussion.

24. See the summary description of the existing manuscripts in JMS 1: 80–86 and in Fusako Hamao, "On the Origin of the Twelve-Tone Method: Schoenberg's Sketches for the Unfinished *Symphony* (1914–1915)," *Current Musicology* 42 (1986): 33.

25. These five pages are shown in facsimile in Bailey, *Programmatic Elements,* 107–17.

26. Slonimsky, *Music since 1900,* 1029.

27. Hamao, "On the Origin of the Twelve-Tone Method," 41–43.

28. "Wie diese Symphonie schließlich aussehen wird, weiß ich noch nicht. Zu den beiden letzten Sätzen habe ich mir selbst etwas zusammengedichtet (bei Gelegenheit möchte ich dirs schicken) und denke nun daran, auch für den 1. u. 2. Satz selbst etwas zu schreiben da mir das wohl besser liegen würde, als Dehmels Gedichte, die ursprünglich dafür bestimmt waren. Allerdings habe ich für diese erste Idee schon eine Menge Musik skizziert, so daß ich mich nicht recht entschließen kann." AZB 142.

29. See his letter of that day to Zemlinsky in ibid., 153.

30. See his letter to Zemlinsky dated 13 December 1916 in ibid., 159.

31. The sketches from 1916 are transcribed in SSW, section 4, series B, vol. 11/2: 150–65. The text of "Wendepunkt" is transcribed in the same volume, p. 202, also in JMS 1: 175.

32. "Ich habe jetzt endlich wieder an der vor 2 Jahren begonnenen Dichtung zu meinem Chorwerk gearbeitet und habe nun auch den II. Theil im Groben fertig. Wenn ichs überarbeitet habe, sende ich dir eine Abschrift." AZB 165.

33. The fragments are transcribed in SSW, section 6, series B, vol. 24/2: 155–65.

34. See the analysis by Harald Krebs, "Schoenberg's 'Liebeslied': An Early Example of Serial Writing," JASI 11 (1988): 23–37.

35. Balzac, *Séraphita*, 123.

36. Ibid., 144.

37. Ibid., 138.

38. Ibid., 139.

39. Ibid., 142.

40. Schoenberg, *Texte*, 65.

41. Christensen, "Arnold Schoenberg's Oratorio *Die Jakobsleiter*," 2:60–63.

42. Karl Wörner, "Musik zwischen Theologie und Weltanschauung," in *Die Musik in der Geistesgeschichte: Studien zur Situation der Jahre um 1910*, Abhandlungen zur Kunst-, Musik- und Literaturgeschichte, 92 (Bonn: H. Bouvier, 1970): 171–200; Michael Mäckelmann, "Auf der Suche nach dem Gottesgedanken: Zum geistigen Hintergrund von Arnold Schönbergs unvollendetem Oratorium *Die Jakobsleiter*," in *Musikkulturgeschichte: Festschrift für Constantin Floros zum 60. Geburtstag*, edited by Peter Petersen (Wiesbaden: Breitkopf & Härtel, 1990); Mäckelmann, *Arnold Schönberg und das Judentum: Der Komponist und sein religiöses, nationales und politisches Selbstverständnis nach 1921*, Hamburger Beiträge zur Musikwissenschaft, 28 (Hamburg: Karl Dieter Wagner, 1984): 421–42.

43. Karl Wörner, *Schoenberg's "Moses and Aaron*," translated by Paul Hamburger (New York: St. Martin's, 1963): 23.

44. Rufer, Sketchbook IV; Maegaard, Sk15–22.

45. See Christensen, "Arnold Schoenberg's Oratorio *Die Jakobsleiter*," 1: 30–37.

46. Letter of 27 June 1951, ASL 288.

47. Christensen, "Arnold Schoenberg's Oratorio *Die Jakobsleiter*," 1: 37.

48. The consistency and thoroughness of Zillig's version have been judged harshly by Christensen, based on her extensive study of the source materials. See ibid., I: 263–86, and her review in *Notes* 46 (1990): 1056–58.

49. Arnold Schoenberg, *Die Jakobsleiter: Oratorium für Soli, gemischten Chor und Orchester*, piano score by Winfried Zillig (Los Angeles: Belmont Music, 1974); Schoenberg, *Jacob's Ladder: Oratorio (Fragment)*, scored for performance, following the composer's instruction by Winfried Zillig, revised for publication by Rudolf Stephan (Vienna: Universal Edition, 1980); SSW, section 9, series A (1985).

50. See the analysis of this music by Fusako Hamao, "The Origin and Development of Schoenberg's Twelve-Tone Method" (Ph.D. diss., Yale University, 1988): 38–75.

51. Schoenberg, *Texte*, 50.

52. The note is given in full in Christensen, "Arnold Schoenberg's Oratorio *Die Jakobsleiter*," 1:419–20.

53. Arnold Schoenberg, *Coherence, Counterpoint, Instrumentation, Instruction in Form*, edited by Severine Neff, translated by Charlotte M. Cross and Severine Neff (Lincoln: University of Nebraska Press, 1994).

54. Ibid., 39.

55. Ibid., 29.

56. A detailed study of the evolution of the Struggler's text is given in Christensen, "Arnold Schoenberg's Oratorio *Die Jakobsleiter*," 1:112–43.

57. Leonid Sabaneyev, "*Prometheus* von Skrjabin," *Der blaue Reiter* (Munich: R. Piper, 1912): 55–67. Schoenberg remarked at least twice on the connection of *Die Jakobsleiter* with Scriabin, once in a marginal note to an article published in 1922, "Sphärenmusik," by Josef Matthias Hauer, and again in his lecture "Komposition mit zwölf Tönen," ca. 1922–23. Concerning the former, see Bryan R. Simms, "Who First Composed Twelve-Tone Music, Schoenberg or Hauer?" JASI 10 (1987): 124–25;

concerning the latter, see Rudolf Stephan, "Ein frühes Dokument zur Entstehung der Zwölftonkomposition," in *Festschrift Arno Forchert zum 60. Geburtstag am 29. Dezember 1985*, edited by Gerhard Allroggen and Detlef Altenburg (Kassel: Bärenreiter, 1986): 296–302.

58. "Alle melodischen Stimmen sind auf den Klängen der begleitenden Harmonie [auf-]gebaut, alle Kontrapunkte sind demselben Prinzip untergeordnet." Sabaneyev, "*Prometheus* von Skrjabin," 61.

Chapter 8

1. "Composition with Twelve Tones" (1941), SI 218.

2. See Erwin Stein, "Neue Formprinzipien," *Musikblätter des Anbruch* (special issue "Arnold Schönberg zum fünfzigsten Geburtstage") 6/8–9 (1924); translated by the author ("New Formal Principles") in Stein, *Orpheus in New Guises* (London: Rockliff, 1953): 57–77; Stein, *Form and Performance* (New York: Limelight Editions, 1989): 69–125; and Josef Rufer, "Begriff und Funktion von Schönbergs Grundgestalt," *Melos 38* (1971): 281–84. Schoenberg himself touched briefly on the notion of *Grundgestalt* in notes that he compiled in 1934 for a theoretical treatise that remained incomplete and unpublished during his lifetime. See Schoenberg, *The Musical Idea and the Logic, Technique, and Art of its Presentation*, edited, translated, and with a commentary by Patricia Carpenter and Severine Neff (New York: Columbia University Press, 1995): 168–69.

3. Stein, "New Formal Principles," 60.

4. Ibid., 62–63.

5. Printed in Nicolas Slonimsky, *Music since 1900*, 5th ed. (New York: Schirmer, 1994): 1030.

6. "Ich [sprach] damals noch von 'neuen Motiven,' wo ich seither an das Vorhandensein bloss eines einzigen Motives glaube." Marginal comment dated 1939 in Heinrich Schenker's *Erläuterungsausgabe* of Beethoven's Piano Sonata in C Minor, Op. 111 (Vienna: Universal Edition, 1915). Cited in full in Bryan R. Simms, "New Documents in the Schoenberg-Schenker Polemic," *Perspectives of New Music* 16/1 (1977–78): 120–24.

7. Described in JMS 1: 94.

8. The piece is transcribed by Reinhold Brinkmann in SSW, section 2, series B, vol. 4: 120–21.

9. Examples are shown in Martina Sichardt, *Die Entstehung der Zwölftonmethode Arnold Schönbergs* (Mainz: Schott, 1990): 48–49.

10. Fusako Hamao, "The Origin and Development of Schoenberg's Twelve-Tone Method" (Ph.D. diss., Yale University, 1988): 99.

11. See Ethan Haimo, *Schoenberg's Serial Oddyssey: The Evolution of His Twelve-Tone Method, 1914–1928* (Oxford: Clarendon Press, 1990): 65; and Arnold Schoenberg, "Vortrag/12/T/K/Princeton," translated by Claudio Spies, *Perspectives of New Music* 13 (1974–75): 85.

12. "Arbeiten kann ich gar nicht. Ich kann den Kopf nicht frei bekommen. Sorgen um den Lebensunterhalt, um die politischen und die Sicherheitszustände; außerdem gebe ich jetzt sogar in den Ferien noch immer 15 Stunden wöchentlich." AZB 208.

13. See Ethan Haimo, "Redating Schoenberg's Passacaglia for Orchestra," *Journal of the American Musicological Society* 40 (1987): 470–94, and also the critique of this article in Hamao, "The Origin and Development of Schoenberg's Twelve-Tone Method," 292–316. Haimo's questioning of the accuracy of the date 5 March 1920 for the eleven-measure fragment is unnecessary.

14. See the letter to Webern dated 29 March 1926 in Ernst Hilmar, "Arnold Schönberg an Anton Webern: Eine Auswahl unbekannter Briefe," in *Arnold Schönberg Gedenkausstellung 1974*, edited by Ernst Hilmar (Vienna: Universal Edition, 1974): 46; and the excerpt from a letter dated 7 March 1926 to Rudolf Kolisch, printed in "Communications," *Journal of the American Musicological Society* 41 (1988): 393.

15. Jan Maegaard, "A Study in the Chronology of Op. 23–26 by Arnold Schoenberg," *Dansk aarbog for musikforskning* 2 (1962): 97–98.

16. After the concert Berg described the piece by Stravinsky as "something really very fine." See Alban Berg, *Letters to His Wife*, translated and edited by Bernard Grun (London: Faber and Faber, 1971): 275.

17. "How One Becomes Lonely" (1937), SI 53.

18. Letter dated 12 February 1923, ASL 83.

19. Rufer, "Begriff und Funktion von Schönbergs Grundgestalt," 282.

20. Stein, "New Formal Principles," 66–67.

21. George Perle, *Serial Composition and Atonality: An Introduction to the Music of Schoenberg, Berg, and Webern*, 3d ed., revised and enlarged (Berkeley: University of California Press, 1972): 48.

22. See the analysis in ibid., 48–51.

23. Stein, "New Formal Principles," 69.

24. See Arnold Schoenberg, *Coherence, Counterpoint, Instrumentation, Instruction in Form*, edited by Severine Neff, translated by Charlotte M. Cross and Severine Neff (Lincoln: University of Nebraska Press, 1994): 39–41.

25. Transcribed by Reinhold Brinkmann in SSW, section 2, series B, vol. 4, 63–64.

26. Martha M. Hyde, "Musical Form and the Development of Schoenberg's Twelve-Tone Method," *Journal of Music Theory* 29 (1985): 93–95.

27. Sichardt, *Die Entstehung der Zwölftonmethode Arnold Schönbergs*, 90–93.

28. Transcribed by Reinhold Brinkmann in SSW, section 2, series B, vol. 4: 60–61.

29. "Das ist nachträglich!! konstruiert und stellt sich heraus als der 2te Takt: die Form, die ich mit vieler [*sic*] Mühe hier gesucht habe, ist mir im 2. Takt sofort richtig eingefallen." Ibid., 61.

30. Reinhold Brinkmann has put forward four sketches for the beginning of a triple-time piano piece made in July 1921 as preliminaries for Op. 23, No. 5. See ibid., 64–65. The relation between the sketches and the Waltz is vague.

31. HL 420.

32. "Composition with Twelve Tones" (ca. 1948), SI 246.

33. "Innerhalb einer gewissen Tonreihe [darf] sich kein Ton wiederholen und keiner ausgelassen werden." Josef Matthias Hauer, *Vom Wesen des Musikalischen* (Leipzig: Waldheim-Eberle, 1920): 53.

34. See Hans Oesch, "Pioniere der Zwölftontechnik," *Basler Studien zur Musikgeschichte* 1 (1975): 273–304

35. "Opinion or Insight?" (1926), SI 262.

36. "Im Angesicht der Erfahrung, daß keine Form mehr existiert, es sei denn die aus dem Abgrund der subjektiven Innerlichkeit heraufsteigt, wird ihm die Erfahrung des äußersten Gegenteils: daß keine Innerlichkeit hier leben kann und Dauer gewinnen im ästhetischen Abbild, es sei denn, daß sie objektive Haftpunkte findet außerhalb ihrer selbst. Die Dialektik dieser konträren Grunderfahrungen—Grunderfahrungen eben des sich entfaltenden Wesens, keine psychologischen Akte und gewonnen in der reinsten materialen Immanenz—wird zum Ursprung von Schönbergs Ironie." "Schönberg: Serenade, Op. 24," *Pult und Taktstock* 2 (1925), in AGS 18 (1984): 326–27.

37. These two fragments, called Op. 24A and Op. 24B by Jan Maegaard, are transcribed by him in JMS, *Notenbeilage:* 41–42.

38. ASL 83.

39. A short score is now at the Library of Congress, and a full score is known only in a photocopy in Schoenberg's legacy. See Martina Sichardt, "In Search of a Lost Manuscript," JASI 9 (1986): 232–35.

40. See the facsimile of one page of this arrangement in R. Wayne Shoaf, "From the Archives: The Felix Greissle Collection," JASI 10 (1987): 79.

41. Schoenberg's correspondence with Hansen is summarized in Sichardt, *Die Entstehung der Zwölftonmethode Arnold Schönbergs,* 188–89.

42. Archives of the Arnold Schönberg Center, Vienna. The contents of the page are transcribed in JMS, *Notenbeilage:* 4.

43. JMS 1:99.

44. Sichardt, *Die Entstehung der Zwölftonmethode Arnold Schönbergs,* 187–88 n12.

45. See the detailed information about the manuscripts in JMS 1: 97–107.

46. Arnold Schoenberg, "On Wilhelm Werker's *Studies of Fugal Symmetry,* etc. in BACH," in Leonard Stein, "Schoenberg: Five Statements," *Perspectives of New Music* 14 (1975–76): 169. In her 1988 dissertation ("The Origin and Development of Schoenberg's Twelve-Tone Method"), Fusako Hamao identified sketches for the Variations theme on a page of an undated sketchbook (Maegaard's Sk [17]) used primarily for *Die Jakobsleiter,* probably in 1917 and 1918. She concludes reasonably that the Variations sketches were entered there after 1920.

47. See Günter Hausswald, *Mozarts Serenaden: Eine Beitrag zur Stilkritik des 18. Jahrhunderts,* Taschenbücher zur Musikwissenschaft (Wilhelmshaven: Heinrichshofen, 1975).

48. Arnold Schoenberg, "The Orchestral Variations, Op. 31: A Radio Talk," translator unidentified, *Score* 27 (1960): 36.

49. These are all published in a single volume of Wolfgang Amadeus Mozart, *Neue Ausgabe sämtlicher Werke, Series IV, Werkgruppe 13, Abteilung 1,* vol. 2 (Kassel: Bärenreiter, 1978).

50. See David Lewin, "Inversional Balance as an Organizing Force in Schoenberg's Music and Thought," *Perspectives of New Music* 6 (1967–68): 8–10.

51. JMS, *Notenbeilage:* 73–74.

52. See the very different conclusions in Sichardt, *Die Entstehung der Zwölftonmethode Arnold Schönbergs,* 148–58, and in Hamao, "The Origin and Development of Schoenberg's Twelve-Tone Method," 256–72.

53. Facsimile in Clara Steuermann, "From the Archives: Diaries," JASI 2 (1978): 148.

54. Francesco Petrarca, *Die Sonette,* translated by Karl August Förster [1784–1841] (Leipzig: Philipp Reclam jun. n.d.): 113. English translation by the author. Unlike virtually all modern editions of Petrarch's *Canzoniere,* Förster's edition did not use the final version, containing 366 poems. The sonnet that he gives as no. 217 ("Far potess' io vendetta di colei") is numbered 256 in the complete version.

55. Arnold Schoenberg, *Texte: Die glückliche Hand, Totentanz der Prinzipien, Requiem, Die Jakobsleiter* (Vienna and New York: Universal Edition, 1926): 29–36. Partial translation in Willi Reich, *Schoenberg: A Critical Biography,* translated by Leo Black (New York: Praeger, 1971): 142–43.

56. "Schmerz, tobe dich aus, / Leid, klage dich müd! . . . Hoffnungslos: wir gehen vielleicht / ewig aneinander vorbei, / treffen uns nie mehr." Schoenberg, *Texte,* 31–36.

57. Sichardt, *Die Entstehung der Zwölftonmethode Arnold Schönbergs,* 167.

58. Heautontimorumenus [Fritz Heinrich Klein], *Die Maschine: Eine extonale Selbst-satire, Op. 1* (Vienna: Carl Haslinger Qdm Tobias; Berlin: Schlesinger'sche Musik-handlung [Rob. Lienau], n.d. [ca. 1923]).

59. See Arved Mark Ashby, "The Development of Berg's Twelve-Tone Aesthetic as Seen in the *Lyric Suite* and Its Sources" (Ph.D. diss., Yale University, 1995): 111–89; and Dave Headlam, "Fritz Heinrich Klein's 'Die Grenze der Halbtonwelt' and *Die Maschine*," *Theoria* [University of North Texas] 6 (1992): 55–96.

60. "Trifft nicht zu. In Weberns Händen, der mir deren erzählte, ohne mich aber dafür interessieren zu können. Ob ich das in Händen gehabt habe, insbesondere aber, ob ich es angesehen habe und gar ob ich wusste, was es vorstellt, bezweifle ich. Jedenfalls hat er mit der Komposition mit 12 Tönen nichts grundlegendes gemein: Kompositionelles, welches je bei mir 2–3 Jahre vorher als 'Arbeit mit Tönen' (ohne das ich die 12 noch als letzte Notwendigkeit gefunden hat) seinen ausscheidenden Vorläufer hätte." Quoted in Bryan R. Simms, "The Society for Private Musical Performances: Resources and Documents in Schoenberg's Legacy," JASI 3 (1979): 135.

61. Hausswald, *Mozarts Serenaden,* 37–38.

62. Stein, "New Formal Principles," 73.

63. "On Revient Toujours" (1948), SI 110.

Bibliography

Adorno, Theodor W. "Arnold Schönberg: Fünfzehn Gedichte aus 'Das Buch der hängenden Gärten' von Stefan George, Op. 15; Anton Webern: Fünf Lieder nach Gedichten von Stefan George, Op. 4." Liner notes to the recording *Fünfzehn Gedichte aus "Das Buch der hängenden Gärten . . . ,* Bärenreiter Musicaphon BM 30 SL 1523 (1963). Reprinted in *Gesammelte Schriften,* vol. 18: 418–21. Edited by Rolf Tiedemann and Klaus Schultz. Frankfurt: Suhrkamp, 1984.

———. "Atonales Intermezzo?" (1929). In *Gesammelte Schriften,* vol. 18: 88–97. Edited by Rolf Tiedemann and Klaus Schultz. Frankfurt: Suhrkamp, 1984. Defends Schoenbergian atonality against Alfredo Casella's theory of Neoclassicism.

———. "Atonalität." In "Neunzehn Beiträge über neue Musik" (1945). In *Gesammelte Schriften,* vol. 18: 57–58. Edited by Rolf Tiedemann and Klaus Schultz. Frankfurt: Suhrkamp, 1984.

———. "Die Musik zur 'Glückliche Hand'." *Die Tribüne* (Cologne) 24/18 (May 1955): 161–63. Reprinted in *Gesammelte Schriften,* vol. 18: 408–10. Edited by Rolf Tiedemann and Klaus Schultz. Frankfurt: Suhrkamp, 1984.

———. *Philosophy of Modern Music* (1948). Translated by Anne G. Mitchell and Wesley V. Blomster. New York: Seabury, 1973.

———. "Schönberg: Fünf Orchesterstücke, Op. 16." *Pult und Taktstock* 4 (1927): 36–43. Reprinted in *Gesammelte Schriften,* vol. 18: 335–44. Edited by Rolf Tiedemann and Klaus Schultz. Frankfurt: Suhrkamp, 1984.

———. "Schönberg: Serenade, Op. 24." *Pult und Taktstock* 2 (1925): 113–18. Reprinted in *Gesammelte Schriften,* vol. 18: 324–30. Edited by Rolf Tiedemann and Klaus Schultz. Frankfurt: Suhrkamp, 1984.

———. "Stilgeschichte in Schönbergs Werk." *Blätter der Staatsoper und der Städtischen Oper Berlin* 10/32 (1929–30): 4–9. In *Gesammelte Schriften,* vol. 18: 385–93. Edited by Rolf Tiedemann and Klaus Schultz. Frankfurt: Suhrkamp, 1984. Deals primarily with *Erwartung* and *Die glückliche Hand.*

———. "Über einige Arbeiten Arnold Schönbergs." *Forum* 10 (1963). Reprinted in *Gesammelte Schriften,* vol. 17: 327–44. Edited by Rolf Tiedemann. Frankfurt: Suhrkamp, 1982. Deals with *Herzgewächse* and Three Pieces for Chamber Orchestra among other works.

———. "Zu den Georgeliedern." In *Arnold Schönberg: Fünfzehn Gedichte aus "Das Buch der hängenden Gärten" von Stefan George,* 76–83. Wiesbaden: Insel, 1959. Reprinted in *Gesammelte Schriften,* vol. 18: 411–17. Edited by Rolf Tiedemann and Klaus Schultz. Frankfurt: Suhrkamp, 1984.

Auner, Joseph H. "'Heart and Brain in Music': The Genesis of Schoenberg's *Die glückliche Hand.*" In *Constructive Dissonance: Arnold Schoenberg and the Transformations of Twentieth-Century Culture,* 112–30. Edited by Juliane Brand and Christopher Hailey. Berkeley: University of California Press, 1997.

———. "In Schoenberg's Workshop: Aggregates and Referential Collections in *Die glückliche Hand.*" *Music Theory Spectrum* 18 (1996): 77–105.

———. "Schoenberg's Aesthetic Transformations and the Evolution of Form in *Die glückliche Hand.*" *Journal of the Arnold Schoenberg Institute* 12 (1989): 103–28.

———. "Schoenberg's Compositional and Aesthetic Transformations 1910–1913: The Genesis of *Die glückliche Hand.*" Ph.D. dissertation, University of Chicago, 1991.

———. "'Warum bist du so kurz?' Schoenberg's Three Pieces for Chamber Orchestra (1910) and the Problem of Brevity." In *Festskrift Jan Maegaard, 14.4.1996,* 43–64. Edited by Mogens Andersen, Niels Bo Foltmann, and Claus Røllum-Larsen. Copenhagen: Engstrøm & Sødring, 1996.

Avshalomov, David. "Arnold Schönberg's 'Five Pieces for Orchestra,' Op. 16: The Story of the Music and Its Editions, with a Critical Study of His 1949 Revision." D.M.A. dissertation, University of Washington, 1976.

Babbitt, Milton. "Three Essays on Schoenberg: Concerto for Violin and Orchestra, Opus 36; *Das Buch der hängenden Gärten,* Opus 15, for Voice and Piano; and *Moses and Aaron.*" In *Perspectives on Schoenberg and Stravinsky,* rev. ed., 47–60. Edited by Benjamin Boretz and Edward T. Cone. New York: Norton, 1972.

Bailey, Kathryn. "Formal Organization and Structural Imagery in Schoenberg's Pierrot lunaire." *Studies in Music from the University of Western Ontario* 2 (1977): 93–107.

Bailey, Walter B. *Programmatic Elements in the Works of Schoenberg.* Studies in Musicology, 74. Ann Arbor: UMI Research Press, 1984. Chapter 5 deals with the Symphony (1914–15).

Ballan, Harry. "Schoenberg's Expansion of Tonality, 1899–1908." Ph.D. dissertation, Yale University, 1986.

Barkin, Elaine. "Registral Procedures in Schönbergs Op. 23/1." *Music Review* 34 (1973): 141–45.

———. "A View of Schoenberg's Op. 23/1." *Perspectives of New Music* 12 (1973–74): 99–127.

Bartók, Béla. "Das Problem der neuen Musik." *Melos* 1 (1920): 107–10. English translation by Bryan R. Simms in *Composers on Modern Musical Culture: An Anthology of Readings on Twentieth-Century Music,* 44–49. New York: Schirmer Books, 1999.

Beinhorn, Gabriele. *Die Groteske in der Musik: Arnold Schönbergs "Pierrot lunaire."* Musikwissenschaftliche Studien, 11. Pfaffenweiler: Centaurus, 1989.

Bekker, Paul. "Schönberg: 'Erwartung.'" *Musikblätter des Anbruch* 6 (1924): 275–82.

Berg, Alban. "Was Ist Atonal?" *23: Eine Wiener Musikzeitschrift* 26–27 (1936): 1–11. English translation by Bryan R. Simms in *Composers on Modern Musical Culture: An Anthology of Readings on Twentieth-Century Music,* 61–71. New York: Schirmer Books, 1999.

The Berg-Schoenberg Correspondence: Selected Letters. Edited and translated by Juliane Brand, Christopher Hailey, and Donald Harris. New York: Norton, 1987.

Boss, Jack. "Schoenberg's Op. 22 Radio Talk and Developing Variation in Atonal Music." *Music Theory Spectrum* 14 (1992): 125–49.

Biringer, Gene. "Musical Metaphors in Schoenberg's 'Der kranke Mond' (*Pierrot lunaire,* No. 7)." *In Theory Only* 8/7 (1984): 3–14.

Brinkmann, Reinhold. *Arnold Schönberg: Drei Klavierstücke Op. 11. Studien zur frühen*

Atonalität bei Schönberg. Beihefte zum Archiv für Musikwissenschaft, 7. Wiesbaden: Franz Steiner, 1969.

———. "Arnold Schönbergs *Fünf Orchesterstücke* Op. 16." In *Komponisten des 20. Jahrhunderts,* 63–70. Basel: Paul Sacher Stiftung, 1986.

———. "Ausdruck und Spiel: Zwei Ansichten eines Stückes" [Op. 11/2]. In *Bericht über den 2. Kongreß der Internationalen Schönberg-Gesellschaft: "Die Wiener Schule in der Musikgeschichte des 20. Jahrhunderts,"* 31–41. Edited by Rudolf Stephan and Sigrid Wiesmann. Vienna: Elisabeth Lafite, 1984.

———. "The Lyric as Paradigm: Poetry and the Foundation of Arnold Schoenberg's New Music." In *German Literature and Music: An Aesthetic Fusion, 1890–1989,* 95–129. Edited by Claus Reschke and Howard Pollack. Houston German Studies, 8. Munich: Wilhelm Fink, 1992. Concerns Op. 15, No. 14, and *Pierrot lunaire,* among other works.

———. "On Pierrot's Trail." Translated by Paul A. Pisk. *Journal of the Arnold Schoenberg Institute* 2 (1977): 42–48.

———. "Schönberg und George: Interpretation eines Liedes [Op. 15, No. 14]." *Archiv für Musikwissenschaft* 26 (1969): 1–28.

———. "What the Sources Tell Us . . . : A Chapter of *Pierrot* Philology." Translated by Evan Bonds. *Journal of the Arnold Schoenberg Institute* 10 (1987): 11–27.

———, editor. *Arnold Schönberg Sämtliche Werke,* section 6, series B, vol. 24, part 1. Mainz: Schott; Vienna: Universal Edition, 1995. Documents concerning *Pierrot lunaire.*

Brown, Julie. "Schoenberg's Musical Prose as Allegory." *Music Analysis* 14 (1995): 161–93.

Buchanan, Herbert H. "A Key to Schoenberg's *Erwartung* (Op. 17)." *Journal of the American Musicological Society* 20 (1967): 434–49.

Budde, Elmar. "Arnold Schönbergs Monodram *Erwartung:* Versuch einer Analyse der ersten Szene." *Archiv für Musikwissenschaft* 36 (1979): 1–20.

Burkhart, Charles. "Schoenberg's *Farben:* An Analysis of Op. 16, No. 3." *Perspectives of New Music* 12 (1973–74): 141–72.

Busoni, Ferruccio. *Ferrucio Busoni Selected Letters.* Translated, edited and with an introduction by Antony Beaumont. New York: Columbia University Press, 1987. Contains the complete letter exchange between Schoenberg and Busoni, pp. 381–423.

Christensen, Jean Marie. "Arnold Schoenberg's Oratorio *Die Jakobsleiter.*" 2 vols. Ph.D. dissertation, University of California, Los Angeles, 1979.

———. "Schoenberg's Sketches for *Die Jakobsleiter:* A Study of a Special Case." *Journal of the Arnold Schoenberg Institute* 2 (1978): 112–21.

Christensen, Thomas. "Interval Ordering and Reordering in Schoenberg's Opus 11/1." *In Theory Only* 4/8 (1979): 27–29.

———. "Schoenberg's Opus 11, No. 1: A Parody of Pitch Cells from *Tristan.*" *Journal of the Arnold Schoenberg Institute* 10 (1987): 38–44.

Cohen, John. "Gloses sur le *Pierrot lunaire:* Forme et expression." *Analyse musicale* 9 (1987): 29–32.

Cone, Edward T. "Sound and Syntax: An Introduction to Schoenberg's Harmony." *Perspectives of New Music* 13 (1974–75): 21–40.

Craft, Robert. "Schoenberg's Five Pieces for Orchestra." In *Perspectives on Schoenberg and Stravinsky,* rev. ed., 3–24. Edited by Benjamin Boretz and Edward T. Cone. New York: Norton, 1972.

Crawford John C. "*Die glückliche Hand:* Further Notes." *Journal of the Arnold Schoenberg Institute* 4 (1980): 68–76.

————. "*Die glückliche Hand:* Schoenberg's *Gesamtkunstwerk.*" *Musical Quarterly* 60 (1974): 583–601.

————. "Schoenberg's Artistic Development to 1911." In *Arnold Schoenberg, Wassily Kandinsky: Letters, Pictures and Documents,* 171–86. Edited by Jelena Hahl-Koch. London: Faber and Faber, 1984.

Dahlhaus, Carl. "Expressive Principle and Orchestral Polyphony in Schoenberg's *Erwartung*" (1974). In *Schoenberg and the New Music,* 149–55. Translated by Derrick Puffett and Alfred Clayton. Cambridge: Cambridge University Press, 1987.

————. "Schönbergs Lied 'Streng ist uns das Glück und spröde.'" In *Neue Wege der musikalischen Analyse,* 45–52. Veröffentlichungen des Institut für Neue Musik und Musikerziehung, 257. Berlin: Merseburger, 1967.

Dale, Catherine. "Schoenberg's Concept of Variation Form: A Paradigmatic Analysis of *Litanei* from the Second String Quartet, Op. 10." *Journal of the Royal Musical Association* 118 (1993): 94–120.

————. *Tonality and Structure in Schoenberg's Second String Quartet, Op. 10* (New York: Garland, 1993).

Deutsch, Max. "Das dritte der 'Fünf Orchesterstücke' opus 16 ist eine Fuge." In *Musik-Konzepte: Sonderband Arnold Schönberg,* 20–28. Edited by Heinz-Klaus Metzger and Rainer Riehn. Munich: edition text + kritik, 1980.

De Zeeuw, Anne Marie. "A Numerical Metaphor in a Schoenberg Song, Op. 15, No. XI." *Journal of Musicology* 11 (1993): 396–410.

Dick, Marcel, and Anne Trenkamp. "Reminiscences of Schoenberg as Conductor." *Journal of the Arnold Schoenberg Institute* 2 (1978): 107–10.

Diettrich, Eva. "Schönbergs *Herzgewächse.*" In *Festschrift Othmar Wessely zum 60. Geburtstag,* 103–11. Edited by Manfred Angerer et al. Tutzing: Hans Schneider, 1982.

Dill, Heinz J. "Schoenberg's *George-Lieder:* The Relationship between Text and Music in Light of Some Expressionist Tendencies." *Current Musicology* 17 (1974): 91–95.

Dineen, Murray. "Schoenberg's 'Vergangenes,' Op. 16, No. 2: Social Critique and Analysis." *Ex tempore: A Journal of Compositional and Theoretical Research in Music* 8/1 (1996): 132–50.

Doflein, Erich. "Schönbergs Opus 16 Nr. 3: Geschichte einer Überschrift." *Melos* 36 (1969): 209–12.

————. "Schönbergs Opus 16 Nr. 3: Der Mythos der Klangfarbenmelodie." *Melos* 36 (1969): 203–5.

Döhring, Sieghart. "Schönbergs 'Erwartung.'" In *Arnold Schönberg,* 35–40. Berlin: Akademie der Künste, 1974.

Dossier de presse de "Pierrot lunaire" d'Arnold Schönberg. Edited by François Lesure. Anthologie de la Critique Musicale: Dossiers de Presse, 2. Geneva: Editions Minkoff, n.d. (ca. 1985).

Dümling, Albrecht. *Die fremden Klänge der hängenden Gärten: Die öffentliche Einsamkeit der neuen Musik am Beispiel von Arnold Schönberg und Stefan George.* Munich: Kindler, 1981.

————. "Öffentliche Einsamkeit: Atonalität und Krise der Subjektivität in Schönbergs Op. 15." In *Stil oder Gedanke? Zur Schönberg-Rezeption in Amerika und Europa,* 10–23. Edited by Stefan Litwin and Klaus Velten. Schriftenreihe der Hochschule des Saarlandes für Musik und Theater, 3. Saarbrücken: PFAU, 1995.

Dunsby, Jonathan M. "'Pierrot lunaire' and the Resistance to Theory." *Musical Times* 130 (1982): 732–36.

————. *Schoenberg: "Pierrot lunaire."* Cambridge Music Handbooks. Cambridge: Cambridge University Press, 1992.

———. "Schoenberg's *Premonition, Op. 22, No. 4,* in Retrospect." *Journal of the Arnold Schoenberg Institute* 1 (1977): 137–49.

Ehrenforth, Karl Heinrich. *Ausdruck und Form: Schönbergs Durchbruch zur Atonalität in den George-Liedern Op. 15.* Bonn: Bouvier, 1963. Concerns the String Quartet No. 2.

———. "Schönberg und Webern: Das XIV. Lied aus Schönbergs Georgeliedern Op. 15." *Neue Zeitschrift für Musik* 126 (1965): 102–5.

Falck, Robert. "Marie Pappenheim, Schoenberg, and the *Studien über Hysterie.*" In *German Literature and Music: An Aesthetic Fusion, 1890–1989,* 131–44. Edited by Claus Reschke and Howard Pollack. Houston German Studies, 8. Munich: Wilhelm Fink, 1992.

———. "Schoenberg's (and Rilke's) 'Alle, welche dich suchen.'" *Perspectives of New Music* 12 (1973–74): 87–98.

Forte, Allen. "Concepts of Linearity in Schoenberg's Atonal Music: A Study of the Opus 15 Song Cycle." *Journal of Music Theory* 36 (1992): 285–382.

———. "The Magical Kaleidoscope: Schoenberg's First Atonal Masterwork, Opus 11, No. 1." *Journal of the Arnold Schoenberg Institute* 5 (1981): 127–68.

———. "Schoenberg's Creative Evolution: The Path to Atonality." *Musical Quarterly* 64 (1978): 133–76.

———. "Sets and Nonsets in Schoenberg's Atonal Music." *Perspectives of New Music* 11 (1972–73): 43–64.

———. *The Structure of Atonal Music.* New Haven: Yale University Press, 1973.

Förtig, Peter. "Analyse des Opus 16 Nr. 3." *Melos* 36 (1969): 206–9.

Friedheim, Philip. "Rhythmic Structure in Schoenberg's Atonal Compositions." *Journal of the American Musicological Society* 19 (1966): 59–72.

Frisch, Walter. *The Early Works of Arnold Schoenberg, 1893–1908.* Berkeley: University of California Press, 1993.

Ganter, Claus. *Ordnungsprinzip oder Konstruktion? Die Entwicklung der Tonsprache Arnold Schönbergs am Beispiel seiner Klavierwerke.* Munich: Katzbichler, 1997.

Gervink, Manuel. "Einsamkeit und Isolation: Interpretationsansätze für die Innovationen im Werk Arnold Schönbergs." *Archiv für Musikwissenschaft* 53 (1996): 160–76.

Gilbert, Jan. "Schoenberg's Harmonic Visions: A Study of Text Painting in 'Die Kreuze.'" *Journal of the Arnold Schoenberg Institute* 8 (1984): 116–30.

Gostomsky, Dieter. "Tonalität—Atonalität: Zur Harmonik von Schönbergs Klavierstück Op. 11, Nr. 1." *Zeitschrift für Musiktheorie* 7 (1976): 54–71.

Graziano, John. "Serial Procedures in Schoenberg's Opus 23." *Current Musicology* 13 (1972): 58–63. Deals mainly with Piece No. 1.

Haimo, Ethan. "Atonality, Analysis, and the Intentional Falacy." *Music Theory Spectrum* 18 (1996): 167–99.

———. "The Evolution of the Twelve-Tone Method." In *The Arnold Schoenberg Companion,* 101–28. Edited by Walter B. Bailey. Westport, Conn.: Greenwood, 1998.

———. "Schoenberg and the Origins of Atonality." In *Constructive Dissonance: Arnold Schoenberg and the Transformations of Twentieth-Century Culture,* 71–86. Edited by Juliane Brand and Christopher Hailey. Berkeley: University of California Press, 1997.

———. *Schoenberg's Serial Odyssey: The Evolution of His Twelve-Tone Method, 1914–1928.* Oxford: Clarendon, 1990.

Hamao, Fusako. "On the Origin of the Twelve-Tone Method: Schoenberg's Sketches for the Unfinished *Symphony* (1914–1915)." *Current Musicology* 42 (1986): 32–45.

———. "The Origin and Development of Schoenberg's Twelve-Tone Method." Ph.D. dissertation, Yale University, 1988.

Hamilton, David. "Schoenberg's First Opera." *Opera Quarterly* 6/3 (1989): 48–58.

Hansen, Mathias. *Arnold Schönberg: Ein Konzept der Moderne.* Kassel: Bärenreiter, 1993.

Hofmannsthal, Hugo von. "Gedichte von Stefan George" (1896). In *Ausgewählte Werke,* vol. 2: 306–13. Edited by Rudolf Hirsch. Frankfurt: Fischer, 1957.

Hough, Bonny, "Schoenberg's *Herzgewächse* and the *Blaue Reiter* Almanac." *Journal of the Arnold Schoenberg Institute* 7 (1983): 197–221.

———. "Schoenberg's *Herzgewächse,* Op. 20: An Integrated Approach to Atonality through Complementary Analyses." Ph.D. dissertation, Washington University, 1982.

Hyde, Martha M. "Musical Form and the Development of Schoenberg's Twelve-Tone Method." *Journal of Music Theory* 29 (1985): 85–139. Deals mainly with Op. 23, No. 4.

Kaufmann, Harald. "Struktur in Schönbergs *Georgeliedern.*" In *Musik-Konzepte: Sonderband Arnold Schönberg,* 82–92. Edited by Heinz-Klaus Metzger and Rainer Riehn. Munich: edition text + kritik, 1980.

Keathley, Elizabeth L. "Schoenberg's Opus 16/IV: An Examination of the Sketches." *Theory and Practice: Journal of the Music Theory Society of New York State* 17 (1992): 67–84.

Kirchmeyer, Helmut. Liner notes to the recording *Erwartung,* Wergo 50 001 (1963).

Klemm, Eberhardt. "Der Briefwechsel zwischen Arnold Schönberg und dem Verlag C. F. Peters." *Deutsches Jahrbuch der Musikwissenschaft* 14 (1970): 5–66.

Konold, Wulf. "Struktur und Klangfarbe: Bemerkungen zu Original und Bearbeitung von Schönbergs *Fünf Orchesterstücken* Op. 16." In *Musik-Konzepte: Schönbergs Verein für musikalische Privataufführungen,* 43–64. Edited by Heinz-Klaus Metzger and Rainer Riehn. Munich: edition text + kritik, 1984.

Kopfermann, Michael. "Über Schönbergs Klavierstück Op. 19, Nr. 2." In *Musik-Konzepte: Sonderband Arnold Schönberg,* 35–50. Edited by Heinz-Klaus Metzger and Rainer Riehn. Munich: edition text + kritik, 1980.

Kramer, Lawrence. *Music and Poetry: The Nineteenth Century and After.* Berkeley: University of California Press, 1984. Schoenberg's Op. 15 is discussed on pp. 161–68.

Kravitt, Edward F. "The Joining of Words and Music in Late Romantic Melodrama." *Musical Quarterly* 62 (1976): 571–90.

Krebs, Harald. "The 'Color Crescendo' from *Die glückliche Hand:* A Comparison of Sketch and Final Version." *Journal of the Arnold Schoenberg Institute* 12 (1989): 61–67.

———. "New Light on the Source Materials of Schoenberg's *Die glückliche Hand.*" *Journal of the Arnold Schoenberg Institute* 11 (1988): 123–41

———. "Three Versions of Schoenberg's Op. 15 No. 14: Obvious Differences and Hidden Similarities." *Journal of the Arnold Schoenberg Institute* 8 (1984): 131–40.

———. "Tonalität in Schönbergs 'atonaler' Musik." *Musiktheorie* 4 (1989): 223–34.

Krenek, Ernst. "Atonality" (1936). In *Music Here and Now,* 141–65. Translated by Barthold Fles. New York: Norton, 1939.

Laborda, José Maria García. *Studien zu Schönbergs Monodrama "Erwartung" op. 17.* Laaber: Laaber, 1981.

Lessem, Alan Philip. *Music and Text in the Works of Arnold Schoenberg: The Critical Years, 1908–1922.* Studies in Musicology, 8. Ann Arbor: UMI Research Press, 1979.

Lester, Joel. "Pitch Structure Articulation in the Variations of Schoenberg's Serenade." *Perspectives of New Music* 6 (1967–68): 22–34.

———. "A Theory of Atonal Prolongations As Used in an Analysis of the Serenade, Op. 24, by Arnold Schoenberg." 2 vols. Ph.D. dissertation, Princeton University, 1970.

Lewin, David. "Inversional Balance as an Organizing Force in Schoenberg's Music and Thought." *Perspectives of New Music* 6 (1967–68): 1–21.

———. "Some Notes on Schoenberg's Opus 11." *In Theory Only* 3/1 (1977): 3–7.

———. "Toward the Analysis of a Schoenberg Song (Op. 15, No. XI)." *Perspectives of New Music* 12 (1973–74): 43–86.

———. "Vocal Meter in Schoenberg's Atonal Music, with a Note on a Serial Hauptstimme." *In Theory Only* 6/4 (1981–82): 12–25. Deals with Op. 20, Op. 21/2, and Op. 15/5.

———. "A Way into Schoenberg's Opus 15, Number 7." *In Theory Only* 6/1 (1981): 3–24.

———. "Women's Voices and the Fundamental Bass." *Journal of Musicology* 10 (1992): 464–82.

Mack, Dana. "Schoenberg and the Battles of Modern Music" (1988). Reprinted in German translation ("Der französische 'Pierrot': Ein Kapitel aus Schönbergs Kampf um die moderne Musik") in *Österreichische Musikzeitschrift* 44 (1989): 25–32.

Mäckelmann, Michael. *Arnold Schönberg: Fünf Orchesterstücke Op. 16.* Munich: Wilhelm Fink, 1987.

———. "Auf der Suche nach dem Gottesgedanken: Zum geistigen Hintergrund von Arnold Schönbergs unvollendetem Oratorium *Die Jakobsleiter.*" In *Musikkulturgeschichte: Festschrift für Constantin Floros zum 60. Geburtstag,* 399–413. Edited by Peter Petersen. Wiesbaden: Breitkopf und Härtel, 1990.

———. "'Die glückliche Hand': Eine Studie zu Musik und Inhalt von Arnold Schönbergs 'Drama mit Musik.'" In *Musiktheater im 20. Jahrhundert,* 7–34. Edited by Constantin Floros, Hans Joachim Marx, and Peter Petersen. Hamburger Jahrbuch für Musikwissenschaft, 10. Laaber: Laaber, 1988.

Maegaard, Jan. "Om den kronologiske Placering af Arnold Schönbergs Klaverstykke Op. 23 Nr. 3." *Musik und forskning* 3 (1977): 5–10.

———. *Studien zur Entwicklung des dodekaphonen Satzes bei Arnold Schönberg.* 3 vols. Copenhagen: Wilhelm Hansen, 1972.

———. "A Study in the Chronology of Op. 23–26 by Arnold Schoenberg." *Dansk aarbog for musikforskning* 2 (1962): 93–115.

Massow, Albrecht von. "Abschied und Neuorientierung–Schönbergs Klavierstück Op. 19, 6." *Archiv für Musikwissenschaft* 50 (1993): 187–95.

Mauser, Siegfried. "Arnold Schönbergs *Erwartung* und Alban Bergs *Wozzeck.*" In *Alban Berg Symposion,* 91–96. Alban Berg Studien, 1. Vienna: Universal Edition, 1980.

———. *Das expressionistische Musiktheater der Wiener Schule.* Regensburg: Gustav Bosse, 1982.

Metzger, Heinz-Klaus. "Zu Schönbergs Orchesterliedern Op. 22." In *Musik-Konzepte: Sonderband Arnold Schönberg,* 51–57. Edited by Heinz-Klaus Metzger and Rainer Riehn. Munich: edition text + kritik, 1980.

Morris, Robert D. "Modes of Coherence and Continuity in Schoenberg's Piano Piece, Opus 23, No. 1." *Theory and Practice: Journal of the Music Theory Society of New York State* 17 (1992): 5–34.

Morrison, Charles D. "Syncopation as Motive in Schoenberg's Op. 19, Nos 2, 3 and 4." *Music Analysis* 11 (1992): 75–93.

Naumann, Peter. "Untersuchungen zum Wort-Ton-Verhältnis in den Einaktern Arnold Schönbergs." 2 vols. Ph.D. dissertation, University of Cologne, 1988.

Nelson, Robert U. "Schoenberg's Variation Seminar." *Musical Quarterly* 50 (1964): 141–63. Contains an analysis of the third movement of Op. 24.

Neuwirth, Gösta. "Schönbergs George-Lieder Op. 15: Die Entwürfe zum XIV. Lied." In *Bericht über den 1. Kongreß der Internationalen Schönberg-Gesellschaft*, 147–58. Edited by Rudolf Stephan. Vienna: Elisabeth Lafite, 1974.

Nono-Schoenberg, Nuria, editor. *Arnold Schönberg, 1874–1951: Lebensgeschichte in Begegnungen*. Klagenfurt: Ritter, 1992.

Oesch, Hans. "Schönberg im Vorfeld der Dodekaphonie: Zur Bedeutung des dritten Satzes aus opus 23 für die Herausbildung der Zwölfton-Technik." *Zeitschrift für Musiktheorie* 5 (1974): 2–10.

Ogdon, Will. "How Tonality Functions in Schoenberg's Opus 11, Number 1." *Journal of the Arnold Schoenberg Institute* 5 (1981): 169–81.

Penney, Diane Holloway. "Schoenberg's Janus-Work *Erwartung*: Its Musico-Dramatic Structure and Relationship to the Melodrama and Lied Traditions." Ph.D. dissertation, University of North Texas, 1989.

Perle, George. "Pierrot lunaire." In *The Commonwealth of Music*, 307–12. Edited by Gustave Reese and Rose Brandel. New York: Free Press, 1965.

———. *Serial Composition and Atonality: An Introduction to the Music of Schoenberg, Berg, and Webern*, 3d ed., revised and enlarged. Berkeley: University of California Press, 1972.

Pfisterer, Manfred. *Studien zur Kompositionstechnik in den frühen atonalen Werken von Arnold Schönberg*. Tübinger Beiträge zur Musikwissenschaft, 5. Neuhausen-Stuttgart: Hänssler, 1978.

Raab, Claus. "Der Fleck im 'Mondfleck': Zu den Takten 8 bis 12 der Nr. 18 in Arnold Schönbergs 'Pierrot lunaire' op. 21." *Die Musikforschung* 46 (1993): 411–16.

Rahn, John. *Basic Atonal Theory*. New York: Longman, 1980.

Reich, Willi. *Schoenberg: A Critical Biography*. Translated by Leo Black. New York: Praeger 1971.

Réti, Rudolph. *Tonality, Atonality, Pantonality: A Study of Some Trends in Twentieth-Century Music*. New York: Macmillan, 1958.

Richter, Lukas. "Schönbergs Harmonielehre und die freie Atonalität." *Deutsches Jahrbuch der Musikwissenschaft* 13 (1969): 43–71.

Ruf, Wolfgang. "Arnold Schönbergs Lied 'Herzgewächse.'" *Archiv für Musikwissenschaft* 41 (1984): 257–73.

Rufer, Josef. "Begriff und Funktion von Schönbergs Grundgestalt." *Melos* 38 (1971): 281–84.

———. "Noch einmal Schönbergs Opus 16." *Melos* 36 (1969): 366–68.

Samson, Jim. *Music in Transition: A Study of Tonal Expansion and Atonality, 1900–1920*. New York: Norton, 1977.

———. "Schoenberg's 'Atonal' Music." *Tempo* 109 (1974): 16–25.

Schäfer, Thomas. "Wortmusik—Tonmusik: Ein Beitrag zur Wagner-Rezeption von Arnold Schönberg und Stefan George." *Die Musikforschung* 47 (1994): 252–73.

Schoenberg, Arnold. "Analyse der 4 Orchesterlieder op. 22." In *Stil und Gedanke: Aufsätze zur Musik*, 286–300. Edited by Ivan Vojtêch. Arnold Schönberg Gesammelte Schriften, 1. N.p.: Fischer, 1976. Translated by Claudio Spies ("Analysis of the Four Orchestral Songs Opus 22"), *Perspectives of New Music* 3 (1964–65): 1–21.

———. *Arnold Schoenberg Letters*. Edited by Erwin Stein. Translated by Eithne Wilkins and Ernst Kaiser. New York: St. Martin's, 1965.

———. *Arnold Schönberg Sämtliche Werke*. Rudolf Stephan, general editor. Mainz: Schott; Vienna: Universal Edition, 1966–.

———. *Arnold Schoenberg, Wassily Kandinsky: Letters, Pictures and Documents.* Edited by Jelena Hahl-Koch. Translated by John C. Crawford. London: Faber and Faber, 1984.

———. *Berliner Tagebuch.* Edited by Josef Rufer. Frankfurt: Propyläen, 1974.

———. "Breslau Lecture on *Die glückliche Hand.*" In *Arnold Schoenberg, Wassily Kandinsky: Letters, Pictures and Documents,* 102–7. Edited by Jelena Hahl-Koch. Translated by John C. Crawford. London: Faber and Faber, 1984.

———. *Coherence, Counterpoint, Instrumentation, Instruction in Form.* Edited with an introduction by Severine Neff. Translated by Charlotte M. Cross and Severine Neff. Lincoln: University of Nebraska Press, 1994.

———. *Fundamentals of Musical Composition.* Edited by Gerald Strang and Leonard Stein. New York: St. Martin's, 1967.

———. *Theory of Harmony.* Translated by Roy E. Carter. Berkeley: University of California Press, 1978.

[———]. "Komposition mit zwölf Tönen" (ca. 1922–23). In Rudolf Stephan, "Ein frühes Dokument zur Entstehung der Zwölftonkomposition." In *Festschrift Arno Forchert zum 60. Geburtstag am 29. Dezember 1985,* 296–302. Edited by Gerhard Allroggen and Detlef Altenburg. Kassel: Bärenreiter, 1986. English translation ("Composition with Twelve Tones") by Arved Mark Ashby in "The Development of Berg's Twelve-Tone Aesthetic As Seen in the *Lyric Suite* and Its Sources," 229–33, Ph.D. dissertation, Yale University, 1995.

———. *The Musical Idea and the Logic, Technique, and Art of Its Presentation.* Edited, translated, and with a commentary by Patricia Carpenter and Severine Neff. New York: Columbia University Press, 1995.

———. "Notes on the Four String Quartets" (1936). In *The String Quartets: A Documentary Study,* 31–78. Edited by Ursula von Rauchhaupt. Liner notes to the recording *Neue Wiener Schule: Schönberg, Berg, Webern.* Deutsche Grammophon no. 419 994–2 (1987).

———. *Stil und Gedanke: Aufsätze zur Musik.* Edited by Ivan Vojtěch. Arnold Schönberg Gesammelte Schriften, 1. N.p.: Fischer, 1976.

———. *Structural Functions of Harmony* (1954). Revised edition with corrections. Edited by Leonard Stein. New York: Norton, 1969.

———. *Style and Idea: Selected Writings of Arnold Schoenberg.* Edited by Leonard Stein. Translated by Leo Black. Berkeley: University of California Press, 1984.

———. *Texte: Die glückliche Hand, Totentanz der Prinzipien, Requiem, Die Jakobsleiter.* Vienna: Universal Edition, 1926.

———. "Warum neue Melodien schwerverständlich sind." *Die Konzertwoche* (Vienna: Universal Edition, 1913). Reprinted with translation by Bryan R. Simms ("Why New Melodies Are Difficult to Understand") in *Perspectives of New Music* 16 (1977–78): 115–16.

Schorske, Carl E. *Fin-de-siècle Vienna: Politics and Culture.* New York: Knopf, 1980.

Schuller, Gunther. "A Conversation with Steuermann." *Perspectives of New Music* 3 (1964–65): 22–35.

Schwab, Heinrich W. "'. . . in einer Art psalmodischem Ton angeblicher Lieder': Zur Struktur der Vertonung in Schönbergs Op. 15." In *Festskrift Jan Maegaard, 14.4.1996,* 81–96. Edited by Mogens Andersen, Niels Bo Foltmann, and Claus Røllum-Larsen. Copenhagen: Engstrøm and Sødring, 1996.

Sichardt, Martina. *Die Entstehung der Zwölftonmethode Arnold Schönbergs.* Mainz: Schott, 1990.

———. "In Search of a Lost Manuscript." *Journal of the Arnold Schoenberg Institute* 9 (1986): 232–35.

Simms, Bryan. "Arnold Schoenberg." In *Schoenberg, Berg, and Webern: A Companion to the Second Viennese School*, 129–84. Edited by Bryan R. Simms. Westport, Conn.: Greenwood, 1999.

———. "Line and Harmony in the Sketches of Schoenberg's 'Seraphita,' Op. 22, No. 1." *Journal of Music Theory* 26 (1982): 291–312

———. "Schoenberg: The Analyst and the Analyzed." In *The Arnold Schoenberg Companion*, 223–50. Edited by Walter B. Bailey. Westport, Conn: Greenwood, 1998.

———. "Whose Idea Was *Erwartung?*" In *Constructive Dissonance: Arnold Schoenberg and the Transformations of Twentieth-Century Culture*, 100–111. Edited by Juliane Brand and Christopher Hailey. Berkeley: University of California Press, 1997.

Stadlen, Peter. "Schoenberg's Speech-Song." *Music and Letters* 62 (1981): 1–11.

Stein, Deborah. "Schoenberg's Op. 19, No. 2: Voice-Leading and Overall Structure in an Atonal Work." *In Theory Only* 2/7 (1976): 27–43.

Stein, Erwin. "Die Behandlung der Sprechstimme in 'Pierrot lunaire.'" *Pult und Taktstock* 4 (1927): 45–49.

———. "New Formal Principles" (1924). In *Orpheus in New Guises*, 57–77. London: Rockliff, 1953.

———. "Schönberg's 'Glückliche Hand.'" *Die Oper: Blätter des Breslauer Stadttheaters*, No. 16 (1927–28): 3–7.

Stein, Leonard. "The Atonal Period in Schoenberg's Music." In *The Arnold Schoenberg Companion*, 83–100. Edited by Walter B. Bailey. Westport, Conn.: Greenwood, 1998.

Steiner, Ena. "The 'Happy' Hand: Genius and Interpretation of Schoenberg's *Monumentalkunstwerk*." *Music Review* 41 (1980): 207–22.

Stenzl, Jürg. "Die apokalypse einer Liebe: Arnold Schönbergs Monodram 'Erwartung' (1909)." In *Bericht über den 2. Kongreß der Internationalen Schönberg-Gesellschaft: "Die Wiener Schule in der Musikgeschichte des 20. Jahrhunderts,"* 64–72. Edited by Rudolf Stephan and Sigrid Wiesmann. Vienna: Elisabeth Lafite, 1984.

Stephan, Rudolf. "Überlegungen zum Thema 'Schönberg und Mozart.'" In *Mozart in der Musik des 20. Jahrhunderts: Formen ästhetischer und kompositionstechnischer Rezeption*, 105–16. Edited by Wolfgang Gratzer and Siegfried Mauser. Schriften zur musikalischen Hermeneutik, 2. Laaber: Laaber, 1992.

Sterne, Colin C. "Pythagoras and Pierrot: An Approach to Schoenberg's Use of Numerology in the Construction of 'Pierrot lunaire.'" *Perspectives of New Music* 21 (1982–83): 506–34.

Steuermann, Edward. "*Pierrot lunaire* in Retrospect." *Juilliard News Bulletin*, 1963. Reprinted in *Journal of the Arnold Schoenberg Institute* 2 (1977): 49–51.

Street, Alan. "The Obbligato Recitative: Narrative and Schoenberg's Five Orchestral Pieces, Op. 16." In *Theory, Analysis and Meaning in Music*, 164–83. Edited by Anthony Pople. Cambridge: Cambridge University Press, 1994.

Stroh, Wolfgang Martin. "Schoenberg's Use of Text: The Text as a Musical Control in the 14th *Georgelied*, Op. 15." Translated by Barbara Westergaard. *Perspectives of New Music* 6 (1967–68): 35–44.

Stuckenschmidt, H. H. "Arnold Schönbergs 'Erwartung.'" *Der Scheinwerfer* (Essen) 4/9 (January 1931): 1–4.

———. "Opus 19, Nummer 3: Eine Schönberg-Analyse." *Orbis musicae* 1 (1971): 88–90.

———. *Schoenberg: His Life, World and Work*. Translated by Humphrey Searle. New York: Schirmer Books, 1977.

Thrun, Martin. *Neue Musik im deutschen Musikleben bis 1933.* 2 vols. Bonn: Orpheus, 1995.

Truman, Philip. "Synaesthesia and '*Die glückliche Hand.*'" *Interface* 12 (1983): 481–503.

Vlad, Roman. "Una Pagina di Schoenberg." *Studi musicali* 14 (1985): 171–92. Concerns Op. 19.

Webern, Anton. *The Path to the New Music.* Edited by Willi Reich. Translated by Leo Black. Bryn Mawr: Theodore Presser, 1963.

———. "Schönbergs Musik." In *Sammelband: Arnold Schönberg,* 22–48. Munich: Piper, 1912. Reprinted 1980.

Weissweiler, Eva. "'Schreiben Sie mir doch einen Operntext, Fräulein!': Marie Pappenheims Text zu Arnold Schönbergs 'Erwartung.'" *Neue Zeitschrift für Musik* 145/1 (1984): 4–8.

Wickes, Lewis. "Schoenberg, *Erwartung,* and the Reception of Psychoanalysis in Musical Circles in Vienna until 1910/1911." *Studies in Music* 23 (1989): 88–106.

Wiesmann, Sigrid. "Arnold Schönbergs *Glückliche Hand* und die Aporien des expressionistischen Dramas." In *Geschichte und Dramaturgie des Operneinakters,* 309–16. Edited by Winfried Kirsch and Sieghart Döhring. Thurnauer Schriften zum Musiktheater, 10. Laaber: Laaber, 1991.

Wintle, Christopher W. "Schoenberg's Harmony: Theory and Practice." *Journal of the Arnold Schoenberg Institute* 4 (1980): 50–67.

Wittlich, Gary. "Interval Set Structure in Schoenberg's Op. 11, No. 1." *Perspectives of New Music* 13 (1974–75): 41–55.

Wörner, Karl. "Musik zwischen Theologie und Weltanschauung: Das Oratorium 'Die Jakobsleiter.'" In *Die Musik in der Geistesgeschichte: Studien zur Situation der Jahre um 1910,* 171–200. Abhandlungen zur Kunst-, Musik- und Literaturgeschichte, 92. Bonn: Bouvier, 1970.

———. "Schönbergs 'Erwartung' und das Ariadne-Thema." In *Die Musik in der Geistesgeschichte: Studien zur Situation der Jahre um 1910,* 91–117. Abhandlungen zur Kunst-, Musik- und Literaturgeschichte, 92. Bonn: Bouvier, 1970.

———. "Symbolismus und Expressionismus: *"Die glückliche Hand."* In *Die Musik in der Geistesgeschichte: Studien zum Situation der Jahre um 1910,* 145–69. Abhandlungen zur Kunst-, Musik- und Literaturgeschichte, 92. Bonn: Bouvier, 1970.

Wurstbauer, Michael. "Uraufführung der *Erwartung*–Erwartung der Uraufführung: Von der Entstehung bis zur Uraufführung des Monodrams *Erwartung* op. 17." In *40.000 Musikerbriefe auf Knopfdruck,* 75–96. Edited by Ernst Hilmar. Tutzing: Hans Schneider, 1989.

Youens, Susan. "Excavating an Allegory: The Texts of *Pierrot Lunaire.*" *Journal of the Arnold Schoenberg Institute* 8 (1984): 94–115.

Zemlinsky, Alexander. *Briefwechsel mit Arnold Schönberg, Anton Webern, Alban Berg und Franz Schreker.* Edited by Horst Weber. Briefwechsel der Wiener Schule, 1. Darmstadt: Wissenschaftliche Buchgesellschaft, 1995.

Zillig, Winfried. "Notes on Arnold Schoenberg's Unfinished Oratorio *Die Jakobsleiter.*" *Score* 25 (1959): 7–16. German version ("Arnold Schönbergs 'Jakobsleiter.' ") *Österreichische Musikzeitschrift,* 5 (1961): 193–204.

Index